Veritatis Splendor:
American Responses

Edited by
Michael E. Allsopp
and
John J. O'Keefe

Sheed & Ward

Sheed & Ward™ is a service of The National Catholic Reporter Publishing Company.

━━━━━━━━━━━━━━◆━━━━━━━━━━━━━━

Library of Congress Cataloguing-in-Publication Data

Veritatis Splendor : American responses / edited by Michael E. Allsopp and
    John J. O'Keefe.
        p.   cm.
    Includes bibliographical references and index.
    ISBN: 1-55612-760-X (alk. paper)
       1. Catholic Church. Pope (1978-   : John Paul II). Veritatis splendor.
    2. Christian ethics—Papal documents. 3. Catholic Church—Doctrines.
    I. Allsopp, Michael E. II. O'Keefe, John J., 1961-
    BJ1249.C19   1995
    241'.042—dc20   94-23533
                                                        CIP

━━━━━━━━━━━━━━◆━━━━━━━━━━━━━━

Published by: Sheed & Ward
                  115 E. Armour Blvd.
                  P.O. Box 419492
                  Kansas City, MO 64141

To order, call: (800) 333-7373

Cover design by Emil Antonucci.

Contents

Introduction, *Michael E. Allsopp* vii

1. "Then Who Can Be Saved?": Ethics and Ecclesiology
   in *Veritatis Splendor, Maura Anne Ryan* 1

2. No Place for Failure? Augustinian Reflections
   on *Veritatis Splendor, John J. O'Keefe* 16

3. An Interpretation of *Veritatis Splendor* and the
   Discussion of War and Peace within the Roman Catholic
   Community, *Stephen E. Lammers* 38

4. "If You Wish to Be Perfect . . .": Images of Perfection
   in *Veritatis Splendor, Katherine M. TePas* 48

5. The Pope on Proportionalism, *James Gaffney* 60

6. A Matter of Credibility, *Clifford Stevens* 72

7. Morality on the Way of Discipleship: The Use of Scripture in
   Veritatis Splendor, William C. Spohn 83

8. Will the Church of the Twenty-First Century Be a Holy
   and Discerning People?, *Mary Frohlich* 106

9. *Veritatis Splendor:* Papal Authority and the Sovereignty of Reason,
   Ronald R. Burke 119

10. The Role of the Connaturalized Heart in *Veritatis Splendor,*
    Andrew Tallon 137

11. *Veritatis Splendor et Rhetorica Morum:* "The Splendor of Truth"
    and the Rhetoric of Morality, *Edward R. Sunshine* 157

12. Judaism and Catholic Morality: The View of the Encyclical,
    Rev. John T. Pawlikowski, ... 177

13. Natural Law and Personalism in *Veritatis Splendor, Janet E. Smith* 194

14. *Veritatis Splendor* and Sexual Ethics, *James P. Hanigan* . . . 208

15. *Veritatis Splendor:* A Revisionist Perspective, *Charles E. Curran* 224

16. The Nature of Christian Love, *John Giles Milhaven* 244

17. *Veritatis Splendor:* Some Implications for Bioethics,
    B. Andrew Lustig 252

18. *Veritatis Splendor* and Our Cover Stories, *John C. Haughey,* . . 269

19. The Moral Act in *Veritatis Splendor* and in Aquinas's
    Summa theologiae: A Comparative Analysis, *Jean Porter* . . . 278

20. *The Splendor of Truth:* A Feminist Critique, *Kathleen Talvacchia*
    and *Mary Elizabeth Walsh* 296

Index 311

Contributors

Michael E. Allsopp teaches moral theology and bioethics in the Department of Theology and Philosophy, Barry University, Miami Shores, Florida.

Ronald R. Burke (Ph.D., Yale) is a member of the Department of Philosophy and Religion, University of Nebraska at Omaha.

Charles E. Curran is Elizabeth Scurlock University Professor of Human Values, Southern Methodist University, Dallas, Texas.

Mary Frohlich is a member of the Department of Historical and Doctrinal Studies, Catholic Theological Union, Chicago.

James Gaffney teaches in the Religious Studies Department, Loyola University, New Orleans.

James P. Hanigan (Ph.D., Yale) is Chair of the Theology Department at Duquesne University, Pittsburgh.

John Haughey teaches moral theology at Loyola University in Chicago.

Stephen E. Lammers is Helen H.P. Manson Professor of the English Bible, Department of Relgion, Lafayette College, Easton, Pennsylvania.

B. Andrew Lustig (Ph.D., University of Virginia) is a member of the Center for Ethics, Medicine, and Public Issues, Baylor College of Medicine, Houston, Texas.

J. Giles Milhaven teaches ethics in the Department of Religious Studies, Brown University, Providence, Rhode Island.

John J. O'Keefe (Ph.D., Catholic University) is a member of the Department of Theology, Creighton University, Omaha, Nebraska.

John T. Pawlikowski, a specialist in Jewish-Catholic relations, is a professor of theology in the Catholic Theological Union, Chicago.

Jean Porter is Associate Professor of Moral Theology at the University of Notre Dame, Indiana.

Maura Anne Ryan (Ph.D., Yale) is a member of the Department of Theology, University of Notre Dame, Notre Dame, Indiana.

Janet E. Smith teaches in the Department of Philosophy, University of Dallas, Irving, Texas.

William C. Spohn (Ph.D., Chicago) is John Nobili University Professor at Santa Clara University, Santa Clara, Calfornia.

Clifford Stevens is a priest of the Archdiocese of Omaha, Nebraska.

Edward R. Sunshine teaches moral theology in the Department of Theology and Philosophy, Barry University, Miami Shores, Florida.

Andrew Tallon is a member of the Department of Philosophy, Marquette University, Milwaukee, Wisconsin.

Kathleen Talvacchia teaches theology at Union Theological Seminary, New York.

Katherine M. TePas (Ph.D., Catholic University) is a member of the Department of Religion, La Salle University, Philadelphia.

Mary E. Walsh is a graduate student at Union Theological Seminary, New York.

Introduction

"Great things are done when men and mountains meet."

—William Blake

It was threatening to rain in Rome on Thursday, October 11, 1962, the day the Second Vatican Council opened. A thunderstorm like the one at the end of the First Vatican Council had moved in over the city. As Pope John reached St. Peter's bronze doors, the blunt and cynical recalled the remark Cardinal Spellman is said to have made about him, "He's no Pope—he should be selling bananas." However, after the assembly had seen John order the bearers of the *sedia gestatoria* to allow him to descend, and watched him walk down the main aisle between the banked rows of prelates—Roman, Byzantine, Melkite, Coptic, and Maronite—the astute sensed that there was more to this "peasant" pope than the Cardinal from New York had observed.

And at the close of the Council's opening ceremony (it took six-and-a-half hours), and John was finishing his address (during which he broke with tradition by wearing a bishop's miter, not a papal tiara), the astute knew they were correct.

John's was the speech of a lifetime. For Church historians John Jay Hughes and Peter Hebblethwaite, the address should be seen as the yardstick of the Council. That evening at dinner in the "Venerable" English College, as bishops talked about the day, some felt they had witnessed an "epiphany," one of those rare moments in life, when (to recoin T.S. Eliot's words), time and the timeless intersect. John's appearance, his optimism, his deference to his fellow bishops, his hopes that the Council would make the Church greater in spiritual riches, gain new strength and energy, and look to the future without fear—his ironic but none too subtle rebukes to some sitting close to him—caused the sensitive to recall that other "peasant" at another Council, the first, who also launched the Church into uncharted seas.

Read in the context of his life, John's address is filled with memories and dreams. It contains his thorough knowledge of the writings of Charles Borromeo, the lessons of his 20 years among Orthodox Christians in Greece, the Balkans, and Turkey, and his eight years of contacts with Protestants in France. When we examine the text, the impression grows that John's words are based upon Carl Becker's thesis that people living today find Aquinas' scholastic theology difficult to accept not because of flaws in the Angelic Doctor's logic, but because they do not sympathize with his medieval climate of opinion; because they are uncomfortable with his feudal political theory, and they do not share his pre-Copernican worldview. John seems aware that we who are living in this postmodern era see ourselves as fact-gatherers and experimenters, as mobile rather than docile, as women and men called by God and the times to fashion our own fates, as well as the fate of the cosmos. He seems conscious that people today do not consider themselves as passive individuals who are subservient to ready-made laws, whether divine or natural. John shows (because of his knowledge of literature, his fluency in Russian) that he appreciates that we are children of Darwin and Einstein, and citizens of a global village.

I do not accept Malachi Martin's contention that John was ignorant of the internal condition of the Church, and out-of-touch with the theological undercurrents running strongly through Catholic universities and seminaries in Europe, the United States, and Latin America. The address shows, on the contrary, that John was sensitive to the signs of the times, and that history was his great teacher; that he had a feeling for the relative and the concrete, for the world's great pain; that he appreciated that the past will never return, and that new situations require new attitudes and approaches.

These beliefs are the wellsprings of John's dreams for the Council: that it be a pastoral rather than a reforming Council; a Council for the times; a forgiving and renewing Council with three goals (that were repeated by Pope Paul VI in his opening address at Vatican II's second session in September 1963):

- the unity of Catholics among themselves.
- the reunion of Catholics with other Christians through a deepening of self-understanding.
- the unity and peace of the whole human family.

Both *Veritatis Splendor* and this volume of responses to the encyclical are conscious efforts to achieve John's goals, and to further the work of the Council.

*   *   *

Veritatis Splendor is another of Pope John Paul II's historic efforts to proclaim the truth about the human person, the truth that frees. In this, his tenth encyclical, John Paul does not reflect on an area of morality (human sexuality, the family, political life), but on the foundations of the Church's moral teaching, "with the precise goal of recalling certain fundamental truths of Catholic doctrine which, in the present circumstances, risk being distorted or denied" (n. 4). Addressed to the bishops of the Church, and arising from a decision made in 1987 (hints about the contents of the document can be found as early as 1984), the 40,000-word encyclical has a definite pastoral purpose: to set forth principles of moral teaching based upon Sacred Scripture and the living apostolic tradition, and "at the same time to shed light on the presuppositions and consequences of the dissent which that teaching has met" (n. 5).

The encyclical, the first authoritative magisterial statement on the foundations of morality, has three parts, each of which possesses insights that reflect John Paul's personal understanding of Christian ethics, as well as his concerns about some of the efforts to renew the Church's moral theology as mandated by Vatican II. Chapter One (it has received high praise) contains an extended meditation on the exchange between Christ and the rich young man (Matthew 19:16-22), in which the pope emphasizes that the moral life means following Christ, empowerment by the Holy Spirit, and a community tradition. "Future generations may find the splendor of *Veritatis Splendor* here in these pages," writes Oliver O'Donovan, Regius Professor of Moral and Pastoral Theology in the University of Oxford. Chapter Two, the most technical and difficult, provides a review of trends in moral theology that lead (in the pope's opinion) to relativism, subjectivism, and individualism, to undermining the universality and immutability of the moral commandments. Here John Paul takes up such subjects as freedom and law, conscience and truth, the fundamental option, and the moral act. Throughout, the pope emphasizes that freedom cannot be separated from the truth about the human person.

The final chapter deals with the place of morality in the life of the Church, the teaching responsibility of bishops, and the role of theologians. It sees martyrdom (Christ's death) as the paradigm of perfect humanity.

The encyclical embodies both the pope's awareness of the seriousness of the moral crisis of our times and some of the finest insights in the 2,000-year-old Christian moral tradition. For example, the document is Christocentric. In John's eyes, "Jesus reveals by his whole life, and not only by his words, that freedom is acquired in love, that is, in the gift of self" (n. 87). The Sermon on the Mount (Matthew 5-7) is called "the Magna Carta of Gospel morality" (n. 15). The document's extended meditation on the rich young man serves as "a useful guide for listening once more in a lively and direct way to his (Jesus') moral teaching" (n. 6). Further, the pope presents the moral life not in terms of servile obedience to laws but as "the response due to the many gratuitous initiatives taken by God out of love for man" (n. 10).

This volume of responses to *Veritatis Splendor* arose from the desire to provide a set of essays that would do justice to the encyclical, and enable both nonspecialists and specialists to understand the document, in particular its presentation of Christian ethics, and to assess its criticism of tendencies seen to be dangerous and erroneous. More complete than the responses that have been published in *The Tablet*, *Commonweal*, *America*, the 20 studies deal with specific aspects of the encyclical, for instance, its use of Scripture (Spohn), the influence of Augustine (O'Keefe), its concept of perfection (TePas). Other essays examine the pope's use of rhetoric (Sunshine), his concept of discernment (Haughey, Frohlich), his understanding of love (Milhaven), his criticism of proportionalism (Gaffney). Some studies look at the document from a feminist perspective (Talvacchia and Walsh), in the light of Rahner and Levinas (Tallon), while other essays assess the implications of the pope's teaching for medical ethics (Lustig), for sexual ethics (Hanigan), for discussions of war and peace (Lammers).

The essays have been written by respected American scholars who represent diverse backgrounds and approaches, that richness which John A. Boyle sees as characteristic of contemporary American Catholic moral theology. Each study has been undertaken as a service to the Church (as Newman saw the work of theologians), to "serve this single end: that each person may be able to find Christ, in order that Christ may walk with each person the path of life" (*Redemptor Hominis*, n. 13).

* * *

I must thank, first, those who responded to the invitations to contribute to this volume, both those who were willing to take part in this project, and those who were prevented because of other responsibilities.

I am indebted to Robert Heyer, Editor-in-Chief at Sheed & Ward, for his interest in this project, for actively seeking contributors, and agreeing to publish the collection when it was still in its adolescence.

Finally, my sincere thanks to John O'Keefe, for his assistance, and encouragement; to Mary Kuhlman, and Diane Kriley, for their secretarial support; and to the friends and colleagues in Sydney, Rome, Spokane, Omaha, and Miami who have added their suggestions, read the essays, and given editorial advice.

Postscript. Great things have taken place as a result of the Second Vatican Council, because of Pope John's dreams and memories. Both *Veritatis Splendor* and this volume are two further examples of William Blake's perceptiveness.

Michael E. Allsopp

1

"Then Who Can Be Saved?": Ethics and Ecclesiology in *Veritatis Splendor*

Maura Anne Ryan

Pope John Paul II's encyclical on moral theology[1] is rich in powerful imagery. It opens with the dramatic confrontation between Jesus and the rich young man recounted by Matthew in the 19th chapter of his gospel. The story is familiar: the earnest young man begs to be told the Way, the path to eternal life; Jesus answers with a call to radical self-surrender. The young man departs in sorrow, an enduring portrait of the would-be disciple who can meet every religious and moral challenge but one: "Come, follow me." *Veritatis Splendor* closes with a broad summons to martyrdom, the challenge to sacrifice property and security for the Kingdom by this point intensified, having taken on the memory of long-dead Christians whose lives were their testimony. In between, sharply contrasting images weave in and out of highly technical theological analysis. Jesus Christ, "the true light," (Jn. 1:9) stands against the darkness of relativism and skepticism, genuine human freedom against illusory autonomy, the church as trustworthy teacher against deceptive culture, transformation by spiritual renewal against conformance to the world, redemption by Christ against domination by lust, faithful magisterium against dissenting moralist. Although the encyclical's weight is in its critical assessment of the state of contemporary moral theology, its force is in its many images. Not only do they coalesce in a striking picture of the moral life, but they convey important (and complex) assumptions about the church, its role as moral guide and interpreter of revelation, its relationship to the world and its internal mechanisms for determining rules and practices.

Veritatis Splendor has been called an "encyclical of restoration." It appears, many argue, as part of a program launched during the present pontificate to restore the Roman Catholic church to its former place as the voice of moral and religious certainty and the unquestioned arbiter of conscience.[2] Whether this is or isn't the case, I am not prepared to say. However, in what follows I will argue that, when read from the perspective of Vatican II ecclesiology, *Veritatis Splendor* displays subtle but nonetheless dramatic shifts of emphasis. Such shifts are most obvious in the encyclical's treatment of legitimate sources for moral wisdom, but are also evident in two related areas: in the encyclical's presentation of the church as teacher and mediator of moral truth, i.e., in its view of the relationship between the magisterium and the individual believer, and its treatment of the relationship between the church and the world, or more precisely, between the church as guardian of faith and "secular culture." In its imagery and its argument, *Veritatis Splendor* makes important and troubling claims about the nature and mission of the church.

1.
Intersections: Ethics and Ecclesiology

A. *Jesus, the Church and the Rich Young Man*

Veritatis Splendor is addressed to the world's bishops. Its stated purpose is to "reflect on the whole of the church's moral teaching, with the precise goal of recalling certain fundamental truths of Catholic doctrine which, in the present circumstances, risk being distorted or denied" (n. 4). This is not an encyclical addressed to "all people of good will" or written, for the most part, in the style of pastoral exhortation. It is a parochial document, intended primarily for the education of the episcopate in the face of a perceived internal crisis, a crisis generated within a particular theological discipline. We should not expect, therefore, to find much here either in the way of focused moral counsel for the perplexed believer or textual attention to the broad issues of church life and practice. Indeed, those looking for a systematic and comprehensive exposition of Roman Catholic doctrine are directed to the *Catechism of the Catholic Church* (n. 5), the publication of which preceded the release of *Veritatis Splendor*. It might be argued, therefore, that reflection on the ecclesiological dimensions of this encyclical—on its implicit theology of membership, authority or church-world relations—is misguided or inappropriate.

Yet, how is the moral life characterized in *Veritatis Splendor*? It is, from the start, fundamentally a matter of *encounter* and *response:* for every believer, just as for the rich young man of Matthew's gospel, "the moral life presents itself as the response due to the many gratuitous initiatives taken by God out of love for man. It is a response of love . . ." (n. 10). The invitation to "Come, follow me" (Mt. 19:21) is extended to all who approach Jesus in search of eternal life; to follow is "not a matter only of disposing oneself to hear a teaching and obediently accepting a commandment. More radically, it involves holding fast to the very person of Jesus, partaking of his life and his destiny, sharing in his free and loving obedience to the will of the Father" (n. 19).

In the encyclical's lengthy and dense second chapter, explicit links are made between faith properly expressed and particular moral actions (that is, faith is given a normative moral content). Still, the underlying dynamic of the encyclical is one of a free, spontaneous, affective cleaving to the person of Jesus Christ (n. 15, 19, 20, 88). Observance of the commandments is not a condition for relationship with Jesus, but an outgrowth of the profoundly intimate encounter which occurs between Jesus and the potential disciple. That the primary religious obligations are love of God and love of neighbor follows naturally, for the love at work in the faith encounter begs, even impels expression in gratitude and imitation (n. 15).

Nonetheless, imitating and living out the love of Jesus are ultimately impossible as human achievements; only by virtue of grace and through the action of the Holy Spirit can the life to which the disciple is invited truly be lived (n. 22, 23, 27). Love and life according to the Gospel, argues John Paul II, "cannot be thought of first and foremost as a kind of precept" (n. 23); rather, they are a *promise,* extended by Jesus Christ, guaranteed by the presence of the Spirit. Perfection is a "possibility opened up to man exclusively by grace," a possibility which the Christian must nonetheless actively seek in disposition and action (n. 24).

But to appreciate the sense in which conclusions about ethics imply ecclesiological presuppositions in *Veritatis Splendor*, we need to ask a further question: What role does the church play in this encounter between Christ and the disciple? In *Veritatis Splendor*: 1). The church is the immediate locus for the divine-human encounter; it is the body, the extension of Christ wherein the believer meets the Teacher (n. 7, 21); it is the site where the deepest questions of faith and morality are posed and answered (n. 117); and it is the witness to God's great deeds in history and "to the inviting splendor of that truth which is Jesus Christ himself" (n. 27, 83); 2) The church, through the function of its magisterium, "receives and hands down the Scripture," promoting and preserving both the conditions for faith encounter and the community's understanding of the normative Christian life (n. 27). Taking the role of Jesus in the meeting between searching disciple and the God who alone is good (cf. Mk. 10:18; Mt. 19:17; Lk. 18:19), the church faithfully expounds God's commandments, correctly interpreting divine law in whatever historical circumstances obtain (n. 25, 95); 3) The church is the "pillar, the bulwark of the truth" (1 Tm. 3:15); its teaching magisterium not only promotes witness to the truth of Jesus Christ, but defends against error and division within the community (n. 26-27). In seeking out the most adequate expression of faith in a particular time or in the face of particular problems, its magisterium evaluates and coordinates the insights of individual believers—it "runs interference," so to speak—by way of its access to transcendental truths (n. 53); 4) Finally, the church is an agent of hope in an increasingly (dangerously) dechristianized world (n. 97; 106-109). The path Jesus offers the rich young man is a universal invitation to true human fulfillment. By keeping the challenge and the promise alive for itself, the community preserves an essential human legacy.

Emphasis on magis. leads to sense of complacency, or overriding guilt → b/c sense of sin fundamentally EXTRINSIC to my life

We see in *Veritatis Splendor*, therefore, a progressive movement from a view of the moral life as an encounter between Jesus and the seeker of eternal life to a view of the moral life as an encounter between Jesus and the seeker in and through the institutional church. Later, I will raise some critical questions of this account; for now, it is important simply to see how John Paul II sets the stage for his critique of trends in contemporary moral theology by locating in the church—and specifically in the activity of the magisterium—the burden of responsibility for preserving the conditions for a genuine encounter. This burden takes on a certain urgency in the encyclical as the church is seen as battling the influence of a threatening culture.

B. The Church and "Secular Culture"

The church and the world stand in complex relationship in *Veritatis Splendor*. On the one hand, Pope John Paul II presents the church as possessing the only morality capable of sustaining genuine democracy, indeed the only morality capable of guaranteeing "the ethical foundation of social coexistence, both on the national and international levels" (n. 96, 97). A viable defense against totalitarianism or "democracy without values" (both long-standing concerns of John Paul II) rests on a personal and communal acknowledgment of the absolutely binding character of those moral norms which pertain to the protection of human dignity (n. 101). The commandments of the second table of the Decalogue—the propositional heart of this morality—are not merely faith practices but the "indispensable rules of all social life" (n. 97).

The church, therefore, offers witness to more than a believer's truth (the reality of Jesus Christ expressed in a particular way of life); it testifies as well to a universal truth (the necessity of an uncompromising regard for personal dignity in the creation and promotion of "truly human" societies). Only this "transcendent truth" (n. 99) which the Roman Catholic Church holds and teaches—the truth about God's intentions for humanity—can lead the way beyond the ethic of self-interest which so often governs human relations of all kinds, from interpersonal to international. Thus, the church has a necessary evangelizing function in *Veritatis Splendor*, one which is intimately linked with its responsibility for articulating a universally binding and objective morality. The long involvement of the Roman Catholic Church in world affairs is affirmed, while the importance of keeping social ethics rooted in a traditional natural law morality is underscored.

We find here a church very much concerned with the world and its people, very much engaged in the struggle for political renewal and social transformation. On the other hand, however, the church in *Veritatis Splendor* is an institution under siege, its ability to promote a specific, ecclesially defined morality threatened by the negative influence of a "prevalent and all-intrusive culture" (n. 88).[3] Cast in the visual imagery of *Veritatis Splendor,* today's "rich young man" wanders in the darkness of subjectivism and relativism, his moral compass possibly so compromised that he does not even know how lost he really is. Existing in a social milieu where "God is dead" and freedom makes its own law, he turns to the church for answers to the mystery of his own existence. For its part, the institutional church must act as a beacon: it must present the uncompromised truth about freedom's duty to the moral law, transmit without distortion the gospel tradition, and protect him (and all the faithful) from doctrines which would obscure or falsify God's moral demands (n. 116, 119).

But some of the church's own theologians are infected, so to speak, with the relativism, subjectivism and individualism which have taken root in the post-modern period. "Even in seminaries and in faculties of theology," systems of thought are being introduced which cast doubt on the very possibility of access to an objective moral order and thus erode confidence in the magisterium's authority to teach an objective morality (n. 4). Culture—enveloping, septic, pernicious—thus becomes even more dangerous as it is carried into the life of the community in the guise of theological renewal. Believers seeking the comfort of truth might well meet a false lantern-bearer who, perhaps even unwittingly, leads them further away from what is truly good.

The emergence of proportionalism and consequentialism in contemporary Roman Catholic moral theology testifies, in John Paul II's view, to the degree to which moral theology has already become "conformed to the world"; in both, abstract moral reasoning is modified by attention to the contextual and experiential features of particular choices. Widespread dissent to magisterial teachings concerning artificial contraception and remarriage after divorce is the unhappy consequence of inappropriate or naive teaching concerning moral certainty and freedom of conscience. The pope's perception that such dissent can only be read as a crisis for the church is the occasion for the publication of *Veritatis Splendor* and the rationale for its three-fold strategy: reaffirmation of hierarchical authority, systematic reflection on moral methodology, and reassertion of traditional doctrines concerning intrinsically evil acts. Seekers of the way must turn "to God alone who is good" (cf. Mk. 10:18; Lk. 18:19), but this occurs properly through the activity of the magisterium; the disciple who approaches Jesus in the encyclical's first chapter approaches the magisterium by the end (n. 27).[4]

We could argue that *Veritatis Splendor* shows evidence of two different ways of understanding church-world relations. To borrow loosely from H. Richard Niebuhr's classic typology, we see strains here of both "Christ above culture" and "Christ against culture."[5] To the extent that the church can serve as a witness to the inbreaking of God's grace in history and as an agent of moral seriousness in its particular context, it is to engage the world freely. But while it ought to shape culture, the church must guard vigilantly against being shaped by it, especially by trends and popular schools of thought which may ultimately undermine it as a community capable of teaching the truth. As we have already seen, John Paul II shows a particular concern in *Veritatis Splendor* for the seepage of negative cultural forces into the community through the influential work of revisionist moral theologians. Given the subtlety and pervasiveness of those worrisome aspects of culture identified (e.g., relativism, subjectivism and individualism), the church must control not only who speaks in its name, but what sources of moral wisdom are to be employed (or, in other words, how much of the world's wisdom is to be sought). Control is thus gained by setting "truth" against "the world's thinking" and locating rightful apperception in the magisterium. The moves John Paul II makes in this regard are subtle. I will now show how they represent important and troubling departures from the visionary ecclesiology of Vatican II.

C. Sources of Moral Wisdom

In his reflections on contemporary moral theology, Richard McCormick counts among its characteristics (indeed, its achievements) the appreciation of human experience and reflection as a rich and indispensable source of moral knowledge.[6] He argues that in adopting the personalist moral criterion, that is, "the human person adequately considered," Vatican II committed the church to "an inductive method in moral deliberation about rightness and wrongness in which human experience and the sciences play an indispensable role."[7] Asking "what a given intervention (or choice) as a whole means for the promotion of the human persons who are involved and for their relationships," as this criterion requires, expands the legitimate sources for moral theology to include the many disciplines which offer insight into broad human experience.[8] Post-conciliar moral theology, having taken seriously the complexity of human personhood—recognizing that persons exist in history, as male and female, within relationships of various kinds, at the same time embodied and spiritual, self-determining but with a finite grasp of the nature of their own existence—necessarily emerges (in principle and potential, if not always in practice) as pluralistic, interdisciplinary, collegial, and, at least more so than it had been, epistemologically humble.

As McCormick reads the documents of Vatican II, the turn to human experience as a rich source of moral wisdom is reflected positively in two ecclesiological moves. First, it is affirmed in the Council's insistence that the *whole church* is a learning and teaching church. *Gaudium et spes* acknowledges the role of all members of the Body of Christ in the discernment of God's will:

> With the help of the Holy Spirit, *it is the task of the whole people of God, particularly of its pastors and theologians, to listen to and distinguish the many voices of our times and to interpret them in the light of the divine Word*, in order that the revealed truth may be more deeply penetrated, better understood, and more suitably presented.[9]

Without negating the special role of the hierarchical magisterium in transmitting and explicating divine revelation, Vatican II honors the transformative charism of the Holy Spirit at work in the entire community.[10] Authority resides ultimately in the Gospel; the legitimate exercise of authority in the church, therefore, facilitates rather than replaces the genuine and trustworthy response in faith of the individual disciple to the Word of God. That there is no "merely passive participation in the people of God"[11] is underscored in *Lumen Gentium's* discussion of the *sensus fidei*:

> The holy People of God shares also in Christ's prophetic office: it spreads abroad a living witness to him. . . . The whole body of the faithful who have an anointing that comes from the holy one (cf. 1 Jn 2:20 and 27) cannot err in matters of belief . . . when "from the bishops to the last of the faithful" they manifest a universal consent in matters of faith and morals. By this appreciation of the faith, aroused and sustained by the Spirit of truth, the People of God, guided by the sacred teaching authority and obeying it, receives not the mere word of men, but truly of God. . . .[12]

While it would be incorrect to call the church envisioned in Vatican II a democracy, the council nonetheless shattered the "supposed division between those whose way of life and activity deals with 'the sacred' and those who are engaged with the 'secular'."[13] Vatican II gives theological weight (indeed prophetic power) to ordinary faith experience; in so doing, it explicitly recognizes lay men and women as subjects of revelation rather than objects of doctrine. In Richard McBrien's words, in the distinctive ecclesiology of Vatican II, "the whole People of God participates in the mission of Christ, and not just in the mission of the hierarchy."[14]

The turn to experience is also affirmed, according to McCormick, in the council's acknowledgment of the particular competence of the laity. In several places, lay persons are urged to take up their special role, and pastors are urged, as they face complex modern problems, to draw on the assistance of those with "worldly expertise." We read in *Gaudium et spes*, for example:

> Nowadays when things change so rapidly and thought patterns differ so widely, the Church needs to step up this exchange [between the Church and different cultures] by calling upon the help of those who are living in the world, who are expert in its organizations and its forms of training, and who understand its mentality. . . .[15]

> It is to the laity, though not exclusively to them, that secular duties and activities properly belong. . . . It is their task to cultivate a properly informed conscience and to impress the divine law on the affairs of the earthly city. For guidance and spiritual strength let them turn to the clergy; but let them realize that their pastors will not always be so expert as to have a ready answer to every problem (even every grave problem) that arises. . . .[16]

And in *Lumen Gentium*:

> By reason of the knowledge, competence or preeminence which they
> have, the laity are empowered—indeed sometimes obliged—to manifest
> their opinion on those things which pertain to the good of the Church.[17]

In such documents, we find pastors challenged to empower the laity
according to their own expertise and to foster broad interest in theological
education. We find theologians encouraged to engage in fruitful collaboration with experts in various fields of human study.[18] Optimism about the
possibilities for growth and renewal in the church is joined here by an assumption that all members of the church community do not enjoy equal
competence in all matters and that open dialogue among persons with different experience and spheres of knowledge enriches the life and ministry of
the community (despite the potential for disagreement).[19] The church of
Vatican II is in many ways a community *in via,* a pilgrim people, "at the
same time holy and always in need of being purified, incessantly [pursuing]
the path of penance and renewal."[20]

What of the church in *Veritatis Splendor*? What of this turn to experience and its ecclesiological expression? In his description of the search for
truth in the Roman Catholic Church, what place does John Paul II give to
the faith testimony of the laity, for example, or to the contributions of the
human sciences? While it would be incorrect to say that John Paul II denies
the theological and ethical significance of particular faith experience or the
weight of broad human knowledge, or that he negates the role of the laity in
the Church's evangelizing mission, his conclusions regarding moral methodology (or legitimate paths to truth) nonetheless represent a clear retreat from
the optimistic openness of Vatican II. In several places, the pope notes
positively the turns taken by contemporary moral theology: its deepened appreciation of history and the diversity of cultures, expanded use of scientific
knowledge and systematic empirical data, attention to the dignity of conscience and the dynamism of human freedom, and concern to view the
moral life as a matter not of mere acts but of agency. But every such nota-
tion is immediately followed by a caution and a discussion of the excesses
and abuses to which each turn is subject.

John Paul II acknowledges the invitation extended by Vatican II to
theologians to "live in the closest contact with others of their time and . . .
work for a perfect understanding of their modes of thought and feelings as
expressed in their culture" (n. 29)[21]; however, he quickly voices alarm at the
price of cultural contact: the influx of intuitionism and subjectivism into
mainstream theology (n. 29-32). He supports modern theology's heightened
respect for the unique dignity of each individual (n. 31), but decries its
adoption of modernity's exalted view of freedom (n. 32). The behavioral
sciences can "rightly [draw] attention to the many kinds of psychological
and social conditioning which influence the exercise of human freedom,"
but some individuals have gone beyond legitimate conclusions to "question

or even deny the very reality of human freedom" (n. 33). Agreeing in principle with the council's teaching that "the moral life calls for that creativity and originality typical of the person, the source and cause of his own deliberate acts," John Paul II nevertheless expresses concern over popular interpretations of the principle of autonomy of reason wherein "reason itself creates values and moral norms" (n. 40).[22] Each individual has a right to "be respected in his own journey in search of truth," he grants, but "there exists a prior moral obligation, and a grave one at that, to seek the truth and to adhere to it once it is known" (n. 34); moral theories which fail to acknowledge freedom's dependence on truth have fallen prey to distortion (n. 34).

The cumulative effect of a naive appropriation of modern theories concerning freedom and reason, such as occurs, in John Paul II's view, in proportionalism and consequentialism, is a generalized "lack of trust in the wisdom of God" (a term which in this encyclical is often used as synonymous with "the wisdom of the magisterium"). Failing to feel bound in conscience by an objective and universal truth, by the absolute demands of the law of God, the modern Christian unknowingly risks his or her very salvation (n. 84). The pope's response to this problem is not, as we might expect, to provide suggestions as to how theology might forge more useful (less distorting) alliances with the behavioral sciences or draw more wisely from modern theories concerning cognition and rationality. Rather, he seeks to restore the faithful to a posture of trust by restricting moral "truth" to magisterial interpretations of the divine law. "Participation in the communal search for truth" thus becomes, for theologians, "expounding the validity and obligatory nature of the precepts [the magisterium] proposes . . . " (n. 110) and for the laity in general "witnessing to the absoluteness of the moral good"—to the point of martyrdom, if necessary (n. 93). The pope accepts Vatican II's teaching that the universal body of the faithful "cannot be mistaken in belief"; however, he cites *Lumen Gentium* n. 12 at the beginning of a discussion concerning the moral theologian's responsibility to be an example of loyal assent to the magisterium's dogmatic and moral teaching despite the human limitations under which it may labor (n. 109-111). When read in the context of the encyclical's critique of culture, it is clear that certain widespread disagreements in the church today, e.g., over the licitness of artificial contraception within marriage, are not to be interpreted as possible signs of the transformative wisdom of the Holy Spirit at work in the community, as they might be from some readings of the meaning of the *sensus fidei*,[23] but as evidence of failed pedagogy or as symptomatic of a climate of insufficient respect for God's law. Moral teachings are not established by vote, therefore "exchanges and conflicts of opinion" have no epistemic or revelatory role to play in the search for truth (n. 113).

Indeed, the possibility of genuine (perhaps productive) disagreement over moral norms within the community is closed off in two ways in *Veritatis Splendor:* it is closed off in principle—the discerning believer who cannot in good conscience proclaim a given teaching "reasonable" is lacking in awareness of dormant truths (n. 64)—and it is closed off in practice: public dissent is illegitimate and is to be suppressed for the sake of ecclesial cohesion (n. 113). No distinction is made here between fallible and infallible teachings; the strong and unnuanced argument for religious obedience offered leaves one with the impression that traditional distinctions bear no weight for the believer. Further, the potential for newly discovered facts or refinements in interpretation to give rise to revisions in traditional teachings is limited by the prior designation of all ethical questions as religious questions, and all religious questions as falling within the deposit of faith (n. 1, 9, 53).

Although John Paul II uses the terms "community of believers" and "community of faith" to describe the church, the picture of the moral life which emerges in *Veritatis Splendor* is finally one of a relationship between an individual disciple and a Master; it is a deeply personal call to obedience expressed in fidelity to institutional norms. To be sure, the encounter with Jesus which gives rise to moral action occurs through the sacramental, educational and social life of the Roman Catholic Church, and the church in the world witnesses in and through the lives of all its members; still, there is little sense in this encyclical of the church as a *body* of seekers, assisting and challenging one another, calling forth from within the unique gifts of all in a common effort to discern the most appropriate response to God's initiatives. Indeed, the community considered as a whole, as including those who question the conclusions of its leaders on some matters, poses dangers for the disciple. For salvation, the disciple must turn to the magisterium (or church teachings), for only there can he or she be assured of not being misled. The church is sinful—a great many believers need to be reminded "not to allow themselves to be tainted by the attitude of the Pharisee, which would seek to eliminate awareness of [their] own limits and [their] own sin"—but there is little acknowledgment of the sin of the Church (n. 104-105). In an almost ironic omission, there is no admission that the weaknesses to which its members fall prey also mark its leaders as human. In the same way, the believer may be a pilgrim, groping her way to God in the complexity and ambiguity of modern life, uncertain as to what a proper gratitude might be; but the institutional church in this encyclical is not *in via,* at least with regard to the specification of morality.

What is evident, therefore, is a shift from Vatican II's church as the people of God to the church as a relation of disciples to a Master; from the church in the midst of history to the church as the beacon of light in the darkness of modernity; from an openness to culture and a variety of sources of human knowledge in the service of its mission to a hostility toward all which might lead to intellectual unrest in the community; from an appreciation of the unique contribution of the laity (in various disciplines) in the search for truth to a posture of "laity-protection." In our attention to the important issues of moral methodology which arise in this encyclical, we should take care not to overlook these assumptions regarding the character and mission of the church.

2.
In Conclusion: How Many Roads to the Truth?

Responses to *Veritatis Splendor* have been numerous, passionate and generally mixed. Many readers have praised the encyclical's reassertion of the existence of an objective moral order, its expression of confidence in traditional natural law methodology, its prescient diagnosis of contemporary moral malaise. A great many more have found fault with its presuppositions and its arguments. They dispute the implication, for example, that revisionist moral theologians are canonizing relativism, individualism and subjectivism and that the church is in a state therefore of moral crisis. They disagree with the conclusion that moral and spiritual renewal in the Roman Catholic Church requires the cultivation of obedience to papal authority.

Some of the praise seems to me to be warranted and much of the criticism. Like many readers, I grant that there is a worrisome moral subjectivity in the air, and I agree that communities of faith have a special duty to cultivate moral responsibility. *Veritatis Splendor's* Christo-centric ethic, based on the experience of gratitude expressed in the performance of particular acts—acts which are defined in light of the self-identity of the community—is attractive in many ways. Pope John Paul II's arguments regarding the necessary relationship between Christian freedom and the divine claim are compelling, if not always convincing. His recognition of the need for vigilant attention to the health of Roman Catholic sacramental life is welcome.

It is difficult, however, to find his description of the cultural crisis facing the church today persuasive, and thus to accept as necessary his plan for institutional damage control (what some would call a plan of martial law). For one thing, "culture" is a far more complex phenomenon than this encyclical grants. To really assess the influence of culture on contemporary moral theology, we would have to give attention to a great many trends, for example, to the rise of religious fundamentalism and the popularity of gangs, clubs and fraternal associations among the young. Moreover, by targeting revisionist moral theologians as the conduits of negative social forces into church life, the pope greatly oversimplifies the problems facing the global church today; thus, the solutions he offers are untenable. Finally, I am not convinced that the picture of the moral life offered in *Veritatis Splendor* is theologically coherent. I am not sure that an ethic based on faith as "a decision involving one's whole existence," "a promise," "not simply a set of propositions to be accepted with intellectual assent," but "an encounter, a dialogue, a communion of love and of life between the believer

and Jesus Christ" (n. 88) can in fact be reconciled with one requiring assent
to hierarchically proposed "moral facts," even those which are counter-intui-
tive.

However, in closing I want to raise what seems to me to be the most
important question, given the focus of this essay: that is, whether *Veritatis
Splendor* has accurately described the possible ways we might seek the truth
in the Catholic church. The encyclical construes the choice starkly: it is
either democratic vote or hierarchical pronouncement. Since the church's
"moral teaching . . . is in no way established by following the rules and
deliberative procedures typical of a democracy" (n. 113), opposition, exchanges and conflicts of opinion are out of place in this institution. The
church is not a democracy; therefore conversation regarding practices need
not run both ways between leadership and membership.

Some have argued that there is no reason why the church *could not* be
organized democratically, that, indeed, there are good theological reasons
for it being so organized. In his *Church: The Human Story of God*, Edward
Schillebeeckx argues, for example, quoting Matthew 20:25-26, Mark 10: 42-
43, and Luke 22:25, that while there is a place for authority and leadership
in the church, there is no proper place for hierarchy, for "master-slave" relationships; all the baptized are subject in the same way to the authority of the
Word of God.[24] That the church took a hierarchical form is more a reflection of historical setting or inculturation than theological impetus. Recognizing the lure of sinful power, the Christian church should attempt to
approximate as much as possible the "non-authoritative, vulnerable, even
helpless, rule of God."[25] Further, to the extent that the ministerial teaching
authority overlooks the "manifold ecclesial mediations of the work of the
Holy Spirit"—particularly the voice of the Holy Spirit in the believing community, it "runs the risk of not having listened faithfully to the word of
God."[26] Thus, while he does not lay out a model for the coordination of
ministries in the church, Schillebeeckx argues that the sort of democratic
structures which would inspire dialogue, multiple expressions of faith, and
accountability in leadership are intrinsic to the nature and mission of the
church. Elisabeth Schüssler Fiorenza and Heinrich Fries have argued along
similar lines.[27]

But even if one wants to accept the position that the "church is not a
democracy," or more precisely that the development of doctrine ought not
be a matter of popular opinion or majority rule, does it follow that the
unilateral exercise of hierarchical authority is the only other form of appropriate leadership? Couldn't we argue, as the early Avery Dulles and others
have done, for a pluralistic model of authority, one in which "several distinct organs of authority" coexist in a relationship of assistance and mutual
critique?[28] The theological rationale for such a model can be found both in
the doctrine of the priesthood of all believers and in traditional beliefs
regarding the diverse and spontaneous gifts of the Holy Spirit. We could

conceive of the church as a community with various organs of leadership, e.g., pastoral, prophetic, and doctrinal, some offices appointed and some arising from the grassroots, each of which performs a particular function in the governance and development of the community.[29] To say how these various organs might relate in practice would require a more fully developed theory than it is possible to provide here; a case might be made that their mode of relation ought to depend upon the community's specific historical, social and ministerial context. But a pluralistic model would at least rule out the "a priori" trump of one office over the other and would presuppose that doctrine cannot be authentically developed without adequately broad consultation and dialogue. A pluralistic model also assumes the probability of genuine disagreements that are not just expressions of sinful disobedience. Various processes might be developed to adjudicate such disagreements, but to legitimate the equal and unique contribution of each office is to recognize disagreement as a sign of the vigor of the community and the continual reformative, transformative action of the Holy Spirit.

To support a hierarchical model of leadership, to agree that moral and religious truth can be proclaimed unilaterally in all cases, such as we are being asked to do in *Veritatis Splendor*, requires that we accept two statements: 1) that the magisterium does not make mistakes; and 2) that truth can be ascertained without attention to "the manifold ecclesial mediations of the work of the Holy Spirit." If historical reflection does not dissuade us from accepting those statements as true, then theological reflection ought.

Notes

1. *Veritatis Splendor,* signed by Pope John Paul II, was released on August 6, 1993. All references herein are to the English translation which appeared in *Origins* 23/18 (October 14, 1993): 297-334.

2. See Gabriel Daly, O.S.A., "Focus on Veritatis Splendor: Ecclesial Implications," *Doctrine & Life* 43 (November, 1993), pp. 532-537. Also, "Veritatis Splendor" *Commonweal* CXX/18 (October 22, 1993), p. 39. Those who see *Veritatis Splendor* as part of a "restoration project" relate its publication to such things as the oath of fidelity, ordinances proposed for Catholic higher education, censure of theologians, the publication of the universal catechism, instructions and letters discussing the ecclesial vocation of the theologian, and trends in the appointment of bishops.

3. I am using the term "culture" as it is used in the English translation of *Veritatis Splendor,* that is, without nuance or precise definition. However, it seems to me that what the term "culture" connotes in this encyclical is something like "Western liberalism."

4. Todd David Whitmore traces this movement from a morality of "invited response" to one of "commanded obedience" (see n. 25-45) in his commentary "Three Cheers and a Number of Hard Questions: 'Veritatis Splendor',￼" in *Bostonia: The Magazine of Culture and Ideas.* To Whitmore's observation that the magisterium

has virtually replaced Jesus as the "Good Teacher" by n. 27, I would add that "church" has virtually collapsed into "magisterium" by n. 95.

5. H. Richard Niebuhr, *Christ and Culture* (New York: Harper and Row), pp. 45-83; 116-149.

6. "Moral Theology from 1940 to 1989," and "Moral Theology in the Year 2000," in *Corrective Vision* (Sheed and Ward, 1994): 1-40.

7. McCormick, "Moral Theology from 1940 to 1989," p. 15. As evidence for the adoption of a personalist criterion in Vatican II, McCormick cites the official commentary on *Gaudium et spes* (re: n. 51) [*Schema constitutionis pastoralis de ecclesia in mundo huius temporis: Expensio modorum partis secundae*] Vatican Press, 1965: 37-38. See also, John Mahoney, *The Making of Moral Theology: A Study of the Roman Catholic Tradition* (Oxford: Clarendon Press, 1987), pp. 301-347.

8. Louis Janssens, "Artificial Insemination: Ethical Considerations," *Louvain Studies* 8 (1980): 3-29 at 24. See also, "Personalism in Moral Theology," in *Moral Theology: Challenges for the Future.* Edited by Charles E. Curran (Mahwah, N.J.: Paulist, 1990).

9. Vatican II, *Gaudium et spes*, n. 44 (7 December 1965) in *Vatican Council II: The Conciliar and Post Conciliar Documents*, edited by Austin Flannery, O.P. (Collegeville: Liturgical Press, 1975), p. 946. Emphasis added.

10. In his "A Half Century of Ecclesiology" [*Theological Studies* 50 (1989):419-442], Avery Dulles explains:

> In the council documents, the theme of the Church as an organized society or institution is clearly subordinated to those of the Church as mystery, sacrament, and communion of grace. Yet the image of the people of God, which holds a major position in the Constitution on the Church, is developed in such a way as to imply institutional and hierarchical structures (p. 429).

Many commentators have pointed out that conciliar documents fail to give clear direction as to how the hierarchical and charismatic forms of authority are to be reconciled.

11. Heinrich Fries, "Is there a *Magisterium* of the Faithful?" in *The Teaching Authority of the Believers* Concilium 180, edited by Johann Baptist Metz and Edward Schillebeeckx (Edinburgh: T & T Clark LTD), p. 83. See also, John Burkhard, "*Sensus Fidei:* Theological Reflection Since Vatican II. II. 1985-1989," *The Heythrop Journal* XXXIV (1993), pp. 134-135.

12. Vatican II, *Lumen gentium*, n. 12, in Flannery, p. 363. Vatican II expressed both the infallibility of the People of God and the infallibility of the magisterium— once again, how these are to be related practically is finally unspecified.

13. Bernard Cooke, "Obstacles to Lay Involvement," in *The Teaching Authority of the Believers*, p. 69.

14. Richard P. McBrien, *Catholicism.* New edition (San Francisco: HarperSanFrancisco, 1994), p. 688.

15. *G.S.*, n. 44. The *Declaration on Religious Liberty* also acknowledged the contribution of all persons of good will to the search for truth. See Flannery, p. 801-803.

16. Ibid., n. 43.

17. *L.G.*, n. 37.

18. See, e.g., *L.G.*, n. 12, 33, 37; *G.S.*, n. 43, 62.

19. See *L.G.*, n. 37, *G. S.*, n. 43.

20. L.G., n. 8. See Avery Dulles, "Doctrinal Authority for a Pilgrim Church," in *Readings in Moral Theology*. No. 3. Edited by Charles E. Curran and Richard A. McCormick, S.J. (Mahwah, N.J.: Paulist Press, 1982), pp. 247-270; and McBrien, pp. 683-689.

21. *G.S.*, n. 62.

22. *G.S.* n. 41.

23. See, e.g., Dulles, pp. 253; also, Hans Waldenfels, "Authority and Knowledge," in *The Teaching Authority of the Believers*, p. 41.

24. Edward Schillebeeckx, *Church: The Human Story of God* (New York: Crossroad, 1993), pp. 187-228.

25. Ibid., p. 221.

26. Ibid.

27. See Elisabeth Schüssler Fiorenza, "Claiming Our Authority and Power" and Heinrich Fries, "Is There a Magisterium of the Faithful?" in *The Teaching Authority of the Believers*, pp. 45-54; 82-92.

28. Dulles, p. 253. See also Christian Duquoc, "An Active Role for the People of God," in *The Teaching Authority of the Believers*, pp. 73-81; Daniel Maguire, "Morality and Magisterium," in *Readings in Moral Theology*, No. 3, pp. 34-67.

29. Dulles, p. 255.

2

No Place for Failure?
Augustinian Reflections
on *Veritatis Splendor*

John J. O'Keefe

Reacting to the publication of John Paul II's encyclical, *Veritatis Splendor*, Richard McCormick paused briefly before launching into his criticism of the document. "All Catholic moral theologians," he wrote, "should and will welcome the beautiful Christ-centered presentation unfolded in Chapter One and the rejection of the false dichotomies identified by John Paul II."[1] As a moral theologian, McCormick was eager to proceed to an evaluation of "the key second chapter,"[2] where the Pope outlines the main features of his critique of certain trends in contemporary moral theology. For my part, as a scholar trained in patristic theology with a strong interest in early Christian exegesis, I was struck by the number of references to patristic authors, especially to Augustine.[3] The Pope cites early Christian literature more than 35 times in the encyclical; 13 of these are references to Augustine. Eight of these 13 references to Augustine appear in the first chapter.[4] This information suggests that Chapter One plays a critical role in this encyclical that can easily be missed if we are too eager to move on to the moral argument of Chapter Two.

There is, of course, nothing particularly startling in the Pope's use of ancient sources. He specifically states that the purpose of the document is, in part, "to set forth . . . the principles of a moral teaching based upon Sacred Scripture and the living apostolic tradition. . . ."[5] His appeal to Augustine, Ambrose, Gregory of Nyssa, and Cyril of Alexandria—to mention a few of the ancient authors whose names appear in the course of the argument—flows from this effort at presenting a synthesis of the whole tradition. In this effort the document largely succeeds; in a way, the encyclical is remarkably "patristic." Following the venerable tradition of church documents—which steadfastly resist modernity—it proceeds with what some might call a reckless disregard for the historical circumstances and the original context of the texts from which it quotes. Something like the "rule of faith," impelled by the urgency of contemporary theological turmoil, rather than historical criticism, guides the selection not only of biblical texts, but also of writings from the Christian past. This tradition, which illuminates the major conclusions of this encyclical, can only be described as compelling. Still, this ecclesiastical approach is not without its dangers; the texts that are chosen often reflect the agenda and purpose of the one using them, rather than the agenda and purpose of the original author. The particular theological perspective of the original author may be lost in the process and, with it, the power of the text to challenge by its difference.

Since the theology of Augustine has been for me a source of both consternation and illumination, I could not help but notice that the way Augustine is used in *Veritatis Splendor* does not necessarily correspond to the way Augustine understood his own work. Through an exegetical reflection on Matthew 19, which fills the first chapter, the Pope develops a model of Christian life based upon a particular vision of human perfection. This vision, which surfaces repeatedly throughout the document, rests firmly upon the foundation of the church's ascetical tradition.[6] Augustinian notions of grace and human freedom help John Paul develop this vision, but in the process, Augustine's words lose their ability to challenge. The original difference of Augustine's theology has been subsumed by the needs of the current moment. Augustine certainly believed that the goal of human life was perfection in God. Indeed, he would agree with most of what the Pope has to say in this document about human freedom, the relationship between who we are and what we do and, to some extent, about the nature of perfection itself. However, for Augustine, the horizon toward which human beings advance was ever receding, and always unattainable. For him, we live now by grace in the hope that one day the perfection we seek, which cannot ever be reached while we live, will be ours in the freedom Christ brings at the end of time. If *Veritatis Splendor* lacks one thing that it should have learned from Augustine, it is Augustine's eschatology. Without it the document runs the risk of being pressed into the service of a self-righteousness that has little room for human failure.

1.
"Teacher, What Good Must I Do?":
The Pope's Exegesis of Matthew 19

Few scriptural texts have influenced, at least indirectly, the Catholic tradition more than Matthew 19:16-21. By choosing it as the foundational text for his reflection on Catholic moral doctrine, the Pope implicitly draws the reader into the world of Christian asceticism. In the middle of the 3rd century, Anthony of Egypt, upon hearing this text read in church, promptly sold all his possessions, moved to the desert, and spent the rest of his life engaged in the pursuit of Christian perfection.[7] This text, and the example of Anthony, inspired Augustine in his own conversion,[8] just as it inspired his opponent, Pelagius[9] in his efforts to excise from the church all forms of mediocrity. Indeed the pursuit of perfection constitutes one of the pillars of the monastic spirituality that has dominated the Catholic imagination for nearly 1500 years.

For most of that 1500 years, Christian perfection has been conceived as the domain of the elite, of the religious who give up family, wealth, and self in complete service to the Gospel. These are the heroes of Christian life whose names crowd the pages of the Roman calendar. Yet this view of perfection is itself constructed on an older model. The conversion of Constantine, early in the 4th century, brought an end to the age of Christian martyrs and inaugurated an age when it was possible to be a Christian without cost. The establishment of Christianity as the religion of the Roman empire raised difficult questions about the nature of Christian commitment and about how to live that commitment in a world where being a Christian was all too easy.[10] Monasticism, and the asceticism that came with it, was conceived, to a large degree, as the new martyrdom. The monks and the ascetics were the new martyrs who shed their blood not in the arena, but in the rigors of self-denial. The history of this transition is complicated, and the particulars of it need not concern us here.[11] However, it is clear that John Paul II wants his own remarks to be understood within the framework of Christian martyrdom and Christian perfection.

Chapter Three of *Veritatis Splendor* reveals this especially. Here the Pope reflects on what has become a familiar theme of his pontificate: the real challenges facing the church are secularism and individualism. In this encyclical the illness is localized especially in the divorce of freedom from truth. The Pope urges Christian people to undertake a new evangelization that resists the "dechristianization, which weighs heavily upon entire peoples and communities once rich in faith and Christian life. . . ." (n. 106). He recommends that Christians regain the confidence to "witness" to the power of the moral life proposed by the Gospel. The kind of witness the Pope has in mind is the ultimate witness of Christian martyrdom:

> The unacceptability of "teleological," "consequentialist" and "proportionalist" ethical theories, which deny the existence of negative moral norms regarding specific kinds of behavior, norms which are valid without exception, is confirmed in a particularly eloquent way by Christian martyrdom, which has always accompanied and continues to accompany the life of the church even today (n. 90).

The witness of the martyrs, the Pope explains, consists in their unwillingness to compromise God's law, even "for the sake of saving one's life" (n. 91). The Pope acknowledges that the martyrdom of blood characteristic of the persecuted church of the early centuries is rare in today's world. Still, he explains, there is a kind of martyrdom to which all are called:

> . . . there is nonetheless a consistent witness which all Christians must daily be ready to make, even at the cost of suffering and grave sacrifice. Indeed, faced with the many difficulties which fidelity to the

moral order can demand even in the most ordinary circumstances, the Christian is called . . . to a sometimes heroic commitment (n. 93).

The church can never conceal its "demands of radicalness and perfection" (n. 95), even if, the Pope implies, the price is martyrdom.

This tradition of asceticism and perfection, which derives from the ideal of the martyr, guides John Paul's exegesis of Matthew 19. The Pope's interpretation of the first part of the text, Matthew 19:16-17, develops the notion that, as a first step, the Christian life requires keeping the commandments. For the Pope, this means not only the Decalogue, but also the commandments contained in the natural law inscribed on the human heart (n. 12). Obedience to God's law, in his view, is the beginning of the freedom of the Christian life and the foundation upon which much of the message of Chapter Two is constructed. The rich young man, however, is not satisfied with this and asks Jesus, "What more must I do?" At this point the Pope turns to the church's ascetical tradition:

Jesus shows that the commandments must not be understood as a minimum limit not to be gone beyond, but rather as a path involving a moral and spiritual journey toward perfection, at the heart of which is love (n. 15).

Similarly, in the next paragraph, the Pope explains that Jesus' response to the young man's desire for more is an invitation for him "to enter upon the path of perfection" (n. 16).

For the rich young man this invitation included a renunciation of his family and property, the greatest of all possible sacrifices for a man of his culture. The Pope, however, says nothing at all about the dangers of wealth, preferring instead to continue development of the theme of perfection.[12] Jesus' invitation to the man becomes, in the exegesis of the Pope, an invitation to live the Beatitudes, especially to be "poor in spirit" (n. 16). The Beatitudes recommend a certain openness to eternal life and, most importantly, provide one with a basic "orientation toward the horizon of perfection" (n. 16) that directs our moral life. For John Paul, the life Jesus offers the rich young man should not be understood in a way that perpetuates the elitism mentioned above. Perfection is not the goal of monks only, it is "not restricted to a small group of individuals," but is a vocation extended to every faithful Christian. The ascetical ideal, he suggests, applies to every person who would follow the gospel (n. 18).

The moral theology of Chapter Two, then, is sandwiched between two chapters presenting an ascetical view of Christian life. The ideal of perfection, developed in Chapter One and reiterated in Chapter Three, emerges at strategic points throughout the encyclical. On the one hand, the Pope should be commended for his efforts to ground moral theology more firmly both in the scriptures and in the Christian life itself. Still, the ascetical tradition carries its own set of difficulties, especially in the area of the relationship between grace and human freedom. These difficulties merit some discussion.

2.
Asceticism and Grace:
The Pope's Effort to Nuance His Presentation

The ascetical movement that gathered momentum during the late 4th and early 5th centuries emphasized the importance of radical commitment to the gospel through heroic acts of self-control and self-denial.[13] In this way, ascetic Christians demonstrated both the depth of their conversion to the gospel and the extent to which their Christian life differed in quality from the ordinary Christianity gaining ground around them. Many were convinced that this radical choice was open to all and the choice to embrace such a life remained, despite the Fall, within the purview of human freedom. The pursuit of perfection was not only demanded, it was also possible for any who desired it strongly enough and pursued it with enough strength of will. Something like this seems to be behind the teaching of Pelagius,[14] and resistance to this view occupied Augustine during the last several decades of his life. Augustine developed his theology of grace, to a significant degree, in response to this tendency to view perfection as a realizable object of the human will.

John Paul II, of course, knows this. He cites Augustine frequently throughout the first chapter to remind the reader that, although we are called to perfection, only God gives us the ability to achieve it. Indeed, the first chapter should strike any reader trained in the Patristic tradition as quite intentionally Augustinian. Not surprisingly, Augustine's theology figures prominently in John Paul's exegesis of two critical passages: Matthew 19:21 ("If you wish to be perfect . . .), and 19:26 ("With God all things are possible.").

We have already seen how the Pope reads Matthew 19:21 as a universal call to a higher moral life beyond the mere observance of the commandments. At the center of his exegesis of this passage, however, he carefully inserts a long quotation from Augustine's *Tractates on the Gospel of John*, much of which dates from the period following the outbreak of the Pelagian controversy. The Pope has just finished explaining that God's law—which requires that we follow the commandments—does not conflict with human freedom: we can enter the path of perfection "if we wish" (n. 17). Augustine is enlisted for two reasons. First, the Pope wants to demonstrate support from the tradition for his understanding of freedom. Second, he wants to remind us that achieving this goal cannot be achieved without God's grace. Augustine, in the text quoted, was attempting to explain how, while we live on earth, our freedom is not yet fully realized. Similarly, the Pope cautions the reader of *Veritatis Splendor* to take care because our "journey" on the way to perfect freedom is "fragile . . . as long as we are on earth." It is made possible only "by grace, which enables us to possess the full freedom of the children of God" (n. 18).

More explicit Augustinian correctives materialize in the Pope's exegesis of Matthew 19:26. After hearing Jesus tell the rich young man to abandon everything he loved and cherished, the apostles, in dismay, exclaim, "Who, then, can be saved?" Jesus replies, "For people this is impossible, but for God all things are possible." According to John Paul, this text clearly indicates that the moral life he is advocating in the encyclical cannot be lived apart from the grace of God. Referring first to Paul's epistle to the Romans, the Pope explains:

> (Paul) recognizes the pedagogic function of the law, which, by enabling sinful man to take stock of his own powerlessness and by stripping him of the presumption of his self-sufficiency, leads him to ask for and to receive "life in the Spirit." Only in this new life is it possible to carry out God's commandments (n. 23).

A quotation from one of Augustine's later works, *The Spirit and the Letter*, provides confirmation from the tradition:

> St. Augustine . . . admirably sums up this Pauline dialectic of law and grace: "The law was given that grace might be sought; and grace was given that the law might be fulfilled" (n. 23).

The Pope then explains that the perfection to which we are called remains inaccessible without God's grace. He insists that this gift of grace does not contradict human freedom but is the very ground of that freedom. Once again Augustine provides support:

> This inseparable connection between the Lord's grace and human freedom, between gift and task, has been expressed in simple yet profound words by St. Augustine in his prayer: *"Da quod iubes et iube quod vis"* ("Grant what you command and command what you will.") (n. 24).

The Pope concludes Chapter One, and with it his exegesis of Matthew 19, by reminding the reader that the invitation Jesus extends to the rich young man is an invitation extended to all people. Chapter Two, with its detailed assessment of contemporary moral theology, follows. Chapter One, then, is more than a pious homily or an interesting introduction. It actually sets the tone for the document and places the contents of Chapter Two firmly in the context of Christian asceticism. The first chapter identifies the call, the second explains the demands of the call. The third exhorts us to live the call.

3.
Veritatis Splendor and Human Perfection

McCormick's reaction accurately reflects the compelling message of this chapter: "All Catholic moral theologians should and will welcome (this) beautiful Christ-centered presentation." However, I am not a moral theologian, and, as a scholar who has read a great deal of Augustine, there is something about the Pope's presentation of perfection in this encyclical that is troubling. Clearly, by recounting the story of the rich young man, the author of Matthew intended to convey a sense of the radical commitment required by the Gospel. Properly understood, Matthew's message is even more radical than the Pope implies: Jesus basically asked the rich man to give up that which he treasured more than anything else, wealth. Undeniably the call to a moral perfection beyond the letter of the law resides at the very heart of the message of the Gospel. Even if one translates the Greek word *tevleio* as "completeness" rather than "perfection," the radicalness of the Gospel invitation is not diminished. The Pope has tied this moral encyclical to a well-credentialed and correct interpretation of the demands of Christian discipleship.

Still, reading John Paul's ethic of perfection with Augustinian eyes raises some nagging questions: Where is this perfection found? When is it achieved? Who, really, is responsible for its fruition? For Augustine, as we will see in the next section, the perfection to which we are all called belongs to the eschatological future and can only be experienced partially in this world. To think otherwise invites the deception of prideful arrogance, an insurmountable obstacle both to human community and to communion with God. Augustine's theology was constructed, in many ways, to clear a space for imperfect Christians. *Veritatis Splendor* does the opposite: the church, it implies, has room only for heroes.

"Implies" is the operative word here. The Pope does not, in my view, think that Christian perfection can be fully achieved in this life. Indeed, at several points in the document he underlines the provisional nature of the church in time: our "participation in God," he explains, is "attained in its perfection only after death" (n. 12), and our life here on earth is characterized as a "fragile journey" (n. 18). His acknowledgment that the "human arguments" employed by the document are subject to limitation (n. 110) seems to indicate an awareness that human understanding will find its perfection only with the advent of God's reign. Moreover, his exegesis of the Pharisee and the tax collector recognizes human weakness (n. 104). In struggling with sin, the Pope writes that we should not attempt to redefine morality to accommodate our failure, but rather that we should repent and hope for God's mercy (n. 105). For the most part, however, these conciliatory statements are lost in the document which, as a whole, deemphasizes the eschatological nature of Christian perfection.

I have, for example, already mentioned that John Paul, quoting Augustine, presents the observance of the commandments as the beginning of freedom. Certainly, living them is difficult because the journey of this life is "fragile," but, the Pope explains, "It is one made possible by grace, which enables us to possess the full freedom of the children of God and thus to live our moral life in a way worthy of our sublime vocation . . ." (n. 18). Having said this, the Pope then declares that the "vocation" to perfection is open to all: all, like the rich young man, are invited to sell their possessions, though not literally, and enter into the radical commitment of Christian discipleship. He implies that this perfection is available here and now, to all who seek it earnestly enough. His position contrasts significantly with Augustine's.

Augustine, in the lines leading to and following the text cited by the Pope, follows a different course. Keeping the commandments is indeed the first step, and Augustine explains that all Christians should be free of major sins such as murder, adultery, fornication, theft, etc. Yet the text quoted by the Pope is a prologue not to a reflection on the possibility of living a perfect life, but to a reflection on the impossibility of such a venture. For in this life, although we are clearly called to sinlessness, we cannot achieve it. We may, Augustine explains, not act on our lust, but we still lust, and perfect freedom is freedom not just from acts associated with lust, but from lust itself. So Augustine quotes Paul (Rom 7:18): "To will . . . is there for me, but to perfect the good is not." Augustine takes this to mean that we can and must work to live a moral life, but we must recognize that perfection remains elusive.[15] The perfected Christian life must wait for the fulfillment of Christ's promise:

> What, then, is that full and perfect freedom in the Lord Jesus who said "If the Son will make you free, you will be free indeed"? When will there be full and perfect freedom? It will be when enemies are no more, when "the last enemy, death, is destroyed."[16]

A second example of the way in which *Veritatis Splendor* deemphasizes the eschatological nature of perfection can also be seen through a comparison with the work of Augustine. Reflecting on the story of the tax collector and the Pharisee (Lk 18:9-14), the Pope cautions against the "sin" of "self-justification." "The Pharisee," he writes, "is self-justified, finding some excuse for each of his failings." The "self-justified," in the Pope's view, turn out to be those who attempt "to adapt the moral norm to (their) own capacities and personal interests" and who reject the idea of norms altogether (n. 105). Jesus' point, however, seems to be that the Pharisee was in fact sinless, at least with respect to the Law. His sin was not any particular act but, rather, that his pride prevented him from recognizing that observance of the particular acts of the law was not sufficient. The point seems to be that one can keep the commandments and still fall short of the demands of the Gospel.

Augustine's exegesis of this text, although missing the point to some extent, comes closer to the mark:

> . . . therefore he who would be strong, trusting in his own strength and boasting of his own merits, whatever they may be worth, will be like that Pharisee. . . . Where, then, was his pride? Not that he thanked God for his good deeds, but that he exalted himself above another by reason of those same deeds. . . . Now there may exist some heretics who really are convinced that almost the whole world has fallen into error, and since all heretics form little groups and factions, they would like to boast that what had perished from the world at large still survived among themselves.[17]

Augustine implicitly compares the Pharisee to the Donatist church, which had broken communion with the Catholics over the issue of the church's purity. Augustine goes on to invite his audience to pray that God will deliver them from their sins as the Publican prayed for deliverance from his. It may be true, as the Pope suggests, that the Pharisee trusted in himself, not in God's grace, but that sin can be committed by people who uphold "moral norms" just as easily as it can by people who deny them. In Augustine's view, the elitism of the Donatists, which insisted on the church's perfection here and now, was their most pervasive mistake.[18] I suggest that this can, and will be, the mistake of many who read *Veritatis Splendor*.

A third way in which the document sidesteps the eschatological nature of perfection is exemplified in the Pope's use of Gregory of Nyssa. Discussing how human freedom and divine law interact in the moral life, the Pope quotes Vatican II: the Council, he explains, wanted to emphasize that because we have been created in God's image, we have in our own power to seek God and "arrive at full and blessed perfection by cleaving to God" (n. 38). To support this position the Pope draws upon Gregory of Nyssa. The text chosen as an illustration recalls the great dignity and autonomous character of the human will. By selecting this text, although perfectly orthodox and traditional, the Pope embraces a tradition of theological anthropology decidedly different from that developed by Augustine.[19] Indeed, here the Pope embraces a theology of human freedom that Augustine consistently and vehemently opposed. Gregory of Nyssa, Jerome and, of course, Pelagius, all believed that if human freedom could not be preserved, God's justice would be incomprehensible.[20] Making sense of God's justice in Augustine's system is extremely difficult. In fact, Augustine's radical notions of grace—which lead inevitably to the notion of predestination—were, quite simply, not embraced.[21] The Pope, then, reflects a tension that Catholicism has long been willing to tolerate. Still, elitism remains the danger of overconfidence in human freedom, and it needs correction. *Veritatis*

Splendor implies a static notion of perfection, a state that can be achieved, like tightening a belt notch by notch until no notches remain. Gregory of Nyssa seems to have known this. In his view, because God is ever greater, human perfection can be achieved only imperfectly:

> For though it may not be possible completely to attain the ultimate and sovereign good, it is most desirable for those who are wise to have at least a share in it. We should then make every effort not to fall short utterly of the perfection that is possible for us, and to try to come as close to it and possess as much of it as possible. For it may be that human perfection consists precisely in this constant growth in the good.[22]

Gregory's notion of human perfectibility is more optimistic than Augustine's, yet, for him, the important thing was progress. Human progress in perfection could be begun here but, since God's perfection is infinite and ever greater, progress continued even after death. Hence, moral transformation begun in this life, far from being the end, represents a first step in an unending journey toward God. The Pope's use of Gregory reflects a much more realized and static notion of perfection.

While the Pope's treatment of Augustine and Gregory indicates a realized notion of human perfection, other evidence from the encyclical suggests that this perfection extends to the church itself. This evidence represents the final way in which the document tends to stress the realized nature of perfection. Hence, at the end of the first chapter, the Pope quotes a passage from Vatican II's *Dei Verbum* which explains that the task of authentically interpreting scripture belongs to the church's living magisterium. By extension, the Pope suggests, this interpretative authority includes "the truth regarding moral action" (n. 27). Now, on the one hand, this statement is true: this is the prerogative of the church's leadership. Yet, on the other, statements such as these ignore the reality that, as it journeys in time, the church's judgment has often been clouded and even wrong.[23] Similarly, although the document professes to recognize the possible limitations of human arguments, it proclaims, as if they were in no way provisional, many of the conclusions based upon those very arguments. The strong language of Chapter Two, which declares that "the negative precepts of the natural law are universally valid," and obliges all people, in every circumstance and admits no exceptions, is clearly true if we are sure of the moral reasoning in question. But even if we are, it seems to me that such statements should be balanced by correctives which recognize that the church itself has often failed to provide moral leadership when such leadership was clearly needed and that people, in spite of their best efforts, frequently fail. Finally, the Pope speaks of the church as if it were already what it is called to be. Hence, the document explains that freedom of conscience is not destroyed by the authority of the church (n. 62-63), and moral theologians are required to submit themselves to the "magisterium which has been charged with the

responsibility of preserving the deposit of faith" (n. 109). Again, this is true
but not absolute and the reader is left wondering what provision there is for
correcting the magisterium when it strays from the tradition it is charged
with preserving.

The overall impression of *Veritatis Splendor* is that the Pope wants a
church of morally pure, perfect Christians who will be able to stand against
the onslaught of consumerism and selfishness. Where are such people?
Have such people ever existed? What place for failure is there in such a
vision of the church? Is moral elitism the way the church should attempt to
resist the dechristianization that the Pope correctly fears? Certainly the
claims made about human perfection in the encyclical fall well within the
confines of the "ascetical and mystical theology" of the tradition. Yet, it is
also certain that they do not mesh well with the view of perfection espoused
by Augustine. Since John Paul attempts, in the first chapter especially, to
root the theological perspective of the document in an Augustinian theology
of grace, some reflection on what Augustine actually thought is in order.
The notions that perfection in the moral life should be a goal of human
striving, and that this perfection can only be achieved with the help of divine grace were foundational principles for Augustine, just as they are for
John Paul II. The difference between them has more to do with emphasis
than with content. Because Augustine stressed the eschatological nature of
perfection, he had more room in his system for ambiguity, especially when
measured against the ascetical standards of his age. I do not mean to suggest that we should necessarily prefer Augustine's vision to John Paul's.
Nor would I claim that Augustine's theology contains no inherent problems
of its own. The Catholic theological tradition is in no way beholden to the
formulations of a single person, even if that person has achieved the greatness of Augustine. Still, I am convinced that in this particular case the message of *Veritatis Splendor* would be more convincing and more livable had
it appreciated the forces that motivated Augustine to develop his theology of
grace.

4.
Augustine's Eschatological Notion of Human Perfection

According to Robert Markus, Augustine's theological perspective was
radically transformed by a rereading of Paul during the 390's.[24] According
to Markus, Augustine developed a profound sense of the inadequacy of the
human will which, he perceived, was unable to choose the good without the
help of God. For Augustine, even the desire to do good was the result of
God's grace. Augustine's words, "Give what you command, command what
you will," quoted by John Paul, express vividly his sense of dependence
upon God[25] (n. 24). This view of grace provides the backdrop to
Augustine's account of his conversion: his reading of "the Platonists" pro-

vided the intellectual tools he needed to accept Christianity, but he lacked the will to take the final step. Only God could move a broken human will in the direction of the good.

This view of grace had profound consequences in Augustine's thought. First, even though he tried to preserve a place for human freedom, in the end he could not.[26] Human beings, in their fallen condition, could choose only evil without God's assistance. There is no place in his mature thought for any autonomous human turning to God. Human beings in their fallen state are radically unfree; they are slaves. Freedom, for Augustine, is not freedom of choice, but freedom from the bondage and oppression of sin. A perfectly free person, having been liberated from the very possibility of evil, would choose only to follow God's commands and God's will. Hence perfect freedom and perfect obedience are one and the same. In this sense, *Veritatis Splendor* accurately reflects an Augustinian view: keeping the commandments, submitting the conscience to the wisdom of the church, and conforming one's life to the moral demands of the Christian life are all a part of what Augustine meant by freedom. Yet *Veritatis Splendor* parts company with Augustine in one significant way: as I argued above, it strongly suggests that this grace-filled liberty is available now to those who answer the call to perfection. Augustine was not so sure. His own experience had convinced him of the futility of any effort to will one's way to conversion. Likewise, his own failure to achieve perfection in the years following his conversion convinced him of the futility of any expectation of achieving perfection on this side of the kingdom.[27]

From the vantage point provided by his theological synthesis, Augustine interpreted all the major challenges he encountered as a bishop. This is evident, for example, in his dealings with the Donatist church. The church, the Donatists argued, was obliged to preserve the legacy of the martyrs; it was a spotless virgin, without stain or wrinkle. Within its walls there was no room for sinners and apostates: it lived already its eschatological nature, not as sign but in fact. Augustine, as Catholic bishop of Hippo, had to refute these compelling Donatist claims, and he did so primarily through his Pauline theology. The church's vocation to perfection belonged not to the present, but to the future. The evidence of the continued sinfulness of human beings, even after baptism, was strong enough to refute any claims to a stainless church.[28]

Similarly, Augustine used his theology of grace to construct a theology of history. In the 4th and 5th centuries (and in many ways throughout the Middle Ages), the historical vision of Eusebius dominated the Christian perspective. In Eusebius's view, all of human history had been moving toward a glorious climax in the establishment of the Christian empire. The truth of Christian claims seemed undeniable in the light of the magnificent achievements of the church. In a real sense, the church had conquered the world. In the year 410, however, catastrophe struck: Rome was sacked, and the end of the Western empire was at hand. Two groups of refugees found their way to North Africa. One group claimed that Rome had fallen because the ancient gods had been forsaken. Another group, Christians who thought like Eusebius, wondered how such a catastrophe could happen in Christian times. Augustine's *City of God* is, to a great extent, a response to the challenge posed by these two groups.

In the course of his massive achievements, Augustine developed a new theology of history consistent with his reading of Paul: the church, as it is called to be, cannot be associated with any temporal government. The church's perfection, the city of God, exists only eschatologically at the end of history. In this present age, the city of God and the earthly city travel side by side, completely intertwined and mixed until the end of time. Practically, this means that the present is fraught with an impenetrable ambiguity. One simply cannot tell through observation of changes in government what God was doing. Neither could one tell, with absolute certainty, who belongs to the city of God and who will be excluded: all of this is hidden in the mystery of God. Augustine explains that:

> the pilgrim City of Christ must bear in mind that among (its) enemies are hidden her future citizens. . . . In the same way, while the City of God is on pilgrimage in this world, she has in her midst some who are united with her in participation in the sacraments, but who will not join with her in the eternal destiny of the saints. Some of these are hidden; some are well known. . . . At one time they join (Christ's) enemies in filling the theaters, at another they join with us in filling the churches. But, such as they are, we have less right to despair of the reformation of some of them, when some predestined friends, as yet unknown even to themselves, are concealed among our most open enemies. In truth, those two cities are interwoven and intermixed in this era, and await separation at the last judgment.[29]

Augustine did not argue that the earthly and the eschatological cities were unrelated.[30] He did, however, insist that as they exist in time, the membership of these two cities could not be definitively linked to any institutional structure, not even to the church.[31] For Augustine, the church was not the kingdom, but a sign pointing to that kingdom. The earthly Jerusalem, Augustine explains, anticipates its heavenly referent:

> A certain shadow, or prophetic image of this City (the heavenly) served here on earth to signify rather than to present this City. . . . It (the earthly Jerusalem), too, was called a holy city, on account rather of its symbolic meaning than of any factual truth, whose realization still lay in the future. . . . A part, therefore, of the earthly city is here made into an image of the heavenly city, signifying not itself (the earthly Jerusalem) but another (the heavenly Jerusalem). . . .[32]

According to Markus, Augustine's eschatological vision of the church represented a radical revisioning of the Eusebian view of history. Augustine's

view "is bound to be unremittingly critical of all and any human arrange-
ments, any actual and even any imaginable forms of social order."[33]

Eusebius' vision, however, prevailed, and the crisis of the 5th century
that provoked Augustine's thinking gradually eased. The church went on to
become the medieval church whose legacy still dominates the thought of
contemporary Catholicism. Augustine's radical vision of history was not
understood by those who came later. Markus, in a most illuminating passage, explains:

> By a supreme paradox, it was a writer who took—or thought he took—
> his inspiration for his great panoramic vision of universal history from
> Augustine's *City of God*, Otto of Freising, who, in the 12th century,
> saw the process of human history as a growing together of the heavenly
> and the earthly cities. Since the time of Constantine, and especially
> since Theodosius, "not only the peoples, but even their rulers, for the
> most part, have become Catholics. From then on, it seems to me," he
> wrote, "that I have been writing the history not of two cities but, al-
> most, of one, which I call 'Christendom.'"[34]

Markus concludes by noting that Augustine's vision of history has been
completely reversed. His "two cities," instead of pointing toward the eschatological future, have become "the theological prop of a sacral society, of
a Christian political establishment in which the divine purpose in history lay
enshrined."[35] In such a view, it seems to me, little space for ambiguity
remains: the church is no longer an icon, but an idol.

Augustine's conflict with the Donatists and the political crisis of the
5th century contributed significantly to his view of Christian perfection. In
the later 4th and early 5th centuries, the Roman empire entered a period of
rapid and dramatic Christianization. By the time the process was complete,
the identity that had served the pre-Constantinian church so well had collapsed. The idea that the Christian church was the church of the martyrs
quickly began to fade. Robert Markus writes that for Christians of this new
age:

> . . . the age of the martyrs retained something of the flavor of a heroic
> age; but it was growing daily harder to recognize it as the heroic age of
> their own Church, increasingly wealthy, prestigious and privileged.
> Somehow they needed to reassure themselves that their Church was the
> heir of the persecuted Church of the martyrs.[36]

In short, it became increasingly difficult for Christians to answer the question: What does it mean to be a Christian? In increasing numbers, the way
Christians both answered this question and forged a link with the church of
the martyrs was through the ascetic pursuit of perfection. "Asceticism,"
Robert Markus explains, "was coming to be the mark of authentic Christianity in a society in which to be a Christian no longer needed to make any
very visible difference in a man's life."[37] Inevitably, two classes of Chris-

tians began to emerge: the elite monks, who followed the way of perfection, and all the other mediocre Christians who did not.[38]

This view was not universally received. Some Christians—Jovinian,
for example—seeking to close the rift separating the elite from the ordinary,
resisted the very notion that asceticism made one a better Christian.[39] Embracing an opposite position, but equally concerned with closing the rift,
was Pelagius. In his view the call to perfection belonged to all Christians,
regardless of their state in life. Writing to a young aristocratic woman, Demetrias, who had recently embraced the virginal life, Pelagius remarked:

> It is, however, very hard to deal with the character of one in whom
> there is such desire to learn, such eagerness for perfection that no teach-
> ing, however admirable, can really meet her needs: she rightly remem-
> bers what worldly wealth and honor she has rejected, what pleasures
> she has renounced, in a word, what attractions of this present life she
> has spurned, and for that reason she is dissatisfied with this common,
> mediocre kind of life of ours. . . . What outpouring of talent will ever
> satisfy a mind so enthusiastic and dedicated, so thirsty for a high degree
> of perfection?[40]

Yet, although Pelagius was here exhorting to the virginal life, it is clear that
he believed the call to perfection extended to everyone, without exception.
He explains that " . . . in the matter of righteousness we all have one obligation: virgin, widow, wife, the highest, middle and lower stations in life, we
are all without exception ordered to fulfill the commandments. . . ."[41] Pelagius scoffs at the notion that God would command something we cannot do:
it may be difficult, but God has given us the ability not only to obey his
commands, but to go beyond them.[42] In the identity crisis of the 5th century, Robert Markus explains, "Pelagius' brand of puritanic revivalism offered a means of establishing one's Christian identity."[43] Yet it was against
this very understanding of Christianity that Augustine protested.

Augustine's reading of Paul compelled him to react to Pelagius in the
same way he had reacted to the Donatists and the calamitous events of the
early 5th century: he transposed the possibility of Christian perfection into
the eschatological future. This does not mean that he eschewed the pursuit
of perfection. He did not. Still, Augustine simply did not believe that the
fullness of perfection was available to anyone before entering into life with
Christ. According to Markus, Augustine and Pelagius differed most dra-
matically in "their view on what baptism achieved in renewing a man."[44] In
Augustine's opinion, Pelagius "left no place, in the baptized Christian, for
God's merciful healing; Pelagius would replace Augustine's urgent prayer
for grace with an austere call to cast off all weakness, a remorseless demand
for perfection."[45] Such perfectionism invited a prideful arrogance that was
ultimately destructive of Christian community.[46] In a sermon with a clearly
anti-Pelagian ring, Augustine reflects on Jesus' invitation to the rich young
man (Matthew 19:21). He focuses on the call to imitate the Lord as a way

of following him, and he urges all to work for the perfection implicit in that call. Yet, he ends with a caution:

> We are all imperfect, you see, and will only be made perfect where all things are perfect. The apostle Paul says, "Brothers, I do not consider that I have obtained it." He says himself, "Not that I have received it, or have already been made perfect (Phil 3:13). And can any human being at all dare pride himself on perfection? Rather, let us confess how imperfect we are, in order to deserve to be made perfect."[47]

Not only was perfection God's to command, the possibility of reaching it was God's to give. Only from such a perspective could Augustine write, "Give what you command, command what you will."

The result of Augustine's theology of grace was ambiguity. Just as the mingling of the "two cities" introduced ambiguity into his conception of the church on earth, so his defense of Christian imperfection introduced ambiguity into the Christian life. Even a mediocre Christian, "who will put up with wrongs done to him with less than complete patience, but burn with angry desire for revenge . . . , who guards what he possesses and gives alms, though not very generously . . . if his faith is right and he acknowledges his own failure, will be saved with Christ."[48] Like Pelagius, Augustine overcame the division of Christians into two groups, one elite and the other ordinary. Unlike Pelagius, however, this division was not overcome by extending the call to perfection to all people, but by insisting upon our absolute need for grace. "All are called to pursue perfection," Markus explains. "None attain it here, but all are commanded to run so as to obtain the prize." (1 Cor. 9:24; Phil. 3:12)[49]

Augustine's conflict with Pelagius led Augustine to transform his thinking about the monastic life he had chosen. One student of Augustine's monastic rule notes that as the bishop grew older his fascination with Matthew 19:21 and Anthony's call—which figured prominently in the *Confessions*—is eventually "upstaged" by the portrait of the Christian community of Acts 4:32-35.[50] Concretely, this meant that Augustine abandoned the notion that "what distinguished the monastic life from other forms of Christian living was the pursuit of perfection through self-denial."[51] Instead, he conceived of the monastery as an eschatological sign of the future Christian community, which will be revealed in its fullness at the end of time. Augustine held up the communal life of the monk as something to be imitated not because it followed a more perfect path, but because it served as a countercultural sign that revealed the fallenness and inadequacy of "all other forms of social existence."[52]

To sum up, in Augustine's view, while we live we necessarily confront the tension introduced by two facts of Christian life: the gift of salvation has already and definitively been given by Christ, but the fullness of the gift has yet to be realized. Human life, then, is fraught with ambiguity. The church, history, human effort, all struggle under the cloud of obscurity char-

acteristic of life in time. This does not mean, as some have suggested, that
the church, as it is now, is not in any way related to the church as it will be,
nor does it deny that human beings can and should attempt to conform their
lives to the rigors of the gospel. Rather, it means simply that God's intention for humanity is often unclear, God's church often stumbles, and our
own efforts, more often than not, fall far short of the demands of Christian
life. Grace, for Augustine, was in many ways a means to provide space for
Christian failure. The Donatists had no room in their church for those who
lapsed under the torments of persecution, and Pelagius envisioned a church
of perfected men and women radically conformed to the Gospel. Augustine
preferred instead to place his trust in the mysterious working of God's
grace; the perfection of the church and the perfection of Christians was
something that belonged to the future, not the present. Still, now, in this
time, Christians could try to anticipate that future reality through their life
together: "Live then, all of you, in harmony and concord; honor God mutually in each other; you have become his temples."[53]

5.
Veritatis Splendor and Augustinian Eschatology

In my view, the Pope has embraced a view of Christian perfection
similar to that resisted by Augustine. In doing so, the Pope is in good company. The ascetical tradition, to which he has attached the moral arguments
of this encyclical, became a means by which the church attempted to stand
as counterculture and to preserve its link to the pre-Constantinian church of
the martyrs. As Christianity became enculturated, it became increasingly
difficult for the church to remember the radicalness of its central vision:
monastic asceticism, through its numerous reforms, helped preserve that vision. Still, this same tradition also helped perpetuate a two-tiered Christianity, one perfect, the other less perfect; one lay, the other clerical. Even
though the Pope has rejected the notion of two classes of Christians, he has
basically placed his hope in this tradition and asked it once again to rise to
the occasion and bring renewal to the church. The question is, can it still
serve that function?

Unlike Augustine, we do not live at a time of Christianization.[54] Our
time is characterized by the process of dechristianization and of secularization. What image of Christian life is likely to preserve the church's mission
and promote Christian life in a social climate such as ours? My reading of
Augustine suggests that focusing on moral perfection as the source of renewal in the church is a mistake. Would it not have been more compelling
to choose Acts 4:32-35 instead of Matthew 19:16-22 as the scriptural foundation for the Christian life? The contemporary church is faced with a crisis
in Christian life that goes to the very heart of the Christian experience. The
crisis in morality identified by the Pope is really a symptom of this greater

problem. Our Christian communities fail to present Christian life as a plausible alternative to the consumerism and individualism that characterizes our social world. We need far more than authoritative pronouncements to resist these cultural forces. We need communities where Christian life is demonstrated to be possible, where the eschatological church to which such communities point is made present as a real, vital, and compelling alternative to the cultural assumptions that surround us. Only in such communities will the Christian moral life begin to make sense as something worthy of our passion and devotion. In the work of building such communities, Acts 4 has more to offer than Matthew 19.

Clearly the church can and should speak boldly about what is and is not characteristic of that Christian moral life. *Veritatis Splendor* has done this, but at what cost? Many people who read this text will, doubtless, take it either as a commendation or as a condemnation. Others, perhaps most, will ignore it. The realized notion of perfection, which is so strong in this encyclical, is, in the end, destructive of community. Even if we reject, as we should, Augustine's more extreme conclusions about the nature of grace, we should at least learn from him that no one ever earns God's favor. Although we should strive to live our lives in conformity with the Gospels, the goal of that striving remains forever beyond our grasp, in God's kingdom. John Paul asserts that unchanging moral norms call us to perfection, while his opponents—the unnamed "theologians"—redefine perfection to reflect what we do. Both come very close to asserting a primacy of works on the path to salvation. Augustine, while clearly closer to John Paul in his understanding of a transcendent moral order, would have rejected both: the church is not a gathering of morally perfect people; it is a sign of God's gracious favor, of the new and restored humanity, and of that life that none has deserved, but which is, nevertheless, given.

Perhaps the real question is: what kind of church do we want? Do we want a church of perfect heroes, or do we want a church with a little more room for mediocrity? In what is certainly unintended irony, the Pope quotes Novation to illustrate how a great variety of gifts contributes to the church's holiness. Through the gifts of teachers, tongues, healings, etc., God "completes and perfects the Lord's church everywhere and in all things" (n. 108). For Novation, and apparently for this Pope, this perfection should be a present reality. Yet, as the document recognizes (if only with an allusion), in the eyes of the tradition, Novation was an antipope, a heretic. His crime was not any particular sin, indeed his life seems to have been exemplary. Yet, in the wake of the Decian persecution (ca. 250), a question arose about what to do with apostates. The church chose to allow them to be reconciled. For Novation, such a move compromised the church's perfection and holiness. In his church there was no room for sinners because there was no distance between the church on Earth and the church of the kingdom.[55]

Clearly, many will read *Veritatis Splendor* as Novation read the persecution of the 250s: in our church, there is no place for failure.

Notes

1. R. McCormick, "Veritatis Splendor and Moral Theology," *America* 169, no. 13 (October 30, 1993): 9. Compare the similar reaction to this chapter by R. J. Neuhaus, "The Splendor of Truth: A Symposium," *First Things* no. 39 (January, 1994): 15.

2. McCormick, "Veritatis," 9.

3. Only Thomas Aquinas (about eighteen times) and Vatican II (about fifty times) are mentioned more than Augustine.

4. Not surprisingly, all but two of the references to Aquinas appear in the second chapter.

5. *Veritatis Splendor,* n. 300. All references to *Veritatis Splendor* are taken from the English translation that appears in *Origins* Vol. 23, No. 18 (October 14, 1993).

6. The Pope explicitly states his intention to do this: "In this way, moral theology will acquire an inner spiritual dimension in response to the need to develop fully the *imago Dei* present in man, and in response to the laws of spiritual development described by Christian ascetical and mystical theology" (n. 111).

7. *Life of Anthony* 2, PG 26, 841C.

8. *Confessions,* 8.6,12.

9. See, for example, his letter "On Riches," in B. R. Rees, ed. and trans. *The Letters of Pelagius and his Followers* (Rochester, NY: Boydell Press, 1991), pp. 171-211.

10. For a discussion of the relationship between the church and society in Late Antiquity, see Peter Brown, *The Body and Society: Men , Women, and Sexual Renunciation in Early Christianity* (New York: Columbia, 1988), and now Avril Cameron, *The Mediterranean World in Late Antiquity: AD 395-600* (New York and London: Routledge, 1993), pp. 57-80.

11. For a good discussion of the emergence of monasticism in Christian antiquity, see Derwas Chitty, *The Desert a City* (Crestwood, New York: St. Vladimir's Seminary Press, 1966).

12. The Pope's reading of the text ignores insights gleaned from modern scripture study. New testament scholars point out that the Aramaic word "tam," which the Greek translates with "tevlwio", means something closer to "complete," or "well-rounded" than it does "perfect." They also point out that Jesus was teaching about the dangers of wealth. While the later monastic tradition adopted the Greek teleological notion of perfection, it did preserve a keen sense of the text's challenging message about the dangers money presents to the spiritual life. The Pope's exegesis preserves the former but ignores the latter. Indeed, the text's message about the renunciation of wealth is subsumed by the rubric of moral perfection that dominates his reading of the text. Cf. Daniel Harrington, *The Gospel of Matthew* (Collegeville, Minnesota: Liturgical Press, 1991), pp. 277-281, and Bruce Malina and Richard

Rohrbaugh, *Social-Science Commentary on the Synoptic Gospels* (Minneapolis: Fortress, 1992), pp. 123-124.

13. See, for example, Theodoret of Cyrus, *A History of the Monks of Syria* (Kalamazoo, Michigan: Cistercian Publications, 1985). For an assessment of the role ascetics played in late antique society, see Peter Brown, "The Rise and Function of the Holy Man in Late Antiquity," in *Society and the Holy in Late Antiquity* (Berkeley and Los Angeles: University of California, 1982): 103-165.

14. B. R. Rees, *Pelagius A Reluctant Heretic* (Woodridge, Suffolk: Boydell Press, 1988), gives a good presentation of the state of scholarly research on Pelagius.

15. *Tractates on the Gospel of John* 41, CCL 36, 12.23-40.

16. Ibid. 13.1-10.

17. *Discourses on the Psalms,* CCL 38, 32.II, 10-11. The translation is taken from S. Hebgin and F. Corrigan, *St. Augustine: On the Psalms* (New York: Newman Press, 1960).

18. The Donastists believed that the Catholic church was compromised because some of its leaders had, so they claimed, apostatized during the great persecution. Cf. W. H. C. Frend, *The Donatist Church* (Oxford, 1952).

19. For a recent discussion of the anthropology of Gregory of Nyssa see Robin Darling Young, "Gregory of Nyssa's use of Theology and Science in Constructing Theological Anthropology," *Pro Ecclesia* 2, no. 3 (Summer, 1993), pp. 345- 363.

20. This point is well documented by Elizabeth Clark, *The Origenist Controversy: the Cultural Construction of an Early Christian Debate* (Princeton: Princeton Universtiy Press, 1992), pp. 194-244.

21. Cf. Jaroslav Pelikan, *The Christian Tradition: A History of the Development of Doctrine. Vol 1: The Emergence of the Catholic Tradition (100-600)* (Chicago: University of Chicago), pp. 319-331.

22. Gregory of Nyssa, *The Life of Moses*, as quoted by Jean Daniélou, *From Glory to Glory,* trans. Herbert Musurillo (Crestwood, New York: St. Vladimir's Seminary), pp. 82-83. Cf. GNO VII.1, 4.20-5.4.

23. John T. Noonan, "Development in Moral Doctrine," *Theological Studies* 54 (December, 1993): 662-677, details modifications in Church teaching on usury, marriage, slavery, and religious freedom.

24. Robert Markus, *Saeculum: History and Society in the Theology of St. Augustine* (Cambridge: Cambridge, 1970), pp. 80-81.

25. Cf. *Confessions,* 10.29.40.

26. While musing upon a work of his youth Augustine says the following: "I worked hard on behalf of the free choice of the human will, but the grace of God was victorious," *Retractationes, Oeuvres de Saint Augustin 12: Les Révisions,* Gustave Bardy, ed. (Paris: Desclée, 1950), XXVIII.1.

27. Margaret Miles, *Desire and Delight* (New York: Crossroad, 1991), explains in her fourth chapter, "Textual Harassment," how Confessions 10-13 understood this failure.

28. Markus, *Saeculum,* pp. 105-132.

29. *City of God,* CCL 47, 1.35. Henry Bettenson, trans., *St. Augustine: City of God* (London and New York: Penguin, 1972).

30. Gerhard Lohfink, *Jesus and Community: the Social Dimension of Christian Faith,* trans. John Galvin (Philadelphia: Fortress, 1984), pp. 181-185, misunderstands Augustine here.

31. Markus, *Saeculum,* pp. 157-166.

32. As quoted by Markus, *Saeculum,* p. 184.

33. Markus, *Saeculum,* p. 168.

34. Ibid. p. 164.

35. Ibid.

36. Robert Markus, *The End of Ancient Christianity* (Cambridge: 1990), p. 24.

37. Ibid. p. 36.

38. Peter Brown, *The Body and Society in Late Antiquity* (New York: Columbia, 1988), p. 204 f.

39. Hunter, D. G., "Resistance to the Virginal Ideal in Late Fourth Century Rome: the Case of Jovinian," TS 48 (1987), pp. 45-64.

40. Letter to Demetrias 1.2, PL 30, 16A. Translations of this letter are taken from Rees, *The Letters of Pelagius.*

41. Ibid. 10.1, PL 30, 25B.

42. Ibid. 16.1, PL 30, 30B.

43. Markus, *End,* p. 43.

44. Ibid. p. 53.

45. Ibid. p. 54.

46. Ibid. p. 55.

47. Sermon 142.14. The translation is taken from Edmund Hill, *The Works of Saint Augustine: Sermons* (Brooklyn, New York: City Press, 1992).

48. Markus, *End,* 54-55. Peter Kaufman, "Augustine, Martyrs, and Misery," *Church History* 63, no. 1 (March, 1994): 14, suggests (basically supporting Markus' thesis), that Augustine rejected perfectionism because it promoted false expectation. True expectation must always be directed toward the pilgrim city in heaven.

49. Markus, *End,* p. 65.

50. George Lawless, *Augustine of Hippo and his Monastic Rule* (Oxford, 1987), p. 15.

51. Markus, *End,* p. 77.

52. Ibid. p. 81.

53. Lawless, *Augustine of Hippo,* p. 83.

54. See the illuminating discussion of "secularity" in Markus, *End,* 1-17. He argues that one of the distinctive cultural shifts marking the end of anciety Christianity was the gradual collapse of the secular: from the fifth century, all areas of society

were increasingly viewed as religiously significant. Our situation is, of course, the exact opposite. Cf. Peter Berger, *The Sacred Canopy: Elements of a Sociological Theory of Religion* (New York: Doubleday, 1967), pp. 105-171.

55. To say that there is distance between the kingdom and the church does not mean that there is no continuity between them. The kingdom of God is not radically distinct from the church in time. Cf. Hans Küng, *The Church* (Garden City, New York: Doubleday, 1976), pp. 124-144.

3

An Interpretation of
Veritatis Splendor and the
Discussion of War and Peace within
the Roman Catholic Community

Stephen E. Lammers

1.
Introduction

Right at the beginning it must be said that the focus of *The Splendor of Truth* is not politics, nor is the document intended to be a commentary on war and peace issues. The announced agenda is quite clear: the focus is on the fundamentals of moral theology. This does not mean that there may not be other agendas in this document. I will not venture an interpretation of why the pope issued the encyclical now.

Having said that, it must also be said that it is not difficult to interpret the encyclical so that it appears to have some implications for further reflection upon issues of war and peace within the Roman Catholic community. The reason for this is simple. The encyclical pays a great deal of attention to politics and our lives together in community. The examples of the pope are drawn from the realm of the political as much as they are from any other realm of human endeavor.[1] I hope to show how much of what is said is in continuity with past Roman Catholic reflection on these matters. Also in continuity with past reflection is the repeated claim of the pope that much of what we do as moral agents not only has an effect upon others but shapes us as well. At the same time, the ongoing discussions within the Roman Catholic community on issues of war and peace should not be dramatically affected by the encyclical. I will develop this point more fully later.

If one could stop there, that might be enough. Unfortunately, there are some curious omissions on the part of the encyclical, omissions which are crucial if the encyclical was supposed to be helpful to those within the Roman Catholic community. I will discuss one of these omissions, because I think it points to some of the fundamental difficulties of this particular letter.

Thus when reflecting on the implications of the encyclical for further Catholic discussion of war and peace issues, one has to be cautious. Given the focus on fundamental theology, the encyclical could have no effect whatsoever on discussions of war and peace. But, then again, it is possible that the encyclical will have little effect on future discussions within fundamental theology. This is because no theologian recognizes him or herself in the pope's discussion of proportionalism. The positive implications for discussions of war and peace I note in this brief essay could very well be ignored.

First, to what is included in the document. Although there will be other, more complete, summaries of the encyclical in this collection, I will offer a brief summary here which will form the backdrop for my discussion.

The focus of the encyclical is the whole of the church's teaching, not a particular sphere of that teaching. Among the particular concerns addressed will be the pluralism of opinions in the sphere of morality (n. 4).

The pope is concerned to defend the importance of the truth of revelation and the connection between authentic freedom and revelation (n. 34). He rejects positions which are not clear on those connections (n. 39). He likewise rejects positions which see freedom as primarily the overcoming of nature (n. 46).

The pope claims that there are immutable norms. He recognizes that the formulation of these norms may change but insists that the norms themselves are unchangeable (n. 53). Conscience applies these norms to a particular situation but does not determine the content of the norms (n. 59).

The encyclical goes on to reject certain interpretations of the fundamental option (n. 69-70) and proportionalism (n. 75). It is in the context of the latter discussion that the pope, quoting Vatican II, lists a number of acts which are always wrong, independent of any circumstance in which they occur and any goods being sought. The list is worth repeating here:

> Whatever is hostile to life itself, such as any kind of homicide, genocide, abortion, euthanasia and voluntary suicide; whatever violates the integrity of the human person, such as mutilation, physical and mental torture and attempts to coerce the spirit; whatever is offensive to human dignity, such as subhuman living conditions, arbitrary imprisonment, deportation, slavery, prostitution and trafficking in women and children; degrading conditions of work which treat laborers as mere instruments of profit, and not as free responsible persons: all these and the like are a disgrace, and so long as they infect human civilization they contaminate those who inflict them more than those who suffer injustice, and they are a negation of the honor due to the Creator (n. 80).[2]

In the next section of the encyclical, the pope argues that faith and morality are connected. Furthermore, this connection extends to his claim that there are "moral norms which prohibit without exception actions which are intrinsically evil" (n. 90). Here the tradition of the martyrs is invoked (n. 91), martyrdom understood as a witness to moral truth (n. 92).

Lest he be misunderstood, the pope returns to the question of unchanging norms. They are not simply to be found in the sphere of interpersonal relation but are part of our lives together in community and are demands which public authorities at all levels are required to follow (n. 93).

2.
Commentary

In this section I will first develop an interpretation which would show how what the pope says has implications for the discussion of war and peace. After that, I will try to indicate why it might legitimately be argued that the Roman Catholic discussion on war and peace remains essentially where it was, open to further reflection and clarification. Finally, I will discuss how the encyclical missed an opportunity to bring to our attention the multiple sources of the very "proportionalism" it is determined to reject.

1. In order to understand why the encyclical is both relevant to and yet leaves most questions about just war discussion open, one first has to understand that just war discussion has four homes or social locations in the modern world. The first social location is that of policy planners and politicians. One example of this would be the discussion of just war during the preparation for the Gulf War in 1991.[3] The second social location is the military, which not only uses just war thinking in planning operations but also teaches just war principles to future officers as part of what it means to be a leader in the military.[4] The third social location is that of the academy, where just war discussion often is part of a critique or defense of governmental policy or military practice.[5] Finally, the just war discussion is also a part of the life of the Christian church.[6] It is here, for example, that questions are raised about the continuity, if any, between just war and pacifism within the Roman Catholic tradition.[7]

If there is a contribution to be noted, the pope's is clearly to the fourth locus of discussion, although there may be relevance for the other three. The reason is that the pope, after claiming that acts of genocide and torture are always and everywhere forbidden, goes on to draw our attention to the martyrs. The argument being put forth here is that one must be willing to say "No" to those forces which would ask one to perform immoral acts, even if it means that one loses one's life. The tradition of the martyrs is here invoked in discussions of morality. These are not empty words in a world in which men are killed because they refuse to rape their neighbors' daughters or their neighbors' wives or in which men, women and children are killed simply because they are of the wrong ethnic group. At the same time, the discussion of martyrdom is not one that comes easily to governmental planners or academic discussions of justifiable war. The pope has insisted upon a religious dimension to the discussion of morality and thus maintains the possibility of a distinctively *Christian* justifiable war position.[8]

   The pope has done this in an interesting fashion, given that he was not focusing upon peace and war. The usual methodological discussion within Catholicism on just war and pacifism focuses on whether there is a shared presumption against the use of force within just war and pacifist thought. Those who claim such a common presumption argue that the gulf between pacifism and just war is not as wide as formerly thought. The pope's approach suggests a new direction. He points to the possibility of dying rather than doing evil acts. This may in fact be a far more fruitful approach to matters at hand.[9] The pope provides at least the beginnings of an answer to those pacifists who have asked what in fact is forbidden under just war teaching and, more importantly, what should one be prepared not to do as part of waging justifiable war.[10] By pointing out that the church's primary mission is one of witness, and by not separating out the realm of politics from the activity of witnessing, the pope points us to the possibility of seeing once again justifiable war discussion as part of that larger discussion of witness and not simply a discussion of policy and statecraft. Here I take it he has advanced the discussion, or better, returned the discussion to where it should have been all along.[11]

   The pope's setting of the problematic makes it possible to argue that within Christian just war discussion, at least, there is a connection between that discussion and the pacifist tradition in the Christian community. The connection is not only that both are willing to insist on boundaries around the use of force nor is it that both instruct people on how to live in a world which is violent and a world within which persons kill others in the name of some great good. If this reading is correct, the important point is that no matter whether one is a pacifist or a defender of justifiable war, one has to recognize that one may be required to die rather than to do evil.

2. I think that the part of the rhetoric of the encyclical which is effective concerns the list of acts which are forbidden always and everywhere. Part of that list (I would in no way claim that all of it would so qualify) should prove unexceptional to Catholic theologians. Which prominent theologian writing today, for example, defends genocide or torture? This is not to say that they have not been defended and we do not need to be reminded that they are always wrong. Here the encyclical sets up an interesting tension between the theoretical stance it wishes to condemn, proportionalism, and the particular acts which it reiterates from previous conciliar documents.

   Given the reading above, there are two issues at stake. The first point is methodological, and the second concerns the list of particular actions which are to be condemned. The encyclical connects the two matters in a way which is not helpful. On the methodological issue, the approach of the encyclical might have been helped if the authors of the encyclical had been aware of certain discussions on the American theological scene. What the pope's theologians seem unable to imagine is a situation in which different theological methods yield similar results. Obviously, this is not always the case, but it is sometimes the case with the very list which the encyclical quotes from *The Pastoral Constitution*.[12] It is thus not surprising that many writers do not recognize anyone, much less themselves, in the encyclical's criticisms of proportionalism.

The second issue is the list of acts always forbidden. Here it simply is the case that these acts have been defended under some circumstances. On the methodological issue, the encyclical may well have it wrong on the details of certain positions and that certainly is relevant to the methodological discussions going on in Catholic moral theology. The pope does not have it wrong on these actions, which continue to be defended and, more importantly, done in our day.[13] But whether they are done because of a supposedly faulty moral method or for some other reason(s) is a discussion where the encyclical is, to say the least, not always helpful.

Thus to repeat my reading of the encyclical: given that some of the examples of acts forbidden always and everywhere have to do with acts of war, the encyclical does have some relevance for discussion of the just war tradition within the Christian community, but only if one is willing to think about the justifiable war tradition within the context of that community. What is finally left unresolved within the encyclical is the tension between two of its claims: the first is that morality is something that is part of the natural law and thus demonstrable by reason; the second is that martyrdom is the witness of some members of the community to the truth of the teaching of the religious community. What is left open is not only the issue of whether there is a natural law open to all to understand, but also how one responds when one is asked to participate in violations of norms supposedly derived from the natural law. Martyrdom as witness is not part of the vocabulary of contemporary politics, nor has it been part of the vocabulary of late of the just war tradition. Martyrdom is a relevant issue when one speaks of the truth of revelation, but again, that is not a matter of interest in modern politics. Insofar as martyrdom is a response to revelation and not to some truth knowable solely by reason, the pope fails to distinguish between those within the Christian community who may be asked to suffer as witnesses to the truth of revelation, and those outside the community who may affirm the same norm but who are not responding to it *as revelation*. It is not clear that they are asked to be martyrs.[14]

The irony of this view of the encyclical is that it leads to a number of questions about the encyclical's basic methodological position. That is, just as the pope makes possible a viable *Christian* just war position, he sets up a tension by insisting that the basic claims of his position are in principle knowable to all.

Now lest I be misunderstood, I want to add that this point cuts both ways. It seems to me that much of modern Roman Catholic theology has acted as if it were written for everyone, and that on matters of politics there might not be special obligations on the part of Roman Catholic Christians.

The pope's focus on the possibility of martyrdom as witness to the truth should remind us that matters are more complex. It might not change the moral evaluation of particular actions but it does affect how we think about our response to those actions, especially when we are asked to participate in them.

3. It must be said, however, that even with the above interpretation the basic discussions of war and peace within the Roman Catholic community are still open. Let me highlight just a few.

A. The first issue open for discussion concerns a central issue in modern Roman Catholic discussion of war and peace, namely the debate between pacifism and just war. The issue might be framed in the following way: How should one witness to the truth and confront the evildoer? Does one do this in and through the life of a nonviolent religious community or should one participate in the organization of the political community so that the evildoer is confronted with force, if necessary? Nothing in this document changes that choice or that debate.

Nor does the encyclical change anything in terms of how the religious community might be organized, if one chooses that form of witness. For example, debates between pacifists on what the appropriate strategy should be are still open for discussion. Nothing new appears here.

B. Given the focus of the encyclical, it is not surprising that the pope is not clear what one should do in the political arena when one is confronted by those who perform those actions always and everywhere immoral. What is intriguing is that the pope does not anywhere discuss the use of force in these circumstances; the focus of attention is the church and what it might do to a person who persists in teaching error. That leaves open that hard part of the discussion when one is charged with the welfare of the body politic and, in the case of the United States, the *de facto* welfare of other nations. What are one's obligations?

If one follows the spirit of the pope's letter, what one must first do is figure out the best way to witness to the truth of the matter at hand. That is to say, the first question may well not be "Is force required in this circumstance?" but "How may I let people and the world know what I think of this particular evil in this time and place?" The next step may well be the use of force but the first activity, at least for a Christian who is a politician, is to witness to what is in fact the truth of the case and to the fact that the evil being done is not acceptable. This does not mean that hard work does not remain. Readers are familiar with the difficult questions which still confront the politician who determines that there is evil being done and that it must be stopped, if necessary, by the use of force. It does, however, bring the issue of truth and witnessing to the truth to the fore, and this is a discussion of which we have seen too little of late in politics.

These two examples should make it clear that discussions of war and peace remain where they were before the encyclical was written. Nothing fundamental has changed, although the letter has opened up some new possibilities for reflection.

4. Having said all of this, I want to say that there are foci within the encyclical which I think are at odds with one another in thinking about war and politics in our world. I will use just war discourse as an example, but my concern applies to other areas as well. The issue in just war discourse long has not been major disagreement about the contours of that tradition of discussion. There have been disagreements, but these have always been carried on in the context of major agreements.

What has not been thought through in this document are the implications of the correct claim that we need to develop ourselves in order to judge correctly. The encyclical is clear in arguing that doing evil acts harms not only others but the agent of the act as well. What is not attended to but only mentioned is the development of the moral agent. In an ironic way, the emphasis upon acts absolutely forbidden turns out to make less important any discussion of the virtues in general and of the virtue of prudence in particular. The way in which the encyclical appears to construct the matter is that acts which are absolutely forbidden are also absolutely obvious. What is lacking is any sense that prudence involves not simply knowing how one might respond to evil actions but also in determining that evil actions are being committed. Even in the discussion of response to evil, there is almost a too quick discussion of martyrdom. I am not taking back what I said earlier; it is that if one is going to teach, one should nuance one's teaching and attempt to be clear on critical issues. What is necessary is the development of persons who would live and think through this teaching in their lives - in the context of this essay, their military or governmental lives. How the church intends to assist in this development is unclear. Further, what is not made clear is how essential all of this is for just war discussion, or for any other discussion of morality as well.

The pope is certainly correct in arguing that martyrdom remains one possibility of witness in the face of grave evil; he does not connect this to his discussion of training in the virtues and the other forms of witness which are possible. In this sense, the pope lost an opportunity to contribute to ongoing discussions within Roman Catholic moral theology. He is clear that Christians must understand martyrdom as one possibility of their witness. What are the possibilities here other than martyrdom are left unexplored.[15]

There is also an emphasis within the document which I think is misleading in the context of the modern world. The most disappointing part of the encyclical is the rancor shown to theologians within the church and the failure to confront the pretensions of the modern nation state.

The issue here is the list of actions which violates human dignity and human rights, as the pope understands them. It certainly is the case that religious leaders have blessed their followers when those followers have done many, if not all, of these actions. But many of the sources of the violations of human rights are not found in religious doctrines and only rarely are they to be found in the writings of theologians. The modern nation state often does demand participation in these actions. The pretensions of the state go unaddressed.

At one level this failure to address the nation state is understandable. After all, the focus of the document is the life of the church. In fairness, too, it should be noted that the underlying claim of some violations of human dignity, that we have value only insofar as we serve human purposes, is roundly rejected. Thus it is clear that there is the foundation for a rejection of the pretentions of any body, religious or political, which would argue otherwise. Yet it is still regrettable that this was not more candidly addressed.

The regret here extends to the basic methodological claims of the pope. More than any other entity, the modern nation state has been able to convince its citizens that they ought to treat others badly when it might serve the purposes of the nation state. If the pope were looking for examples of proportionalism, he really did not have to look further.[16]

Conclusion

In the end, there are some interesting hints for future discussion of issues of peace and war within the Roman Catholic community. Helpful, in my view, with the qualification noted above, is the reminder that witness is the appropriate response to others' urging us to evil, even witness unto death. At the same time, in no sense did this encyclical "settle" anything in Roman Catholic discussions of war and peace. What the pope did was point to some potentially fruitful areas for further reflection. The hard work of theological reflection and Christian living is ahead.

One of the interesting questions which remains is whether the mention of human rights in the document is helpful at all. This leads to a discussion of human rights within recent Catholic theology and the relationship of that discussion to the usual discussion of rights within liberal political theory.

The terminology of rights, as generally used by liberal theorists, is a way to protect individuals from decisions of the larger community, even decisions which were democratically adopted. In the process of attempting to protect individuals from what they thought were unjust decisions, liberal theorists often isolate the individuals from the communities in which they are found. What critics of liberalism charge is that rights and its attendant baggage should be jettisoned in favor of a framework which points to persons as connected with others and in the web of relationship sometimes needing protection but always needing affirmation.

Such a criticism is not unfamiliar to Roman Catholic thinkers. The individualism which often attended rights talk has always been antithetical to the central claims of that tradition. And it must be said on the first level of analysis that rights do not provide the framework for this document. In that sense, liberalism has not been so much rejected as much as bypassed. The document has another starting point.

Notes

1. Thus I do find it curious that among the reactions to the encyclical there are those who think that the central issue is the relationship of the hierarchy and the theologians within the church. Further, it is curious that there is such a concentration upon issues of sexuality in materials I have read about this document.

2. Pastoral Constitution on the Church in the Modern World, *Gaudium et Spes,* 27. It should be pointed out that the context of this statement in the original makes it clear that the evils mentioned should be understood as offenses against human persons in community. The methodological point of the pope does not appear to be of interest to the Council.

3. Cf. the speech by President George Bush to the National Religious Broadcasters, January 28, 1991. This can be found in James Turner Johnson and George Weigel, eds., *Just War and the Gulf War* (Washington, D.C.: Ethics and Public Policy Center, 1991), pp. 141-146.

4. For a good example of someone who has been influenced by being a teacher in this location, cf. Paul Christopher, *The Ethics of War and Peace: An Introduction to Legal and Moral Issues* (Englewood Cliffs, NJ: Prentice Hall, 1994).

5. There are numerous examples of this. The preeminent historian of just war is James Turner Johnson, *Just War Tradition and the Restraint of War* (Princeton, NJ: Princeton University Press, 1981).

6. A collection of documents reflecting this is Richard B. Miller, ed., *War in the Twentieth Century: Sources in Theological Ethics* (Louisville, KY: Westminster/John Knox Press, 1992).

7. It is important that the reader understand that this description of four social locations is not intended to imply that the thinkers who are situated in one of those locations do not have conversations with those who are differently situated. The difficulty has been that thinkers from the various social locations thought that everyone else was talking about the same thing they were. In my view, this is not always the case.

8. I am not arguing that other positions could not affirm that these actions are not always forbidden. Indeed, the pope's claims are ones most defenders of justifiable war would affirm, no matter what the social location of the commentator.

9. In saying this, I am not arguing that pacifism and just war do not share a presumption against the use of force. However, even if true, that presumption still

leaves open the question about what one ought to do when confronted with evildo-ers, both those evildoers who initiate evil actions and those doers of evil who resist evil through the illegitimate use of force.

10. John Yoder has been among the most persistent in pressing this question on just war thinkers. Cf. John Yoder, *When War is Unjust: Being Honest in Just-War Thinking* (Minneapolis: Augsburg Pub. House, 1984).

11. Lest I be understood as offering only praise on this point, I hasten to offer a caution. The discussion of martyrdom appears to apply to the individual who re-fuses to do immoral acts; what the response of collectivities ought to be is not discussed at all.

12. For one account of this, cf. Jeffrey Stout, *Ethics After Babel: The Languages of Morals and Their Discontents* (Boston: Beacon Press, 1988).

13. One needs to look no further than Bosnia or Rwanda.

14. In saying this, I am not arguing that they are not asked to be martyrs. I take it that this is a point of contention.

15. Perhaps it is inevitable that they would be unexplored in a document such as this. What one misses, however, is a reference to a real or fictionalized account of a martyr which gives one some sense of the texture of those decisions and how they might be taken in the context of politics. Here, Robert Bolt's *A Man for All Seasons* (New York: Vintage Books, 1962), the fictionalized account of Thomas More's journey to the headsman's axe, is much more helpful.

16. Obviously, theologians and religious leaders who bless these activities ought to be reminded that they bear a special responsibility for the continuation of evil.

"If You Wish to Be Perfect . . .": Images of Perfection in *Veritatis Splendor*

Katherine M. TePas

The moral life, according to *Veritatis Splendor*, is essentially teleological in that it "consists in the deliberate ordering of human acts" to the "ultimate end (*telos*) of man" (n. 73). How one envisions the end and perfection of human life appropriately determines the path one chooses to arrive there. Thus differences in images of human perfection lead to differences in guidelines on how to live now in order to attain that end. Aristotle, for example, imagined that the sole activity of the most perfect beings, the gods, was contemplation. Humans, likewise, were encouraged to develop the virtues which would allow them to live, as much as possible, a life of contemplation. In contrast, Francis of Assisi's rule used for its model the physically poor, humble and celibate Jesus Christ. The friars minor, therefore, were mendicant preachers who embraced lady poverty, obedience and chastity. What are John Paul II's predominate images of perfection? How does he describe the *telos* appropriate to human beings? What is the ideal model he envisions humans following as they sculpt themselves through their actions?

The following pages explore the various images of perfection offered in *Veritatis Splendor*. The principal image, the incarnate Jesus Christ, is explored first, followed by a more general image of God and the heavenly Father, then the model of Mary mentioned in the final pages of the encyclical. The essay notes what John Paul II focuses on in describing each image and in explaining what it means for humans to follow it. The images are also compared to themes in John Paul II's earlier works. The last section of the essay briefly analyzes some conflicts between the images of perfection, and critiques *Veritatis Splendor*'s approach to human perfectibility.

1.
Jesus, the Way, Truth and Life

We must first of all show the inviting splendor of that truth which is Jesus Christ himself. In him, who is the Truth (cf. Jn 14:6), man can understand fully and live perfectly, through his good actions, his vocation to freedom in obedience to the divine law summarized in the commandment of love of God and neighbor (n. 83).

The predominant image of perfection, offered throughout *Veritatis Splendor*, is Jesus Christ. Jesus, however, is a multifaceted image who has been approached in a wide variety of ways throughout the history of Christian spirituality: Holy Infant, King of Kings, Suffering Servant, Teacher, Miracle Worker, Good Shepherd, Judge, Prince of Peace, Prophet or Revolutionary. For John Paul II, the focus is on Jesus as the one who freely and obediently gives himself in love for God and for all of humanity. Humans attain perfection by imitating this self-sacrificing love for God and others in a freely chosen obedience to God's commands.

Unlike Francis' rule, the encyclical does not focus on a literal following of Jesus' life; nor does it interpret Jesus' words to the rich young man as a special call to the evangelical counsels of poverty, chastity and obedience. Instead, the encyclical regards the vocation to perfection as addressed to all and capable of being fulfilled in any state in life. John Paul II does not ignore the fact that the words to the young man include a call to poverty, "Sell your possessions and give the money to the poor . . . then come, follow me" (Mt 19:21). To make the call inclusive, he interprets poverty in the context of Matthew's Sermon on the Mount. The first Beatitude is "of the poor, the 'poor in spirit' as Saint Matthew makes clear (Mt 5:3), the humble." The encyclical sees in the Beatitudes a "self-portrait of Christ" which "speak of basic attitudes and dispositions in life" (n. 16). Christians in every walk of life can strive to take on Christ's humility, meekness, mourning, hunger for justice, mercy, purity of heart, peacemaking, and acceptance of persecution for the sake of righteousness.[1]

Likewise, later in the encyclical, it is solidarity, temperance and justice that are discussed in connection with Christ's poverty. Citing the new Catechism, temperance is required "to moderate our attachment to the goods of this world"; justice is required "to preserve our neighbor's rights and to render what is his or her due"; as well as "solidarity, following the Golden Rule and in keeping with the generosity of the Lord, who 'though he was rich, yet for your sake . . . became poor'(2 Cor 8:9)" (n. 100).

Thus *Veritatis Splendor* approaches the imitation of Christ in terms of imitating Christ's heart and interior life. The interior life, however, is necessarily manifested in works of love. Jesus is the one who has fulfilled the commandments "by interiorizing their demands and by bringing out their fullest meaning. Love of neighbor springs from a loving heart which, precisely because it loves, is ready to live out the loftiest challenges" (n. 15). The primary definition of love used in the encyclical is "the total gift of self." This is the character of Jesus' love which is to be imitated by all who follow him. It is a gift of service to others shown through the washing of the disciples' feet. It is the love perfectly shown through Jesus' passion, where he gave up his life for his friends (cf. n. 15, 18-21, 85, 87).

This description of perfection through giving oneself to others is common in John Paul II's writings and echoes a phrase he quotes often from *Gaudium et Spes*: "Man can fully discover his true self only in a sincere giving of himself" (24). In *The Acting Person*, written in 1969, the future pope argued that when one perceives that a community is founded on the common good, and that one's actions can serve this common good,

> he will readily relinquish his individual good and sacrifice it to the welfare of the community. Since such a sacrifice corresponds to the ability of participation inherent in man, and because this ability allows him to fulfill himself, it is not "contrary to nature."[2]

This theme is again present in a Lenten retreat he gave to Pope Paul VI in 1976.

> The human will—or rather the human heart—impels man to be "for others," to have generous relationships with others. It is in this that the essential structure of personal and human existence consists. Man exists not merely "in the world," not merely "in himself"; he exists "in relationship," "in self-giving." Only through disinterested giving of himself can man attain to full discovery of himself.[3]

A significant element in John Paul II's descriptions of the way Jesus loves is the ease in which he speaks of the self-giving as done both for God's sake *and* for humanity's sake. He does not argue that God is the only Being which can be loved for his own sake, nor that loving humans, for humans' sakes, is a misdirected love. Both God and humans can be loved for their own sake. Indeed, God loves humans for humans' sakes. Working with the same passage from *Gaudium et Spes*, John Paul II notes that this is the unique dignity of humans among all of God's creatures, for "man is the only creature on earth that God has wanted for its own sake" (n. 13). A corollary to this is that a person is to be loved "as an end and never as a mere means" (n. 48).[4] Perfect love as manifest in Jesus Christ, therefore, has a type of interdependent twofold end: humanity and God. Christ's actions, especially his passion and death, "are the living revelation of his love for the Father and for others" (n. 20). The cross is "the sign of his indivisible love for the Father and for humanity" (n. 14). Thus Christ illuminates human nature's "dynamism of charity towards God and neighbor" (n. 53).

The image of Jesus Christ is also used in *Veritatis Splendor* to explore the obedient and free nature of human perfection.

> It is in the Crucified Christ that the Church finds the answer to the question troubling so many people today: how can obedience to universal and unchanging moral norms respect the uniqueness and individuality of the person and not represent a threat to his freedom and dignity? . . . The Crucified Christ reveals the authentic meaning of freedom; he lives it fully in the total gift of himself and calls his disciples to share in his freedom (n. 85).

Because Christ's self-giving is to fulfill the commandments of love and the will of the Father, it is obedient (cf n. 87). Yet, because the obedience is a conscious choice to love, it is also necessarily free.

Human freedom is not an end in itself. It is a means to achieve perfection through "passing beyond self to knowledge and love of the other" (n. 86). The nature of the perfection to which freedom is called has been predetermined by the Creator as self-giving love (n. 17, 35). If freedom chooses to obey the commandments consummated in love for God and neighbor, the human finds eternal life. If freedom seeks to create and follow a different route to perfection, the human remains unfulfilled. There is thus seen to be an unavoidable relationship between freedom and God's law (n. 17). Those who desire to serve others find in the divine law the "fundamental and necessary way in which to practice love as something freely chosen." Moreover, they feel an interior "necessity," different from "a form of coercion," to live out the demands of the law in their fullness (n. 18).

Veritatis Splendor's most common image of perfection is Jesus Christ who, in loving obedience to the Father, freely gives himself for God and humanity. All humans are called to strive for this perfection by adhering to the person of Christ and imitating his example of love. Such love fulfills the law and the attitude of heart portrayed in the beatitudes. The central ideal held up by the encyclical is, in union with Christ, to love as Christ loved, even to the point of laying down one's life for others.

2.
Be Perfect as the Heavenly Father Is Perfect

> It is Jesus who leads to the Father, so much so that to see him, the Son, is to see the Father (cf. Jn 14: 6-10). And thus to imitate the Son, "the image of the invisible God" (Col 1:15), means to imitate the Father (n. 19).

The image of the Son is the image of the Father. While recognizing that these images are ultimately the same, the next section explores what the encyclical chooses to focus on when discussing perfection in terms of the image of God, in general, or the image of the Father. The theme of human freedom reappears in conjunction with reason as part of a traditional interpretation of the image and likeness of God. Mercy is the characteristic of God highlighted when the text explicitly addresses perfection according to the image of the Father's perfection.

Human freedom is "patterned on God's freedom" (n. 42) and, quoting *Gaudium et Spes*' section on freedom, is "an outstanding manifestation of the divine image" (n. 38).[5] Again quoting from the council, "Human dignity requires man to act through conscious and free choice, as motivated and prompted personally from within, and not through blind internal impulse or merely external pressure" (n. 42). The central Scriptural quote for the discussion is Sirach 15:14, where God is said to have willed that man should "be left in the power of his own counsel." This freedom gives humans a share in God's dominion and is an imitation of God as king. Corresponding to this image, the soul is free and self-governed, ruling over itself by its own will (n. 38, cf 34).

Because humans are free and self-governing, they are responsible for "personally building up that perfection" in themselves (n. 39). In this they image God as Creator. Through freely chosen acts, humans determine their own character. In a sense, they create themselves. To describe this process, *Veritatis Splendor* cites Gregory of Nyssa:

> All things subject to change and to becoming never remain constant, but continually pass from one state to another, for better or worse. . . . Now, human life is always subject to change; it needs to be born ever anew . . . but here birth does not come about by a foreign intervention, as is the case with bodily beings . . . ; it is the result of free choice. Thus we are in a certain way our own parents, creating ourselves as we will, by our decisions[6] (n. 71).

The theme of humans as free and self-governing is central to John Paul II's personalism. Throughout his previous works he argues that persons are essentially their own masters. According to his interpretation of "the beginning," man is first revealed as a subject, alone, faced with a choice of self-determination.[7] This solitude is recognized through a person's unique ability to rule over himself, which sets him apart from the rest of creation and likens him to God.[8] In *The Acting Person*, freedom means that each person "depends chiefly on himself for the dynamization of his own subject."[9] To be fully human is to be able to will and execute one's own acts of self-determination.[10] Through their free choices, persons are said to guide and create themselves. They mold themselves into the type of person who does such things.[11] Events which "happen" to individuals without their understanding and free choice do not create the individual.[12] Similarly, a man who simply "conforms," rather than exercising fully his self-determination and free choice, makes himself "but the subject of what happens instead of being the actor or agent responsible for building his own attitudes and his own commitment to the community."[13]

The capacity to reason is discussed in *Veritatis Splendor* hand-in-hand with freedom of choice and self-determination. As free will is seen as a reflection of God's dominion, so the ability to reason is viewed as a reflection of and participation in God's wisdom. Through the reason proper to human nature, humans can discern good from evil. Such moral truths are not created by the human mind, rather they are determined by God and subsequently discovered by the mind. The encyclical thus grants a "rightful autonomy of practical reason" whereby humans possess in themselves their own law, and also acknowledges that this law is received from God (n. 40-44).

Such optimism about a person's capacity to know truth is a characteristic of John Paul II's earlier works. For example, in *Love and Responsibility*, he argued that "by giving man an intelligent and free nature," God

> . . . has thereby ordained that each man alone will decide for himself the ends of his activities, and not be a blind tool of someone else's ends. Therefore, if God intends to direct man towards certain goals, he allows him to begin with knowledge of those goals, so that he may make them his own and strive towards them independently.[14]

Truth is made accessible to the human mind in such a way that each individual can, within himself or herself, come to know it.[15]

From the beginning, humans have been made in the image of God in their abilities to know and freely choose the good. Thus they participate in God's wisdom and imitate God as creator and ruler. Nevertheless, it is not to the image of God as creator or ruler that John Paul II directs those wishing to follow the exhortation in Matthew's Gospel to "be perfect as your Heavenly Father is perfect" (Mt 5:48). He points instead to the Gospel of Luke, where "Jesus makes even clearer the meaning of perfection, 'Be merciful, even as your Father is merciful' (Lk 6:36)" (n. 18).

In the conclusion of *Veritatis Splendor*, John Paul II returns again to God's mercy and explains in more detail what he means by mercy.

> No human sin can erase the mercy of God, or prevent him from unleashing all his triumphant power, if we only call upon him. Indeed, sin itself makes even more radiant the love of the Father who, in order to ransom a slave, sacrificed his Son: his mercy towards us is Redemption (n. 118).

Mercy "offers liberation from the slavery of evil and gives the strength to sin no more." Jesus Christ is the ultimate revelation of God's mercy, dwelling among humans and sacrificing his life for them. So, too, is mercy the quality of the Spirit who makes possible a new life for sinners. Yet, mercy is equally the quality of the Father, who sacrificed his only Son for sinners (n. 118).

In stressing mercy as a defining characteristic of the Father's love, the encyclical returns to the theme of John Paul II's 1980 encyclical, *Dives in Misericordia*. This earlier work describes merciful love as that love which is particularly manifest in the situations of suffering, injustice, poverty and sin.

> For mercy is an indispensable dimension of love; it is, as it were, love's second name and, at the same time, the specific manner in which love is revealed and effected vis-à-vis the reality of the evil that is in the world, affecting and besieging man, insinuating itself even into his heart.[16]

Mercy is more powerful and more profound than justice because it prevails over sin, "restores to value, promotes and draws good from all forms of evil."[17] Furthermore, mercy is revealed with a certain intimacy and affection. It takes on "an anxious solicitude to ensure for each individual every true good and to remove and drive away every sort of evil."[18]

3.
Mary, the Mother of Mercy

The final pages of *Veritatis Splendor* consider Mary, whom John Paul II calls a "model of morality." In light of his previous comments on mercy, it is not surprising that he chooses "Mother of Mercy" out of all the possible titles for Mary. She is said to participate in God's mercy such that "together with Christ" she asks for "forgiveness for those who do not know what they do." She, too, loves sinners and experiences God's love opening her heart to embrace all of humanity (n. 120). As a model of perfect love, she freely gives herself for God, which allows her to participate in God's giving of himself to the world. In these ways the image of Mary is similar to the other models of perfection in the text. She is merciful, as the heavenly Father is merciful. She also freely gives herself for love of God and others.

This final section, however, also highlights Mary's full acceptance of what she does not always understand. She is praised for her "perfect docility to the Spirit." "By accepting and pondering in her heart events which she did not always understand (cf. Lk 2:19), she became the model of all those who hear the word of God and keep it." Furthermore, "Mary invites everyone to accept this Wisdom," which is Christ. To all she commands, "Do whatever he tells you" (Jn 2:5) (n. 120).

4.
Critique of the Images of Perfection

Created in the image and likeness of God, redeemed by the sacrifice of the Son, graced by the power of the Holy Spirit, humans, according to the encyclical, are capable of perfection. "With God all things are possible" (n. 22, Mt 19:26). In Jesus Christ "man can understand fully and live perfectly" his vocation to love God and others (n. 83). Throughout *Veritatis Splendor*, John Paul II admits real and crippling effects of sin on the human will and intellect, yet always goes on to describe what people are capable of through grace. For him, it is not so much a question of what a sinful person can accomplish, as what a redeemed person can accomplish (n. 103); and the Spirit "makes possible the miracle of the perfect accomplishment of the good" (n. 118).

Is the encyclical too optimistic about the capacity of the human mind to *know and understand what is the good to be done* in a given situation? Even if one grants that Jesus reveals the fullness of truth and that humans are able to die for the truth, one could still question whether or not humans can determine with certitude, in a particular instance, what is the good for which they should die. Furthermore, even if humans are graced with the ability to know what God asks in a particular situation, they still may not be able to understand what God asks. The Christian spiritual tradition commonly speaks of the saints' graced capacity to love outstripping their graced capacity to know. Might there be a corollary in moral theology? Might the Spirit's gift of love, enabling humans to give themselves completely for love of God and others, surpass, in some sense, the gift to understand completely what love would call them to do?

The encyclical's concluding remarks on Mary, noted above, seem to admit that humans will not always understand the commands of God. These are intriguing remarks for a text that also stresses the capacity of the human mind to understand the will of God, and the importance of the reason and will working together in morally good human acts. The idea of obedience is not new. However, previous discussions of obedience were in the context of accepting God's commands, which are understood because they are in accord with the law written on the human heart. In contrast, the references to the annunciation and the wedding at Cana point to situations where God's will could not have been foreseen by human reason: a virgin birth and the transformation of gallons of water into fine wine. The image of Mary, used in this way, seems to point to an incomprehensible aspect of God's will which must be embraced and acted upon before it is understood by the intellect.[19] Moreover, it seems that John Paul II intends this type of obedience to be now a model for obedience to God's moral commandments.

John Paul II's approach to human acts usually champions the importance of full understanding and free choice. From this perspective, the most perfect human acts are those which are freely chosen and fully understood to be in accord with the truth. Nevertheless, this is the pope who did a dissertation on faith in John of the Cross. He also acknowledges a *Deus absconditus* and his meditations have quoted John of the Cross' *via negativa*: "To attain to this which you know not, you must pass through that which you know not."[20] Thus, John Paul II views God's mind as both in harmony with human reason and beyond the understanding of the human mind. He argues that humans should obey God's truth as personally understood through the law written on their hearts, yet also follow docilely the revealed word when they cannot understand it.

This, possibly, can explain some apparent contradictions in John Paul II's works. On one hand, *The Acting Person* condemns passive conformism and even argues for the necessity of responsible opposition.[21] On the other hand, later works including *Veritatis Splendor* call for internal assent to the teachings of the Magisterium and condemn certain forms of organized dissent: "Opposition to the teaching of the Church's Pastors cannot be seen as a legitimate expression either of Christian freedom or of the diversity of the Spirit's gifts" (n. 113, 110). According to the former, truth is knowable to human reason, and vigorous and open dialogue is one of the best ways to discover it. From the latter perspective, the Holy Spirit works especially through the magisterium, and the faithful are called to assent in a manner similar to the servants who obeyed Mary's "Do what he tells you."

John Paul II's use of the story of Susanna also indicates a problem with his optimism regarding humans' ability to know and understand moral truths. The encyclical calls Susanna a "prime example" of someone willing to die rather than sin. The story does work as an image of someone willing to give herself completely for God's law. However, it is less convincing as an image of knowing what sin is in a given situation. Indeed, it seems to highlight the difficulties even the pure of heart can have in knowing with certitude what God's commands require.

According to the story, Susanna refused to cooperate with the lustful advances of two unjust judges. She refused them, knowing the judges would therefore have her condemned to death. The story concludes with her life being spared through the clever intervention of Daniel. "Susanna," the encyclical explains,

> bears witness not only to her faith and trust in God but also to her obedience to the truth and to the absoluteness of the moral order. By her readiness to die a martyr, she proclaims that it is not right to do what God's law qualifies as evil in order to draw some good from it (n. 91).

In the story, Susanna did perceive this to be her situation. Nevertheless, is this a fair example of choosing to die rather than sin? What absolute truth in the moral order was Susanna upholding? What exactly was the evil, condemned in God's law, that Susanna chose not to do? From the context, it looks as if she was choosing not to be raped more so than choosing not to commit adultery. The latter is obviously condemned in the sixth commandment. Being raped, however, is a significantly different act on the part of the victim.

John Paul II uses the encyclical to argue for the existence of intrinsically evil acts. To do so, he focuses on "the object of the act" rather than the consequences or intentions of the subject who performs the act. Nonetheless, the encyclical does not deny that the intention and circumstances can, at times, effect the morality of the act (n. 76-83). Yet it fails to note that the story of Susanna is one that demands that the circumstances and intentions be taken into account. Sex is certainly not an intrinsic evil. The circumstances and intentions surrounding the behavior can make the human act adultery, rape or a component of the sacrament of marriage.

Even if the Scriptural story had clearly portrayed Susanna's choice as a choice against adultery instead of a choice against being raped, others have argued that one should die rather than be raped. The ideal of giving up one's life rather than committing a sin against chastity has been applied to situations where a woman is threatened with rape. Not all that long ago, Catholic children were taught to jump out a window rather than "lose their chastity." Today, most Catholics are justly scandalized if a rape victim is accused of sinning against chastity.[22] Thus the example of Susanna and the conflicting opinions on what is the right choice to make when faced with rape seem to indicate that "the pure of heart" may not always agree on what is the perfect thing to do in a difficult situation. They may be willing to die rather than sin, but not agree on what must be done in a particular situation.

Veritatis Splendor is consistent in holding up self-sacrificing love as the primary model of perfection. From this perspective, humans are fulfilled by giving themselves in love for God and others. In doing so, they follow Jesus who freely and obediently gave his life for humanity. The encyclical, however, is not so consistent when it discusses humans' ability to know and understand what must be done to love perfectly God and others. On one hand, human reason and free will are in the image of God, and, through grace, persons are able to understand and follow the law of God written on their hearts. On the other hand, humans are called to imitate Mary and the servants at Cana by docilely following what they do not personally understand. Moreover, in looking for an example of someone who is willing to die rather than trespass a moral absolute, *Veritatis Splendor* cites an ambiguous story. It is not clear that Susanna risked her life rather than commit an evil against God's law. One could admire the character's willingness to die without agreeing with her conviction that giving into another's advances, under the threat of death, is sinful.

Notes

1. The encyclical also summarizes the invitation to the rich young man as a call to follow Jesus in "poverty, humility and love" (n. 114).

2. Karol Woytyla, *The Acting Person,* trans. by Andrzej Potocki, vol. 10 of *Analecta Husserliana* (Boston: D. Reidel Publishing Company, 1979), p. 283.

3. *Sign of Contradiction* (New York: Seabury Press, 1979), p. 132.

4. This, too, is a longstanding theme for John Paul II. Note, for example, the argument in *Love and Responsibility* that not even God, the Creator, would use a person as a means (trans. H.T. Willetts [New York: Farrar, 1981] p. 27).

5. *Gaudium et Spes,* 17.

6. *De Vita Moysis,* II, 2-3; PG 44, 327-378.

7. John Paul II, *Original Unity of Man and Woman: Catechesis on the Book of Genesis* (Boston: St Paul Editions, 1981), p. 51. See also *Mulieris Dignitatem,* 6-7.

8. See also *Sign of Contradiction's* discussion of "munus regale" which connects a Christian's participation in the kingship of Christ with the dominion given in Genesis. "Man's obedience to his conscience is the key to his moral grandeur and the basis of his 'kingliness,' his 'dominion'; and this—ethically speaking—is also a dominion over himself" (p. 141).

9. P. 120.

10. Ibid., p. 107. See also *Love and Responsibility*, p. 24.

11. While a person's existence and value is certainly prior to any actions, "it is in actions that the person manifests himself" (*The Acting Person*, p. 265).

12. Cf. pp. 134-135. See also Ronald Lawler, *The Christian Personalism of Pope John Paul II*, paper presented at Symposium held at Trinity College (Chicago: Franciscan Herald Press, 1982), pp. 40-43.

13. *The Acting Person*, p. 289.

14. P. 27.

15. For a concise summary of this see Lawler, *Personalism of John Paul II*, p. 22. Lawler later notes that Cardinal Wojtyla intervened twice during the drafting of the "Declaration on Religious Liberty." Wojtyla objected to the statement that an individual's right to act according to conscience could be impeded for the sake of "the just requirements of public order." Wojtyla preferred to explain this limitation by rooting the interference with this right to requirements in the moral law itself. In doing so, he argued for an objective moral authority which could be grasped by the rational mind, rather than an extrinsic authority wielded in the public arena (pp. 104-105).

16. *Rich in Mercy, Encyclical, Dives in Misericordia,* November 30, 1980 (Washington, D.C.: Publications Office, USCC, 1981), p. 26.

17. Ibid., p. 22.

18. Ibid., p. 52.

19. Note that in *Sign of Contradiction,* John Paul II posits the possibility of Mary's knowing God's will at the wedding at Cana. Earlier in the retreat he had meditated on Mary pondering things she did not understand. Yet when reflecting on her directive to the servants at Cana, he suggests: "From this it is possible to conclude that Mary knew what the Father willed. And that she also knew, without any doubt, that her son would not reject her request. Mary's request and the Father's will coincided" (p. 66). Nevertheless, the meditations do not suggest that the servants understood what God intended to do when they were called to follow Mary's command.

20. *Sign of Contradiction,* p. 17, cf. p. 49.

21. Opposition must be allowed in order to guarantee solidarity and authentic communion. The members of the community need the freedom to bring to light what they see to be right and true, even if it conflicts with the accepted understanding of the common good. Such openness to dialogue may strain the community, but it is necessary for the elimination of "partial, preconceived or subjective views and trends" (pp. 286-287).

22. Centuries ago, Augustine also argued that a woman commits no sin against chastity by being violated by another's lust against her will. "While the mind's resolve endures, which gives the body its claim to chastity, the violence of another's lust cannot take away the chastity which is preserved by unwavering self-control" (*City of God* I, 18). Furthermore, it is not appropriate for her to choose suicide in order to avoid being raped. To choose suicide would be to choose to sin to avoid a horrible event that, in itself, is not a personal sin (ibid., I, 16-20).

5

The Pope on Proportionalism

James Gaffney

In the Vatican's official summary of *Veritatis Splendor* the matter with which this essay is concerned is identified as the encyclical's "opposition to the moral theories called *teleologism*, *consequentialism*, and *proportionalism*."[1] What is held in opposition to these undefined "moral theories" is that "the moral evaluation of human acts is not drawn solely from the weighing of their foreseeable consequences or from the proportion of 'premoral' goods or evils resulting from them."[2] Immediately afterwards comes the very strange statement that "even a good intention is not enough to justify the goodness (*sic*) of a choice."[3] Sense can best be made of this statement by simply omitting "the goodness of"—since goodness hardly needs justifying.

These negative assertions are then followed by an affirmative one that apparently states an ethical theory. "The morality of an act, while certainly taking into account both its subjective intention and consequences, depends primarily on the object of the choice which reason grasps and proposes to the will."[4] This statement requires us to distinguish three factors in moral behavior, namely the action of a particular moral kind that one has rationally chosen to perform (the "object" in a peculiar Scholastic sense of that word), the purpose for which one has chosen to perform it (the "subjective intention"), and the effects expected to result from its having been performed.[5] What is meant by saying that the "object" is what the morality of an act depends on "primarily" becomes clear in two assertions which immediately follow, that "it is possible to hold as "intrinsically evil" certain kinds of behavior opposed to the truth and the good of the person" and that "the choice by which they are made can never be good, even if that choice is made with a subjectively good intention and with a view to positive consequences."[6]

Simply stated, the pope's teaching thus far seems to be that a deliberately chosen course of action may fall within a category of moral classification every instance of which is *ipso facto* immoral, quite regardless of intentions however high-minded, or results however desirable in themselves. Since this is proposed in opposition to "teleologism, consequentialism, and proportionalism," those "moral theories" are understood to reject this doctrine.

The doctrine as I have stated it can hardly be dismissed as patently absurd. Indeed it is in no way extraordinary, and seems to have had defenders, including some very illustrious ones, in every age of serious ethical analysis. It can even lay claim to a firm place in popular moral wisdom, as reflected in such familiar proverbial admonitions as "the end does not always justify the means" and "the streets of hell are paved with good intentions." Probably most educated citizens of modern democracies think of at least some "human rights violations" precisely as kinds of behavior whose moral condemnation is simply not negotiable on a plea of lofty intentions or useful results.[7] And in the history of the Roman Catholic and of other Christian churches, the pope's position, as stated above, can certainly claim to be solidly traditional.

That is not, of course, to claim that there is not or has not been any serious opposition to that doctrine. Within the history of Christian theology, the name of Peter Abelard is associated with a doctrine asserting the primacy of intention in determining the morality of an act. But since the intention he had in mind was the intention of pleasing God, if he were persuaded that God had revealed that certain kinds of behavior were never pleasing to him, his position could, in practice, be equivalent to the pope's.[8] Much more serious is the opposition offered by a school of thought that for the past two centuries has been called utilitarianism, and in particular what has been subdistinguished as "act utilitarianism."[9] In its unqualified form, act utilitarianism directs us to judge the morality of each action by whether or not it "will or is likely to produce the greatest balance of good over evil in the universe."[10] If "teleologism" means emphasizing intended goals, and "consequentialism" means emphasizing results, and "proportionalism" means emphasizing the ratio of good results to bad ones, these labels are all appropriate for act utilitarianism. However, forthright endorsements of act utilitarianism would be hard, if not impossible to find among the public statements of any Catholic moral theologians, whereas the three "isms" have often enough been applied to, and even accepted by Catholic moral theologians whom no informed ethicist could possibly confuse with act utilitarians, and who would certainly not repudiate the pope's doctrine as I have summarized it from the Vatican's official summary of the encyclical. For further light on whom the pope is opposing under these labels, and why he is opposing them, it is necessary to turn from the official summary of the encyclical to the encyclical itself. Unfortunately, while the encyclical abounds in footnote references to specific texts with which the pope agrees, not one specific text, or even a specific author, is cited as an unequivocal example of the "teleologism, consequentialism, and proportionalism" with which he so vehemently disagrees. Thus, of course, suspicions are generated: among the timorous, suspicions of persecution; among the censorious, suspicions of heterodoxy; among the cynical, suspicions of straw men.

Turning to the encyclical, we find that the material whose summary we have just analyzed is to be found in the second of the work's three chapters, where it comprises Section IV, headed "The Moral Act."[11] Here the matters under consideration are treated at much greater length. It is arguable whether or not they are treated with greater clarity.

"Teleology," we are told, is characteristic of the moral life, for moral life is life oriented towards its ultimate goal (*telos*), and morally good acts are those conducive to that ultimate purpose. Moral acts express and determine the moral quality of persons who perform them; they do not simply better or worsen the external world in which they produce their effects.

But actions cannot express and determine the positive moral quality of a life directed towards a divine goal unless they are kinds of acts that lead in that direction. That was what concerned the rich young man who asked Jesus what he must do to gain eternal life—a Gospel narrative about which the encyclical presents a lengthy commentary that actually comprises a fundamental moral theology.[12] And that was why Jesus directed the rich young man first to the commandments and then to self-denial and discipleship. The commandments are precisely God's warnings against kinds of action that diminish moral character and divert human life from its divine goal.

Against this frankly theological background the pope considers modern efforts to answer traditional questions concerning what constitutes the morality of a free human act. He envisages the three alternatives outlined by Thomas Aquinas.[13] They are "the intention of the acting subject, the circumstances—and in particular the consequences—of his action, or the object itself of his act."[14] It is important to recall that the term "object" has here that technical Scholastic significance explained previously—an esoteric usage unlikely to be even guessed at by modern readers whose education has not included medieval philosophical vocabulary!

The encyclical calls "teleological" theories that base the moral evaluation of acts on a "weighing of the nonmoral or premoral goods to be gained and the corresponding nonmoral or premoral values to be respected."[15] Thus the measure of being (morally) good would be the extent of doing (nonmoral) good—an idea of morality not without appeal for the common sense of conscientious people, regardless of their religious beliefs or disbeliefs. The pope acknowledges that many Catholic moralists who encourage this point of view do not themselves subscribe to utilitarian principles so completely as to disregard the ultimate divine goal of human life. And he recognizes that such theorizing in the direction of an "autonomous morality" is strongly motivated by a commendable desire to find, in pluralistic societies, authentic common ground for moral discourse. What, then, does the pope find ominous and reprehensible in the "teleological" theorizing of modern Catholic moralists?

The terms "consequentialism" and "proportionalism" seem always or nearly always to be used by the pope in a pejorative sense. The former relies on "a calculation of foreseeable consequences deriving from a given choice," the latter on "the proportion acknowledged between the good and bad effects of that choice"—a distinction that is intelligible but uneven.[16] But the pope further attributes to what he calls "proportionalism" and "consequentialism" an additional tenet that is the real basis of his opposition. For "while acknowledging that moral values are indicated by reason and by revelation," they "maintain that it is never possible to formulate an absolute prohibition of particular kinds of behavior which would be in conflict in every circumstance and in every culture with those values."[17] The crucial issue for the pope seems therefore to be the admission of at least the possibility of formulating negative moral norms that admit absolutely no exceptions.

Most negative moral norms are originally and familiarly formulated in ways that admit, and indeed demand numerous exceptions. Thus the biblical prohibition, "Thou shalt not kill," is obviously understood within the Bible itself to admit several kinds of exceptions, including cases of self-defense, legitimate warfare, and capital punishment. Biblical commentators sometimes recommend the rendering "Thou shalt not commit murder." And thus reformulated, the prohibition might well seem to be unexceptionable. But that is only because the word "murder" precisely *means* illicit homicide— without shedding any light on the practical question of just what kinds of homicide are illicit. One must already know the exceptions to "Thou shalt not kill" in order to know what counts and what does not count as murder. "Murder" implies immorality. "Killing" does not. Hence "morally justified murder" is a contradiction in terms whereas "morally justified killing" or "homicide" is a coherent hypothesis. Strictly speaking, "Thou shalt not murder" merely forbids us to commit whatever kinds of homicide are not morally permissible!

But is it possible to formulate a prohibition of *all* and *only* those kinds of homicide that could never be morally permitted? Such a prohibition would, no doubt, be very complex and lengthy, hard for most people to learn and harder to remember. Universal agreement with the formulation would surely be too much to hope for. And yet it is by no means evident that such a formulation is absolutely unattainable. And if the pope could be satisfied with the mere admission of that sort of possibility, he could find little to object to among most even of those willing to be labeled "consequentialists" and "proportionalists." Most ethicists of even the most quibbling kind could, if pressed, come up with *some* description of *some* kind of behavior that they could not in *any* circumstances imagine being justifiable. But the arguments of professional ethicists would not likely be required to persuade normal people of the moral wrongness of such behavior, nor indeed would divine revelation or the authoritative teaching of a church.

Rather clearly, what is really bothering the pope is not the blanket denial of any possibility of formulating an unexceptionable moral prohibition, but rather the denial that certain familiar and traditional moral prohibitions, as they are usually stated, admit no exceptions. One must, therefore, seek definite examples of what the pope regards as, in the words of the Catechism, "specific kinds of behavior that are always wrong to choose, because choosing them involves a disorder of the will, that is, a moral evil,"[18] "objects of the human act which are by their nature 'incapable of being ordered' to God,"[19] "acts which, in the church's moral tradition, have been termed 'intrinsically evil,'"[20] "acts which per se and in themselves, independently of circumstances, are always seriously wrong by reason of their object."[21] Far from evading this question, the pope furnishes an actual list, taken from the Second Vatican Council, of what he calls "examples of such acts." It will be useful to cite this list in its entirety and to review it with some care. It needs to be noted, however, that the Second Vatican Council, in the passage that the encyclical cites, had no intention of addressing the issue that the pope wishes to address in citing it. Even without consulting records of the conciliar discussions, the text itself of *Gaudium et Spes* makes it entirely clear that the Council is not at this point addressing any issue of ethical theory or methodology, much less proposing any exemplary list of "acts which *per se* and in themselves, independently of circumstances, are always seriously wrong by reason of their object." In fact, what the Council does list is not confined to "acts" at all, but includes deplorable social conditions which are not acts but are very often *consequences*, and much more likely to be consequences of *in*action than of "acts." This is entirely consistent with the conciliar context, which had just previously urged the obligation of active neighborly intervention as contrasted with selfish disregard, but it contributes nothing whatever to the pope's argument in the encyclical, that certain acts can be categorically condemned without reference to their consequences. Oddly enough, the translation of this misappropriated passage in the official English version of *Veritatis Splendor* serves the pope's argument even less well than more familiar earlier translations of the Council document, as for example in preferring the term "homicide" to "murder," and "voluntary suicide" to "willful self-destruction."[22] The following citation of the passage is from the official English version of the encyclical.

> Whatever is hostile to life itself, such as any kind of homicide, genocide, abortion. euthanasia and voluntary suicide; whatever violates the integrity of the human person, such as mutilation, physical and mental torture and attempts to coerce the spirit; whatever is offensive to human dignity such as subhuman living conditions, arbitrary imprisonment, deportation, slavery, prostitution and traficking in women and children; degrading conditions of work which treat laborers as mere instruments of profit, and not as free responsible persons: All these and the like are a disgrace, and so long as they infect human civilization they contaminate those who inflict them more than those who suffer injustice, and they are a negation of the honor due to the Creator.

The Council's characterization of this list of social abuses is unexceptionable. The pope's characterization of it is exceptionable at nearly every point. And if all that the pope is saying is that *somewhere* in this list examples can be found of what he means by "intrinsically evil" acts, that information is hardly helpful unless he tells us *which* ones they are!

The same strange mystification reoccurs when the pope appeals to the Bible, producing again an unwieldy list, containing no "acts" whatsoever, but rather a loose itemization of what might be called "immoral" or "vicious types." "In teaching the existence of intrinsically evil acts, the church accepts the teaching of Sacred Scripture. The apostle Paul emphatically states: 'Do not be deceived: Neither the immoral, nor idolaters, nor adulterers, nor sexual perverts, nor thieves, nor the greedy, nor drunkards, nor revilers, nor robbers will inherit the kingdom of God.'"[24] Clearly, what Paul is teaching in this passage is what he states in introducing it, namely that "the unrighteous will not inherit the kingdom of God." The list comprises simply a conventional set of what might be called unrighteous types. The list contains no "acts," but rather habitual offenders in various areas of morality. To be sure, immoral persons are perpetrators of immoral acts, at least potentially. But that the characteristic behavior of each of the types cited is, in every instance, an act whose malice is independent of circumstances and consequences is patently absurd. To pinpoint the intrinsically evil act of "the immoral," or even of "the greedy" or "drunkards," would be a challenging task indeed. And as for "thieves," Thomas Aquinas himself responds affirmatively to his own question, "Is it licit to steal on account of need?", thus implying that the morality of thieves is indeed dependent on circumstances.[25] Here again, the text cited, even when torn from its context, contributes nothing whatsoever to support the argument to which it is applied.

In fact, there is only one example cited in this portion of the encyclical where an authoritative document definitely is referring to what John Paul II means by an "intrinsically evil act," here characterized as "something which of its very nature contradicts the moral order and which must therefore be judged unworthy of man, even though the intention is to protect or promote the welfare of an individual, of a family or of society in general." This is indeed what the pope is talking about and the authority he cites does indeed propose an example of "intrinsically evil acts." The authority is Pope Paul VI, referring in his famous encyclical *Humanae Vitae* to "contraceptive practices whereby the conjugal act is intentionally rendered infertile."[26] Thus the one unequivocal example the pope cites of an authoritatively specified "intrinsically evil act" turns out to be the most vigorously contested and widely rejected moral teaching in the entire modern history of the papacy. It is not easy to avoid a sense of profound anticlimax, combined with a strong suspicion that what purported to be a critique of certain moral theories was after all only one more assault against critics who find no real plausibility in certain official Catholic teachings about sex and, in particular, about contra-

ception. It is certainly true that for a great many people who take morality
very seriously the mere description of a bit of human behavior as, say, "sexual intercourse with the use of a condom" is morally insignificant; the statement, of itself, communicates nothing to elicit moral blame, moral praise, or
even moral interest. To those people, of whom I am certainly one—and one
who has read and pondered countless dreary pages on this subject—it is
alternately funny and sad that an official doctrine of the Catholic church
holds that anything identifiable as "contraceptive practices whereby the conjugal act is intentionally rendered infertile" can be denounced as "intrinsically evil" and "gravely disordered" behavior without knowing anything at
all about the motives or results of these practices in individual cases. If one
has any reason to question the morality of such practices, the questions will
almost certainly be the kinds of questions associated with what the pope
calls "teleologism," "consequentialism," and "proportionalism," questions
like "Why are they doing it?" "Are there any bad effects?" And, "Do the
good effects compensate sufficiently for the bad effects?" Questions of the
most unsubtle kind, the answers to which can usually be reliably guessed
before they are even asked.

It is no longer imaginable that any new arguments will be advanced
either for or against the reasonableness of the Catholic church's official doctrine concerning the morality of contraception. At present it is extremely
difficult to find any theologian, philosopher, or conscientious man or woman
outside the Catholic church who finds that doctrine morally admirable or
defensible. Inside the Catholic church the doctrine is rejected in practice by
a great majority, in theory by an even greater majority, and accepted by
most of those few who do accept it on grounds of authority alone. It is no
contribution to this controversy, or to the issues with which it is concerned,
to suggest or pretend that opposition to this official church teaching by
moral theologians and philosophers is rooted in their adherence to one or
several indistinct "moral theories." As observed at the beginning of this essay, the pope's clearest identification of these "theories" is to be found in
the two statements he proposes in opposition to them: (1) "The moral evaluation of human acts is not drawn solely from the weighing of their foreseeable consequences or from the proportion of "premoral" goods or evils resulting from them." (2) "Even a good intention is not enough to justify . . .
a choice."[27] If an anonymous questionnaire were to be distributed among
Catholic moral theologians and philosophers, requiring them simply to mark
"True" or "False" on each of those two propositions, I do not believe the
resulting tally of "Falses" would be even statistically significant. And I am
certain that among the many, myself included, who accepted the two propositions as "True," would be vast numbers of those who regard the papal
teaching about contraception as not only rationally untenable but a serious
disservice to social morality. The intellectual adversaries whom the pope
addresses in the portion of the encyclical under consideration in this essay

are, in reality, straw men—and, to be sure, straw women! The pope's employment of these straw figures appears to be a rhetorical stratagem intended to imply that criticism of some of the Church's most dubious official tenets concerning sexual morality derives from certain broad theoretical premises which he defines under the labels "teleologism," "consequentialism," and "proportionalism." That implication is certainly false. If the pope believes it, his misinformation is dangerous. If it is merely a rhetorical exaggeration intended to support the greater good of what he deems to be moral orthodoxy, it would seem to exemplify the very kind of "results-dominated" moralizing that he deplores. In any case, it is scarcely an enhancement of the "splendor of truth." If these judgments are too severe, and the adversaries as the Pope describes them are a real and present danger, it would not seem too much to ask that out of one hundred and eighty-two footnotes at least a few would identify in some bibliographically verifiable way, the persons and writings that explicitly profess the "moral theories" to which he objects. The recognition of "proportionate reason" as a significant factor in moral choice has been a part of Catholic moral theology since its earliest beginnings and among its most illustrious practitioners. Arguments about "proportionalism," variously defined and redefined, have been with us for about thirty years, associated most often during this period with practical issues of sexual morality (n. 28). What this period has actually witnessed in Catholic moral theology has been a progressive application to sexual morality of principles and patterns of argumentation that had long been commonplace in treating virtually every other area of human morality. Some incautious and even rather foolish statements have been published during this controversy and on different sides of it. Most of them were subsequently modified in response to criticism. None of the participants in the controversy have, to my knowledge, consistently professed anything like the positions characterized by the pope's rejection of "teleologism," "consequentialism," and "proportionalism." Most of them have made considerable positive use of the teachings of Thomas Aquinas, including the Thomistic doctrine about the "sources of morality" which the pope employs against them.[29] It may be useful to conclude this essay with a brief review of that doctrine (itself by no means as clear as one could wish) and of its relevance to the issues here under consideration. Since the doctrine is restated in a form that is both contemporary and authoritative in the *Catechism of the Catholic Church* recently promulgated by the pope, I shall base my observations on that text, which is very faithful to that of Thomas Aquinas.[30]

"The object, the intention, and the circumstances form the "sources" or constituent elements of the morality of human acts. . . . The *object* chosen is a good towards which the will deliberately tends. . . . The end is the first term of the intention and represents the purpose pursued in the action. The intention is a movement of the will towards the end. . . . The circumstances, which include the consequences, are secondary elements of a moral act.

They contribute to increasing or reducing the moral goodness or malice of human acts. . . . The circumstances cannot of themselves modify the moral quality of the acts themselves; they cannot render good or just an action that is evil in itself."[31] The doctrine is evidently rooted in common sense, and focuses upon the questions common sense normally raises in attempting to judge the morality of human conduct, once it is established that the conduct is deliberate. "What did he (or she, or they) do?" is the first such question. "Why did he (she, they) do it?" is the second. "Were there any aggravating or extenuating circumstances, including foreseeable effects?" is the third. Sometimes the answer to the first question sheds no light on the moral question, whereas the others leave no doubt as to the moral quality of the behavior under consideration. "John Doe extracted all Mary Roe's teeth" is meaningful but morally opaque. One kind of moral light dawns when we learn that John did it in order to appropriate Mary's gold fillings. And that moral light grows more intense when we learn additionally that the operation was performed without anaesthesia, in a Nazi concentration camp, and that Mary was a Jewess." Moral judgment swings to the opposite pole if we learn instead that John was a dental surgeon by whose timely intervention Mary was spared the consequences of a progressive disease of the jaw, and that he provided the surgery and subsequent care without fee because Mary was a very poor woman. What such examples indicate is that sometimes, at least, to describe the object of a human act without any indication of its purpose or circumstances provides no basis for moral judgment. What it might further suggest is that the line of demarcation between "object," "intention," and "circumstances" is a line much sharper in abstract theory than in concrete application.

"John Doe copulated with Mary Roe" might also seem to be a meaningful but morally opaque statement. If we learn that they are a loving couple, eager for children, on their wedding night, we are unlikely to inquire further about their intentions or other circumstances. The circumstances and intentions would matter greatly if Mary were the victim of John, an armed rapist. The distinction between "object" and "intention," understood as simply the distinction between what one is doing and why one is doing it, is fairly clearcut and often immediately usable. The same cannot be said of the distinction between "object" and "circumstances." Throughout the history of moral theology this confusion, in the very nature of things, between "object" and "circumstances" has been signalled by laborious redefinitions of actions deemed intrinsically evil, or evil from their very "object," in order to eliminate circumstances in which they seemed not to be evil. The first really celebrated example of this kind of thing was a tedious Augustinian discussion of the lie. The received doctrine was that lying is immoral, hence sinful. Common sense retorted that sometimes lying is not immoral, and sometimes it may be praiseworthy and even obligatory. Initially, to lie was understood as the dictionary still defines it, to "speak falsely." But progressively that definition, though sanctioned by usage, was subjected to a series of qualifications whereby at last what the "experts" meant by a lie could indeed be regarded as always immoral, while departing wildly from what ordinary people meant by a lie. "Thou shalt not kill" was similarly made an unexceptionable prohibition by simply defining away all permissible kinds of killing. Christian readjustments of the meaning of usury proved necessary in order to pay continued lip-service to the biblical condemnation of lending money at interest without weakening the foundations of modern capitalism.

In these and many other such instances, what the history of moral theology records is the consistent ethical condemnation of a named category of behavior while the description or definition of the behavior is subjected to endless revision, as circumstances are noticed in which it cannot reasonably be condemned. As a result, the Church's moral norms may undergo considerable evolution, but behind a facade of unchanging verbal formulation. Although it would be hard to deny that something very like sophistry enters this process, it has undoubtedly protected certain Catholic moral teachings from fossilization. Basically, it is a process of refining the classification of kinds of behavior considered to be immoral. One who freely indulges in such behavior may be said to perform a human act that is evil from its very object. One might express the same idea by calling it a kind of human act that is evil by moral definition. So long as one accepts the moral definition one cannot refute a moral judgment consistent with it. Commonly, once the moral definition wins acceptance, the behavior it describes is given a name that connotes the moral definition. And, of course, to attempt to defend the morality of a kind of behavior whose very name implies its immorality is logically absurd. Consequently, those who do wish to defend such behavior are likely to begin by replacing its morally pejorative name by one that is morally neutral. Thus, for example, persons who believe that morally innocent sexual intercourse can take place between an unmarried man and woman will naturally prefer to call such behavior not "fornication," but "pre-marital sex." "Fornication" has become an unpopular term with many people precisely because it seems to them to beg the very question they wish to argue. The rejection of a moral label typically reflects scepticism about a prevailing moral definition of some kind of behavior.

Nowadays, a number of traditional moral definitions, and the labels that imply them, are indeed widely rejected. Many others, however, are not. A great many people, for example, who would object to the morally pejorative term "fornication," do not in the least object to the morally pejorative term "rape." Nor, if they used that kind of vocabulary, would most of them object to calling rape intrinsically evil or evil from its very object. That is, whereas to identify a kind of behavior as sex between an unmarried man and woman seems to many people an insufficient basis for moral judgment, it is quite otherwise with behavior defined as sex forced upon an unwilling partner. Of the many people who are "proportionalist" in their assessment of pre-marital sex, very few are prepared to argue that rape might be quite all right as long as the rapist's satisfaction sufficiently exceeded the victim's distress! In other words, many people who would consider the pope's categorical condemnation of "fornication" short- sighted, would have no similar complaint about his categorically condemning rape. The difference is not between two general moral theories, but between two particular moral judgments.

In the same connection, it should not be overlooked that certain kinds of behavior that most modern Christians would readily define as immoral, would not have been so defined by such traditional authorities as Thomas Aquinas, for example enslavement and torture. In discussions of such behavior by moral theologians and by Christians generally, one would look far indeed to find those whom the pope stigmatizes as proportionalists. Once again, proportionalists, as the pope defines them, appear to be straw men. What the pope is really complaining about is the use of proportionately good and bad consequences to assess the morality of certain quite particular kinds of behavior, pertaining to sexuality, that have indeed been traditionally defined as immoral in Catholic teaching, but which many modern thinkers believe cannot be judged apart from considerations of intentions and circumstances. What most of these thinkers are in fact doing is applying to sexual behavior ethical theories and methods that have long been commonly applied, by Catholic philosophers and theologians and by church authorities, to other kinds of human behavior. And what the pope appears to be doing is resisting this critical enterprise under the confusing pretext of exposing an erroneous general moral theory called "proportionalism." Unfortunately, "proportionalism," as presented here by the pope, is quite simply a bugaboo.

Notes

1. "The Vatican's Summary of *'Veritatis Splendor'*," *Origins* 23 (1993) 334-336, p. 336. [Hereafter abbreviated as *Summary VS*]

2. Ibid.

3. Ibid.

4. Ibid.

5. This traditional threefold distinction derives from Thomas Aquinas, *Summa Theologiae*, IaIIae, q. 18.

6. *Summary VS*, p. 336.

7. To acknowledge that certain rights belong to human beings simply in virtue of the fact that they are human beings, and that these rights are inalienable, implies that any violation of these rights is, *ipso facto,* wrong. The point of affirming such rights is, of course, to indicate moral limits of the state's authority.

8. Petrus Abelardus, *Ethica* in J. P. Migne, ed., *Patrologia Latina*, vol. 178, pp. 640A, 650B.

9. See William K. Frankena, *Ethics* (Englewood Cliffs: Prentice-Hall, 1973), p. 35.

10. Ibid.

11. John Paul II, *"Veritatis Splendor,"* Origins 23 (1993) 298 334, pp. 313-322. [Hereafter abbreviated as *VS*.]

12. *VS*, 300-306.

13. *VS*, 321.

14. *VS*, 319.

15. Ibid.

16. *VS*, 320.

17. Ibid.

18. *Catéchisme de l'église catholique* (Paris: Mame, 1992), p. 374.

19. *VS*, p. 321.

20. Ibid.

21. Ibid.

22. See, e.g., Walter M. Abbott, ed., *The Documents of Vatican II* (NY: America Press, 1966), p. 226.

23. *VS*, 321.

24. Ibid.

25. Thomas Aquinas, *Summa Theologiae*, IaIIae, q. 66, a. 7.

26. *VS*, 321.

27. *Summary VS*, 336.

28. For an historical resume, see Bernard Hoose, *Proportionalism: The American Debate and Its European Roots* (Washington: Georgetown, 1987).

29. For a synthetic account of a common trend of this recent work in moral theology, see John Mahoney, *The Making of Moral Theology* (Oxford: Clarendon, 1987), pp. 311-315.

30. *Catéchisme de l'éqlise catholique*, pp. 373-375.

31. Ibid., p. 374.

6

A Matter of Credibility

Clifford Stevens

1.

For several years, it has been clear that the Holy See was not happy with the state of moral theology in the Church and with certain conclusions in moral matters drawn by Catholic theologians. That these conclusions were chiefly about sexual morality was also clear and several documents facing these issues have preceded the encyclical. It was also clear that certain moral theologians were not listening, were carrying on public controversy in the matter, and were making their views known through the instruments of public opinion. *Veritatis Splendor* is the definitive and authoritative statement of this pontificate on the matters in question and it is a masterly response to what the Holy See regards as a growing evil.

It is clear that the Holy See looks upon it as a scandal that its public position on these matters should be openly questioned by those who should be its official teachers, and the encyclical is a well-reasoned response to positions that have been thoroughly discussed in magazines and journals and in the public forum. That it should want its voice to be heard in such serious matters should be surprising to no one, and what is notable is that no individuals are singled out for censure. It is a teaching *document*, not a juridic one, and it sets forth its own positions clearly, cogently and authoritatively, touching on the whole field of the moral sciences: moral theology, ascetic theology, spirituality and mysticism, deeply rooted in a Thomistic tradition which is the special province of this Pope. What the Pope shows is a remarkable grasp of the issues in question, and he gives a carefully detailed response to the positions he is opposing. What is clear also is that he is not condemning systems of moral theology as such, and does not enter into the debate, carried on in this country, regarding *proportionalism* and *consequentialism*. He is concerned about certain *conclusions* of these systems. These conclusions are the main thrust of the encyclical and the reason for its promulgation.

What will be questioned are its *timeliness*, its *style*, its *grasp of the issues* and its *moral content*. There is no question about its *authority*. Its authority will be questioned by those who hold different positions on the moral matters faced in the encyclical, but those voices are weakened by the encyclical itself and that, indeed, is the very purpose of the document. This

Pope is concerned about the tangle of voices in the Church and the debates among moral theologians about critical moral matters. This encyclical will certainly not put an end to the debate, but it does take certain conclusions out of the public forum, with an authoritative voice, and the Pope has faced the confusion of voices that he believes is disturbing the Catholic community.

The only real question is: how effective will the encyclical be? Will it bring about the unity that is intended by its promulgation? Will it silence the critics of this kind of exercise of authority? Will it persuade those who disagree with certain of its conclusions? Will it be the prophetic voice that is needed in the face of a massive breakdown of public morality? Will it help to stem the tide of unbridled sexual license that is its paramount concern? My answer to this must be "No," because it is mainly in the form of a *moral exhortation*, and except for official statements and commentaries, it will have no impact on those who are not already convinced by its teaching. The encyclical leaves no doubt about the *what* of Catholic moral teaching: what is lacking is the why that makes sense out of that teaching. It is a mere repetition of negative moral precepts, with no insight into the reality under discussion. The contemporary need, in my opinion, is a clear exposition of a theology of sexuality, throwing light on the sexual life of human beings and the realism of the Gospel precepts. What has been lost is a teaching moment of great significance. I doubt if that teaching moment will ever come again in this pontificate.

This encyclical highlights two contrasting convictions of what is at stake in the pastoral mission of the Church in the wake of the Second Vatican Council: those who are convinced that the chief pastoral problem is one of doctrinal orthodoxy, and those who are convinced that it is one of pastoral effectiveness. There is no doubt about the conviction behind the encyclical, and to disagree with this conviction is not necessarily an act of disloyalty. To disagree with a policy or an exercise of authority is not to question the validity of that authority, but only the judgment that fashioned it. Such disagreement, if it is reasonably stated and modestly presented, is simply part of that dialogue which is constantly at work in the Church and is critical to the pastoral mission of the Church in any age.[4] My disagreement is not with the *substance* of the encyclical, but with the style and manner of its presentation and with the pastoral judgement behind it.

2.

Why am I dissatisfied with *Veritatis Splendor*, in spite of the fact that I consider it a necessary response to a very critical problem: the breakdown of sexual morality in all parts of the world? I am dissatisfied because it is merely a negative response, is peripheral to the real pastoral problems of the Catholic community,[5] and makes the *exhortative mode* the chief vehicle of moral doctrine. My concern has been, for several years now, that what is gradually being eroded by this kind of exercise of authority is the *credibility* of the Church in the human dialogue and the complete disappearance of the Church as a partner in this dialogue. The Church is no longer a credible witness to its own teaching, except for a very vocal group of loyalists, who have made themselves the guardians of orthodoxy and often mix their politics with their religion.

This disappearance of the Church as a credible witness of its own teaching is most evident in the case of abortion, where it is helpless to prevent legislation sanctioning abortion, from the conviction that the mere voicing of its opposition is sufficient in the dialogue. It does not reach into the depths of its own intellectual tradition, the philosophical and theological riches it has stored up through the centuries, but is satisfied with empty polemics that convince no one, or with moral indignation that is not persuasive. By reducing its dialogue with its own and with the world community to the exhortative mode, it makes dialogue with the riches of its tradition impossible by making dialogue a mere exercise of authority. It does not seem to realize that what is at stake is not its authority, but its *credibility*.

Why do I find this an embarassment? Because I am aware of the philosophical and theological tradition out of which the Church speaks, and I see little of this in evidence in this encyclical. It does not turn to the world its best face, but only that face that conjures up the most distasteful and most unacceptable side of its own history, and an image of itself totally contrary to what it really is.[6] I have never been disturbed by those who reject the Church for what it claims to be, but it disturbs me greatly if the Church is rejected for what it is not. The image that the Church is projecting of itself in this encyclical is not the Church as I have come to know it, and that saddens me.

Let me give an example of the kind of response to moral evil that I am talking about, one that reached into the depths of the Catholic tradition for cogent reasonings to face a critical moral problem, and which brought respect for that teaching by the clarity of its presentation.

In the wake of the Spanish conquest of the New World, colonial settlements were set up in the Caribbean and in Mexico for the economic exploitation of the new territories by Spanish colonists. That economic exploitation soon involved the forced labor of the native islanders and mainland Indians, simple in their economic pattern of living and totally unprepared to defend themselves against the military and political force that was used against them.[7]

They were seen by most of the Spanish colonists as having no rights under Spanish law, completely in the power of the landowners who employed them, and subject to their Christian owners because they were unbaptized pagans.

One of the voices raised against the enslavement and forced labor of the native Indian was one of the landowners himself, Bartolomé de Las Casas, who recognized the legal right of the Indian to his own land, the obligation of the Spanish government to recognize that right, and the total injustice of the Spanish system of *encomienda*, which justified the enslavement and exploitation of the Indian.

Unsuccessful in his battle to put an end to the system, Las Casas became a priest and a Dominican, spent 10 years in seclusion making himself thoroughly familiar with the Catholic tradition on justice and right,[8] allying himself with a qroup of Spanish Dominican scholars[9] who were facing the same problems. What was created by this effort to solve a particular moral problem was a totally new juridic science, *International Law* and what is known as the Spanish Theological-Juridical Renaissance, a flowering of Catholic thought unique in history, and layinq the groundwork for the establishing of the United Nations 400 years later.

Drawing upon the riches of their own philosophical and theological tradition, Las Casas and his Dominican confreres created a new body of thinking on an important moral question,[10] making themselves credible partners in the moral dialogue of their own times. It is this kind of dialogue, it seems to me, that is desperately needed in the world community today and that I see lacking in this encyclical.

Moreover, there seems to be no conviction that anything more is needed than the mere stating of Catholic teaching, as if this alone were sufficient to make it credible. Besides, that Catholic teaching is not exposed in the depth and wealth of its human riches, but is stated in merely negative terms, as if moral precepts were the mere repetition of moral imperatives, having a basis in nothing more than naked duty.

It is this failure of the encyclical that I find the most distressing, and one which, I believe, will make it totally ineffective in facing the very dangers it is addressing.

3.

The real dangers for Catholics in the moral climate of today is not an ignorance of Catholic moral teaching, but the persuasive arguments of those who think differently. In the erosion of moral values so prominent in today's society, what is needed is a counterbalance that is cogent in its anthropology, convincing in its behavioral norms and genuinely human in its insights into affective life.

My own view is that the real conflict in the Church is not over moral issues, even though these always surface as objects of controversy. The real conflict is *anthropological* and *ecclesiological*, and what is painfully being born in the Catholic community is a new *anthropology* and a new *ecclesiology*, of which the Second Vatican Council was the herald and the embodiment. The real achievement of Vatican II is not the new theological and pastoral principles embodied in the documents of the Council, the *aggiornamento* proclaimed by Pope John XXIII as the goal of the Council. These documents merely embody the real achievement.

The achievement is something more remarkable still, something begun 1,000 years before in the pontificate of another great Pope, one who ushered in the second millenium of Christianity, as Pope John closed it. The Pope was Sylvester II, known as Gerbert before his election, and the achievement of his four years is not unlike that of the five years of Pope John.[11] In both cases, the pastoral mission of the Church was refashioned as a new millennium was about to begin.

What Pope John brought about was the complete victory of Catholic theology over the dualism[12] of the Middle Ages, a hardfought battle begun in the bitter conflicts surrounding the Councils of Nicaea, Ephesus and Chalcedon, the Christian *ontology of creation* that came out of those battles, the superb intellectual achievements of St. Athanasius, St. John Chrysostom and the Cappadocians, the councils and synods of the Eastern and Western Churches over 1500 years and the theological labors of St. Maximus the Confessor and St. Gregory Palamas in the East and of St. Thomas Aquinas and John Henry Newman in the West. Pope John brought all of this huge theological and intellectual effort together in his own person, and in doing so remade Catholicism for the next thousand years.

With this final victory over a dualism that threatened the very concept of God and of His good will towards the human race, Catholic theology could face the critical pastoral dimensions of the Church in the modern world. What was defined was a future for the Catholic Church in history: what Pope John gave to the Church was a new mandate and a new vision of itself, one that looked, not just to the concerns of Catholics, but to the needs and aspirations of the whole of humanity.[13]

To understand the achievement, one must understand the hard-fought battle extending over almost 2,000 years, a battle that emerged in the early Christian Church in the face of two intellectual traditions which today are merely footnotes in the history of philosophy. The first was the *cosmology* of Gnosticism, which proclaimed the material universe as evil, and the second was the *ontology* of Platonism, which proclaimed the visible universe, not as the creation of a beneficent God, but as an emanation of His very substance.[14]

Gnosticism denied the goodness of creation, and Platonism denied a *Creator*. Both struck at the very concept of God in the Scriptures: the essential and inherent goodness of creation, the reality of the Incarnation as a loving act of God, as the Creator Himself in human flesh, the inviolable dignity of the human person, and human history as embodying the intentions of a gracious and provident God.

The hard-fought battle was fought and won in the early centuries and embodied in the documents of the great councils and in the writings of those known as the Fathers of the Church. But the philosophies took new forms down through the centuries and great minds emerged to do battle with them again, usually in the form of various kinds of pessimism that struck at the very root of Christian consciousness, obscuring the reality of God the Creator and the historical reality of that Creator in human flesh, the Incarnation of Jesus Christ, as the emergence of God into human history. It was the pastoral genius of Pope John which saw the significance of the Incarnation for human beings and the startling implications it held for the welfare of human beings and the future of humanity.

Pope John was convinced, in the light of the Incarnation and the Christian doctrine of creation, of the infinite worth of every single human being, that God deeply loves every single human person and that creation itself and the individual creation of each human being is the gift of love. The wonder of God hovering over the human race and directing human events to final fulfillment in Himself is the substance of Pope John's vision. Like the pontificate of Sylvester II at the end of the first millennium, Pope John aligned his pontificate with the millennium to come.

The conflict that I see in the Church is a conflict between two different visions of what the Church is and of its role in human affairs. I do not see an end of that conflict and I believe it will continue into the third millennium. This encyclical, it seems to me, does not end that conflict, but continues it by the very manner of its presentation. For me, this is a matter of great sadness, considering the riches of the Catholic tradition of which I am heir and my own experience in trying to share those riches with the world.

4.

What I see, then, in this encyclical, is a battle going on between two mindsets in the Church, two mindsets incompatible and in fierce opposition. I, for one, see no reason for this encyclical and simply do not agree that there is a crisis in moral theology in the Church or any real doubt among Catholics about the substance of Catholic teaching on these matters. This seems to be a police-action in an ongoing war that the Holy See is waging with some of its best minds and most devoted members,[15] under the belief that authority and orthodox doctrine are under siege. I believe this is a mistaken judgment and in consequence, a climate of mistrust and suspicion has been set up which is destroying morale among priests and bishops, arresting the development of Catholic teaching into critical areas of contemporary concern[16] and is contributing to a pastoral crisis of immense proportions.

And I see no end to the battle or the crisis. Priests are leaving the priesthood and will continue to leave, vocations to the priesthood and religious life will continue to dwindle for the simple reason that discouragement has become a way of life and the climate in the Church has become oppressive. It is hard to convince those responsible for this encyclical that this encyclical itself is one of the reasons for the pastoral crisis in the Church and will only contribute to the priestly shortage and loss of vocations. And those who will suffer are the Catholic people themselves, who see themselves without priests, because those in authority do not realize that it is their style of leadership that is the root of the problem.

The pastoral crisis in the Church has not been brought about by the debates of theologians and the hair-splitting distinctions of *proportionalism* or *consequentialism;* it has been brought about by the death of hope. There is almost no note of hope in this encyclical. It is filled with warnings, admonitions, exhortations, aimed at problems that do not exist, persons who are nameless, issues not in debate and minds not in contention. Its pessimistic appraisal can only add another weight to the already depressed spirits of those carrying on the pastoral mission of the Church on the front lines, bewildered by yet another document which they did not ask for and do not need.

5.

What, in my opinion, could have furthered the credibility of the Church at this critical moment in history? First of all, by bringing the hidden agenda of this encyclical into the open: its concern for the breakdown of sexual morality all over the world and its effects upon Catholics. What could have been given to the Catholic community and the world that was listening was a theology and anthropology of sexuality and of the man-woman relationship in marriage drawn from the rich sources of Catholic theology, the fruits of the best minds of the Eastern and Western tradition, the most valid insights of the Scriptures and of those minds in the contemporary Church who have grappled with this problem.[17]

What the world and the Catholic community waited for in this encyclical was a *Pacem in Terris* of married love, a new reading of the Catholic tradition of sexuality and marriage, brought up to date in its expression and continuing the vision of the Marriage Covenant laid down in *Gaudium et Spes*, the Pastoral Constitution of the Church in the Modern World. It seems to me that a rich opportunity was lost and a teaching moment of great significance.

What do I see that is needed, then, that is lacking in this encyclical as a statement of the mind of the Church on this critical matter? A touch of genius. A rich exposition, drawn from the riches of the Catholic tradition and the wisdom of the Scriptures of the noblest of human loves, the sacramentality of sex in marriage[18] and the priceless gift of that nuptial communion that is the greatest earthly gift that God has given to the human race.

Something *more* than mere moral exhortation to avoid evil, but some insight into the *goodness* to be cultivated and the rich human harvest that God has placed in the man-woman relationship in marriage.

How would I begin such an encyclical, how would I draw attention to the riches of Catholic truth in this matter and the priceless gift of man to woman and woman to man that is bound up in the Sacrament and Covenant of Marriage? I would begin it with: *Gaudia Dulces Amoris Nuptialis*: "The sweet joys of married love have inspired the love songs of the human race, and every nation and people has its passionate love poems and love songs. In Sacred Scripture, too, God has enshrined as a gem among its books the incomparable *Song of Songs*, reflecting the beauty and joy, the hopes and longings of married lovers, leading to the consummation of their love in wedded bliss."

Then I would give a masterly exposition of marriage as a Communion of Persons and Community of Love, drawing from the very nature of marriage itself the human values that are the heart of that relationship and which embody its moral structure. And then I would root this Covenant of Love in the very philanthropy of God, the Mystery of the Trinity,[19] which is a Communion of Persons in Love, and in the Mystery of the Incarnation, which is the Mystery of the Creator-in-human-flesh, drawing by Sacramental bonds all human beings into loving intimacy with Himself.

The service of the Church to humanity, to the world community and to its own members, it seems to me, is more than a mere statement of its teaching, but for its own credibility and acceptance of its teaching, it should expose the inner *rationale* of that teaching in all its Divine wisdom and human dimensions, as a precious legacy to the human race. My great disappointment with the encyclical and my chief criticism of its failure is that it does not truly reveal the *Veritatis Splendor* of the Catholic teaching on sexuality and marriage, which is the main focus of its concerns. By its very title and promulgation it held out a promise of immense proportions and inestimable value. Its failure to live up to that title and promise is what my criticism of the encyclical is all about.

Notes

1. "Declaration on Certain Questions Concerning Sexual Ethics," *Personal Humana*," Dec. 29, 1975, AAS 68(1976) 80.

"Instruction on Respect for Human Life in its Origin and the Dignity of Procreation," *Donum Vitae*, Feb. 27, 1987, AAS 80 (1988) 74.

Apostolic Letter, "Spiritus Domini," Aug. 1, 1987, AAS 79(1987) 1374.

2. Cf. "Statement Criticizing the Book Human Sexuality, New Directions in Ammerican Catholic thought, for its Manipulation of the Concept or Definition of Human Sexuality, and for other reasons," Congregation of the Doctrine of the Faith. English translation, Origins, 9:167-9, Aug. 30, 1979.

"Letter of the Congregation for the Doctrine of the Faith and Father Charles Curran," Doc. Cath. 83:854-5, Oct. 5. 1986; "Authority and Dissent in the Church," *Origins,* 16:375-6, Nov. 6, 1986; "Anxiety in the Academy," *Tablet,* 239:1171-8, Nov. 9, 1985.

3. "Certainly the Church's magisterium does not intend to impose upon the faithful any particular theological system, still less a philosophical one." *Veritatis Splendor,* Ch. II, para. 29.

4. Cardinal Newman, in a letter to one of his most vocal critics, William George Ward, who thought that some of Newman's views bordered on disloyalty to the Church, thus comments on legitimate differences in opinion in the Church, which do not touch the essentials of the Faith: "I do not feel our differences such a trouble as you do: for such differences always have been, always will be the Church; and Christians would have ceased to have spiritual and intellectual lives if such differences did not exist. It is part of their militant state. No human power can hinder it; nor, if attempted, could it do more than make a solitude and call it peace. And thus thinking that man cannot hinder it, however much he try, I have no great anxiety or trouble. Man cannot and God will not. He means such differences to be an exercise of charity. Of course I wish as much as possible to agree with all my friends, but if, in spite of my utmost efforts, they go beyond me, or come short of me, I can't help it, and take it easy.

He recognized, however, that there was an acceptable way of speaking out, one that did not help the cause of genuine dialogue in the Church, but furthered, rather, one's own sense of personal triumph: "There is a time for everything, and many a man desires reformation of an abuse, or a fuller development of a doctrine, or the adoption of a particular policy, but forgets to ask himself whether the right time has come; and, knowing that there is no one who will be doing anything in his own lifetime unless he does it himself, he will not listen to the voice of authority, and he spoils a good work in his own century, in order that another man, as yet unborn, may not have the opportunity of bringing it happily to perfection in the next."

5. The real pastoral problems in the Catholic community have to do with violence and war, peace and harmony among peoples, the creation of a truly Christian *paideia,* and the poverty that keeps half of the world in domestic and economic misery. For the facing of these problems, more than moral exhortation is needed. It is these problems that seem to go unheeded in the clash of opinions in the Church. The greatest scandal in the Church today is this war going on within the Catholic community.

6. "It is so ordered on high that in our day Holy Church should present just that aspect to my countrymen which is most consonant with their ingrained prejudices against her." Thus did Newman comment on a similar image problem in his own time. And in another place, he comments: "Instead of aiming at being a world-wide power, we are shrinking into ourselves, narrowing the lines of communion, trembling at freedom of thought, and using the language of disarray and despair at the prospect before us, instead of, with the high spirit of a warrior, going out and conquering and to conquer."

He expressed his mind again in another passage: "We are in a strange time. I have not a shadow of a misgiving that the Catholic Church and its doctrine are directly from God—but then I know well that there is in particular quarters a narrowness which is not of God. And I believe great changes before now have taken place in the direction of the Church's course, and that new aspects of her aboriginal doctrines have suddenly come forth, and all this coincidentally with changes in the world's history, such as are now in progress: so that I never should shut up, when new views are set before me, though I might not take them as a whole."

7. Cf. "Bartolomé De Las Casas In History," edited by Juan Friede and Benjamin Keen (Dekalb, Illinois: Northern Illinois University Press, 1971), pp. 67-127 309-349.

8. Ibid. Part II: "The Spanish Theological-Juridical Renaissance and the Ideology of Bartolomé de Las Casas." p. 237.

9. The list of his collaborators include: Francisco Vitoria, Dominic Diego de Deza, Soto, Melchior Cano, Luis de Valladolid.

10. The works that embodied their thought and achievement are: La Casas' three major works: "Historia de las Indias," "Apologetica historia de las Indias," "De unico vocationis modo." Vitoria's major works: "Reelection de Indis" and "On the Law of Conquest," Cano's "De justitia et jure," and Matias de Paz's, "De dominio regum Hispaniae super Indias."

11. Gerbert was the most learned man of his time, the greatest teacher of his age, who summed up in himself the intellectual currents that would take the Church into the Second Millennium. His person and his history reflect the new age into which Christian Europe was emerging and he pioneered in his own person and in his pastoral concerns, the new directions that the Church would be taking for the next thousand years.

He was not only learned in Sacred Scripture and theology, he had studied under Arabic teachers in Spain, immersed himself in Arabic learning and mastered every known science of his age. He became tutor to two emperors, helped to give unity and stability to Christian Europe as advisor to four emperors and laid the foundations for the rise of the medieval university.

As pope, he consecrated the first archbishops of Poland and Hungary, helped to stablize Christianity in Norway under the first Christian king, Olaf Tyrggvason, and began diplomatic relations with Russia, under its first Christian ruler, the grand prince Vladimir of Kiev. When he died in 1003, after a short pontificate, he had given unity and stability to Christian Europe by far-seeing papal policies and by encouraging learning and education on every level of society. He gave the papacy a position and character it would hold for the next thousand years and showed that the Christian Faith was a religion, not of the past, but of the future. He laid the seeds for every major development that Europe would take for the next thousand years.

12. The *dualism* that at various times threatened the unity of these: the conflict that was seen between: matter and spirit, body and soul, senses and mind, passion and reason, nature and grace, intellect and will, creation and redemption, freedom and authority, sin and human worth, marriage and celibacy, Church and State, faith and reason, time and eternity, secular and sacred, clergy and laity. All were based on a certain *dualistic* view that saw conflict and opposition between the two.

The great minds of Christianity brought them into unity by clear concepts of the nature of God, the inherent goodness of creation, the good-will and good intentions

of God to His creation, the closeness of Providence, God watching over His creatures, a loving human affairs, the inherent dignity of the human person, the gift of
one's individual creation as a gift of love, the real meaning of the Incarnation as the
Creator in human flesh, the significance of the Eucharist, evil and sin as not consti-
tuting the *nature* of things, but arising from the exercise of freedom, *redemption* as
not only deliverance from sin, but as orientation to Eternal Life, the unity of religion
and culture.

This unitive view flows from two basic Christian doctrines: 1) the Biblical doctrine of Creation *ex nihilo*, and, 2) the Gospel revelation that Jesus Christ is the
Creator in human flesh. The genius of Pope John XXIII, Sylvester II and other seed
thinkers of Christianity was to see the *implications* in human life and history of
these key doctrines of the Christian Faith. What Pope John did was to re-shape the
pastoral mission of the Catholic Church by drawing out the contemporary significance and implications of these doctrines.

13. Pope John's optimism is shown in his opening address to the Second Vatican
Council, with the prophetic statement: "In the present order of things, Divine Providence is leading us to a new order of human relations which, by men's efforts and
beyond their expectations, are directed toward the fulfillment of God's superior and
inscrutable designs. And everything, even human differences, leads to the greater
good of the Church."

"Now, more than ever, certainly more than in past centuries, our purpose is to
serve human beings as such, and not only Catholics, to defend above all and everywhere, the rights of the human person, and not only those of the Catholic Church.
"Present-day circumstances, the needs of the last fifty years, and deeper doctrinal
knowledge have placed before us new realities. . . . it is not the Gospel that changes,
but rather we who begin to understand better. . . . The moment has arrived to recognize the *signs of the times*, to seize the opportunity and to look far ahead.

14. Cf. "Being as Communion" by John Zizoulias, St. Vladimir's Seminary Press,
Crestwood, N.Y.

15. Edward Schillebeeckx, Hans Küng, Bernard Häring, Leonardo Boff and Charles
Curran are five names that come to mind.

16. The serious theological problems raised by *liberation* theology, the oppressive
political regimes that arise in countries that are nominally Catholic, developing a
theology of women.

17. To mention only a few: Dietrich von Hildebrand's "Man and Woman" opened
up a whole new theology of marriage; Bernard Häring, whose monumental writings
on the subject have all but been ignored in official circles; Paul Endokimov, whose
"Sacrament of Theology Love" brought the riches of Eastern Christianity to the
West, and numerous European studies little known in this country.

18. Cf. "The Noblest Love: the Sacramentality of Sex in Marriage," by Clifford
Stevens, BMH Publications, Schuyler, Nebraska, 1993.

19. Cf. "The Trinitarian Roots of the Nuptial Community" by Clifford Stevens, *St.
Vladimir's Theological Quarterly*, Fall, 1991.

Morality on the Way of Discipleship: The Use of Scripture in *Veritatis Splendor*

William C. Spohn

John Paul II indicates the historical importance of the encyclical, *Veritatis Splendor* (*VS*), when he states that it is the first authoritative magisterial statement on the foundations of Christian morality (n. 4).[1] Responding to certain currents in contemporary culture and theology, particularly the separation of morality from truth, *VS* articulates basic positions which previous magisterial documents had left unexpressed. Although the text defends at length the Church's competence to state universal and invariant moral norms, its description of the relation between morality and Christian discipleship may reorient moral theology in a more biblical and Christological direction.

No papal document in history has concentrated to such an extent on the role of Jesus Christ in the Christian moral life or relied as much on Scripture as the source of its argument. The opening chapter presents a lengthy meditation on the encounter between Jesus and the rich young man in Matthew 19, which locates the role of moral commandments in the assent of faith to Jesus Christ. Although this chapter holds out the promise of a Christological ethics, the rest of the encyclical narrows the focus of discipleship to following Jesus' respect for the commandments and imitating his obedience to God's will, even to the point of death. The lengthy second chapter shifts attention to the controversies over moral autonomy, relativism, conscience, and proportionalism. It reverts to a more familiar philosophical form of magisterial ethics, which can be described as "theonomous naturalism," that is, a realist ethics in the natural law tradition which grounds morality in the divine law. Although this approach evokes biblical phrases as support, it uses Christology and Scripture to underwrite its ethics of commandments but not to develop a fuller account of the following of Christ. Commandments remain at center stage, leaving practical morality, virtues, imagination and moral development hidden in the wings.

This essay will examine the use of Scripture in the argument of *VS* in three stages: first, the historical context of the Catholic debate on Scripture and ethics; second, the methodological issue of Scripture in relation to the

other sources of moral theology; and third, the incorporation of Scripture
into the encyclical's argument. The principal concern will be whether it succeeds in providing an adequate biblical and Christological foundation for the
moral life of Christians.

1.
Historical Context

The discipline of moral theology has undergone more change in the
past generation than in the previous three centuries combined. From a traditional interpretation of natural law dominated by a deductive application of
moral principles, moral theology has moved to more personalist approaches
which acknowledge the limitations of law and the need to root moral discernment in Christian identity. Currently, the personalism that emerged from
Second Vatican Council is itself being challenged by critics who question
the social context of particular moral dilemmas and insist that the struggle
for social justice is integral to the commitment of faith.[2]

The call for a more biblical moral theology came some time before
Vatican II. Vincent MacNamara describes how three different stages in this
debate emerged in the past 50 years.[3] The first stage began in the 1940s
when a few pioneers decried the religious barrenness of the manualist tradition which had dominated Catholic moral teaching since the 19th century.
The manualists organized their detailed presentation of Christian duties under the headings of the Ten Commandments, and that appeared to exhaust
Scripture's contribution to moral theology. Jesus Christ and the grace of the
Holy Spirit played almost no role in a natural morality which had been established in creation and ratified in the Decalogue. Bernard Häring, Gerard
Gilleman, and others called for a moral theology which was centered on
Christian love rather than on a rationalist conception of human nature. In
order to accommodate *agape* to realist philosophical categories, they attempted to define love as an ontological principle. Unfortunately, the old
wineskins could not contain the new wine.[4]

The second stage of the retrieval of Scripture into moral theology
came prior to Vatican II from the revisionist moral theologians, known as
proponents of "autonomy ethics." The Council endorsed the criticism of the
manualist tradition when it issued a forthright mandate to moral theologians:
overhaul the discipline to make clear the connection between moral duties
and the Christian vocation of the faithful, Scripture, and the mystery of
Christ.[5] For some time before the Council, certain moralists were becoming
sensitive to Protestant critiques that Catholic morality ignored Jesus Christ.
Scholars began to connect natural law morality with New Testament Christology. Josef Fuchs, the principal architect of contemporary moral theology,
grounded natural law morality in the great theological hymns which are pro-
logues to John's Gospel and the letters to the Ephesians and Colossians.[6]

Since humanity was created in Christ and for Christ, Fuchs argued that the basic pattern of humanity is oriented to Christ. Authentic human development will reflect the values of Christ, whether the individual person is aware of it or not.

While moral values and obligations were rooted in God and Christ ontologically, on the experiential level they could be known without explicit reference to biblical revelation. Ontologically, therefore, ethics is "theonomous," that is, grounded in the divine reality. Epistemologically, however, moral values and principles are "autonomous", intrinsic to humanity, rather than "heteronomous," imposed from an external source. According to Bruno Schuller, S.J., Scripture provides motivation for morality, but moral content comes from the reality of what it means to be human.[7] The proponents of the autonomy school point out that the natural law tradition had always respected the human character of morality. Furthermore, Christians need to speak a common moral language with nonbelievers in order to be intelligible in civil society and effective in shaping social policy. Biblical appeals shape the overall goals of Christians and add concreteness and affect to preaching. However, in order to preserve the autonomous character of morality, most revisionist moral theologians considered explicitly religious warrants out of place in public moral discourse.

Moralists who find their inspiration in Immanuel Kant have been even more restrictive about finding any moral content in the person and message of Jesus. To the extent that the proponents of autonomy ethics depend upon the philosophy of Kant, they find it difficult, if not impossible, to qualify the noun "ethics" with the adjective "Christian." If, by Kant's definition, ethics must be universal for all rational beings, and it is presumed that any reference to "Christian" introduces a particular, non-universal limitation, then "Christian ethics" becomes a self-canceling phrase. Although the specific biblical injunction of Matt. 19:21 to sell one's possessions and give the proceeds to the poor may oblige Christians in virtue of their membership in a religious community, it is no more a moral obligation than the practice of keeping kosher.

The third stage of the debate, the proposal of a "faith ethics," was generated in response to the autonomy position. Before becoming head of the Congregation for the Doctrine of the Faith, Josef Ratzinger advocated a "faith ethics" which made commitment to Jesus Christ central to Christian moral reflection. Hans Urs von Balthasar and other conservative European theologians supported this faith ethics, but until the advent of narrative theology, it did not attract much support in the English-speaking world.[8] Although this school insisted that Jesus Christ must be the norm of morality, it failed to specify how he could be normative or how the disparate biblical moral materials could be employed critically in moral discussion.

In contrast to the autonomy school, these authors doubted that human powers unaided by grace and not instructed by the Church could accurately

discern moral values and principles. Secular culture and sinful modern attitudes, including consequentialism, subjectivism and a false autonomy, distorted moral perceptions. *VS* must be counted as the most authoritative magisterial rejection of the autonomy school. Using terms unmistakably derived
from the faith ethics school, the Pope writes, "Jesus' way of acting and his
words, his deeds and his precepts constitute the moral rule of Christian life"
(n. 20)." Whether the encyclical refutes the actual positions of the autonomy
school or only assails a caricature of its position will remain a subject of
debate.

2.
Methodological Context

How should Scripture function in moral theology? Examining the
contours of moral theology's method will complement the historical map.
Most writers in Christian ethics today would agree that there are four
sources for moral reflection: Scripture, tradition, moral philosophy, and the
empirical data relevant to the issue under consideration. Each of them makes
an indispensable contribution. *Scripture* is the canonical revelation of the
reality of God, Christ, and Spirit and spells out the identity of those who
respond in faith. *Tradition* witnesses the wisdom of the believing community extended over time, under the guidance of the Spirit. It includes the
councils and doctors of the church, the wisdom of the saints, the *sensus
fidelium*, and the papal magisterium. Since the early part of the 19th century, the Vatican has assumed a more extensive teaching role through encyclical letters and other authoritative, noninfallible pronouncements. *Moral
philosophy* represents the search for what is humanly normative. Moralists
often expressed this wisdom in various forms of natural law, but in principle
they could draw from other ethical systems as well. *Empirical data* grounds
the discussion in the information provided by relevant social, biological and
psychological sciences. Moral theology pays increasing attention to the experience of those affected by the issues under consideration.[9]

These sources are mutually complementary and corrective. We do not
know exactly what weight each source should have in advance because the
nature of the question will determine which ones will make a greater contribution. Empirical data is descriptive rather than normative because any scientific data must be reckoned within the normative values and beliefs provided by Scripture, tradition and moral philosophy in order to produce an
ethical judgment. An argument which neglects any of these base points
would be deficient. In the past, Catholic moral theology has relied largely
on tradition and natural law, while Protestant Christian ethics has concentrated on Scripture and experiential data.[10] Catholic moralists, when they
invoked Scripture at all, usually wrenched biblical expressions out of their

context and used them to garnish natural law arguments. Recent documents from the magisterium indicate that this practice has not entirely disappeared.

The major obstacle to appealing to Scripture for moral argument is its apparent irrelevance to today's burning questions. Can this collection of ancient texts from diverse cultures offer moral guidance on nuclear weapons, economic justice, or the new status of women? Clearly Scripture would have little to offer on these current issues if one restricts moral guidance to particular concrete moral rules of behavior. However, when ethics is expanded beyond rules and principles to encompass one's fundamental vision of what is worthwhile in life, the shape of one's character, the moral qualities of virtue and vice, and the humane quality of social practices and institutions, then Scripture can play a more extensive role in moral guidance. Biblical events like the Exodus become paradigms for action; psalms are seen to shape the deeper emotions of the heart; and narratives reveal the character of God and intimate a faithful response.[11] In this expanded version of ethics, the moral action is the one that corresponds to the revealed reality of God and Jesus Christ. Even though the moral theologian may be intimidated by the explosion of biblical scholarship and its increasing specialization, some relatively coherent images of God which are central to the canon can function as invitation and norm for Christian responses. However Scripture serves as an indispensable norm, it cannot be the exclusive source of morality.

Three Questions on the Use of Scripture in Ethics

There are three questions that can clarify how Scripture is being used in a theological argument:

1. Selection: What texts are chosen? Because the canon contains a virtual library of books, any author must choose some materials and pass over others. Reasons should be given for these choices and no passage should be used in obvious contradiction to central themes in revelation or in violation of accepted moral wisdom. The process of selection inevitably raises the correlative question: What canonical texts, genres, or historical periods are left out? For example, Martin Luther located the center of Christian ethics in Romans and Galatians, but rejected the Epistle of James. Liberation theologians, by contrast, often ignore Paul entirely while relying on Exodus and Luke. One should also ask whether the author places normative material in the context of the central narratives of Scripture and broader biblical themes, like covenant, justice, and mercy. Is the selection so narrow that other major themes and literature in the canon cannot be considered?[12] Theologians no longer apologize for having "a canon within the canon," but they should provide some rationale for it.

2. Interpretation: Why are these materials morally authoritative? No text is self-interpreting because every passage derives its meaning from broader convictions and assumptions. What central theological themes and methodological commitments make it possible to understand the selected texts? Basic notions of God, humanity and the world, Christological commitments, the relation of sin and grace (or grace and nature) and models of Christian community provide the warrants for using Scripture in a certain way.[13] For example, Josef Fuchs appeals to Karl Rahner's distinctive configuration of nature and grace to justify his use of John 1, Ephesians 1, and Colossians 1 to ground natural law in Christology. In Rahner's theology, creation was established for the sake of the Incarnation, which means that human values are predisposed to fulfillment in the grace of Christ.

3. Application: How are these texts, so interpreted, to be applied practically? Theologians often fail to examine this question adequately because they take a particular form of ethics for granted. They may assume that ethics is simply about norms and principles, or character formation, or nothing but social transformation. The type of ethics assumed in the application often guides the selection by narrowing the range of acceptable biblical resources. Because Luther feared that legalism would undermine the Gospel, he framed an ethics of dispositions which played down biblical action guides and general principles. Or if ethics is assumed to be categorical in the Kantian sense, biblical exhortations based on reward or punishment are dismissed as premoral appeals to self-interest. Only universal rational principles or their biblical facsimiles are selected. Just as with selection and interpretation, any theologian must choose some ethical approach. The author should acknowledge and defend these theoretical options and not assume that they are self-evident.

Turning to the encyclical, we can inquire how it makes these methodological options concerning biblical material and coordinates them with the other sources of moral theology. Since the argument focuses on a particular disputed question, the empirical situation influences the choice of biblical material. The encyclical makes empirical claims about certain attitudes in the Church and secular society concerning truth, freedom, conscience, moral norms, etc.; however, no data are offered to substantiate or analyze these assertions. (How widespread are these tendencies in the Church? Do they differ from one region to another? Are they more prevalent among the educated or the uneducated? Have in fact the writings of revisionist moral theologians caused these attitudes among the faithful?)

The encyclical treats tradition as a relatively unified body of philosophical and theological truths. Augustine and Aquinas are taken to address Christian experience universally; no mention is made of their historical contexts or differences in philosophical and theological method. *VS* takes its stand on a priori grounds as a statement of necessary theological and moral truths, with no examination of the a posteriori history of the moral teachings of the magisterium. Its doctrines have developed smoothly and consistently: "This truth of the moral law . . . unfolds down the centuries: the norms expressing that truth remain valid in their substance, but must be specified and determined *eodem sensu eademque sententia* in the light of historical circumstances by the Church's Magisterium . . ." (n. 53).

Does the actual history substantiate this description of doctrinal development? John T. Noonan, Jr., the foremost historian of Catholic moral teaching in the English world, writes that the Church substantially changed its position on the permissibility of slavery, taking interest on loans, marriage, and religious liberty.[14] These changes cast serious doubt on the presumption of magisterial consistency in *VS*. If the Church has in fact reversed its normative teaching on slavery or religious liberty, should not that history affect the encyclical's assertions about the magisterium's capacity to teach immutable, universal, concrete moral norms?

Tradition and ethics will shape the selection of Scripture in any theological argument; it is virtually impossible to proceed *sola Scriptura*. Biblical material is likely to be interpreted through commitments rooted in the author's tradition in order to yield applications consistent with the tradition. Or ethics may be the controlling factor: the model of ethics which is assumed in the application phase will enlist particular doctrinal and ecclesiological themes of the tradition to select and interpret Scripture. It is legitimate to begin from either a given tradition or a particular ethics, so long as the choice is acknowledged and defended. Unless Scripture also challenges the favored ethical model and traditional themes, it is relegated to a supporting role in the argument which is derived, in fact, from these other sources. Although it is not immediately apparent whether *VS* begins from tradition or ethics, it appears that they dictate any appeal to Scripture. Eschatological and prophetic dimensions of the canon that might challenge the portrait of a stable, consistent moral tradition of theonomous naturalism are not considered in the encyclical. An ethical preference for law pays little attention either to biblical promises of reward and punishment or to the specific guidance of the Holy Spirit through the diverse gifts in the entire Body of Christ.

3.
Scriptural Material in the Argument of *Veritatis Splendor*

There are two sections where the encyclical focuses mainly on biblical material: the entire first chapter, which is structured around the encounter between Jesus and the rich young man (n. 6-27), and the beginning of the third chapter, which defines discipleship in terms of the cross and resurrection of Jesus, and presents martyrdom as the fullest expression of discipleship (n. 84-93). Although a rich array of biblical and patristic citations illuminates the philosophical critique of contemporary moral currents in the second chapter, the argument could stand without them. Here the ancient Christian tradition and Scripture offer corroborating but not substantive testimony.

Selection of Biblical Materials

Beginning with the question of selection, we can examine these primary sections in turn:

1. The first chapter is an extended meditation the text of Mt 19:16-22. Where the manuals began with abstract considerations about "the end of man" and the relation of the natural and supernatural orders, the Pope offers a phenomenology of personal encounter between a particular person and the historical Jesus which "brings the question about morality back to its religious foundations" (n. 9). The dialogue is analyzed according to the two Great Commandments, and each strain incorporates other biblical material:

Mt 19:16-22

A. The Response to God: The First Great Commandment
Mk 10:18 parallel to Mt 19: Who is good but God?
Mt 22:37: The Religious Question behind the Moral One
Ex 20:2-3: Covenant and Gift of the Decalogue
Lev 19:2, Dt 6:4-7: God's Holiness manifest in God's Law
Wis 18, Ez 36: Promise of the New Covenant, internal Law
Mt 5-7: The New Covenant's commands linked to the Kingdom

B. The Response to the Neighbor: The Second Great Commandment
Rom 13:8-10: Second Tablet of Decalogue = Love of Neighbor
Lk 10:25-37: Who is Neighbor? Good Samaritan parable
Jn 3:14-15, 13:1: Love of God and Neighbor in Cross of Jesus
1 Jn 4:20, Mt 25:31-46: Neighbor Love Indispensable

C. Jesus Christ: the New Moses and the New Norm
Mt 5: Sermon on the Mount: Magna Charta of Gospel Morality
Col 3:14: Interiorizing moral demands
Mt 5:3-11: The Beatitudes: Attitudes of Discipleship
Gal 5:13,16 (Rom 7,8): Human Freedom Appealed to by God's Law
Mt 19:21: Following Christ = Foundation of Christian Morality
    (Jn 6:45, Jn 10:11-16, Jn 14:6-10)
Jn 13:14-15, 34-35, Jn 15:12,13: The New Commandment: Jesus
    as Norm and Motive for Christian Morality
Phil 2:5-8, Rom 6:3-11, Gal 5:16-25: Conformity to Christ
Jn 1:17, 1 Jn 3:34, 4, Jn 15:10: The Task Follows the Gift

In summary, citations from the Gospels of Matthew and John predominate, with significant corroboration from some Pauline material and the First Letter of John. The Old Testament materials center on Exodus and appeals to holiness from the Pentateuch.

What is missing from this set? OT narratives, wisdom literature and prophetic material are mostly absent. The Gospels of Mark and Luke, which present a different image of Jesus and of morality, are peripheral at best.

Mark's moral doctrine is heavily shadowed by the imminent eschatology, which *VS* omits. Lukan parables and healing accounts convey the moral message of Jesus more fully than his discourses. John Paul II's 1980 encyclical, *Dives in Misericordia*, relies heavily on the parable of the prodigal son in Lk 15:11-32 as "the analogy that enables us to understand more fully the very mystery of mercy, as a profound drama played out between the father's love and the prodigality and sin of the son. That son . . . in a certain sense is the man of every period. . . ."[15] In *VS* the rich young man plays the same role: in him "we can recognize every person who, consciously or not, *approaches Christ the Redeemer of man and questions him about morality*" (n. 7). This form of analogical thinking, which moves from the particular features of the parable and the encounter with Jesus to every person's situation, shows the moral power of biblical stories. *VS* ignores the analogical imagination in defending commandments as the basis of Christian morality.

VS does not treat the parables, which were one of Jesus' preferred modes of moral teaching. He was not a rabbi who reinforced conventional morality by commenting on the Law. In fact, Mt 19 is one of the few Gospel passages where Jesus explicitly endorses the Decalogue. Instead, he spoke in paradox and parables that challenged his audience's moral presuppositions without specifying what they should do.[16] The encyclical does not examine his exemplary actions of healing and table-fellowship as acts of social inclusion and challenge to the religious establishment. Although the announcement of the inbreaking Reign of God was central to Jesus' preaching, the encyclical avoids this mysterious reality, possibly because its eschatological vagueness might undermine the moral clarity *VS* seeks to buttress. Not that other material is dismissed as irrelevant to discipleship: "Jesus' way of acting and his words, his deeds and his precepts constitute the moral rule of Christian life." The Cross and Resurrection definitively "reveal his love for the Father and for others" (n. 20). Unfortunately, the text concentrates on his precepts with little reference to his other acts, deeds and dispositions. We will see that the encyclical's operative ethical system, which concentrates on rules and principles, determines this narrow selection of biblical materials.

The immediate context of the nineteenth chapter of Matthew receives scant attention, although its dependence on Mk 10 is noted. Most scholars agree that Mt 19 begins the narrative section of the fifth book of the Gospel, which treats the ministry of Jesus in Judea and Jerusalem.[17] The chapter focuses on what four different classes of persons must do to enter the Reign of God: the married, those who do not marry, children, and the rich. In context, therefore, the rich young man is not "Everyman," but a representative of the rich and their particular impediments to discipleship. The immediate response of the disciples to the dialogue supports this reading: if the rich, who are God's favorites, have such difficulty, then who can be saved? (Mt 19:25)

The encyclical does capture the fact that Jesus makes special demands on all these would-be disciples, except the children. He asks more of his disciples than they can comprehend. All are called to radical fellowship with Jesus in joining his journey to the Cross (Mt 20:17-28). The encyclical breaks new ground for moral theology by its highly personal focus; beyond the commandments lies radical attachment to the mysterious and attractive person of Jesus. Discipleship goes beyond learning and obeying commandments. "More radically, it involves *holding fast to the very person of Jesus,* partaking of his life and his destiny, sharing in his free and loving obedience to the will of the Father" (n. 19).

2. The second main appeal to Scripture comes at the outset of the third chapter; it is summarized in the introductory quotations: "Lest the cross of Christ be emptied of its power" (1 Cor 1:17) and "For freedom Christ has set us free" (Gal 5:1). The paradigmatic event of the cross defines Christian freedom as the union of sacrificial love and obedience. The cross of Jesus is replicated in the ultimate witness of martyrdom.

A. Freedom and the Cross
  Rom 12:2:Conversion from Worldly Ways to the Lord's Way
   Eph 5: 8-11, 15-16
  1 Cor 1: 17, 23-24: Christ Crucified Reveals Freedom
  Gen 3:5: Rebellion against Truth and Freedom
  Jn 8:32: Christ the Truth makes Us Free
   Jn 18:37, Jn 4:23
  Jn 15:13, Mt 26:46, 20:28, Phil 2:6-11: Love is the Free Gift of Self
  Jn 15:6, Gal 2:20: The Christian Way: Live as He Lived
  Mt 5:14-16 Witness: Living in the Light
  Eph 5:25, Lk 9:23: Christ's Cross the Model and Means for Disciples
   Eph 5:1-2

B. Martyrdom: the Ultimate Witness
  Dan 13: Susanna: Death rather than Disobedience to God's Law
  Mk 6:17-29: Death of John the Baptist
  Acts 1, 6, Rev 13:7-10, Heb 5:7: Christian Martyrs
  Mk 8:36: Gain the World but Lose Oneself
  Wis 2:12, Is 5:20: Martyrdom Refutes Those Who Deny the Law

VS defines the love enjoined by Jesus' new commandment of Jn 13:34 by the crucifixion. While this emphasis is consistent with the washing of the feet in Jn 13, it reads the symbolic action too narrowly. The washing of feet refers to the entire narrative of the preceding twelve chapters as the full display of "just as I have loved you." *VS* combines the Johannine literature that identifies Jesus as the norm of truth and freedom combined with Paul's concentration on the Paschal event as the summary of Jesus's life. Motivationally, the cross integrated a free and total gift of self in love for humans and in obedience to the Father. *VS* presents the crucifixion as the paradigm and inspiration for self-sacrificing love and obedience to God, even unto death. Like Paul, *VS* ignores the public ministry as a narrative guide for the moral life. Unlike the Apostle, however, the encyclical treats the will of God as an objective moral requirement rather than a forensic standard of justification and acquittal. Paul saw the Law as both gift and curse; it is a player on the stage of history which multiplies transgression and demoralizes humans (Rom 7). In *VS* the law appears here in a more abstract, philosophical guise: "law" is the imperative form of objective truth. It is an embodiment of the truth and not merely a standard.[18] In general, Paul balances the paradox of the cross with the victory of the resurrection. He applies the moral significance of the Paschal Mystery through the Spirit which guides the moral life and conveys "the mind of Christ" to the mature Christian. (Cf. Rom 7, 8, 1 Cor 2) Unfortunately, these themes are not central to the encyclical.

As suggested above, *VS* frequently uses biblical phrases as rhetorical commonplaces to convey its message, but the argument is not derived from their canonical context. For example, it refers to Romans 2: 12-16 as the standard biblical locus for the existence of natural law. No attempt is made to locate this pericope in Paul's overall theological argument of Rom 1-4, that both Jew and Gentile have sinned and stand in need of the justifying grace of Christ (Rom 3:22). *VS* warns and encourages the reader with numerous exhortative passages from Scripture without reference to their original literary or historical context. Although Vatican documents urge that the original historical meaning of biblical texts should have a controlling role in applying them to present problems, *VS* rarely pays any attention to original context or intent.[19] Instead, the biblical material is cited in a timeless manner, just like the selections from patristic sources. Contrary to modern historical interpretations, the encyclical presents Paul, Augustine and Aquinas as having identical understandings of natural law, grace and freedom. No influence stemming from the authors' diverse temporal locations, audiences and theologies seems relevant when they are taken to be addressing the objective order of moral truths, which is universal and immutable.

Interpretation of Scriptural Material

Theologians cannot use historical sources without making sense of them through some key beliefs about God, Christ, the world, the human condition, etc. Since the Bible is more a library than a single book, it requires interpretive principles to order its wider variety of materials. The second stage of analysis asks *why* these materials are relevant to this discussion. The explicit intention of the encyclical gives the most immediate answer. In the face of challenges to moral truth, especially from within the Catholic community, the main question is:

> . . . do the commandments of God, which are written on the human heart and are part of the Covenant, really have the capacity to clarify

the daily decisions of individuals and entire societies? Is it possible to obey God and thus love God and neighbor, without respecting these commandments in all circumstances? (n. 4)

For *VS* the crisis in the Church centers on commandments: are they relevant? Are they the means to love? Are they universally binding? Beneath the crises of relativism, autonomy ethics, proportionalism, false notions of conscience, and the separation of freedom from moral duty lies a fundamental issue: the divorce between moral freedom and objective truth.

1. Christ as the Source and Norm of Morality

The first chapter of the encyclical makes a religious connection between morality and truth by meditating on the person of Jesus Christ. *VS* opens up the possibility of a Christocentric ethics, at least initially. It subordinates a realist epistemology and the natural law to the religious realities of discipleship and the cross, which are the moral core of Christian discipleship. The authority of the commandments becomes personal in the attractiveness of Jesus Christ, the one who makes the Goodness of God tangibly present. However, the encyclical does not sustain this Christological ethics into the remainder of the text. *VS* interprets Jesus through the symbols of the New Moses and martyrdom which are defined in terms that lead easily to a rule-centered ethic of obedience.

A. Christ is both the new Moses and the New Law himself. The One who is the Way, Truth and Life proclaims and embodies objective moral truth. The young man is not drawn to Jesus because of the Law, but is drawn to move beyond obedience to the law by some compelling quality in Jesus who manifests the ultimate authority of Truth and Goodness in history.

Traditionally, the magisterium and Catholic tradition have not made Jesus Christ central to the moral life. Until recently human reason has discovered the moral intentions of God in human nature. Scripture confirmed the values and principles which have resided in human nature since the creation and which remain even after the fall from grace. Catholics expected that a restored human nature mediated between them and their ultimate end. Sanctifying grace was the healing force that brought human capacity beyond itself to the supernatural end of union with God. In morality, *caritas* informed the natural moral virtues so that they led to friendship with God.[20]

The Pope asserts a more theonomous morality, which subordinates natural moral knowledge to the encounter with Christ. Neither the "natural end of man," which the manualists appealed to, nor the graced nature of contemporary theology, which the autonomy school depends upon, serve as adequate mediators of God's call.[21] *"Only God can answer the question about what is good, because he is the Good itself"* (n. 9). Nature can supply an answer to the moral question but not to the religious question that lies behind it. This drive pushes beyond God's directives to the person of God as such. Hence, "the goodness that attracts and at the same time obliges man has its source in God, and indeed is God himself" (n. 9). What the rich young man and every one of us seeks is the personal reality of God, manifest in human form in the person of Jesus Christ. The moral seeker cannot be satisfied with a moral answer devoid of religious content; at the deepest level, the merely moral answer will still be "lacking." Nevertheless, *VS* does not assert a purely theonomous ethic where human reason is blind to God's directives in nature.

Revelation does not supplant nature as a moral source; it confirms the objective moral demands of nature and shows where they lead. Matthew's Jesus fills this role perfectly: "From the very lips of Jesus, the new Moses, man is once again given the commandments of the Decalogue." The Sermon on the Mount parallels the tablets given to Moses; it is "a sermon which contains the fullest and most complete formulation of the New Law (cf. Mt 5-7), clearly linked to the Decalogue entrusted by God to Moses on Mount Sinai" (n. 12). Just as the Old Law was given to guide Israel to the promised land, Jesus mediates the gift of the New Law, which is a means to eternal life. In both cases, moral norms are directed to a religious goal. "God's commandments show man the path of life and they lead to it." (n. 12)

Christ interprets the demands of morality to the disciple. In the most famous 20th-century reading of the Sermon on the Mount, Dietrich Bonhoeffer states that Christ stands between the disciple and the law.[22] While this reading is not surprising for a Lutheran theologian, it is remarkable for the Catholic magisterium to take a similar position. Nevertheless, there are significant differences. Like most Protestants, Bonhoeffer does not retain the same confidence in human nature that *VS* does. He does not believe that fallen human nature can serve as a reliable moral source or that any church can act as a moral teacher. We are not surprised that Bonhoeffer interprets the Sermon on the Mount in far more paradoxical terms, focusing on its hard sayings and challenging parables. He makes Jesus a more prophetic figure, one for whom the demands of God challenge human religious and moral imaginings. The Pope concentrates instead on the Beatitudes and the reaffirmation of the Law in Mt 5. The legal character of *VS*'s Christology stands out in the statement that Jesus "*himself becomes a living and personal Law*, who invites people to follow him" (n. 15).

Other commentators point out that the Jesus of Matthew is not only the New Moses, but also the eschatological prophet of the imminent Reign of God and the Sage who discloses clues to divine ways through the mundane details of the parables.[23] A more comprehensive New Testament Christology would also have to discuss Jesus as socio-political critic (particularly in Luke) and the Johannine Incarnate Word revealing the deepest intentions of the Father, who is equally the servant and friend of his disciples. These perspectives would temper the Matthean emphasis on law and obedience that has dominated Catholic theology since the Council of Trent.[24]

B. Martyrdom is the second Christological symbol that shapes the portrait of Jesus in *VS*. It corroborates the religious interpretation of commandments associated with "the New Moses" because this teacher internalizes the will of God by his obedience unto death. However, the symbol of martyrdom truncates the witness of Jesus to death on the cross and the corresponding witness of the disciple to obedience to God's law. The command of Mt 5:14-16 to "let your light so shine before men" commands Christians to replicate the witness of Jesus. His destiny on the cross normatively defines the Christian meaning of love and

> authentic freedom which is manifested and lived in the gift of self, *even to the total gift of self*, like that of Jesus, who on the Cross "loved the Church and gave himself up for her" (Eph 5:25). Christ's witness is the source, model and means for the witness of his disciples, who are called to walk on the same road: "If any man would come after me, let him deny himself and take up his cross daily and follow me" (Lk 9:23) (n. 89)."

Scripture highlights two central motivations behind the journey of Jesus to the cross: obedience to the will of the Father and love for those who will be saved by his suffering and death. In the technical language of ethics, the deontological element (obedience to command) can be distinguished from the more teleological one (love directed toward the salvation of the world). By giving preference to the deontological motivation for the cross over its teleological significance, *VS* repudiates contemporary moral theologians who would admit exceptions to principles when results seem to warrant them. Since they allow teleological considerations to outweigh deontological ones, they are emptying the cross of Christ of its power and meaning.

VS appeals to the staunch resistance of Susanna in the book of Daniel, the martyrs of Acts, and the heroes of Revelation who refuse to burn incense to the Emperor. They are proof of the doctrine about unexceptionable norms: "The Church has canonized their witness and declared the truth of their judgment, according to which the love of God entails the obligation to respect his commandments, even in the most dire of circumstances, and the refusal to betray those commandments, even for the sake of saving one's own life" (n. 91).

Martyrdom supports the deontological focus of the encyclical because it affirms the ultimate significance of universal, immutable norms. Martyrdom is "the exaltation of the inviolable holiness of God's law" (n. 90). The martyr makes the ultimate gift of self in absolute fidelity to God's law. This obedience is not simply theonomous, since these moral norms also rest on a human foundation. Respect for God and respect for human dignity are closely aligned in this complex ethical naturalism. Faith adds an ultimate and unconditional character to morality, disclosing the *"unconditional respect due to the insistent demands of the personal dignity of every man,* demands protected by those moral norms which prohibit without exception actions which are intrinsically evil" (n. 90).

The theological and moral significance of martyrdom is not exhausted by this deontological reading. Is witness to the faith unto death primarily obedience to a principle? It may embody the principle that loyalty to God takes precedence over all other loyalties, but obedience to law does not fully capture the meaning of martyrdom. The Latin American liberation theologian Jon Sobrino gives a decidedly teleological account of martyrdom, stressing its consequential and social dimensions. It is the supreme act of solidarity with the oppressed, the liberating love which looks more to those whom it embraces than to the ascetical test of self-giving. Sacrifice remains at the heart of the experience, but it is sacrifice in service of solidarity more than sacrifice in obedience to the law of God. He writes that martyrdom "is our lot not only because of the a priori demand of total self-bestowal in testimony and discipleship with Jesus crucified. It is our lot in virtue of the concrete reality of Latin America. . . . [It is] the demand that we give out own lives for the life of the poor." The Catholic Church is undergoing a new era of martyrdom, particularly in Latin America. When *VS* defines that experience as vindicating deontological ethics, one suspects that the self-understanding of today's martyrs is being "colonized" to serve magisterial interests.

Is martyrdom an adequate or exhaustive symbol to express Christian discipleship? While this symbol connotes the furthest reaches of loyalty and self-giving in both *VS* and Sobrino, it may overlook the daily forms of love in favor of the heroic. The generosity and detachment demanded of the rich young man and the promise offered him *"are meant for everyone*, because they bring out the full meaning of the commandment of love of neighbor" (n. 18). Although this stress on the heroic nature of obedience supports *VS*'s defense of unexceptional moral norms, it says little about the rest of life which is not lived at the heroic margins. The same holds true for liberation theology's insistence on a heroic solidarity with the poor which leaves unclear what responsibility one owes to one's children, parents and others whose claim is close but not as urgent as the claims of the poor.[26]

The encyclical states clearly that the call to perfection is not issued only to a particular class in the Church. Gone is the traditional distinction between those who follow the counsels in the way of perfection and those who follow the commandments. Vatican II states that the universal call to holiness comes from Christian baptism, and *VS* reaffirms that equality. "The vocation to perfect love is not restricted to a small group of individuals."

The encyclical's treatment of martyrdom displays one of the more problematic patterns of biblical interpretation in *VS*. In theonomous ethics there is an almost irresistible temptation to make certain norms and values sacrosanct. Attributes that belong to God get transferred to finite moral demands and values; as a result, moral statements become sacrosanct. Even though humanity is created in the image of God, it does not necessarily follow that human statements can or ought to image divine attributes. When the direction of argument proceeds from the transcendent down to the finite, terms can be used univocally instead of analogically.

Several examples of this move from divine qualities to features of the moral life occur in *VS*:

1. From the inviolable holiness of God can one infer the inviolability of certain moral norms endorsed by God? Does inviolability mean the same thing when applied to God and applied to certain humanly formulated moral norms? (n. 90-93) If not, it produces a classic instance of "begging the question," namely, assuming as true what needs to be proved.

2. Does "truth" have the same meaning when used as a Christological title in John's Gospel, in doctrinal matters, and in asserting the objective status of moral norms? (n. 31, 51) The encyclical's undifferentiated notion of truth contrasts with the traditional distinction of Aristotle and Aquinas between truth in the speculative order (such as the necessary truths of geometry) and truth in the practical order (propositions which address contingent matters and rely on virtue for appropriate application).[27] One cannot expect the same level of clarity or certitude in moral questions that can be found in mathematics because the realities they consider are different. There may well be necessary truths in moral matters, like statements about universal human rights, but necessity is predicated differently about statements of human rights than about the axioms of Euclidean geometry.

3. *VS* argues that certain features of human nature are immutable by referring to the permanence of Christ: "The Church affirms that underlying so many changes there are some things which do not change and are *ultimately founded upon Christ* who is the same yesterday and today and forever" (n. 53). In order to ward off charges that certain magisterial teachings have relied excessively on physical and biological processes, the encyclical reasserts the existence of "permanent structural elements of man which are connected with his own bodily dimension." A human nature that transcends cultural and historical change warrants universal and immutable moral norms.[28] Do "universality" and "immutability" mean the same when predicated of Christ and of moral norms? While some inference may be drawn analogically between the permanence of Christ and the continuities of human nature, the limits of the analogy should be carefully noted. Otherwise, certain moral practices may become sacrosanct, because criticism of them could be taken as denying the permanence of Christ. The a priori method of *VS* and its unwillingness to attend to changes in the actual teachings of the Church, contrasted with recent discussions of natural law theology, have accorded a normative status to human nature, while acknowledging its historical character.[29]

These three examples indicate the tendency of a theonomous ethic to leap from qualities of God to corresponding characteristics in the moral life.

After the first chapter, *VS* presents an ethics that could be called a "theonomous naturalism" because it grounds morality in human values and dignity as well as in their transcendent source. It is not a purely theonomous ethic like that of Karl Barth. He would agree that moral obligations make an unconditional demand because they issue from an unconditional source.[30] However, he objected to any appeal to nature as a moral source: Catholic natural law was no better than idolatry, since it confused the absoluteness proper to divinity with the dictates of finite, fallen nature. *VS* outlines a theonomy which is naturalist because moral laws rest on a dual foundation, even though the natural is clearly subordinated to the divine. God does not command by immediate call, as in Barth's account, but through certain values and rational capacities structured by creation into the human species.[31] Human nature is not an autonomous source which is independent from God since it embodies, even in its present state, God's image. Christ is necessary to realize the fullness of that image, and the magisterium of the Church calls the faithful to the moral specifics of discipleship.

Application of Biblical Material

Finally, key methodological choices of method are made about application: How are these biblical materials, so interpreted, applied? What type of ethics is preferred? Are reasons given for this option? We have mentioned that the dominant style of ethics in a work often guides both the selection and interpretive moves. The encyclical opts for a basically deontological ethics since it focuses on commandments as the primary vehicle for articulating the moral content of Christian discipleship. In this ethics of duty, rules and principles are foundational and considerations of the right take precedence over appeals to the good. *VS* gives two sets of examples of these moral boundaries, but nowhere offers an exhaustive list (cf. n. 80, 100). It upholds the magisterium's competence to teach unexceptional moral prohibitions rather than state all the norms as such.[32] There are teleological dimensions, to be sure, where the goodness of God and the role of virtues are noted (cf. 64), but they are subordinate to an ethics of duty. Actions are right because God requires them, not because they lead to good results for the agent or society.

Why does the encyclical employ a deontological approach? The controversies that evoked *VS* may be largely responsible, or deontology may articulate the best defense for the outer boundaries of morality. The revisionist moral theologians hold that the tradition which preceded the moral manuals was primarily teleological. Richard McCormick, S.J., for example, invokes Thomas Aquinas' dictum, "God is not offended by us except insofar as we act against our own good."[33] Proportionalists and consequentialists consider immutable, unexceptional moral norms to be epistemologically problematic and practically rigid. Most principles are prima facie duties

which may be overridden in favor of more important values when they conflict with the values which the principle aims to enshrine.

More significantly, however, the revisionists seek moral insight in the
opposite direction from that of *VS*. They find the primary locus of moral
meaning in particular problems, relations and circumstances, and marshall
more general resources to render the particular features of the case morally
intelligible. They are not situationists since they do not intuit the "loving
thing to do" directly from the facts. They weigh consequences, intentions,
circumstances and more general matters in tandem with the situation. Like
their casuist forebears, these revisionists conceive the good to be what is
possible and beneficial to the actual persons involved. They seek a truth
which is appropriate and practical rather than one which is warranted by
universality and immutability.[34]

By contrast, the a priori method of *VS* moves in the opposite direction.
It finds intelligibility primarily in general and universal characteristics,
metaphysically fixed in the "objective truth." Accordingly, conscience does
not discover appropriate means to good ends or discern the right action
through virtuous insight. Conscience is an intellectual judgment about truth:
"The dignity of this rational forum and the authority of its voice and judgments derive from the *truth* about moral good and evil. . . . This truth is
indicated by the 'divine law,' *the universal and objective norm of morality*."
Nevertheless, teleological elements remain in the ethics of *VS*, since the
practical reason is attracted by law's relation to the supreme good (n. 60).

Virtuous dispositions play a subordinate role, specifically the dispositions mentioned in the beatitudes, which present a portrait of the qualities of
Jesus. These attitudes and dispositions "are above all *promises*, from which
also indirectly flow *normative indications* for the moral life" (n. 16). Virtues
are useful primarily because they lead to normative principles. The encyclical does not consider how Scripture's stories, parables, events and the like
shape the character of Christians by displaying a distinctive set of attitudes
and values. *VS* reads the Gospels through a deontological lens which misses
much of their moral import. Virtues underwrite an ethics of agency in which
what the person becomes is at least as important as what one does.

VS limits its attention to those virtues that support an ethics of rules
and principles. Prudence is exercised only on the positive commands of the
natural law. Because they are open-ended and may have to be adjusted to
other relevant duties, we need prudence to apply them creatively. The virtue
of obedience, however, displaces prudence in applying negative moral precepts because norms "prohibiting certain concrete actions or kinds of behavior as intrinsically evil do not allow for any legitimate exception" (n. 67, cf.
52-53).

One may have to use a deontological approach in order to defend universal, unexceptional norms. Arguably, it offers a better defense of moral
boundaries than teleological methods, especially utilitarianism, which over-

rides any moral principle if doing so leads to the greatest good for the greatest number. *VS*, however, fails to acknowledge that deontology has its own limitations. Life within the moral boundaries calls for a more flexible approach which takes intentions and circumstances seriously, without making them the sole measure of what is right and good. Conscience does not only apply universal principles to cases. It operates differently depending upon what region of moral experience it is exercised on. In human rights, conscience may be a judgment of truth that has deductive import for action; in social policy, conscience will weigh competing goods; in deciding one's vocation in life, it will make a virtuous discernment of what is fitting.[35]

Scripture and tradition witness to the need for greater moral flexibility than *VS* seems to allow. They do not always apply the commandments as deontological absolutes. The final text of Exodus, for example, appends the Holiness Codes to the Decalogue. These casuistical refinements exclude certain types of persons from the commandments' protection and excuse certain acts because of the circumstances and intentions involved (See Ex 21 to 23). The New Testament authors adapted the absolute prohibition of Jesus on divorce (Lk 16:18) to fit new Gentile contexts. Mt 19:9 adds "except for *porneia*" to the prohibition and I Cor 7 permits a Christian convert to divorce a pagan spouse under certain conditions.[36] Traditional moral theology focused on issues like telling the truth, just business practices and other cases where no absolute rule applied and where trade-offs of values and disvalues were inevitable.

Unfortunately, the encyclical truncates the life of Christ to make it morally normative in a deontological way. Like previous expressions of the faith ethics, *VS* fails to show how the life of Jesus is morally normative because it narrows the moral life to obedience to universal moral norms. It reduces the moral import of the life of Jesus to commandments and to a death of heroic fidelity to the will of God: "Christ's witness is the source, model and means for the witness of his disciples, who are called to walk on the same road:'If any man would come after me, let him deny himself, and take up his cross daily and follow me' (Lk 9:23)" (n. 89). A deontology that applies universal, necessary prohibitions to practice is poorly equipped to show how the rest of the story of Jesus can be morally instructive.[37]

What forms of moral reflection can appreciate the full normative significance of Jesus Christ? When the new commandment of Jesus states that the standard of Christian love should be "as I have loved you" (Jn 13:34), it points to a richer meaning of normative than can be found in the deontology of *VS*. Reading Scripture through the lens of virtue ethics or as narrative theology or as an appeal to the moral imagination opens up the moral potential of the text. These approaches show how the Bible can offer moral illumination and not only moral prescriptions. Recent Church documents urge us to interpret economic and social conditions "in the light of the Gospel." Scripture does not tell us what to do about nuclear conflict, for example, but it does "provide us with urgent direction when we look at today's concrete realities."[38]

Parables and other biblical forms show the illuminative power of Scripture. Parables upset our moral presuppositions, paradoxical sayings invite the imagination to new insight, healing encounters with Jesus display forms of behavior and shape dispositions for appropriate response. The entire story of Israel and Jesus shapes the disciples' way of life through remembered paradigms, creative imagination, rituals, and dispositions responsive to God's mercy, justice and love. In order to apply the biblical witness to practice, Christians must engage in analogical reflection above all. They have to heed the constant rejoinder of Jesus' parables and exemplary actions, "Go and do likewise." Moving by analogy, they should ask how present moral challenges invite a response patterned upon, but not slavishly copying, the attitude and action of Jesus in similar situations.

The encyclical promises a Christonomous ethics of discipleship but it cannot deliver because it reduces morality to a matter of rules and principles. The ethics of discipleship gets quickly transformed into a theonomous naturalism which enshrines the natural law realism of the recent tradition. However, natural law reflection is not the medium of application, at least for the individual. Instead the magisterium of the Church mediates between the disciple and the message of Jesus. The transition occurs at the end of the meditation on the dialogue of Mt 19, where it is noted that people of every era ask the question of the rich young man, "Teacher, what must I do to have eternal life?" Christ alone can give the full answer, and how is he present to each era? *"Christ's relevance for people of all times is shown forth in his body, which is the Church."* Immediately the document shifts to the hierarchy as the ongoing moral voice of Christ: "The task of interpreting those prescriptions was entrusted by Jesus to the Apostles and their successors. . . . 'He who hears you hears me'" (Lk 10:16) (n. 25).

In the end, therefore, the Christonomous ethics becomes not a theonomous but a "hieronomous" ethics of the Church's magisterium. The hierarchy of the Church, specifically the Roman magisterium, determines the application of biblical commandments. Theologians have a supporting role to play in helping the magisterium research questions, assist in relevant formulation of the immutable principles, and refrain from dissent about current teaching. The People of God are to be learners and faithful witnesses, but they are given no role in the formulation or confirmation of magisterial teaching. No mention is made of the work of the Holy Spirit through the other charisms of the Body of Christ. In the final analysis, therefore, *Veritatis Splendor* makes the Bible serve as the charter document for the official magisterium, not for the Christian faithful.

Notes

1. Pope John Paul II, *Veritatis Splendor* (Vatican City: Libreria Editrice Vaticana, 1993). References to paragraph numbers cited in text. The encyclical is also available in *Origins*.

2. John Mahoney, S.J., *The Making of Moral Theology;* also, John A. Gallagher, *Time Past, Time Present.*

3. See Vincent MacNamara, *Faith and Ethics: Recent Roman Catholicism* (Washington, D.C.: Georgetown University Press, 1985), pp. 14-36. See also John R. Donahue, S.J., "The Challenge of the Biblical Renewal to Moral Theology," in William J. O'Brien, ed., *Riding Time Like a River* (Washington, D.C.: Georgetown University Press, 1993), pp. 59-80.

4. Ibid., pp. 33-35. See Gerard Gilleman, *The Primacy of Charity in Moral Theology* (London: Burns and Oates, 1959); Bernard Häring, *The Law of Christ: Moral Theology for Priests and Laity,* 4 vols. (Westminster, Md.: Newman Press, 1964).

5. Second Vatican Council, *Decree on the Training of Priests,* no. 16, in Walter Abbot, ed. *Documents of Vatican II* (New York: Association Press, 1966), p. 452.

6. Josef Fuchs, S.J., *Natural Law: A Theological Investigation* (New York: Sheed & Ward, 1965).

7. See Bruno Schuller, "The Debate on the Specific Character of Christian Ethics: Some Remarks;" Charles E. Curran and Richard A. McCormick, S.J., *Readings in Moral Theology No. 2: The Distinctiveness of Christian Ethics* (New York: Paulist, 1980), pp. 207-233.

8. Josef Ratzinger, "Magisterium of the Church, Faith, Morality," in Curran and McCormick, ibid., pp. 174-189; also Hans Urs von Balthasar, "Nine Theses in Christian Ethics," ibid., pp. 190-206.

9. For a good example of how these sources function in practice, see Lisa Sowle Cahill, *Between the Sexes: Foundations for a Christian Ethics of Sexuality* (Philadelphia: Fortress and New York: Paulist, 1985).

10. Cf. James M. Gustafson, *Protestant and Roman Catholic Ethics: Prospects for Rapprochement* (Chicago: University of Chicago Press, 1975).

11. See David Bartlett, *The Shape of Biblical Authority* (Philadelphia: Fortress Press, 1983) for a discussion of the distinctive contributions to moral reflection made by the major literary genre of the canon.

12. Compare Elisabeth Schüssler Fiorenza's *In Memory of Her: A Feminist Theological Reconstruction of Christian Origins* (New York: Crossroad, 1983) and *Bread Not Stone: The Challenge of Feminist Biblical Interpretation,* which bracket the Hebrew Scriptures with the work of Phyllis Trible in *God and the Rhetoric of Sexuality* (Philadelphia: Fortress, 1978) and *Texts of Terror: Literary-Feminist Readings of Biblical Narratives* (Philadelphia: Fortress, 1984). Recently, Schüssler Fiorenza has modified her position on using Hebrew Scripture material in a critical feminist hermeneutic. See her "Biblical Interpretation and Critical Comment," *Studia Theologica* 43 (1989), pp. 5-18.

13. See David H. Kelsey, *The Use of Scripture in Recent Theology* (Philadelphia: Fortress, 1975).

14. John T. Noonan, "Development in Moral Doctrine," *Theological Studies* 54/4 (1993), pp. 662-67.

15. John Paul II, *Dives in Misericordia: On the Mercy of God* (Boston: St. Paul Edition, 1980), p. 18.

16. See John R. Donahue, S.J., *The Gospel in Parable: Metaphor, Narrative and Theology in the Synoptic Gospels* (Philadelphia: Fortress, 1988), pp. 4-27.

17. See John P. Meier, *Matthew,* New Testament Message 3 (Wilmington, Del.: Michael Glazier, Inc., 1980) pp. 211-226. Daniel J. Harrington, S.J. *The Gospel of Matthew,* Sacra Pagina Series 1 (Collegeville, Minn.: The Liturgical Press, 1991) pp. 272-281.

18. John Mahoney points out the limits of the legal analogy. Moral theology has expressed the whole of morality "almost entirely in the language of law as enacted, promulgated and sanctioned by God as the supreme legislator. And yet such language is purely analogical, ascribing to God the words and ideas of human everyday experience raised to the highest power of which they are capable." Mahoney, *The Making of Moral Theology*, p. 248.

In treating God as lawmaker in a univocal manner, the tradition has fallen into serious difficulty: "This is the ultimate literalism and legalism of moral theology and it is, in that respect at least, profoundly untheological." Ibid., p. 252.

19. See Second Vatican Council, *Constitution on Divine Revelation* and Pontifical Biblical Commission, *The Interpretation of the Bible in the Church* in *Origins* 23/29 (January 6, 1994) pp. 497- 524.

20. Accordingly, in Aquinas's *Summa Theologiae,* the Treatise on Law (I-IIae qq. 90-97) comes before the Treatise on Grace (I-IIae, qq. 109-114).

21. In the transcendental anthropology of Karl Rahner, which has so shaped Catholic theology of the past 40 years, nature is permeated with grace, at least as God's offer of self-communication. Nature does not have independent status, but is a "remainder concept," the result of a mental subtraction of grace from the totality of human experience. Nature is the condition for the possibility of the Incarnation, created in Christ and for Christ. As such, graced nature mediates not only God's intentions in creation but to God's redemptive purposes as well.

22. "It is Jesus himself who comes between the disciples and the law, not the law which comes between Jesus and the disciples. They find their way to the law through the cross of Christ." Dietrich Bonhoeffer, *The Cost of Discipleship* (New York: Macmillan, 1963), p. 139.

23. See John P. Meier, *The Vision of Matthew: Christ, Church and Morality in the First Gospel* (New York: Paulist, 1978) and Marcus J. Borg, *Jesus: A New Vision: Spirit, Culture, and the Life of Discipleship* (San Francisco: HarperCollins, 1987).

24. See Mahoney, *The Making of Moral Theology*, p. 174.

25. Jon Sobrino, *Spirituality of Liberation: Toward Political Holiness* (Maryknoll, N.Y.: Orbis Books, 1989), p. 65; see also Sobrino, *The True Church and the Poor*

(Maryknoll: Orbis Books, 1989), pp. 103, 177-185. Also, Sobrino, *Jesus the Liberator: A Historical-Theological View* (Maryknoll: Orbis, 1993), pp. 264- 271.

26. See Stephen Pope, "Proper and Improper Impartiality and the Preferential Option for the Poor," *Theological Studies* 54/2 (1993), pp. 242-271.

27. Cf. Aristotle, *Nicomachean Ethics,* Book Six; Thomas Aquinas, *De Veritate.*

28. This sentence is taken from Second Vatican Council, document *Gaudium et Spes,* 29.

29. See Anthony Battaglia, *Toward a Reformulation of Natural Law* (New York: Seabury Press, 1981); Richard J. Gula, S.S., *Reason Informed by Faith: Foundations of Catholic Morality* (New York: Paulist, 1989), pp. 231-249; Edward A. Molloy, "Natural Law Theory and Catholic Morality," *American Ecclesiastical Review* 169 (1975), pp. 456-469.

30. Karl Barth, *Church Dogmatics II/2: The Doctrine of God* (Edinburgh: T.& T. Clark, 1957), pp. 532-544, 631-661.

31. "Martyrdom, accepted as an affirmation of the inviolability of the moral order, bears splendid witness both to the holiness of God's law and to the inviolability of the personal dignity of man, created in God's image and likeness" VS (n. 92).

32. Many commentators have accepted the argument in principle but found it difficult to understand why artificial contraception would be considered as intrinsically evil acts in the same class as genocide and slavery.

33. Thomas Aquinas, *Summa Contra Gentiles* 3, 122. Cited in Richard A. McCormick, S.J., *The Critical Calling: Reflections on Moral Dilemmas Since Vatican II* (Washington, D.C., Georgetown University Press, 1989), p. 186.

34. For a brilliant exposition of the history and continuing relevance of casuistry, see Albert R. Jonsen and Stephen R. Toulmin, *The Abuse of Casuistry* (Berkeley: University of California Press, 1988). They would dispute the limited role of casuistry in the face of law that is stated in VS 76. "It was a basic tenet of [casuists] that all laws admitted of exceptions, except those explicitly identified as primary precepts of the natural law." Ibid., p. 186.

35. On the ethics of the fitting in comparison to that of the right or the good, see H. Richard Niebuhr, *The Responsible Self: An Essay in Christian Moral Philosophy* (New York: Harper & Row, 1963).

36. See John R. Donahue, S.J., "Divorce: New Testament Perspectives," *The Month* 14 (1981), pp. 113-20; also Joseph Fitzmyer, S.J., "The Matthean Divorce Texts and Some New Palestinian Evidence," *Theological Studies* 37 (1976), pp. 197-226.

37. See William C. Spohn, S.J., "Parable and Narrative in Christian Ethics," *Theological Studies* 51/1 (1990), pp. 110-114.

38. National Conference of Catholic Bishops, *The Challenge of Peace: God's Promise and Our Response* (Washington, D.C.: United States Catholic Conference, 1983) par. 55. See also N.C.C.B., *Economic Justice for All: Catholic Social Teaching and the U.S. Economy,* Origins 16/24 (1986), p. 410, 415; Paul VI, *Octogesimo Adveniens,* 4.

8

Will the Church of the Twenty-First Century Be a Holy and Discerning People?

Mary Frohlich

John Paul II wrote *Veritatis Splendor* because, in his view, humanity is in the midst of a moral and spiritual crisis. Violence, amorality, dehumanization, and alienation seem to be spiralling upward. He believes that Christ, speaking through the Church, has the message which will enable humanity to find its way through the crisis to the fullness of life and joy. For this to take place, however, people must correctly discern both the nature of the crisis and the nature of the various solutions offered. Without this discernment, even devout Christians will be unable to avoid being swept along by the growing wave of dehumanizing attitudes and practices.

The term "discernment" appears frequently in *Veritatis Splendor*. John Paul presents the content of the document as the fruit of his own discernment, and calls his brother bishops to engage in ongoing discernment of contemporary theologies and movements. Properly speaking, discernment is "recognition of the presence or action of God." While the term is sometimes used derivatively to mean "decision-making" or "moral reasoning," its core meaning is rooted in the spiritual experience of knowing God. The goal of this paper is to examine and critique the encyclical's model of discernment from the point of view of spiritual theology.

Although the subject of the encyclical is moral theology, in Part I John Paul quite explicitly makes spiritual life and theology the ground of Christian morality. People are moral because they are first holy (radically open to God) and discerning (able to recognize God). A central question in regard to *Veritatis Splendor* is whether it will, in fact, foster the practical appropriation of this fundamental theology of the moral life by the Christian people of the 21st century, or whether it may actually hinder the achievement of that end.

Part One of the paper explores the spirituality of discernment that is advocated by the document, with special focus on its ecclesiological context. While finding much to appreciate, this analysis also notes some disturbing trends in the Pope's use of classical themes in the spirituality of discernment. Part Two seeks the theological roots of these trends in a critical analysis of the theological anthropology of the encyclical.

1.
The Context of Discernment in *Veritatis Splendor*

A. Basic Spirituality: Discipleship, Humility, and Obedience

The initial spirituality of discernment which John Paul presents in Part I of his encyclical has many strengths. It is, above all, a spirituality of discipleship—of being attracted by the person of Jesus and of opening oneself completely to a life of following him (n. 8). Disciples come to know the truth of themselves and of God in the act of opening themselves to God's revelation, which reaches its fullness in Christ. Discernment, then, is humble reception of revelation: "What man is and what he must do becomes clear as soon as God reveals himself . . . Acknowledging the Lord as God is the very core, the heart of the law, from which the particular precepts flow and toward which they are ordered" (n. 10-11).

In keeping with contemporary trends (both philosophical and popular), John Paul strives for a holistic and relational vision of the human person. Human identity is that of "a spiritual and bodily being in relationship with God, with his neighbor and with the material world" (n. 13). A right relationship with God is the core from which right relationship with neighbor and world flows. Consequently, there can be no dissociation between one's spiritual life and one's relations with other persons as they are expressed in bodily actions; the human person is in every instance to be treated as an integral being, "a soul which expresses itself in a body and a body informed by an immortal spirit" (n. 91; cf. 26 also). The implication for discernment is that any tendency to split off or to downplay the significance of the concrete dimensions of one's behavior is a signal of failure to attend fully to God in the situation.

Tender and generous love of neighbor radiates intrinsically from the personal and affective relation with Jesus that is at the heart of this spirituality. As Jesus gave himself completely for others, so will the fully mature disciple (n. 17-20). True human freedom and fulfillment are not found in having one's own way, but in giving oneself over in service on behalf of communion—even unto martyrdom (n. 85-87). Yet neither the knowledge of exactly how one ought to give oneself so radically, nor the capacity to carry out the deed, is available to the disciple apart from grace (n. 22-23). The disciple in search of holiness and discernment must emulate the humble, supplicating attitude of the tax collector who knows his absolute need of God's help, rather than the self-sufficient attitude of the Pharisee who imagines not only that he knows what to do but also that he has the capability to do it (n. 104; cf. Luke 18:9-14).

The essential elements of this spirituality, as outlined thus far, are quite thoroughly in harmony with the mainstream tradition of Christian spiritual discernment—so much so that it would require a book-length text to discuss all the references that could reinforce its central themes. Some elements that are well represented in the tradition include affirmation of how one must above all begin discernment with acknowledgment, at the core of one's being, of the priority of God and God's ways over one's own ways; how becoming a discerning person is best enhanced by a permeating discipline of forming one's imagination, values, and behavior through attentiveness to the gospel; and how the fruits of evident love of neighbor and of a transparent integrity between one's spiritual affirmations and one's concrete behavior are the key *post facto* confirming signs of genuine discernment.

A theme that permeates the classical literature on discernment, and that is also implicitly foundational for *Veritatis Splendor*, is that of humility. Cassian, summarizing numerous references in the earlier desert and monastic literature, said that "True discernment is obtained only when one is really humble. The first evidence of this humility is when everything done or thought of is submitted to the scrutiny of our elders."[1] A thousand years later Catherine of Siena wrote, "Humility is the governess and wet nurse of the charity into which this branch of discernment is grafted. . . . So only when discernment is rooted in humility is it virtuous, producing lifegiving fruit and willingly yielding what is due to everyone."[2] Literally dozens of other examples of this traditional conviction that discernment is closely linked with humility could be cited.

Many today are suspicious of talk about humility because it has sometimes been associated with self-denigration and blind obedience to authority. Indeed, the classical texts cited (and many others) are not wholly exempt from these attitudes. In the Jewish and earliest Christian traditions, however, the primary referent of humility was not submissiveness, but the joy and freedom which the humiliated discover in knowing God's solidarity with them.[3] A key biblical text for this spirituality of humility is Luke 1:46-48, "My soul proclaims the greatness of the Lord; my spirit rejoices in God my savior. For God has looked upon his handmaid's lowliness;[4] behold, from now on will all ages call me blessed."

In this perspective, the classical emphasis on the close relation between humility and discernment points to the powerless and the humiliated as those who are the most likely recipients of God's gift of discernment. This is very different, however, from the normative context of discernment as presented in *Veritatis Splendor*. To explore this difference, we will next examine the ecclesiology of the encyclical.

B. Ecclesiology: A Hierarchy of Discerners

John Paul frames *Veritatis Splendor* with a very clear-cut ecclesiologi-cal statement. The document is addressed to "Venerable brothers in the episcopate," and at several key points John Paul reminds the bishops that it is firstly his, and secondarily their, responsibility to discern the movements and ideologies that are current in the world. He quotes *Dei Verbum* 10, which said that "the task of authentically interpreting the word of God . . . has been entrusted only to those charged with the church's living magis-terium, whose authority is exercised in the name of Jesus Christ . . . the magisterium, in fidelity to Jesus Christ and in continuity with the church's tradition, senses more urgently the duty to offer its own discernment and teaching . . ." (n. 27).

Discernment, then, is presented as primarily a hierarchical function. While the necessity of the assistance of the Spirit is acknowledged (n. 25; 108), John Paul's theological position seems to be that this gift can be pre-sumed to be given in a unique way to those who are designated as "succes-sors of the apostles" (n. 25). This is not a wholly novel position; it has explicit roots at least as far back as Ambrosiaster, who wrote during the reign of Pope Damasus (366-384). Ambrosiaster interpreted 1 Corinthians 12, the standard scriptural locus for discussion of the charism of discern-ment of spirits, as specifically referring to clergy. He added, "A man put in a rank of ecclesiastical office has a grace, of whatever sort it is, that is not his own but belongs to his rank through the efficacy of the Holy Spirit."[5]

Association of the capacity for discernment with hierarchical office, however, is not as well represented in the early tradition as is association of this gift with spiritual depth. In the desert tradition, for example, the one gifted with the ability to discern spirits was normally the *abba* or *amma*. These men and women of intensive ascetic discipline were revered as having the ability to give their disciples a "word" that could instantaneously both assess and liberate the supplicant's spiritual condition.

As the rigorous life of the desert ascetics was tamed and institutional-ized within monasticism, so was this tradition of extraordinary discernment. The Greek *diakrisis pneumaton* (discernment of spirits) carried connotations of the struggle of the spiritually zealous to distinguish between actual good and evil spirits. Its place was taken in the Latin tradition by the much tamer *discretio* (discretion), which was often depicted as the virtue of finding the mediating position between two extremes.[6]

In a parallel development, the reverence evoked by the charismed *abba* or *amma* was channeled into the obedience owed to the abbot or abbess. By the time of Benedict's *Rule*, it is the religious superior to whom explicit words about discretion are addressed. The abbot is to "use discretion and tenderness as he sees it expedient for the different characters of his brothers . . . he is to examine his commands to see whether they are in accordance with God's will or arise from worldly motives. . . . Discretion is the mother of virtues."[7]

It is easy to see how a literal reading of the highly influential *Rule* could contribute to the tendency to associate *discretio* (discretion or discernment) with hierarchical position. This interpretation, however, is somewhat shortsighted. Benedict's *Rule* is permeated by an urgent appeal to every disciple to listen attentively for the immediacy of God's word, to learn the art of recognizing "the felt presence of Christ," and to choose freely and personally to respond to the Spirit.[8] Benedict's model of discernment certainly involves hierarchical elements, but it also calls each disciple to be personally "holy and discerning."

As even this brief survey indicates, an inevitable tension exists between two ecclesiological models of discernment. One emphasizes the charisms of the "pilgrim people" whom any structure exists to serve; the other emphasizes the authoritative structure within which the people are to find security.[9] We see this tension held in an exquisite balance in Benedict's *Rule*. In *Veritatis Splendor*, however, the balance seems to have shifted strongly toward emphasis on authoritative structure. Even when the document briefly mentions that the Spirit offers all Christians a share in Christ's *munus propheticum* (gift of office of prophecy), it does so only as a prelude to an extended treatment of the subordination of this gift to the teaching of the magisterium (n. 109-117). In this encyclical, then, the Christian people are neither presumed nor encouraged to exercise discernment as an intrinsic dimension of their own personal spiritual journey; rather, the assumption is that the bishops alone are capable of adequate discernment.

This ecclesiology implies, of course, that anyone who disobeys or dissents from magisterial teaching has failed to discern truth correctly. It is interesting to contrast this position with that found in the writings of Jean Gerson, a theologian and university chancellor of the late 14th and early 15th centuries. Between 1401 and 1423, Gerson wrote three treatises on discernment. B.J. Caiger finds in these a progression toward greater emphasis on the hierarchy as chief discerner, and speculates that the ecclesial chaos of the era and the personal trials undergone by Gerson led him to emphasize discipline over truth because he learned that "Truth is not well served by indiscipline."[10]

Yet even in the final treatise, Gerson acknowledged the possibility that a "nonentity"—a person without hierarchical status, but nonetheless gifted by the Spirit—could conceivably be called to discern and teach truth to the Council, Pope, bishops, theologians, and/or the learned. In Gerson's schema, a person lower in this hierarchy might well be censured or even martyred for attempting to teach truth to those above. This does not invalidate the rights of the hierarchy as legally authoritative discerners, but it does relativize the claim that they have a corner on truth.

Gerson's position, born in the fires of personal and public adversity, seems almost tragic in the classical sense of the term: each Christian is called upon to discern and proclaim truth personally, with humble acceptance of the possibility that the official, hierarchical discerners may discern otherwise and martyr him or her as a result. John Paul's stance is far less nuanced. His view is that Christ directly handed over his own teaching office to the apostles; through them it is handed over to the hierarchical magisterium; today, therefore, discipleship means obedience to the magisterium. John Paul's vision, unlike that of Gerson, has little place for the possibility that a Christian without status in the Church's hierarchy might have a God-given insight into truth that would require him or her to take a stand different from that of the magisterium. For him, any dissent from the teachings of the magisterium is evidence of a lack of holiness and discernment.

The lack of nuance in this position makes it problematic—theologically as well as pastorally. The next section of the paper probes more deeply into the theological anthropology of *Veritatis Splendor*, seeking the roots of its weakness.

2.
Analysis of the Theology of Discernment in *Veritatis Splendor*

A. Anthropology: The Image of God and Natural Law

In anthropology as in spirituality, *Veritatis Splendor* begins well. The theological anthropology of the document is rooted in the biblical notion of humanity as created in the image and likeness of God. Since God is supremely free, the human person created in the image of God also is gifted with freedom. The most profound actualization of this divine image is freely chosen action in accord with God's will. It is by coming to know the divine image imprinted on one's deepest being that one can discern which actions are in accord with God's plan. Such morally good action, in turn, "strengthens, develops and consolidates . . . [one's] likeness to God" (n. 39).

Thus far, John Paul's theological anthropology of discernment is very much in line with classical traditions of spiritual theology. Teresa of Avila, for example, develops in great detail the theme of the soul as image and dwelling place of God. She teaches that to know God and God's will, one must first strive to know oneself; eventually God will "enter the center of the soul without going through any door" in an experience that one is incapable of doubting. Such experiences of God's presence in one's deepest being are the foundation of discernment.[11]

For John Paul, however, the main bridge between the divine image imprinted on our beings and our knowledge of what to do is "natural law" as known by reason. He makes repeated references to the teaching of

Thomas Aquinas on this topic: for example, that the natural law "is nothing other than the light of understanding infused in us by God, whereby we understand what must be done and what must be avoided" (n. 12; cf. 19); and that "the light of natural reason whereby we discern good from evil, which is the function of the natural law, is nothing else but an imprint on us of the divine light" (n. 42; cf. 76). The natural law is universal because it is "inscribed in the rational nature of the person," and thus "makes itself felt to all beings endowed with reason and living in history." Only by following this universal law which all have in common can human beings "build up the true communion of persons and, by God's grace, practice charity" (n. 51).

In quoting Thomas Aquinas, John Paul implicitly invokes a common interpretation which regards the virtue of prudence as the heart of Aquinas' teaching on moral discernment.[12] In John Paul's use of this model, the normative act of discernment seems to be prudently rational deliberation. To act according to true and universal reason is to act according to the "imprint of the divine light" within us, and hence according to God's law. At one point he explicitly states that the proper function of conscience is "to apply the universal knowledge of the good in a specific situation and thus to express a judgment about the right conduct to be chosen here and now" (n. 32).

John Paul makes this statement in the context of decrying contemporary tendencies to subjectivism in moral judgment, which he sees as flowing directly from a loss of the "sense of the transcendent." In this part of his exposition, he appears to presume that one who denies the clear-cut availability and applicability of universal truths through reason is, in the same act, declaring independence from God and God's law; such a person cannot possibly be "discerning." This is not, however, an adequate interpretation of the position of Aquinas.[13]

In Aquinas's view, no formulatable law—natural, divine, or human— is sufficient to answer the question of what one ought to do in the particularity of an individual situation. Rather, the Spirit imparts to Christians a connatural wisdom which enables them to recognize the implications of divine wisdom in the here and now. Since the same Spirit is at work in the exterior law as in the interior wisdom, the two are not divergent.[14] Nevertheless, "The guidance which Christians receive from the Spirit enables them to give precision and relevance to the written law within the insight which the Spirit gives into the total situation, and to discern within the total situation the invitation which is being offered here and now to this individual [child] of God."[15]

John Paul's emphasis on universal reason and natural law is out of harmony not only with Aquinas, but also with the best of classical treatments of discernment. Ignatius of Loyola, for example, gives three "times" in which discernment can take place. The first "time" is when conviction of

God's presence and movement is immediate and indubitable. The second "time" is when many experiences of consolation and desolation—of God's apparent presence and absence—follow one another in confusing succession, so that one must gradually sort out what is of God and what is illusory. The third "time" is when one has no particular sense of God moving in one's experience; then—and only then—is it appropriate to attempt to make a decision by reliance on discursive reason alone. Even in this case, however, Ignatius counsels that one ought to try to bring the decision back within the purview of the experience of God and the movements of the heart (the first and second "times")—because they, and not rational deliberation, are the truly normative times for spiritual discernment.[16]

Indeed, other statements in *Veritatis Splendor* itself come closer to this view. John Paul writes, for example, that

> It is the "heart" converted to the Lord and to the love of what is good which is really the source of true judgments of conscience. Indeed, in order to "prove what is the will of God, what is good and acceptable and perfect" (Rom 12:2), knowledge of God's law in general is certainly necessary, but it is not sufficient; what is essential is a sort of "connaturality" between man and the true good (n. 64).

John Paul does not seem to be concerned about the inconsistency between this and his other statements that so strongly emphasize the role of universal reason. Here is the clue to the fundamental weakness in his position. Lacking clarity in regard to basic distinctions among different meanings of the term "reason," he ends by endorsing a seriously attenuated concept of reason that is actually destructive of true discernment. To take the analysis a step further, we will next briefly review some of the history of the Western philosophical understanding of "reason."

B. Deepening the Analysis

In the philosophical and theological tradition from which John Paul attempts to draw, the foundational term for the human capacity to seek and know truth is the Greek *nous*. In the classic Greek philosophers, *nous* is the core dimension of the human being, and its nature is to seek an intuitive knowledge of the divine. As *nous*, the human person is constituted by a dynamic tension between divine and worldly reality. *Nous* is manifested above all in the restless wonder, questioning, and seeking that structure all human activities. This "questioning unrest" is itself evidence that the human person is grounded in the divine, for the human person "is moved to his search of the ground by the divine ground of which he is in search."[17] As the ground of all human experience, *nous* manifests a rationality—that is, a divinely-grounded order—that is infinitely more profound than that of mere discursive "reason."

Nous is to be clearly distinguished from *psyche*, which is the dimension in which concrete perceptions, thoughts, and affections occur. It is also to be clearly distinguished from the structure of concrete discursive thought, which can be named by the term *logos*. As Eric Voegelin summarized with great clarity, at the very beginning of the Greek philosophical tradition "Parmenides had given the name *nous* to man's faculty of ascending to the vision of being, and the name *logos* to the faculty of analyzing the content of the vision."[18]

Both Bernard Lonergan and Karl Rahner have written on this distinction as it is related to discernment. Following Voegelin, Lonergan says of the *nous* or grounding dimension of human consciousness that it is a "luminosity of existence with the truth of reason" that underlies and precedes any articulated insights we may have about where God is calling us. There is, he says,

> . . . an inner light that runs before the formulation of doctrines and that survives even despite opposing doctrines. To follow that inner light is life, even though to worldly eyes it is to die. To reject that inner light is to die, even though the world envies one's attainments and achievements."[19]

This, he continues, is the kind of knowledge to which ascetical and mystical writers refer when they speak of the "discernment of spirits" and strive to formulate rules for distinguishing between the call of the divine and other movements that occupy one's attention.[20]

Rahner does not use the language of *nous*, but speaks of how in the Ignatian tradition discernment depends (at least implicitly, if not always explicitly) on the *consolación sine causa* (consolation without preceding cause). The latter is characterized by an "utter receptivity to God, the inexpressible, nonconceptual experience of the love of God who is raised transcendent above all that is individual, all that can be mentioned and distinguished, of God as God."[21] This nonconceptual experience does not offer a distinct and particular "answer" to an issue under discernment. Rather, one discerns by repeatedly comparing the feelings and direction aroused by the concrete matter being discerned with those associated with the "consolation without preceding cause." The question is whether the object under scrutiny "leaves intact that pure openness to God . . . or weakens and obscures it."[22]

In setting forth a theology of discernment, then, both Lonergan and Rahner are very careful to maintain the distinction between the ground of consciousness (within which God can be "known" nonconceptually) and the content of consciousness (within which knowledge of God is always secondary and imperfect). In classical Greek philosophy, this is the distinction between the knowledge characteristic of *nous* and that of *logos*; in Thomas Aquinas, it is the distinction between knowledge of divine wisdom that is imparted interiorly by the Spirit and knowledge of exterior laws which can be formulated. Serious problems arise when these two are confused—that is, when the underlying luminous, dynamic ground is confused with the concrete structure or contents of thought. When this occurs, "reason" as intuitive participation in the divine is mongrelized into mere systematic thought, and "discernment" becomes nothing more than the spelling out of the system.

In the modern period, this is often spoken about in terms of the misuse of "ideology." An ideology is a formulated worldview—that is, an expression operating on the level of *logos*. Ideologies are not inherently evil; indeed, they are necessary tools in the construction and maintenance of human societies. The problem is that ideologies have an inherent tendency to move toward dogmatism. It seems as if the very act of articulating a worldview with conviction carries the temptation to impose that worldview as "the only one." But, as Adolfo Nicolas puts it, "When we accept an ideology as normative, Christian discernment becomes impossible."[23]

When any ideology is proclaimed as "the only truth," Nicolas continues, . . . there is always a subtle "sacrificing" of human understanding, of true knowledge. The concern for truth and depth becomes secondary to the success of the created movement. There is such a need to keep the ideological program consistent, unified and solidly based that the freedom and agility to think creatively is diminished and eventually lost."[24] In Voegelin's terms, in this process of absolutizing a particular stance, the essential nature of the human person as existing in the *tension* between the divine and the human (never permitted to opt wholly for either one) is lost.[25] As Voegelin sums up, "Once the divine *nous* has been submitted to human construction, God is dead indeed. What has come to life instead is the imperial appeal of the System to the *libido dominandi*."[26]

It appears that the Pope, in his struggle to combat this very error, has gotten himself entangled in its tentacles. His effort to appeal to the classical tradition of the presence of the divine in the human being as manifested in the capacity for "reason" begins well, but disintegrates when it becomes evident that what he means by reason, more often than not, is a particular approach to propositional thought. He is inclined to rely on a truncated concept of discursive reason as the locus of discernment, rather than recognizing that discursive thought is one important, but not necessarily decisive, moment in a dynamic movement that continually cycles among ordinary experience, spiritual experience, reflection, judgment, decision and action—a movement driven by a "rationality" of a far deeper order than that which can be mastered by discursive thought.

Rather than demonstrating how an unwavering intention of openness to God can blossom in a life that always aims for the highest and best while humbly acknowledging that inevitably "its mediations are innumerable, successive, always vulnerable, defectible, and fragile,"[27] John Paul spends his energy in defending a particular mediation—that is, the current ecclesial structure. The ecclesiology of the encyclical makes it unmistakably clear that the social location of this approach is that of an elite hierarchy which aims to strictly control both the deployment and the results of "discernment." Sadly, the encyclical evidences no consciousness whatsoever that it has fallen into the trap of absolutizing an ideology.

Conclusion

In its basic spirituality of discipleship and in its core anthropology of the "divine in the human," John Paul's theology of discernment is quite well-grounded. Its weaknesses are its overemphasis on a hierarchical ecclesiology and its confused use of the "image of God" anthropology, particularly in regard to the nature of "reason." These weaknesses are linked. This link could be traced in the history of theology, especially that of the last two centuries culminating in the type of theology Karol Wojtyla studied during his seminary years in the late 1940s.

In the present situation, however, the immediate link appears to be Pope John Paul's preoccupation with maintaining top-down ecclesial control. The idea that God might move in the lives of Christian individuals and communities apart from their obedience to the hierarchical magisterium seems to be profoundly disturbing to him. If discernment is to be maintained as normatively a task of the hierarchy, it must be the case that the magisterium, in applying universal reason, "does not bring to the Christian conscience truths which are extraneous to it; rather it brings to light the truths which it ought already to possess . . ." (n. 64). Discernment, in this model, is not really a matter of listening to God *per se*; it is enough to listen to God's law mediated through reason and magisterium.

At the end of his three articles on discernment in Thomas Aquinas, John Mahoney sums up: "What constitutes the particular dignity of the individual [children] of God is that each is a unique center of the personally adapted activity of the Holy Spirit."[28] This sense of the potential presence of the gift and art of discernment in the life of each Christian, regardless of hierarchical position, is sadly depleted in John Paul's theology of discernment. Especially disturbing is the loss of contact with the earliest Christian understandings of humility, which suggest that the best discerners may well be those in the lowliest and most humiliating circumstances. When 21st-century Christians look for guidance in the journey to becoming a holy and discerning people, this document will not suffice.

Notes

1. Conference Two, #10, in *John Cassian: Conferences,* trans. Colm Luibheid (New York: Paulist, 1985), p. 67.

2. "The Dialogue," #9, in *Catherine of Siena: The Dialogue,* trans. Suzanne Noffke (New York: Paulist, 1980), p. 40.

3. Klaus Wengst, *Humility: Solidarity of the Humiliated,* (Philadelphia: Fortress, 1988).

4. Wengst, p. 42, points out that the Greek *tapeinosis* can also be translated "humiliation."

5. Ambrosiaster, *In epistulas sancti Pauli* at 1 Cor 12:4 (CSEL 81/2, 133); translation and discussion in Joseph T. Lienhard, "On 'Discernment of Spirits' in the Early Church," *Theological Studies* 41 (1980), pp. 510-11.

6. See Lienhard. See also Augusta Raabe, "Discernment of Spirits in the Prologue to the Rule of Benedict," *American Benedictine Review* 23 (1972), p. 400, where she writes that in the fifth century the word "discretion" came to be used not only to translate *diakrisis,* discernment, but also for *metron,* measure. "This was due to the enrichment of the term in a new sense drawn from the Old Testament motif of the Royal Way, and meaning the ability to discern the right place to be on the royal road to God, that is, neither to the right nor to the left, but measured or moderated as being 'right on.' Based upon a Christian allegorization of Numbers 21:22, this meaning of 'discretion' originated as an image for discernment."

7. "Rule of Benedict," #64, in *Western Asceticism,* ed. Owen Chadwick (Philadelphia: Westminster, 1968), p. 332. In one other reference (#70), monks placed in charge of youngsters are warned that they will be punished if they treat them *sine discretione.*

8. See Raabe, especially p. 406.

9. B.J. Caiger, "Doctrine and Discipline in the Church of Jean Gerson," *Journal of Ecclesiastical History* 41 (1990): 389-407.

10. Caiger, p. 406.

11. See, for example, Teresa of Avila, *The Interior Castle* V:1,11.

12. For discussion of this point, see John J. Mahoney, "'The Church of the Holy Spirit' in Aquinas," *Heythrop Journal* 15 (1974), especially p. 35.

13. See the series of three articles by John J. Mahoney in *Heythrop Journal* 13, 14, and 15 (1972-74).

14. For numerous references to these points in the works of Aquinas, see John J. Mahoney, "The Spirit and Moral Discernment in Aquinas," *Heythrop Journal* 13 (1972): 282-97.

15. Mahoney (1972), p. 296.

16. Ignatius of Loyola, *The Spiritual Exercises,* #175-178.

17. Eric Voegelin, "Reason: the Classic Experience," in *Anamnesis,* trans. and ed. Gerhart Niemeyer (Columbia, MO: University of Missouri, 1978), pp. 95-96.

18. Voegelin, p. 94.

19. Lonergan, *A Third Collection: Papers by Bernard J.F. Lonergan, S.J.,* ed. by Frederick E. Crowe (New York: Paulist Press, 1985) p. 190.

20. Ibid., p. 195.

21. Karl Rahner, "The Logic of Concrete Individual Knowledge in Ignatius Loyola," in *The Dynamic Element in the Church* (New York: Herder and Herder, 1964), p. 135.

22. Rahner, p. 158.

23. Adolfo Nicolas, "Apostolic Discernment and Ideologies," *East Asian Pastoral Review* 20 (1983), p. 93.

24. Nicolas, p. 85. On ideology, see also J. B. Libanio, *Spiritual Discernment and Politics: Guidelines for Religious Communities* (Maryknoll, NY: Orbis, 1982).

25. See Voegelin, p. 104.

26. Voegelin, p. 110.

27. Libanio, p. 42.

28. Mahoney, *Heythrop Journal* 15 (1974), p. 36.

9

Veritatis Splendor:
Papal Authority and the Sovereignty
of Reason

Ronald R. Burke

Introduction

The modern question of authority remains today the greatest problem facing the Roman Catholic church.[1] In this encyclical, *Veritatis Splendor*,[2] Pope John Paul II pledges to bring greater "human dignity" and "true freedom" to the world by reemphasizing objective and universal moral standards that are at the foundation of human existence. This purpose is noble and the text is often beautiful and inspiring. For some reason, however, the Pope's proposal for dignity and freedom around the world also demands diminished "dignity" and "freedom" for Roman Catholics, their bishops and their moral theologians. The Pope requires greater obedience and submission to his moral teachings, especially in regard to sexuality. This combination of grand humanitarian purpose, a *call for greater papal authority,* and a fixation on sexuality make this encyclical the epitome of John Paul's papacy.

The Pope calls quite eloquently for the people of God to live a higher morality.[3] The call is impressively biblical. It begins with a homily on the dialogue between Jesus and the rich young man (Mt. 19:16-21). It proposes that humans[4] are destined for union with God (n. 12).[5] Living and growing toward this destiny is the enactment of "true freedom" and "true morality." It is this destiny, with its morality, which gives "the full meaning of (human) life" (n. 7). Christ is the teacher and example of this morality of self-giving love (n. 2, 19-21). Anything inconsistent with the teachings of Christ or with the dignity and eternal destiny of humanity is immoral.[6]

Many scholars have postulated "real purposes" and "subtexts" in the encyclical, both in its final form and its earlier drafts. Some commentators claim that the Pope responds in the encyclical to widespread Roman Catholic disregard for the papal condemnation of artificial contraception, and that it is this sexual restriction that the Pope is especially anxious to reassert.[7] Others say it is a reprimand against moral theologians for the methods they have used to find fault with such restrictions. European commentators have found it to be an effort to reclaim greater papal authority and to correct

119

"faulty directions" that the church has followed since the Second Vatican Council (1962-65).[8] Some Protestants have said the encyclical is good if it is intended to encourage discussion, but they read the text as meant to stop it.[9]

All of these claims have degrees of truth and accuracy. They share the perception that the Pope finds himself weakened in his ability to influence the moral behavior of people of today. He finds his *authority* in competition with contemporary cultures and their various forms of "reason." The encyclical can best be seen, then, as the Pope sees it himself: as a struggle between the "authority of the papacy" and what the Pope calls the modern "sovereignty of reason" (n. 36).[10]

1.
Three Themes

In general, the encyclical is a condemnation of modern morality. The published version is a *"reaffirmation of the universality and immutability of the moral commandments,* particularly those that prohibit always and without exception *intrinsically evil acts"* (n. 115) Three claims related to this reaffirmation tie together the encyclical's three chapters: (1) modern society is in very bad shape; (2) the church has the responsibility to do everything it can to help improve the condition of modern society; and (3) there is special need for Catholic moral theologians and bishops to help the church to aid society. As we review these themes, we will examine what is actually taught in the encyclical and offer some critical comments. We will then analyze two flaws in the encyclical and three misdirections in its response to problems in the world and in the church.

(1) Problems in Society Today

Modern, contemporary society is in bad shape. Such an assertion is somewhat surprising when it comes from the man who helped to dismantle the threat of atheistic Communism and the very existence of the Soviet Union. One might think the world had improved. But the modern sickness envisioned by the Pope is larger than Communism. It infects democracies as well as tyrannies, the Catholic church as well as secular society. It must be confronted, he says, on a very fundamental level.

The basic problem is a growing secularism. At least since the time of the Enlightenment, more people have begun to "think and live 'as if God did not exist' " (n. 88). There is a new philosophy of "immanentism," one that denies the existence of God and any eternal, transcendent "Truth" or afterlife (n. 99). The result has been the development of a new "subjectivism, utilitarianism, and relativism." That is, there has been a kind of revolution in morality and a new freedom and independence. People think they can decide for themselves what is right and what is wrong.[11] The whole notion of an objective, eternal, natural, moral law is in shambles. This (tragic) development is claimed to have intellectual justification. It is given "full cultural and social legitimacy" (n. 106).

With the disappearance of moral absolutes, there remains only *self-interest*, the self-interest of individuals, classes, and nations, as the force to decide law and morality. "Each person tends to make full use of the means at his disposal to impose his own interests or his own opinion, with no regard for the rights of others" (n. 99). Gone are the universal, negative commandments that protected human rights and dignity (e.g., commandments against killing and stealing, the implications of which gave broad protection to all human life and dignity).

The absence of moral absolutes leads to power struggles, anarchy, disorder, totalitarianism, and disrespect for human rights. Crucial is the disrespect for human rights. This is the source of modern totalitarianism. "The root of modern totalitarianism is to be found in the denial of the transcendent dignity of the human person" (n. 99). No longer seen as "the visible image of the invisible God," the rights of human persons, as individuals or as a minority, can be violated: by the power of other individuals, the class, the group, or the State.[12]

Examples of this modern totalitarianism, with its disregard for human rights, can be seen in Nazism and in Marxism, both of which Karol Wojtyla experienced firsthand.[13] But disregard for moral absolutes and for human dignity is also present in the alliance between democracies and ethical relativism (n. 101). When people are *totally independent*, making their own laws without regard for eternal laws, they take advantage of others. This is the whole history of humanity's sin. The Pope says that he has learned from history and personal experience that the correction of this problem will require a long and difficult journey (n. 98).[14]

The Pope makes more precise the problem of today in regard to Roman Catholics. It is not just among atheists and pagans that moral absolutes have been dismembered. There has also occurred a kind of "dechristianization." (n. 88, 106) "*Within the Christian community itself* . . . (there is) an overall and systematic calling into question of traditional moral doctrine. . . ." (n. 4). Even among Roman Catholics there has been "a decline or obscuring of the moral sense" (n. 106).

The heart of the problem is one of authority. The problem is not just that Catholics call moral doctrines into question. Some Roman Catholics give to the Magisterium, the center of the teaching authority of the church, only "advisory authority," no decisive control:

> certain of the Church's moral teachings are found simply unacceptable; and the Magisterium itself is considered capable of intervening only in order to "exhort consciences" and to "propose values," in the light of which each individual will independently make his or her decisions and life choices" (n. 4).

Moral authority has shifted away from hierarchies and rulers, and toward laity and individuals.

Such emphasis on individual conscience may sound compatible with what was taught at Vatican II. The Council's Declaration on Religious Freedom (*Dignitatis Humanae*), for instance, in articulating the right of free choice in choosing one's religion, demands that people "enjoy the use of their own responsible judgment and freedom, and decide on their actions on grounds of duty and conscience, without external pressure or coercion" (n. 31).

The Pope respects this "journey of conscience" as "one of the positive achievements of modern culture" (n. 31). He is unhappy, however, that this "freedom" has been exalted into an ultimate. It has been distorted into personal independence, a blank check for self-gratification, with no regard for human destiny, immutable morality, or papal authority.

(2) The Church Must Help Society

The Pope proposes that the key problem in today's low morality and disregard for human dignity is the loss of moral absolutes. These are the same as the eternal law of God. The church must speak these absolutes now more boldly than before (n. 87-88). The people of the church must live them with heroism and with beauty, offer a "new evangelization" to the world, and convince it of the reality of God, his Law and Truth (n. 106-9).[15]

The task of the church is not just to "rethink" moral questions, as was encouraged by Vatican II (n. 36). This past effort did exemplify some of the "best tradition of Catholic thought" (n. 36). What followed the Council, however, included "some trends of theological thinking and certain philosophical affirmations (that) are incompatible with revealed truth," (n. 29). "positions incompatible with Catholic teaching" (n. 36). What is needed is a "new evangelization," with the reassertion of moral absolutes.

The Pope recognizes that this reassertion of absolutes may sound like "intolerable intransigence." People might prefer that the church be more compromising, that it allow more freedom and sound "more like a loving mother" (n. 95). But the church has an irrevocable responsibility to teach "the Truth." Hence the Pope must teach what he sees to be the truth. As a motto, he sees the church as necessarily "stern toward sin, and rich in mercy for sinners" (n. 95).

Independence from moral absolutes is equivalent to immorality and sin. It is people desiring self-determination and complete independence in the question of what is good and what is evil (n. 102). The sinfulness of such independence is as old as the story of eating from the forbidden tree of the knowledge of good and evil (Gen 2:16-17), of people proudly determining their own law (n. 35). The church must give strong reaffirmation not only to the reality of God but also to the universality and immutability of his eternal, natural law.[16]

The success of the church's effort to help society see and accept again God's eternal law does not rest only with the Magisterium, and its *proclamation* of God's word. It rests just as much with the People of God and how well they *live* the word that the Magisterium proclaims (n. 107). The Pope's call is for all believers to exemplify a new holiness, following Christ's example (n. 19-21). This is an example and teaching of self-giving love (n. 14-15, 20, 107).

It is noted, however, that simply following the commandments is not enough. We gain an insight into the Pope's goals in the encyclical from his call: not just for self-giving love, but for *humility*. The Pope takes as an example the parable of the scribe and the pharisee (Lk 18:9-14). What is needed today is the scribe's humility and repentance, not the self-satisfaction and independence of the pharisee (n. 104). The Pope concludes this theme with a short prayer of St. Ambrose of Milan on man's proper and complete humility[17] (n. 105).

(Critique) This could be a most appropriate example. The parable and the prayer emphasize *humility before God.* These connect with the story of the rich young man. He was one who had followed the law and wanted something more, something "which would *transcend a legalistic interpretation of the commandments*" (n. 6). What Christ offered the man, the Pope accurately relates, was a call to "maturity in self-giving" (n. 17).

Does the Pope himself follow the example of Christ in this? Is "maturity in self-giving" what he offers the people of the church? If he requests maturity and humility before God, he deserves praise. He deviates from this theme, however. His words do not require of Catholics a struggle of humble conscience before God and an effort to grow in moral maturity. They require, rather, an *immaturity of submission* and a *humility before the hierarchy and Magisterium.*

> An opinion is frequently heard . . . that in the sphere of morality a pluralism of opinions and of kinds of behavior could be tolerated, these being left to the judgment of individual subjective conscience or to the diversity of social and cultural contexts (n. 4).

This is not what the Pope wants. He requires unquestioning obedience. In deviating from his own examples, and calling for immaturity and humility before the Pope, rather than maturity and humility before God, he also requires criticism.

(3) Help from Moral Theologians and Bishops

In struggling against the immorality of modern society, the Pope makes a *call for special help to Catholic moral theologians.* Unfortunately, the requested *help* sounds more like a demeaning chastisement than an empowering exhortation. John Paul II sees Catholic moral theologians as themselves having played a part in the "dechristianization" of society. They have gone too far in the direction of secularization, for they have used "the sovereignty of reason" to question moral absolutes and look for exceptions to the eternal law (n. 36). In the future, they must follow more strictly the teachings of the Magisterium, the "authority of the papacy."

An explanation of the Pope's restrictive attitude toward moral theologians can be found in his view of authority in the church. His is an "exclusivist" and "hierarchical" rather than "inclusivist" and "communal" view of the Magisterium. He proposes that the task of interpreting the Old and New Covenant "was entrusted by Jesus to the Apostles and to their successors, with the special assistance of the Spirit of truth" (n. 25). He takes "successors" to mean, exclusively and hierarchically, the *bishops* of the church and, especially, the bishop of Rome.

Quoting a phrase from *Dei Verbum* (Vatican II's Dogmatic Constitution on Divine Revelation), he writes:

> The task of authentically interpreting the word of God, whether in its written form or in that of Tradition, has been entrusted only to those charged with the church's living Magisterium, whose authority is exercised in the name of Jesus Christ (n. 27).

Who is it, then, who is "charged with the church's living Magisterium"? The Pope takes it to mean bishops. With a phrase that might be read as an anachronism, he refers to "Bishops (as the ones) to whom Jesus Christ primarily entrusted the ministry of teaching" (n. 29).

The Pope, then, begins his "reminder" to moral theologians by excluding them from the Magisterium. Their job is (only) "to . . . give . . . examples of loyal assent, both internal and external, to the Magisterium's teachings in the areas of both dogma and morality." They are to "develop a deeper understanding of the reasons underlying its (the Magisterium's) teachings and . . . expound the validity and obligatory nature of the precepts it proposes" (n. 110). The Pope risks an oxymoron as he asserts that the teachings he "proposes" are "obligatory." But the tone suggests that his (or the Magisterium's) "proposal" has an imperial authority.

The Pope is involved here in serious business. He wants to leave no room for doubt regarding the authority of the Magisterium or the subservient role of moral theologians. There is no constructive contribution, no place for questioning, no place for dissent.

This restriction on moral theologians is not traditional. They here have lost their responsibility for critical and constructive contributions to Catholic morality. Their role is, apparently, reduced to "loyal assent."

The reason for the Pope's restrictive words is suggested by the source from which they are developed. The source is the encyclical of Paul VI, *Humanae Vitae*, which is famous for continuing the church's ban on artificial contraception (n. 110). This ban has been questioned by many Catholic theologians, restricted in its practical importance by many pastors, and ignored by many Roman Catholics.[18] It is as if the Pope's restrictive words to moral theologians were intended to exact some retribution for their role in the disregard often paid the ban on contraception.

Moral theologians must not think that popular dissent permits professional opposition to Magisterial teachings. Popular opinion can be sinful as well as erroneous. Sometimes "believers . . . erroneously consider as morally correct a kind of behavior [such as artificial contraception] declared by their Pastors [read: Pope] as contrary to the law of God" (n. 112). This gives no right of dissent to moral theologians. There is simply no place for dissent in the church.[19]

After completing this restrictive instruction to moral theologians, the Pope concludes with an *instruction for bishops*. They, too, have a special responsibility. They are the Magisterium, the church's "authentic teachers" (n. 113). They are endowed "with the authority of Christ." Answers to questions about morality have been "entrusted by Jesus Christ in a particular way to us, the Pastors of the Church" (n. 114).

What does this responsibility actually mean for bishops? It means they are to serve as watchdogs. The bishops must exercise special "pastoral vigilance" (n. 115). They must "be vigilant that the word of God is faithfully taught" and must take "appropriate measures to ensure that the faithful are guarded from every doctrine and theory contrary to it" (n. 116).[20] For example, bishops must take away the name of "Catholic" from institutions, agencies, schools, universities, or counseling services that exemplify "serious failure" in living up to that title (n. 116). In sum, they must guarantee that members of the church receive Catholic doctrine with "purity and integrity" (n. 113). The question is, who determines the "purity and integrity"?

The bishops have considerable responsibility. It is here, however, in primary part, a *subservient responsibility*, subservient to the Pope. He is, in this document, very much a *"primus inter pares,"* a *"first* among equals." He determines alone, and with his advisors, the "purity and integrity" of moral and theological teachings. As in the case of moral theologians, he has not *asked* the bishops but *told* them what must be done. He plans to leave both groups, bishops and moral theologians alike, very little choice in *how* the church will respond to the modern crises of morality and authority.

2.
Two Problems in the Encyclical

This is the epitome of John Paul II's encyclicals because of the importance of the problem which it faces. It confronts the fundamental modern question of authority in a post-revolutionary age. One of the modern "revolutions" assigned new authority to people themselves and to their use of "reason" in deciding their moral and judicial laws. This revolution brought to modern cultures a loss of moral absolutes.

The Pope's answer to the revolution in morality and authority has been to pit the authority of the papacy against the sovereignty of reason. Because of this answer, he has called especially for *obedience and humility* from members of the church. He has asked the laity to be like humble scribes, not self-satisfied pharisees. He has told moral theologians to give loyal assent and *never any exterior or interior dissent* to Magisterial teachings. From the bishops he has required *a vigilance against anything that seems less than "purely and integrally" Roman Catholic* in their dioceses.

There are good reasons for questioning how literally this document and the plan of the Pope are to be taken. The document can be seen as part of a tradition of hyperbole, of "Pope-Talk." Professionals know there is a kind of "code" involved, requiring a translation between what the Pope says in an encyclical and exactly what he means.[21]

Despite this ambiguity, however, there is a certain amount of clarity. Three points manifest in the encyclical are its delusion of aloneness, its obsession with sexuality, and three instances of a reactionary response.

(1) The Delusion of Aloneness

The tone of the encyclical makes the Pope sound as if he were very much alone. In many ways he is alone, and this is true of almost every world leader. He sounds, however, as if he thought most Catholics and moral theologians were opponents rather than allies in the struggle for an appropriate Christian morality. He is not really alone, although he has been perhaps most alienated by a mistaken stand regarding sexuality. The Pope's differences with Catholic moral theologians are significant, but not so severe as he reads them to be.

The Pope and Catholic moral theologians are in basic agreement. The Pope argues they disagree on his claim that there is a "species of action" that is "intrinsically evil" (*intrinsece malum*). Yet Catholic moral theologians *do* agree.[22] They say there are intrinsically evil actions. Their point of disagreement is that the "species" of intrinsically evil actions cannot helpfully be characterized in general terms.[23] Although the Pope is inconsistent on the point, he wants to claim that broad definitions will suffice. He tends to ignore the places in the encyclical where he agrees that qualifications and descriptions are required (n. 74-79).

Catholic moral theology *must* give an accurate description to (the species of) actions that are inherently evil. The Pope argues to the contrary that Catholics can give "*rational determination of the morality of human acting*" *without worrying* about "the intention for which the choice was made." If such generalization is *not allowed*, he says, the church *cannot affirm* an "objective moral order" (n. 82).

That papal reasoning is false. The Catholic tradition has already and regularly examined motives. That is why it distinguishes from sin and "intrinsic evil" such things as killing "in self-defense," lying on the basis of

"right-to-know," and stealing "for survival" (not to mention stockpiling nuclear weapons "to prevent war"). It is not irregular but traditional in the
church to give qualifications to acts based on motivation. It is essential to
an accurate description of the morality or immorality of an act. It has been
done in most "species" of actions, except for sexual acts like contraception.

The moral theologians are themselves being more "traditional" than
the Pope. They agree that some actions, adequately described, are inherently evil. They are requesting for sexual morality the same careful study
and discussion given to other moral issues in the Catholic tradition. Sinfulness in sexual behavior, like any other behavior, requires adequate specification or description. The Pope's absolutism on the issue, and his call for
silence, are inappropriate. In this sense he is somewhat alone.

(2) The Obsession with Sexuality

There are serious differences between particular positions the Pope has
taken and those of many Catholic moral theologians. The differences are
predominantly in the area of sexuality. As he suggests in the encyclical, the
disregard paid by many Roman Catholics to the ban on artificial contraception is a troubling reality. He interprets it as an instance of alienation from
and disrespect for the papacy and Catholic authority. Catholics do need to
reexamine the reasons for which they use artificial contraception. But the
Pope, too, needs to examine his sweeping disapproval of this practice. It
could be that the people are closer than the Pope to an accurate understanding of the implication of natural law for the morality of sexual behavior in marriage.[24] One fears that the Pope is so concerned about the immorality of much sexuality, and so concerned about Catholic opposition to his
concern, that he has become preoccupied with this issue.[25]

It would be good to explore carefully a number of questions regarding
sexual morality in the concerns of the church.[26] Passing by those contextual
questions for now, let us recall the Pope's central concern in the encyclical
regarding a "species" of action that is "intrinsically evil." Although generally described as violations of "human dignity" (n. 80), most outstanding on
the list of intrinsically evil acts is a great deal of sexuality. In fact, *the only
intrinsically evil acts* that the Pope discusses in this encyclical are *sexual
acts.*

One might summarize the Pope's view of intrinsically evil sexual acts
as: any intercourse that is not directly generative or procreative. This is an
exceedingly narrow and mistaken view of marital intercourse in the human
family. The Pope does not recognize that—whatever the case may be
among "barnyard animals"—sexual intercourse builds more than fetuses in
the human family. It functions naturally for much more than generativity
and procreation.[27] Of its "nature," "sexual intercourse serves the enduring,
committed relationship between partners; openness to life inheres *in the relationship* and not in individual sexual acts."[28] With a misplaced view of

the "nature" of human sexuality, the Pope mistakenly claims that sexual climax is not permissible if there is no "mechanical" possibility of conception.[29] This view of the propriety of human sexuality needs to be widened: not for the sake of *greater freedom* (which the Pope fears) but for greater accuracy regarding *the nature of human sexuality* (which the Pope would want to encourage).

The point the Pope purportedly wishes to make is that "it is never lawful, even for the gravest reasons, to do evil that good may come of it." What is his "example of choice" in regard to "intrinsically evil" acts? It is the sexual sin of contraception,[30] "contraceptive practices whereby the conjugal act is intentionally rendered infertile" (n. 80). He must readjust his understanding of the nature and purpose of human sexuality. It is not the individual actions, but the whole relationship that should be open to procreation.

Surely there are better examples of heinous crimes and intrinsically evil acts. With the feared spread of nuclear weapons, genocide on three continents, worldwide hunger, and homelessness in the world's wealthiest nation, why do condoms and the pill receive "pride of place"?[31] It seems like a very different mind-set, a different culture, a kind of obsession that assigns every instance of contraception such intrinsic evil.

None of this is to demean the importance of many moral questions regarding sexuality. The Pope is not alone on the questions, but on some of the answers. Again, almost all moral theologians are opposed to the "contraceptive mentality" which the Pope especially abhors. They are opposed to "ready abortions" that show little concern for human life. Similarly, they are opposed to adultery, to promiscuous sexuality, and to other sinful sexual behavior.

Where moral theologians differ with the Pope is in *the consideration* of difficult questions. They request further consideration of the legitimacy of artificial insemination, artificial contraception, some instances of masturbation (as when it is used not for autoeroticism but to provide semen for artificial insemination), the morality of homosexuality, and other matters related to sexuality.

The questions do not mean that absolutes have been abandoned. They are remembered, taken seriously, and examined so that they might be, as Thomas required, properly interpreted and applied.[32] These are not instance of unbelief. Sometimes difficult questions do not have easy answers. They require careful consideration, by moral theologians as well as by bishops. They require examination by a broad and faithful, communal Magisterium.

3.
Three Reactionary Responses

The most reactionary acts in the encyclical are its *prohibition of dissent,* its *call for episcopal vigilance,* and its *shrinking of the Magisterium.* The Pope makes it clear that moral theologians must not disagree with the teachings of the Magisterium. They are simply to give "external and internal assent," seeking to understand better why the Magisterium teaches as it does and then work to be sure that Catholics realize that what the Magisterium "proposes," Catholics "must accept."

(1) Prohibition of Dissent

The *opposition to dissent* may be in part a cultural difference. Karol Wojtyla does not come from a tradition of democracy, has no lengthy experience of "loyal opposition" in politics, and probably has little experience of benefits derived from the slow process of seeking consensus. From this background he seems himself to have developed a kind of "absolutist" position in which dissent is interpreted as revolution and unbelief.

To those who do live in the framework of the Enlightenment, as well as the Gospel, his position sounds scandalously dishonest and authoritarian. "How else, from the dawning of the human mind, has truth been ascertained, mistakes corrected, confusion clarified, *except* through properly conducted disagreement?"[33] Why prohibit Catholic moral theologians from expressing their professional opinions and the results of their theological investigations? To allow them only to parrot the teachings of the Magisterium, providing them with biblical and traditional justifications, makes them only sycophants and reduces this age of Catholic history to a single voice. This deeply violates the Catholic tradition.

An indication that his prohibition is an instance of "Pope Talk" or "overspeak" is found in the Pope's earlier position in the encyclical. There he recognized that at least "adequate formulations" for understanding "permanent moral norms" do "unfold down the centuries." The work of the Magisterium in this unfolding "is preceded and accompanied by the work of interpretation and formulation characteristic of the reason of the individual believers and of theological reflection" (n. 53). Here is a more constructive role for theology. The use of reason is admittedly required.

(2) Call for Episcopal Vigilance

The second call that is most extreme to someone familiar with the modern history of Catholicism is the call for *"vigilance" by Catholic bishops.* The word itself is reminiscent of the "vigilance committees" set up by Pope Pius

X to fight against "modern" ideas among Catholic scholars. Because of these committees, jobs were lost and lives were ruined. It was an instance of terrible brutality, terrible violations of the very dignity of human beings that the present Pope has pledged himself to defend. Surely this Pope of human dignity intends no such brutality. After all, even in the encyclical, he chose the motto of "stern against sin, merciful toward the sinner" (n. 95).[34] The modernist crisis was a time of painful transition in the history of the church. Surely such pain does not have to be repeated for its lessons to be learned, even as transition continues.

(3) Shrinking the Magisterium

Finally, as a last sad act of overreaction, the Pope *centralizes the Magisterium.* He condenses it to himself and his advisors. Toward the end of the encyclical, summarizing its exceptional steps in the Magisterium's encyclical regarding morality, he uses the pronoun "I" to name the author of this magisterial work.[35] Such an equation is consistent with a tone of absolutism or imperialism that characterizes especially the last chapter of the encyclical.[36] Tradition has been more inclusive. The Magisterium *informally* includes diverse teachers: parents, scholars, priests, nuns, mystics and theologians. All have contributed. The *formal* Magisterium includes all the bishops, "disagreeing when disagreement is necessary," contributing to the "frank and open acceptance of truth."[37]

The shrinking of the Magisterium to an individual pope is not an example of the "humility before God" that St. Ambrose encouraged. It is the reaction of a person who wants to be in as much control as possible. There is nothing especially virtuous and Christian about that. Where is his humble recollection of the words he put in italics at the start of the encyclical: *"Only God can answer the question about what is good, because he is the Good itself"*? (n. 9).

The Pope has said that every person has some sense of the Good and of God's law because each is ordered at creation:

> with wisdom and love to his final end, through the law which is inscribed in his heart (cf. Rom. 2:15), the "natural law," . . . the light of understanding infused in us by God, whereby we understand what must be done and what must be avoided (n. 12).

If this is infused in all, how reasonable is it to think the Pope *alone* is right, that the Magisterium must be condensed, and that moral theologians and bishops receive little voice?

Conclusion

The Pope refuses reminders of his own humanity and the possibility of human error in his personal interpretation of the law. It is disappointing to find this absolutism to replace the more collegial and communal view that became predominant at Vatican II. The Pope's imperial tone is more divisive, with its authoritarian call to obedience, humility, loyal assent, and vigilance.[38] Taken quite literally, it glorifies the rote proclamation of the Magisterium's law and shows no skill in conveying authoritative teachings to educated and critically reflective Catholics who require information, persuasion, and a sense of intelligent conviction in those who teach. Attention to this encyclical by Catholic laity would worsen the crisis of authority rather than resolve it.

The document contains but does not resound with the broad and deep wisdom of the Roman Catholic tradition. It is a notable effort by a serious and brilliant churchman to solve the problems that deeply beset the world. Yet after a beautiful introduction to the morality and love of Christ, the text seems distracted by sexuality and by a lack of papal control over people's morality. The response is reactionary: demand popular submission; silence professional dissent; threaten official expulsion; and shrink the Magisterium to the papacy. The document is, in these parts, an angry scolding. In its reception by the wider church, when inconsistencies and extremes of one individual's "Pope-Talk" are translated and filtered out,[39] its inspiring greatness will show more strongly and it will make positive contribution to the longer and continuing tradition.

Notes

1. The revolutions of the 18th and 19th centuries raised radical questions in regard to authority. Fundamental changes regarding the rights of individuals, encouraged by such thinkers as John Locke, combined with economic changes to overthrow the rule of European kings. The repercussions shook the halls of the Roman Catholic church, which had held a close alliance with many such kings. These revolutions raised new questions of authority in politics, morality, and religion. The hierarchy of the Catholic church has struggled with the changes in the *Syllabus of Errors,* the so-called "Modernist Crisis" (1890-1910), and the two Vatican Councils (1870 and 1962-65).

2. In the Apostolic Letter, *Spiritus Domini,* of August 1, 1987, the Pope announced his decision to write an encyclical with the aim of treating "more fully and more deeply the issues regarding the very foundations of moral theology." See *AAS* 79 (1987), 1374. Six years in the making, *Veritatis Splendor* was published October 5, 1993. It is 40,000 words and 179 pages in length, with 184 footnotes. For the names and positions of five probable contributors to the encyclical, see Peter Hebblethwaite, "Leaked Encyclical," in *National Catholic Reporter* 29, 36 (13 August 1993), 20.

3. References to the encyclical will be put in parentheses in the text and will be taken from *The Splendor of Truth (Veritatis Splendor),* Vatican Translation (Washington, D.C.: United States Catholic Conference, 1993). The references will be to paragraph numbers as they appear in this official translation.

4. The Pope and his aids in writing this encyclical did *not* use a gender-neutral vocabulary. As Lisa Sowell Cahill says, "It reeks with patriarchal language," much more than his "apostolic exhortation" of 1981, *Familiaris consortio.* See *The Tablet* 74, 8001 (11 December 1993), pp. 1618-9.

5. In his commentary upon the gospel story of Jesus and the rich young man (Mt. 19:16-21), the Pope explains the goal of human life. It is the "Kingdom of Heaven" that is promised in the New Covenant. "This same reality of the Kingdom is referred to in the expression 'eternal life,' which is a participation in the very life of God. It is attained in its perfection only after death, but in faith it is even now a light of truth, a source of meaning for life, an inchoate share in the full following of Christ." Earlier, in the anthropology he developed while a professor at Catholic University, Lublin, Poland he emphasized "eternal life" as "man's" intended destiny. Lasting happiness comes only from approaching this destiny of union with God.

6. For other examples of this theme in the recent writings of the Pope, see his speech at Vilnius University, 5 September 1993, and his speech at World Youth Day in Denver, CO, August 14, 1993. These are recounted by Peter Hebblethwaite, *National Catholic Reporter,* 29, 42 (1 October 1993), p. 9. For the history of the theme in the Pope's writings, see the article by Avery Dulles, "The Prophetic Humanism of John Paul II," *America,* 169, p. 12 (23 October 1993), pp. 6-11.

7. See the insightful criticism by Gregory Baum, "A Letter from the Pope," in *Canadian Forum* 72, 825 (December, 1993), pp. 21-24.

8. See the references to words from Hans Küng and Massimo Aprile in an anonymous article in the *National Catholic Reporter* 29, 44 (15 October 1993), p. 15.

9. See *Christian Century* (October 20, 1993), 1007-8, and Dawn Gibeau, *National Catholic Reporter* 30, 1 (22 November 1993), p. 12.

10. Another name for this "sovereignty of reason" might be "conscience." John Henry Newman called it "the first of all vicars of Christ." John Paul II himself has a high regard for conscience, saying it should be followed "even in the case of error due to invincible ignorance." The possibility of error becomes the Pope's theme. He demands "properly formed conscience." This means a conscience educated in "the biblical Revelation of the moral law, authoritatively interpreted . . . by the Magisterium of the Church." In other words, other consciences have to be dependent upon his! That is not the modern understanding of conscience. See *L'Osservatore Romano* (English version) 26, 45 (1318: 10 November 1993), p. 2.

11. The Pope recognizes that humanity has a "sharing in God's dominion," but it is impermissible that "reason itself *creates values and moral norms*" (n. 38, 40).

12. John Finnis properly praises the encyclical's world concern. I sometimes wonder, however, if he read the concluding two chapters. *The Tablet* 747, 8002 (8 January 1994), pp. 9-10.

13. From Poland, Maciej Zieba offers a significantly "non-Western" perspective on the encyclical. In 1991, John Paul II issued the encyclical *Centissimus Annus,* praising free market economies and relating them to Christian virtues. The encyclical received nodding approval in the West. In Eastern Europe, suffering through a changeover to capitalism, it was largely ignored. *Veritatis Splendor,* however, received more applause in Eastern Europe because it celebrates the transcendent,

counter-cultural "Truth" which gave the people strength under Communism. It emphasizes that truth gives sense and meaning to human freedom. *The Tablet* 247, 7998 (20 November 1993), pp. 1510-2.

14. Clarence Thompson, a scholar of Enneagrams, finds the encyclical to reflect the personality type of the "Perfectionist" (Type One), a person who lacked sufficient early nurture and seeks compensation by angrily and continuously demanding "rightness." Motivated toward "punitive scolding," such a person is discomforted by sensuality. These traits are shown in the Pope's 1981 book, *Love and Responsibility,* in which he sanitizes correct love and shakes a finger at every possible kind of evil. Other people have picked up on the Pope's preoccupation with evils in sexuality, including England's Nicholas Lash [*The Tablet* 247, 7997 (13 November 1993), pp. 1480-2] and Australia's Ronald Conway ("Papal Obsessions," in *World Press Review,* December 1993, p. 45).

15. While himself commenting on his newly-published encyclical, in an *ad limina* address, the Pope emphasized the Church's responsibility to aid society. Referring especially to documents from the Second Vatican Council, *Gaudium et Spes* and *Lumen Gentium,* he said that the Church fulfills this responsibility by helping people "to maintain the path of their authentic liberation" and by dispelling "the crippling confusion in relation to fundamental questions of good and evil, right and wrong." See *Origins, CNS Documentary Service* 23, 20 (28 October 1993), pp. 360-2.

16. Gregory Baum quite sharply disagrees that moral laws have to be immutable in the Catholic church. Change does not need to mean relativism. Change, in fact, can be found to recur in the Catholic tradition. One example is the church's long opposition to freedom of choice in regard to religious affiliation, especially in Catholic countries like Italy and Spain. At the Second Vatican Council, after long discussion, religious liberty was affirmed. Similar changes regarding moral laws have occurred in regard to ownership of slaves, charging interest on loans, the torture of prisoners, and the (hierarchical) relationship between men and women. Even in this encyclical, the Pope is making a change, giving formal affirmation to the words of revolution that were previously condemned, "liberty, equality, fraternity." See Gregory Baum, "A Letter from the Pope," in *Canadian Forum* 72, 825 (December, 1993), pp. 21-24.

17. "What then is man, if you do not visit him? Remember, Lord, that you have made me as one who is weak, that you formed me from dust. How can I stand if you do not constantly look upon me, to strengthen this clay, so that my strength may proceed from your face? *When you hide your face, all grows weak* (Ps 104:29): if you turn to look at me, woe is me! You have nothing to see in me but the stain of my crimes; there is no gain either in being abandoned or in being seen, because when we are seen, we offend you. Still, we can imagine that God does not reject those he sees, because he purifies those upon whom he gazes. Before him burns a fire capable of consuming our guilt (cf. Joel 2:32)."

18. According to a recent Princeton survey, 94% of Catholic women in the United States have used methods of birth control prohibited by the Catholic church. Only 25-30% of Catholic priests in the U.S. consider artificial contraception immoral. See Peter Hebblethwaite, *National Catholic Reporter* 27, 37 (27 September 1993), pp. 12-13.

19. "Dissent in orchestrated protests and polemics is opposed to ecclesial communion." (113) Opposition to the teaching of the church's pastors is *not to be seen* as a Gift of the Holy Spirit.

20. "Ever since Apostolic times the Church's Pastors [Bishops] have unambiguously condemned the *behavior* of those who fostered divisions by their teaching or their actions (italics added)." (27) One hopes that this particular Pope, a strong opponent of dissent as well as division, restricts his condemnation only to "behavior" and does not extend it also to individuals!

21. As Bernhard Häring points out, even though the Pope's call for total submission is absolute, it is not so extreme as earlier documents, by other pontiffs, in reaction to modern times. A friendly "translation" might claim the Pope is requesting serious consideration of the whole context of moral discussion. See *The Tablet* 247, 7994 (23 October 1993), pp. 1378-9.

22. The extremely knowledgeable and traditional Fr. Charles Curran, of Southern Methodist University, who lost his job at Catholic University because of questions he raised regarding sexual ethics, makes this point quite strongly. See *National Catholic Reporter* 29, 44 (15 October 1993), p. 15. Richard McCormick is a good example. He is known as a "proportionalist." That properly means he believes the morality of an act cannot be judged by the physical act alone. The Pope might feel very distant from this Catholic moral theologian. Yet Jesuit McCormick, who holds a chair in ethics at Notre Dame University, writes: "Some acts are objectively wrong (ex objecto), but we must know more than the material happening to say the act is morally wrong." *The Tablet* 247, 7995 (30 October 1993), pp. 1410-11.

23. Mary Tuck has quoted Thomas Aquinas to resolve the issue. Thomas says the ten commandments are absolutes, but adds that "what can alter are the criteria which decide in particular cases whether this or that *is* murder or adultery or theft." She finds this position to avoid relativism without ending debate. *The Tablet* 247, 8000 (4 December 1993), pp. 1583-5.

As Lisa Sowell Cahill also points out, it is not easy to agree on where the description of the "act" ends and that of the "circumstances" begins. Conditions and circumstances separate moral and immoral actions, as in intercourse and adultery. See *The Tablet* 247, 8001 (11 December 1993), pp. 1618-9.

24. In an exceptionally astute article, Dominican priest Herbert McCabe points out that since artificial contraception, homosexual acts, masturbation, and *in vitro* fertilization are not mentioned in the decalogue, we must use reason to rule regarding their morality. They belong to the "natural law." This should make us somewhat "chary" of defining them in terms of mortal sin. They are not so much part of absolute prohibitions as they are of more flexible guidelines toward moral maturity. *The Tablet* 247, 8002 (18 December 1993), pp. 1649-50.

25. For an outstanding and groundbreaking anthropological investigation, which includes culturally different Roman Catholic views on sexuality and authority, see the book by David Schultenover, *A View from Rome: On the Eve of the Modernist Crisis,* New York: Fordham University Press, 1993.

26. Unfortunately, space does not allow answers to the questions here. Why are differences of opinion in regard to sexual morality so great in the Roman Catholic church? Do the differences have anything to do with the focus put upon sexuality

by a tradition of celibacy? Is this one issue of most-private morality (sexuality) especially important in the modern age because this is also the age that has taken from the church its lands, its army, its political connections, its social preeminence, and much of its power, wealth, and *authority*? Are the differences between the Pope's view of sexuality and that of many moral theologians primarily religious or more cultural? Finally, is it important that sexual issues received much less attention in the Old and New Testaments than they do in papal documents of the 20th century?

27. I am indebted in shaping this point to an outstanding article by Robert P. Heaney, M.D. The Pope needs to reexamine the purpose of sex in human relationships. Heaney points out some of the telling biological evidence that intercourse among humans is "naturally intended" for more than simple procreation. It helps to reinforce the nuclear family, which is to raise the child and furthers the couple's openness to life. Similarly, the Pope's position does not recognize the biological evidence that human procreation requires much more than intercourse for the raising of human persons. See "Sex, Natural Law and Bread Crumbs," *America* (26 February 1994), pp. 12-16.

28. Ibid., p. 16.

29. Chapter 3 in the encyclical makes it difficult to disagree with the aged Bernhard Häring. He says (through his artificial voice-box) that the whole point is to demand "total assent and submission to all utterances of the Pope, and above all in one point: that the use of any artificial means for regulating birth is intrinsically evil and sinful, without exception." *The Tablet,* 247, 7994 (23 October 1993), pp. 1378-1379.

30. The best-known previous reference to "intrinsic evil" in papal documents was in 1930. Pius XI, in *Casti Connubi,* called artificial contraception an "intrinsic evil" (*intrinsece malum*). The designation was sent for reexamination to a study committee called by Paul VI in 1964. Ninety percent voted against the ban on artificial contraception and the designation. The phrase was changed in Paul VI's new encyclical, *Humanae Vitae,* to *"intrinsece inhonestum."* But the ban was continued. (Karol Wojtyla was a member of the commission, but attended none of its meetings.) The 1980 Synod on Christian Marriage suggested that not all those who dissent from official church teachings on contraception are necessarily "unfaithful" or "insincere." Some bishops pointed out that *"intrinsece inhonestum* meant something less than *"intrinsece malum."* The Pope made a critical reply in *Reconciliatio et Penitentia.* See Peter Hebblethwaite, in *National Catholic Reporter* 29, 43 (8 October 1993),pp. 8-9 and in *The Tablet* 247, 7992 (9 October 1993), pp. 1286-8.

31. Colman McCarthy, *National Catholic Reporter* 30, 2 (29 October 1993), p. 22.

32. See fn. 23, above.

33. Nicholas Lash, *The Tablet* 247, 7997 (13 November 1993), pp. 1480-2.

34. See p. 7, above.

35. "This is the first time, in fact, that *the Magisterium* of the Church has set forth in detail the fundamental elements of this teaching . . . I have briefly recalled the essential characteristics of freedom, as well as the fundamental values connected with the dignity of the person and the truth of his acts . . ." (n. 115) (italics added).

36. Pope John Paul II expressed a very different and more inclusive sense of the magisterium in his apostolic exhortation of 1981, *Familiaris Consortio*, 5. There he said the Holy Spirit gives the church "a corporate sense of the faithful" in which to discern "the meaning of God's word." He emphasized this was not just a "majority opinion," but was "a consensus achieved through the collaboration of various orders in the church." In this more collegial view, he emphasized the "maturity" mentioned above. The Church's task is "to educate the faithful in an ever more mature evangelical discernment." This is a far cry from the more recent demand for submission and no dissent. See *Familiaris Consortio, The Role of the Christian Family in the Modern World,* Vatican translation, (Boston: St. Paul Books & Media, 1992).

37. Nicholas Lash, *The Tablet* 27, 7997 (13 November 1993), pp. 1480-2.

38. See Dennis Doyle, "Comments on *Veritatis Splendor*," in *Commonweal* (20 October 1993), pp. 12-14.

39. As John Henry Newman pointed out, when a document comes from Rome, two things must happen: the people receive it and the theologians explicate it. See Lawrence Cunningham in "Comments on *Veritatis Splendor*," in *Commonweal* (20 October 1993), pp. 11-12.

10

The Role of the Connaturalized Heart in *Veritatis Splendor*

Andrew Tallon

> ". . . the just man justices;
> Keeps grace: that keeps all his goings graces;
> Acts in God's eye what in God's eye he is . . . ."
> —Gerard Manley Hopkins

Introduction

No important word appears more frequently in *Veritatis Splendor* (hereafter VS) than "heart." Is this the usual irrelevant and trivial use — or misuse — of the term, or does it suggest something worth noticing? Because of a central methodological concern essential to VS, the answer must be that no other term could substitute for heart. Furthermore, because of a particular passage in (n. 64), on the relation of Aquinas's teaching on judgment based on affective connaturality, the thesis of the nontrivial centrality of the concept of heart for VS's attempt to revitalize natural law ethics for today suggests very forcefully that the only correct way to interpret that teaching and apply it is through the concept of virtue, both natural virtues (as good moral habits) and supernatural virtues (as gifts of the Spirit transforming human nature — understood as having an obediential potency for such transformation — to a higher operative ability, vocation, and responsibility than ungraced nature).

This brief essay has a single, modest goal. I offer what is a reflection on VS based on the centrality of the idea of the converted heart to VS's program of reinstating its version of the natural law at the center of contemporary Catholic ethical teaching. I take VS's project to be not only the stated one (the reinstatement of natural law as a theoretical justification) but also the implied, partially proposed, and implicitly required one of suggesting a method for applying natural law to practice in daily life through a heart-based discernment of spirits. In addition to drawing on Lonergan for essential background on the structure of consciousness, I draw upon Karl Rahner — whose presence behind the scenes of VS is pervasive and palpable — for insights on the relation of heart and connaturality to the practice of discerning ethical good and evil, and chiefly upon Emmanuel Levinas, for insight into the theoretical underpinning for any philosophy that today can seriously claim to be an "ethical system (or nonsystem) based on a responsibility for one's neighbor rooted in one's already having been affected, in a past that Levinas calls before the prehistoric" by an infinite Otherness Christians call God, and in one's present and future ability, indeed vulnerability and destiny, to be affected by every finite human "other" I meet. The way I present Rahner and Levinas in relation to VS is to show how Rahner's use of affective connaturality relates to Levinas's dual affectivity in order to throw light upon and thereby make more understandable VS's emphasis on the converted, connaturalized heart as necessary condition for applying the general natural law to concrete particular cases.

My thesis is that we can, through a contemporary phenomenology of affectivity, based mostly on Levinas, at least comprehend the standpoint of VS; agreeing with its applications and conclusions is secondary to this first task of understanding it. Understanding VS's dependence on a natural law theory that moves from the general law to its particulars through the concept of the connaturalized heart is a significant step, if obvious and modest, one that is more likely to identify areas of agreement than of disagreement with VS. This essay thus tries to comprehend VS first and foremost by a valuation of its heart concept. Rather than engage VS in arguing for or against particular conclusions, as a philosopher I deal with the more fundamental question whether and how VS succeeds in its attempt to reinstate natural law. I offer an analysis — one of several possible, but one prompted by VS's own language of the connaturalized heart — that shows VS is on firm phenomenological and metaphysical ground with natural law. To show the limits of my analysis I also distinguish between a natural law established philosophically and the theological additions to it from scripture and tradition. VS does not emphasize the difference between the philosophical and theological content of natural law. VS is addressed to bishops, not to those who might think that calling the law "natural" might seem to exclude the "supernatural" additions coming from God, grace, the Spirit, or anything else added by religion. The result of my approach to natural law in VS is, in fact, to show the compatibility and in itself "natural" continuity between a philosophical natural law and those supernatural theological additions, because once we recognize that the actual operation of the natural law is in practice through the discernment of good and evil felt in affective connaturality, we can then go on to recognize that at bottom that affective connaturality is itself (in this context) but the work of acquired moral habits, the good habits we call virtues; we can finally also recognize that since operationally grace is the infusing of the gifts of the Spirit, which are virtues, then the continuity, through virtue as internal meaning of connaturality, becomes evident.

1.
The Connaturalized Heart

To begin by establishing the validity of choosing the connaturalized heart as central to VS's ethical method, it would not be enough to cite the very numerous occurrences of the word "heart" and knit them together into a quilt of some sort. We must delve beneath the overused and usually unexamined meaning of heart in order to reach especially the meaning of the "new heart" (n. 12), which is a loving heart" (n. 15), because although once deformed by sin it is now transformed—this transformation is crucial to VS—by the gifts of the Spirit (n. 21): God's love has been poured into our hearts through the Holy Spirit which has been given to us" (Rom 5:5) (n. 22). Grace . . . heals, restores, and transforms the human heart . . ." (n. 23). It is therefore not enough to say with Paul that what the law requires is written on their hearts" (Rom 2:15) (n. 46), or with Augustine that . . . "every just law is transcribed and transferred to the heart . . ." unless we also add with Augustine that this is the heart . . . "of the one who works justice" (n. 51), because doing justice brings about an effect Augustine describes as truth being ". . . impressed upon it [the heart], just as the image from the ring passes over to the wax . . .". (Ibid.). This line of reasoning nears its conclusion when the heart of the person is identified (at least in this context) with "moral conscience" (n. 54) and called a voice that speaks to one's heart saying do this, shun that," because one . . . has in one's heart a law written by God" (Ibid.); to conscience is assigned the task of pronouncing moral ". . . judgment of either acquittal or of condemnation, according as human acts are in conformity or not with the law of God written on the heart" (n. 59). We are still nearer the conclusion when we recognize the relation between natural law and conscience: . . . whereas the natural law discloses the objective and universal demands of the moral good, conscience is the application of the law to a particular case. . . ." (Ibid.). And we finally reach the conclusion and decisive point of VS's method when we realize that the entire foregoing argument consists in a developmental concept of what is traditionally called "formation of conscience," or better, a "continuous conversion" (n. 64). This *metanoia* is a process, a continual progress in virtue, never perfect in this life.[2] As Newman says, "here below to live is to change. And to be perfect is to have changed often."[3]

Here we come to the central text for this essay on VS. I will quote the passage before showing how Lonergan, Rahner, and Levinas will contribute to our understanding of VS's claims for a valid theory and practice based on a law found in human nature *qua* transformed by the gifts of the Spirit (i.e., the infused virtues connaturalizing the soul).

> It is the "heart" converted to the Lord and to the love of what is good
> which is really the source of *true* judgments of conscience. Indeed, in

order to prove what is the will of God, what is "good and acceptable and perfect" (Rom 12:2), knowledge of God's law in general is certainly necessary, but it is not sufficient: what is essential is a sort of connaturality' between human nature [man] and the true good.*[4] Such a connaturality is rooted in and develops through virtuous attitudes of the individual person: prudence and the other cardinal virtues, and even before these the theological virtues of faith, hope, and charity. This is the meaning of Jesus' saying: Whoever does what is true comes to the light" (Jn 3:21). (Italics in original.)

The essence of this essay is that VS proposes a particular philosophy of the continually converting heart underlying a theology of grace as effecting the conversion in those of good will, those who try "to do the truth" and thus "see the light," a process called being "connaturalized to the good," and which Aquinas said (in the text cited) happened in two domains, the ethical and the mystical. The "mechanism" or structure of this connaturalization is nothing other than habituation or habit formation, i.e., acquiring virtues (or vices). Put another way, we could call it "attuning our first nature to a new harmony, so that a second nature now mediates our otherwise natural spontaneity with a new, achieved spontaneity."[5] As Lonergan puts it:

> God, the angels, and humans are all proportionate to the true and the good, for all are rational beings. But in God this proportion is such that divine operations cannot be defective; in the angels it implies only that for the most part operations will not fail; while in us humans it gives a mere possibility with no guarantee of success, so that for the most part we do what is wrong. Nevertheless, *it gives us the virtues and in place of the statistical law governing humanity one will have an approximation to the statistical law governing the angels.* Endowed with the virtues one becomes a "perfected agent" (an *agens perfectum*) and, for the most part, one does what is right; thus a will adorned with the virtue of justice performs just deeds with the *spontaneity* and the regularity with which fire moves upwards."[6]

Thus the doctrine of affective connaturality turns out in practice to be another name for virtue. But that insight only raises more questions. Why does virtue function as a source of light for ethical consciousness, and how does connaturalized consciousness manage to perform the task of mediating between the natural law in our hearts and some particular concrete decision here and now before us? Let me suggest something from Levinas and something from Rahner to help us toward an answer to these questions, so that we might give a positive reading to this claim of VS that returning to human nature as graced by the Spirit will guide us to do the good.

2.
Lonergan and Triune Consciousness

As a model for thinking about consciousness's internal relation to it-self as triune, and also about consciousness in relation to grace, let me suggest as symbol for the heart connaturalized by grace the Galway Claddagh ring, a 300-year-old Irish tradition that usually is given another interpretation. It symbolizes the continuously converting heart, both in triune consciousness and as affected by the gifts (virtues) of the Spirit. In the center is the heart—affective consciousness. Left and right, assisting the heart, are cognition and volition, making the three elements of human consciousness: affection, cognition, and volition, or the heart, mind, and will. These three form one consciousness, without separation, but with distinctions among the three based on clearly distinct intentionalities. Affective intentionality is irreducible to the representational intentionality of cognition, or to the volitional intentionality of responsible freedom. Lonergan has presented cognitional and volitional consciousnesses in *Insight*, with the levels of experience, understanding, and judgment forming cognition, and with the fourth level of consciousness being decision. He has presented the heart and affective consciousness, including affective conversion, in his *Method in Theology*, where affection is apprehension of value in a way analogous to the way insight is apprehension of truth. The Claddagh ring can first, therefore, be interpreted as symbolizing triune consciousness, with the heart as the center and queen of consciousness, and with cognition and volition there to inform and transform the heart. To be all heart or all mind or all will is to be unbalanced; we need a synthesis of all three ways of triune consciousness at the service of love of God and neighbor in correct balance. Second, the ring can also be interpreted as symbolizing the advent of grace in the crown coming down to the heart from above, infusing as gifts of the Spirit the transforming virtues, theological and moral, mentioned in the text above from VS.

One could be a person of generous heart, sound mind, and good will and still maintain a distinction between philosophical ethics and moral theology, such that while both acknowledge the natural law, only the latter adds something special, namely, belief in the transformation worked upon human nature by the gifts of the Spirit, which are virtues attuning nature to the good, a transformation the Christian attributes to God's freely given grace. The difference between philosophical ethics and moral theology cannot be ignored without serious confusion. It does not settle the matter to presume all humans of generous heart, sound mind, and good will to be graced whether they know it or not, or like it or not, whether by baptism of desire, anonymous Christianity, or any other explanation. The difference is important because different conclusions to particular cases result, e.g., in suicide, where even a traditional ethics textbook grants that the nonbeliever can morally opt for suicide, while the believer cannot.[7] (Fagothey)

The big condition, namely, that one believes oneself transformed by grace, is a necessary condition for VS's conclusions, although a nonbeliever could also reach some or all of those conclusions without acknowledging the workings of the Spirit. My only intention, a purely philosophical one, is to establish what Kant would call the transcendental *a priori* possibility of VS's position. This is a major point for it rules out any *a priori* dismissal of VS's position. Of course, whether VS is also correct in any of its conclusions, e.g., in claiming that there are as many intrinsically evil acts as it lists, remains to be seen. Many others commenting on VS will engage it in debating those particulars.

3.
Levinas and Ethical Affectivity

Now how does an independent phenomenology, Levinas's primacy of ethical responsibility, contribute to our understanding of VS?

A. Introduction to Levinas

From Levinas we take and adapt the idea of a dual affectivity in human nature, one nonintentional, one intentional (in the phenomenological sense of intention). This idea of a double affectivity explains the power of the other, in the face to face relation, to affect me in a way that transcends the power of the other alone, as just another finite individual equal to me, to command me in the way I experience the moral ought; this concrete experience is specifically ethical and directly related to the idea of the heart as empowered to make moral discernments through affective connaturality. I offer this recourse to and interpretation of Levinas as an outside approach, a supporting witness, and an alternative access to the natural law idea because the whole concept of a natural law has become so familiar as to breed "contempt" in some circles, as VS laments. Levinas's dual affectivity is an original and coherent way in aid of understanding why affective connaturality works, and why it works the way it does in the realm of the ethical (and the mystical).[8]

By Levinas's "nonintentional affectivity," I understand the natural law written in our hearts (by "God," the believer would add). By his "affective intentionality" I understand the face of the other connecting with nonintentional affectivity and experienced as responsibility for my neighbor. Creation can be seen as a nonintentional affectivity disposing us to the affective intentionality we feel in the presence of our neighbor. Affective development (including affective conversion) can be seen as the way the general orientation we feel as the solidarity of the human species to value human persons above everything gets particularized, namely, through the discernment of spirits in concrete instances.[9] But we also feel the good and evil as well as the gravity of the good and evil through the experience of depth of feeling; the spatial metaphor of depth refers to the strength of the affective response and the concomitant experience of responsibility in the concrete case.[10]

B. Levinas's Two Affectivities

There are two affectivities in Levinas. He not only speaks of the face of the other affecting me in the present, but also of another kind of being "affected," one that reaches back into a preconscious and preintentional past, before knowledge, volition, or freedom. This preintentional or nonintentional consciousness, furthermore, is not a lower kind of consciousness, like that mentioned by Scheler and von Hildebrand when they speak of mere physiological or organic appetites or of mere teleological orientations, vectors, or trends, such as fatigue, thirst, etc.; while those affections are conscious, their explanation is causal, and entirely from below; they are not affections that occur because of relations to objects in conscious intentions.

The claim that there is a nonintentional affectivity has in Levinas's employment of it the structure of a practical postulate offered to explain the feeling of responsibility occasioned by the face of the other. Why and how does the face have this power and authority? The way Levinas uses the language of hyperbole (words like obsession, persecution, hostage) to describe this nonintentional affectivity, especially under the name of the presence of the idea of the infinite (the biblical image of God" translated into the Cartesian idea of the infinite) in consciousness, allows and suggests that we call responsibility a projection upon the other of one's own interior archetype, to use the language of psychology, understanding such archetypal projection itself as one kind or part of a general mediation of a diachronic nonintentional affectivity (the root of the general natural law) by a synchronic affective intentionality like the face (the application of the law to particular cases by affective connaturality). The face operates as a symbol, and as a symbol it unites a feeling with an image.[11] The feeling of responsibility is attached to an archetypal image, rooted in the diachronic timeless past of creation (redemption, sanctification). It is this creation that places in oneself, like Descartes's idea of the infinite, an image of God, a dormant image one can wake to find in oneself and in the other in an ethical context.

Together, then, affective intentionality and nonintentional affectivity explain Levinas's philosophy of the face as ethical responsibility in that the synchronic affective intentionality of the face-to-face relation (affective connaturality operating in the present) draws its authority from a diachronic nonintentional affectivity (the general natural law written in our hearts before and without our knowledge and without our free or voluntary consent).

We can try to explain the authority of the face in terms of the two affectivities in either or both of two ways: our created solidarity as one species and/or the image of God in oneself and in the other.[12] One can *postulate* this, and stop there; but we can also try to understand the postulate by pointing to the trace of everyman and everywoman in us all. I am reminded of a *Star Trek* episode where the crew of the Enterprise is indicted for the sins of humanity before a court of sentient species representing all the galaxies. The crew is led from initial rejection of responsibility for its species to an eventual grudging acceptance (while denying any *personal* knowing or voluntary culpability and protesting that humanity as a species had progressed beyond its early barbarism). They denied individual guilt while admitting solidarity with the human species.

What escapes cognitional and volitional intentionality *is,* however, accessible through *affective* intentionality, and the classical name for this, as Ricoeur points out in *Fallible Man,* is *affective connaturality.* There has to be *some* link between the before-the-prehistoric nonintentional origin of our affectability, on the one hand (the natural law), and each present event of one's consciousness of being affected in the face-to-face relation, on the other (through affective connaturality). If we had *no* such consciousness, *no* intentionality to which Levinas could appeal, then his work and his message would remain inaccessible to consciousness, and thus outside assent by his readers. We who hear him must find resonance within ourselves of what he proclaims to us, such as the image of God (the idea of the infinite) found within us—and also met in the other—so long as we remember that the *image* of God is not God nor is the *idea* of the infinite (the) infinite. Now affective connaturality explains the way affective intentionality actually works and operates as a connaturality based on a common affectivity, linking the intentional back to the nonintentional. So how do these two affectivities interact?

Let us analyze affective intentionality, thereby illuminating VS's recourse to connaturality as the necessary and essential something beyond the knowledge of the law, deemed not sufficient "without that connaturality . . . rooted . . . in virtuous attitudes. . . ." Affective intentionality has two moments; according to Ricoeur, feeling is an affection plus an intention, "the first is a being affected" (affection) and the second is the affective response (intention). The first presupposes an affectability, an ability to be affected; the second presupposes a responsibility, an ability to respond. It is to being as important, as good, but especially as value, that feeling responds.

But value imposes a demand, obligation, or call for an *adequate* response, unlike a good that is merely "appealing or subjectively satisfying," and to whom or which one's response is entirely optional. A value puts a claim on us; value commands. The face is in the class of value, demanding an *adequate* response once one is affected. This is the dual structure of affective intentionality, i.e., affectability plus responsibility. But *why* is one so affectable by the face?

It is because affectability itself—the ground of responsibility—is based on something prior to itself, namely, a nonintentional connaturality, affinity, kinship, solidarity with the other: something in me resonates with the other and I am spontaneously affected and so commanded to respond—obsessed, Levinas says, and *therefore* free: I am free because first I am responsible. There is also, of course, an affectability that is intentional, when through our own actions we acquire habits, a second nature. Levinas is addressing the origin of our first nature, in a nonintentional affectivity that is a pure passivity, the absolute receptivity of our very existence and nature, prior to all action.

Recall the story Joseph Campbell tells of the Hawaiian policeman: a deep solidarity with a fellow human, who was in the act of committing suicide by leaping off a cliff, precipitated the policeman into risking his own life to save another's, and even drew, with a strange magnetism, a second policeman into the chain reaction. Clearly this is a *substitution,* a spontaneous action before voluntary deliberation, beyond willingness. Why did the policeman feel so responsible? How did his affective response override reason and will? Campbell quotes Schopenhauer to the effect that at a moment like that, a deep metaphysical (his word) resonance between one's consciousness and the deeper unconscious self that Jung calls the objective psyche occurs within one's subjectivity; this identity with other is rooted more deeply than rational, discursive thought or deliberative, voluntary will. One could invoke the Platonic "like known by like," but it is more than a knowing; it takes affective connaturality to explain how the solidarity, already there beneath and before cognition and volition, breaks through into consciousness as feeling.

Let's analyze the structure of feeling as affective intentionality even further. A *response* is not an operation in the sense of cognitional and volitional operations. We must distinguish between operations, such as looking, seeing, thinking, forming concepts, judging, deciding, and *responses.* Feeling, as affective intentionality,[13] has something specific to it as affection, namely, the dual structure of feeling whereby the feeling or emotion is always feeling of some moving agent, namely, the *other,* but also feeling or emotion for *oneself,* where the emotion consists in being moved, being frightened, made to rejoice or to be sad, etc.; there is a double intentionality of the of "and of the for," a *participating in affectivity from two sides,* since the event in oneself depends on being affected by the other. The essence of affective intentionality is that the term of the intention is not a concept or will act but a *being-affected,* first in the *passive* moment, and then in an *affective response,* in the second, spontaneously *active* moment.[14]

My response, then, while produced by me, depends on the other to whom it is a response and who has affected me in just this way to engender this response. Thus the face works in the present to particularize the law written in the heart in the "prehistoric past" of my creation, redemption, and continual sanctification in the offer of grace. But the point of dual affectivity, nonintentional and intentional, is that the face is a symbol that acts not only with its *own present* power but also as and with the *deeper force* of an *archetype* whereby there occurs a deep communicating between the diachronic past and this synchronic present.[15] In this way affective connaturality operates in the present by connecting with the natural law from an immemorial past. As *face* it speaks for itself, but as *symbol* and *archetype* it says much *more than itself* through its affective link to all humanity, affective because I am passive to this being—affected with a passivity that doesn't even presuppose my existence as a subject, for it is the passive reception of that very existence and nature in my being created in the human species.[16]

Thus I am affectable because, out of my own immemorial past, I project upon or transfer to the other something (the image of God, like the idea of the infinite) from that deep objective psyche that the other and I share as human. The transfer works and has the authoritative power it does because it is grounded in our common created (redeemed, sanctified) solidarity; coming to consciousness as a link between a nonintentional affectivity and an affective intentionality, making the experience possible as qualitatively what it is. It is not an empty projection because the image found in the face is *first* found nonintentionally in myself. Thus, rather than take the power of the face as a mere "projection" in any pejorative sense, we should understand projection itself as a subset of the face as the most fundamental occurrence of an affective intentionality of which projection or transference are instances—in the way Jungian psychology speaks of projection as the first attempt of the Self to bring its unconscious (objective) past to present (subjective) consciousness—and these instances are themselves explainable on the basis of the dual structure of affective intentionality. Thus Levinas's projection of responsibility to and for the other is rooted in the archetype postulated to begin in a diachronic nonintentional affectivity. Interpretatively, this is natural law. This aboriginal affectivity is projected upon the other from a past too remote to be accessed directly by cognition and volition.[17]

Further, if we take Ricoeur's definition of symbol as meaning "other than what is said," then Levinas's face can be taken as a symbol in that sense also, i.e., as a saying other and more than is said, as commanding "Thou shalt not kill," which by interpretation sends us back to the nonintentional affectivity of the trace that is the true diachronic saying embodied in every synchronic said. Symbols, like the face, represent the *fullness of language* in that a symbol, much more than a word, contains an *overdetermination of meaning*. As Ricoeur says in his *Freud and Philosophy*, speaking of full language,

> The movement that draws me toward the second meaning assimilates me to what is said, makes me participate in what is announced to me. The similitude in which the force of symbols resides and from which they draw their revealing power is not an objective likeness; . . . it is an existential assimilation, according to the movement of analogy, of my being to being.[18]

This means that the reason why the face communicates more meaning than itself is that there is an affective connaturality not between my *knowing* and the other but between my *being* and the other. It is what Ricoeur calls an "existential assimilation," or what Sartre calls an affective intentionality when he says that Heidegger's being-with ". . . is not knowledge,"[19] and what VS calls a ". . . connaturality between human nature [man] and the true good."[20]

This way of looking at natural law is a reversal of the Freudian reduction, which is of a present to a past by a hermeneutic of *suspicion* that empties meaning from immediate consciousness in favor of an archeology of the subject who is a pure self-obsessed *narcissist*. In retrieving natural law we perform a hermeneutic of *recovery,* and the self-obsessed narcissist becomes an other-obsessed altruist. The meaning of the present still returns to an immemorial past, but its sign is reversed. Freud's irreligious egoism, which saw in religion "the universal obsessional neurosis of mankind," is replaced in Levinas by an obsession with the other whose authority comes from connecting with the infinite, the *vertical infinite* of God, the creator, and the *horizontal infinite* of a humanity of the other, the created image of God, where creation is the event of a nonintentional affectivity. The "for-it-self" of Freud's amoral egoism becomes the "for-the-other" of Levinas's moral altruism. The two affectivities are linked by the face as real symbol, almost as sacrament, effecting what it signifies.

So there is also a *telos* in Levinas, a reference of the face to the *future* that complements its archeological roots in the prehistoric *past.* Its name is *substitution* as the future to-be-done, the action that complements the passion of having-been-affected by having been created in the immemorial past. Thus the face as symbol is a *janus face,* both a looking *back* and a looking *forward,* a *trace and* a *project,* a nonintentional affectivity and an affective intending of the other. The face has this double intentionality, repeating our childhood, anticipating our adulthood, a present extending back into our past and forward into our future, an archeology and a teleology.[21] Affective intentionality is the present face-to-face moment that links an archeology, created in a nonintentional affectivity, to a teleology, creative responsibility for the other. Archeology and teleology connect through a passivity of the past and an activity for a future still to come, the advent of the other.

Similarly, the dual function of face as symbol shows in that the face conceals and reveals, hides and shows the infinite. The face makes present an immemorial past, but for the sake of a present that becomes its future.

Thus the face is not a *re*presentation but a *present*ation, a presenting and presensing of what can never become old, namely, the other who addresses to me the ever new imperative, "Be responsible." Love thy neighbor as thyself." Each meeting face-to-face with the other is an epiphany both of myself and the other; the question is never asked once and for all, but always anew: Do you accept this responsibility or not?

Thus, there would be no *experience* of responsibility, no *sense* of responsibility, were it not for the dual structure of affectivity, the dual structure of the *janus face* as symbol tracing its power and authority to an affectivity before time, in the solidarity of our creation as one species, for the sake of the other. This archeological-teleological dialectic is experienced as a *present* ability to answer for a *future* because of a *past* that can only be present in this face as real symbol overdetermined with meaning. To employ another language, affectivity, unlike cognitional and volitional intentionalities, is the *heart,* i.e., a capacity to respond that depends on being affected by the other. As Ricoeur says, a feeling is a *mélange* of affection and intention; something in the present symbol communicates with a past for a future. Past, present, and future unite in the face; one is affected and made able to respond, *affected* because face as symbol communicates with an immemorial past affectivity, and *intending* because the transcendence of ego toward Self is felt as a command to respond to the other. As created we are one species; the Self (not the ego) is an other. Transcendence of *ego* is advent and epiphany of both *Self* and *other*. The ego of cognitional and volitional intentionality must be overcome by the Self-Other structure of affective intentionality, and out of this dialectic comes the ethical.

4.
Rahner and Affective Connaturality

Rahner's use of affective connaturality occurs chiefly in the context of his discussion of the discernment of spirits. He connects these themes with the concept of the heart, where heart operating through connaturality is seen as a higher mode of ethical (and mystical) judgment, decision and action, proper to someone of developed virtue, attuned to the good, fulfilling the need VS expresses for something essential to bridge between the law and the deed.

Discursive reason and deliberate will are not the best we can do but are stages of finite spirit on its way to nondiscursive, quasi-intuitive knowing and spontaneous love without will-acts. ". . . [T]he rational version of man found in the western world, especially among the intellectuals, is not necessarily the model and paradigm for the whole of humanity" (*Theological Investigations* XVI, p. 47). Head is ordained to become heart as its perfect development, and faith, love, and hope are truly only comprehensible as affective responses of the heart not in opposition to head as to another faculty, but as the essential meaning of the idea of affective connaturality.

The key Thomist text for this, which VS cites, is *Summa theologiae* IIa IIae q. 45. a. 2. As was noted, what *Summa theologiae* I q. 84 a. 7 was for Aquinas's metaphysics of mind or head, this text is for his metaphysics of heart. Here Aquinas states, addressing the two primary areas of intersubjectivity, the ethical and the mystical, that beyond the perfect use of reason someone with the habit (his example for ethics is the virtue of chastity while for the mystical he just refers to divine things, *res divinae*, in general) judges by connaturality. He also explicitly says that in the latter case (*res divinae*) virtue is a gift of the Spirit. Equally interesting is his quoting Dionysius's saying that such a person not only learns (*non solum discens*) but is affected by divine things (*sed et patiens divina*). Connaturality is both a later and a higher development, making someone *perfectus in divinis*, i.e., more actualized in one's nature and operations than if reason and will were the best we could do. If the heart works by affective connaturality, then heart can be recognized as the highest stage on a developmental continuum above discursive cognition and deliberative volition.

How should we understand this key text for the question of experience of God through grace? Aquinas's simple answer is that the one who has a habit (virtue) is con-naturalized (in the case of grace the word used sometimes is "divinized') to cor-responding good (value) and so operates at a higher level of actualization. How does this work? De Finance states that habit installs between being and doing, perfecting a nature in the direction of action.

> But to know means more than simple [acts of] knowledge. Knowledge can be momentary, occasional, transitory: it is an act. For knowledge really to remedy my limitation and let me conquer the alterity of the object more completely, it must fix itself in me: acting must sediment in being [must settle or sink roots into my being]. In other words, knowing must become a habitus. For habitus is a sort of middle term between being and acting, an acting stabilized in being, a being in tension toward acting and bearing the structure of that action in its being. Fixed in habitus, the act loses its alterity in relation to the subject in losing its casual character. Insofar as I do not have the habitus or habit, the success of my deed . . . remains chancy, depending on the other: There has to be a conjunction of several elements, of which the knot is outside me. Habitus puts this knot in my hands. If it is perfect, there is no need of effort, as though to capture an elusive prey in flight. The act is in me and I can at will make it happen [literally: I can deploy it into actuality]. . . . Knowing is a habitus: it is knowledge that has passed into the structure of the spirit.[22]

All finite being comes to itself through action, as a way of becoming itself, fulfilling itself. Recall Rahner's concept of concupiscence as the inertia of finitude in finite spirit forcing it to self-enact, act after act, in time; so also, act by act, act can become habit; as de Finance says, I remedy my limitation: habitude is remedy for finitude as a quasi-permanent change in one's being. How? By modifying our operative potencies; and we can experience this: what used to be difficult or impossible is now familiar, easier, more pleasurable, connatural, congenial, spontaneous, harmonious. What higher, less finite spirits have by nature, in Denis's hierarchy of spirits—where the highest performance of a lower spirit just touches the lowest performance of the next higher spirit—we acquire by habit or are given as gift.

This is familiar enough stuff to students of Aristotle and Aquinas, but what is easily missed is that for Aquinas and Rahner (and Ignatius) the way of connaturality is the *normal* way, not the exceptional way: the paradigm in ethical discernment is not the child or beginner but the person making progress in virtue in response to God's initiative through the neighbor. Since affective connaturality is the normal way, it is in its failure or absence that we have to default to ethics by the book or try to approach God through a Ph.D. in theology. Habit changes the horizon of one's operations: one can do more and do it better, more reliably, autonomously, spontaneously; one becomes an ethical principle of beneficence almost with the dependability of natural appetite rather than elicited appetite, thanks to virtue. This is not only true in the ethical realm, thanks to acquired virtue, but also in the mystical realm where the gifts of the Spirit, best understood as infused virtues, change human nature by changing our operative powers to know and love. VS's claim for the Church to speak as "expert in humanity" would seem to depend on this developmental idea of human nature as possessing an obediential potency for the grace (both *sanans* and *elevans*) that raises it to a higher level of connaturality with the good.

Lonergan's concept of "vertical finality" is also relevant here. According to this idea, human consciousness has a dynamic impetus to ascend from its lowest to its highest level of performance. Experience, e.g., at the lowest level, naturally is oriented toward understanding, and our incessant questions, curiosity, hunger, and desire to understand propel us upward toward the formation of the insights that are our acts of understanding and the concepts we form as we try to understand. Not content with understanding, we seek to verify and confirm those insights, and so we test our hypotheses, check out our theories and bright ideas; these three levels of consciousness—experience, understanding, and judgment—constitute cognition, and remain incomplete and unfulfilled until cognition leads to volition, to the fourth level of consciousness, where responsible freedom culminates in decision and action. Furthermore, paralleling these four levels of "head" consciousness, i.e., cognitional and volitional consciousness, there is "heart" consciousness, the equally dynamic and vertically final domain of affective consciousness, the realm of feelings, moods, attitudes. These three, as mentioned above, form a triune consciousness, and all share a vertical finality such that the highest human consciousness consists in the union of the three in an affective connaturality where the lower form of reasoning, by rational and discursive thought, and the lower form of deciding, by deliberative volition, is sublated by the intuitive knowing and spontaneous love of the heart's connaturality with the good. Lonergan accounts for the intervention of grace in this vertical finality by speaking of a fifth level of consciousness; his favorite scriptural quotation is about the love of God flooding our hearts through the Spirit who is given us. This is the infusion of the virtues given from above, at this fifth level of consciousness, as gifts that transform consciousness from the top down. Vertical finality confirms the coherence, usefulness, and unity of a concept of natural law that is open to transforming action from above.

A final point comes from Rahner's discussion of discernment of spirits in *Dynamic Element in the Church*. For the mature adult advancing in the spirit, life can be divided into two halves: first, direct vocative prayer (the mystical, consciousness at its most sublime), and, second, our attempt to bring the rest of life into harmony with that direct relation through discernment; thus spiritual life consists of prayer and discernment; prayer (meditation, contemplation) is our direct relation to God and action based on discernment is our indirect relation with God through what we do every day, as it were our *contemplatio in actione* (the ethical). Thus the mystical inspires the ethical, i.e., literally is its spirit, and the ethical is the evidence and sign of authentic mystical life. Now as Rahner has said, and as we know without being told, the experience of grace as grace is not something we can distinguish from some hypothetical state of pure ungraced nature, so we have to include reference to faith in order to do a theology of this experience of God through grace. But for a concept of a head-heart developmental continuum, that presents no problem because faith, self-transcending love, and hope are the *par excellence* examples of just those higher operations beyond discursive reason and deliberative will. Faith, love, and hope, in human intersubjectivity, are high ethical achievements, as theological faith, love, and hope, in divine intersubjectivity, are the mystical gifts that show that the lower operations of reason and will are not ultimate and definitive; thus to take faith and hope seriously means that they qualify as experience of the highest kind. In a strong statement Rahner says that mysticism ". . . [is] . . . a radical experience of faith which destroys the conceptual and the categorical insofar as these claim to be ultimate realities . . . " (*Theological Investigations* XVI, p. 47). Faith, love, and hope are from the heart, above the head on a developmental continuum.

Conclusion

VS may be understood as trying to reinstate an ethics based on natural law, with the additions of scripture and tradition. There is a confidence implicit in VS that succeeding in that attempt would be a major step in reversing the mistakes of the varieties of consequentialism, utilitarianism, and the other "isms" found guilty of undermining what VS would call traditional Catholic teaching. Perhaps that confidence is naive, especially if no useful consensus could be reached on the most basic philosophical content of natural law, not to mention the obviously even more difficult task of bringing nonbelievers to accept the additions of scripture and tradition to that natural law and the conclusions VS would say follow from the perspective of a *graced* human nature and natural law.

But for those of us who do find a way, whether helped by Levinas or someone else, to assent to a human solidarity that could be natural law by another name, VS cannot be dismissed as ill-founded or misguided in its recourse to natural law, despite disagreement about its conclusions. To show (1) the a priori possibility of natural law, (2) the continuity between the philosopher's natural law and the theologian's graced natural law (through the concept of virtue, not only acquired but especially given as gift of the Spirit), and (3) the practical link between these two in affective connaturality, which also serves as practical method of application, is a task worth doing.

Notes

1. "The specific purpose of the present encyclical is this: to set forth, with regard to the problems being discussed, the principles of a moral teaching based upon Sacred Scripture and the living Apostolic Tradition, and at the same time to shed light on the presuppositions and consequences of the dissent which that teaching has met" (n. 5) in the Vatican Translation published by St. Paul Books & Media [Boston, 1993]); I refer to numbered sections; I also correct the language to make it gender inclusive.

It becomes clear in the text that this tradition ("the living Apostolic Tradition") is the one called the tradition of the natural law as modified by grace and interpreted by the Church in scripture and tradition; God has put it in the "depths of [the] heart" (n. 1), through (in part) commandments "written on the human heart" (n. 4), so that keeping that law is the "desire of the human heart" (n. 7), and which "rises from the depths of [the] heart" (n. 8).

2. The natural law is not just the moral law written in/on the heart by nature, but has become somehow the law written by God. How this happens and the difference it makes involves the idea of the converted heart, where heart has become a capacity to be changed from above, by grace (the gifts of the Spirit).

3. John Henry Newman, *An Essay on Development of Christian Doctrine,* ed. Charles Frederick Harrold (New York: Longmans, Green, 1949) 1.1.7, p. 38.

4. VS's endnote 110 (marked by an asterisk in the text above) refers to Aquinas's key text on connaturality, *Summa theologiae* IIa IIae, q. 45, a. 2, a text that is as important for Aquinas's teaching on affective consciousness as *Summa theologiae* I, q. 84, a. 7 is for his teaching on cognitive consciousness. I consider this a crucial text for understanding VS and the claim of the church through John Paul II in VS to

speak authoritatively to and for humanity. Knowledge of natural law in general is not enough; connaturality is essential for its application to particulars. These are key statements.

5. See Charles Davis, *Body as Spirit. The Nature of Religious Feeling* (New York: Seabury, 1976), *passim* in chapter one, "Feeling as the Human Response to Reality."

6. Bernard J.F. Lonergan, *Grace and Freedom. Operative Grace in the Thought of St. Thomas Aquinas* (New York: Herder and Herder, 1971; edited by J. Patout Burns), pp. 44-45; my emphases. The Fathers were not above calling "divinization" this process whereby divine grace transforms the soul into a "connaturalized citizen" of heaven, an adopted child of God, sharing the divine nature in a mysterious way.

7. E.g., see Milton Gonzalves, Fagothey's *Right and Reason,* (Columbus OH: Merrill, 1989; 9th edition).

8. Below, in section V, with Rahner we will go the next step, the practical one of applying natural law, now within a theological context (i.e., that of graced nature) in order to do two things: (1) show how infused virtue (the gifts of the Spirit) can be understood as operationally modifying human nature to attune it to the good, and (2) show how the discernment of spirits works by affective connaturality to guide transformed triune consciousness to choose the good. If the above makes sense, then VS may be regarded as standing on solid ground in attempting to retrieve natural law and cannot be dismissed on the ground, at least, that natural law is unfounded.

9. All this only establishes natural law, not the particular conclusions. VS claims something besides natural law, viz., that the Church as "expert in humanity" (p. 11, quoting Paul VI) adds scripture and tradition. If knowledge of law is not enough and connaturality is also needed, then it becomes clear why some do not recognize what they should do: their hearts have not been connaturalized by grace, i.e., the gifts of the Spirit, which are the virtues operative in affective connaturality (n. 64).

The heart means the ability to respond affectively to value, especially values that touch us as persons, i.e., in our ethical relations to finite human persons (and our mystical relations to the infinite divine persons). Mind and will are there as the other two kinds of consciousness whose task is to bring about the affective conversion needed to ready oneself to receive the gifts of the Spirit, gratuitously given, unmeritable.

In VS connaturality is supposed to function as the way to get from the general natural law to particular cases. My task is to show whether and how that might be so. The connaturalized heart can only work this practically if someone "does justice" and is thus attuned to the good, so that one's resonance with deeds can be a correct discernment. This is circular, since only someone who *is* good *does* good, and only someone *doing* good (justice) is *connatural* to good. Likewise, someone evil is connatural to evil and finds it easy and natural to do evil. For the believer, grace *qua* gift of virtue breaks the circle: the initiative is God's, the Other who affects us by creation (Father), redemption (Son), and sanctification (Spirit).

10. On depth, see Sue L. Cataldi, *Emotion, Depth, and Flesh. A Study of Sensitive Space. Reflections on Merleau-Ponty's Philosophy of Embodiment* (Albany: State University of New York Press, 1993) and Quentin Smith, *The Felt Meanings of the World. A Metaphysics of Feeling* (West Lafayette: Purdue University Press, 1986). Depth is essential to the experience of the difference between mortal and venial sin,

a criterion that must be related to the connaturalized heart in its practical discernings. But we could be numb or oversensitive and thus have to mistrust our feelings, by discounting them or in some way correcting them. Discernment is relevant to metanoia, therefore, i.e., to the transformation occurring when one is graced with the virtues as gifts of the Spirit.

11. "A symbol is an image or a real or imaginary object [e.g., a face] that evokes a feeling or is evoked by a feeling" (Bernard Lonergan, *Method in Theology* [New York: Herder & Herder, 1972, p. 64). "Finally, feelings are related to their subject: they are the mass and momentum and power of his conscious living, the actuation of his affective capacities, dispositions, habits, the effective orientation of his being. The same objects need not evoke the same feelings in different subjects and inversely, the same feelings need not evoke the same symbolic images. This difference in affective response may be accounted for by differences in age, sex, education, state of life, temperament, existential concern. But more fundamentally, there is in the human being an *affective development* that may suffer aberrations. It is the history of that process that terminates in the person with a determinate orientation in life and with determinate affective capacities, dispositions, and *habits*. What such affective capacities, dispositions, *habits* are in a given individual can be specified by the symbols that awaken determinate affects and, inversely, by the affects that evoke determinate symbols" (Ibid., 65; my emphases).

12. When Levinas says "same" and "other," he has to mean "same nature" but not "same person," otherwise there can be no communication or commerce between human beings. Human solidarity is not denied by affirming the otherness of the other. That the other and I are not the same leaves intact that she is my sister, he my brother. Nonintentional affectivity affirms our original solidarity, a humanism of the other and an otherness within humanity. This humanism makes possible a hospitality to the stranger at the same time that it can declare the *totaliter aliter* an absurd notion. It is not that otherness is contained within and by sameness of persons rightly called totalitarian but that it is on another plane, having the intelligibility of judgments of existence rather than that of essence, concepts, definitions, and having the meaning of the saying rather than of the said, of actuality rather than possibility, of person rather than nature, of who rather than what.

13. In an affective intentionality, we have four elements. By accounting for them we account for the nature of affective intentionality as the experience of feeling of the *other*. We have the object intended (the other; the *quod intenditur*). We have the subject intending (oneself, the *qui intendit*). We have the act of intending (the *intendere*), an act known both as the act of the subject. Finally we have the being intended, i.e., one's being affected by the other (the *intendi*). As subject of cognitional intentionality I know myself knowing something or someone; as subject of volitional intentionality I know myself willing something or someone; as subject of affective intentionality I know myself feeling something or someone.

I can also *reflect* on these intentions and *represent* them; I do this by attending not to the *other* but to *myself,* i.e., not to the data of sense (e.g., listening to someone, being in a face- to-face relation with someone) but to the data of consciousness. It is to this second, reflective stage Levinas is anxious to deny primacy; but that denial leaves direct affective intentionality undenied. There would be no *other* without it, nor would there be a conscious subject, only a substance. Substance becomes subject *when it acts,* not when it becomes an object of someone's knowledge. I am therefore in a nonrepresentationally intentional relation with the other affectively *and* know myself to be affected by the other purely and simply in the feeling itself, and only later do I turn that nonrepresentational intentionality into a representation when I think about it, understand it, form a concept of it, reflect on it, judge it. When I do this latter set of operations I am not attending directly to the *other* in my presence, near me, whom I see, address in saying, etc., but am now attending to *myself,* i.e., to my consciousness of my seeing, addressing as said, etc.

In other words, I do not *have* to turn myself into an object (although I can) in order to know myself as a subject: I need only *be in act, be intending, be conscious,* including being conscious of an other. I can do that affectively, cognitively, volitionally. In my intending, *because I am in act,* I know *myself* once. In *reflecting* on my intending, I know myself *twice,* but now I have lost the *other,* because now indeed I myself am the object of my intending. It is this *second* moment Levinas wants to dethrone from the primacy it holds in *representational* intentionality.

14. It is incorrect to say that Levinas's ethics depends on a nonintentional affectivity exclusively, or that he denies an affectivity that is intentional. His rejection of intentionality is a rejection of *representational* intentionality, the reflective, second-order intentions mentioned above, along with a somewhat irrelevant allusion to a nonphenomenological meaning of intention having to do with *purpose, willing,* and *volition;* this latter rejection of the term intention is apparently aimed at those of his readers who do not understand the proper sense of intentionality as consciousness of an object rather than as a term used to describe the doing something intentionally, meaning voluntarily; obviously he wants to deny that our being affected by the other is under our direct voluntary control. A proper understanding of affective intentionality preserves both elements of this phenomenon, both the affection, whereby the agency of the other is affirmed, and the intention, whereby one's consciousness of the face is also given.

In an act of affective intentionality, the subject is known not as an object but as a subject, for the act already has an object, namely, the other. Levinas is obviously doing away with a superfluous representational intentionality; he doesn't need a cognitional intentionality to have a subject and is wary of anyone inserting one. Why? Because that puts freedom first, before responsibility. Natural law written in our hearts is a nonintentional affectivity: we are affected before and beyond cognition and volition.

Again, it is a misunderstanding of Levinas to say that only objects are known. Subjects, too, are known, simply by intending. They do not have to intend themselves in order to be conscious. In intending the other in affective intentionality the subject knows itself as a subject who is affected, and to know oneself as affected is to know oneself as capable of responding, as responsible. He does not say responsive or responding, but responsible, i.e., able to respond, called to respond, empowered to respond, as a capacity to respond, which he usually expresses in the emphatic language of persecution, hostage, obsession. Note that this knowing is not objective but subjective; it is Sartre's presence-to-self that is not knowledge-of-self (a *conscience [de] soi*), where Sartre clearly means a nonconceptual knowing that he, too, called an affective intentionality.

15. The human face, as no other, functions as the symbol *par excellence,* evoking the feeling of responsibility, where "feeling" changes its meaning as the quality of

consciousness changes, especially in persons of more maturity and affective development. Now, "symbols obey the laws not of logic but of image and feeling. . . . The symbol, then, has the power of recognizing and expressing what logical discourse abhors: the existence of internal tensions, incompatibilities, conflicts, struggles, destructions. . . . Finally, it does it in a way that complements and fills out logic and dialectic, for it meets a need that these refinements cannot meet. This need is for internal communication. Organic and psychic vitality have to reveal themselves to intentional consciousness and, inversely, intentional consciousness has to secure the collaboration of organism and psyche. Again, our apprehensions of values occur in intentional responses, in feelings; here, too, it is necessary for feelings to reveal their objects and, inversely, for objects to awaken feelings. It is through symbols that mind and body, mind and heart, heart and body communicate" (Lonergan, *Method,* pp. 66-67).

16. Thus the face, while not "only" or "merely" a symbol, operates like one, i.e., with the overdetermined force of one, i.e., by being more than itself, by being itself plus what Levinas calls the trace, which can be understood as the nonintentional affectivity of the natural law engraved in our hearts.

17. We see this thesis of projected archetype illustrated in the pages on paternity in *Totality and Infinity.* My son and daughter are my vulnerability incarnate in a space and time other than my own, yet somehow still my own. We get an insight into affective intentionality, seeing it writ large in the other. I suffer for the other who is me and not me, as my own embodiment is a kind of vulnerability of me outside me, at least outside the me who is capable of thinking this distinction. In living paternity, e.g., just as in living embodied, I live an intention to be affected by an otherness I have partly generated.

18. Paul Ricoeur, *Freud and Philosophy,* trans. Denis Savage (New Haven: Yale University Press, 1970), p. 31.

19. Jean-Paul Sartre, *Being and Nothingness,* trans. Hazel Barnes (New York: Washington Square Press, 1953), p. 332.

20. The connaturality is not between the general natural law and my knowing, but between that law and my being, my nature; I apprehend that law, then, through feeling, e.g., peace or the inner turmoil that attends my moral inclinations, judgments, decisions, actions, and which are the content of my discernment of spirits. VS maintains that graced nature, the converted heart, is attuned to the true good because it now has something essential, besides knowledge of the law, namely, the infused virtues, gifts of the Spirit; these virtues are operative in the affective connaturality of the converted heart.

21. See Levinas, *Time and the Other* [and additional essays], trans. Richard A. Cohen [Pittsburgh: Duquesne University Press, 1987], p. 79: "Relationship with the future, the presence of the future in the present, seems all the same accomplished in the face-to-face with the Other. The situation of the face-to-face would be the very accomplishment of time; the encroachment of the present on the future is not the feat of the subject alone, but the intersubjective relationship."

22. Joseph de Finance, *L'affrontement de l'autre. Essai sur l'altérité* (Rome: Gregorian University Press, 1973), p. 97; my translation and emphases.

11

Veritatis Splendor et Rhetorica Morum: "The Splendor of Truth" and the Rhetoric of Morality

Edward R. Sunshine

The main concerns and major claims of the papal encyclical on moral theology involve moral truth: the best and correct way to evaluate human conduct. Such claims and concerns provoke varied reactions. For critics they amount to intemperate triumphalism which aborts the slow formation of theological consensus at a time when dissent abounds. For supporters they bring welcome closure to years of rancorous debate and definitively render dissent impotent.

Both supporters and critics are reacting to more than moral doctrine: they are responding to the ways in which that doctrine is presented. Supporters gladly adopt the teaching because its argumentation is agreeable; critics want to be persuaded. In either case, the encyclical's rhetoric is the key to its acceptance.

The Pope's attempts to persuade his varied audiences in *Veritatis Splendor* and how well he succeeds in doing so are subjects worthy of serious study. Understanding rhetoric cannot substitute for coming to terms with content, but rhetorical analysis can show the limits and possibilities of content and reveal the assumptions and values present in it. In this sense, both in the development and appropriation of doctrine, moral rhetoric influences and even determines moral content.

1.
Audience

Pope John Paul II addresses the encyclical specifically to his fellow bishops—those most like himself in power, authority, and background.[1] The hierarchy forms an elite audience of well-educated colleagues who presumably accept the Pope's argument and affirm his teaching. This choice of audience allows the Pope to say what he wants to say, and it motivates him to excel in saying it. By directing his message to bishops, he shows how important he thinks it is, implies that it reflects their thinking, and ensures that it will get serious attention.

If bishops were its only audience, the document would have limited value. But modern popes write encyclicals with other audiences in mind, especially the community of believers and the universal audience of all humans, even though they don't specifically mention these larger groups. "The church's pastors . . . guide and accompany [the faithful] by their authoritative teaching, finding ever new ways of speaking with love and mercy not only to believers but to all people of good will."[2]

The formal audience of bishops includes the informal audiences of both believers and all humans. Bishops embody the audience of believers because believers recognize bishops as their leaders and models. Bishops also represent the universal audience of all humans insofar as what is reasonable to them should be reasonable to all who give careful consideration. Thus the indirect audiences of believers and all humans define the Pope's specific audience of bishops in ways which affect what he has to say to them.

Although these informal audiences influence the encyclical greatly, they are not recognized as participants in the discussion. They are bystanders who may listen in on what is said, but they have no standing to make formal responses. Dissenting moral theologians have special status in this role. Never named, they are the reason why this encyclical was written. Compared to the rich young man who turned down Jesus' call to perfection, they are wayward children whom parents discuss *in absentia*. Their teaching is the anti-model for what correct doctrine should be.

The English text of the encyclical excludes one audience almost completely: all who are concerned about inclusive language. The translation, which is especially one-sided in the use of generic nouns and pronouns, amounts to an exercise in translational fundamentalism. For example: "*Man's* capacity to know the truth is also darkened, and *his* will to submit to it is weakened. Thus, giving *himself* over to relativism and skepticism . . . , *he* goes off in search of an illusory freedom apart from truth itself."[3] The encyclical itself distinguishes different pronoun genders only in a discussion of martyrdom: "The Christian is called . . . to a sometimes heroic commitment. In this *he or she* is sustained by the virtue of fortitude. . . ."[4] Women will find it difficult to recognize themselves in most of this document.

The encyclical's audiences and non-audiences are like concentric circles expanding further and further away from the core of the papal communication.[5] The effects of the message on these varied groups are like the centrifugal ripples of a pond disturbed by a stone. An opposite effect is also present: what the Pope has to say reflects his perception of what his audiences think about his topics. The effects of these audiences on the encyclical's message are like the centripetal currents of a river drawn into whirlpools. Thus *Veritatis Splendor* gauges the ebb and flow of current moral theories, and it discloses Vatican perceptions about their relevancy and orthodoxy.

2.
The Starting Points

Ideas held in common among the various audiences of the encyclical are agreements of the universal audience. These agreements are useful bases for developing its argument, but they are often very abstract. More specific agreements, which are shared by particular audiences only, are what we call values: "objects of agreement which do not claim the adherence of the universal audience."[6]

When agreements get specified, the differences between particular audiences and their values become apparent. Everyone esteems "freedom" in general (an agreement of the universal audience), but not everyone gives it the same meaning (a value of a particular audience). For example, the Pope says that freedom is "man's free obedience to God,"[7] while others think of it as the primacy allocated to individual conscience in the exercise of moral responsibility. In the abstract, everyone would agree on the importance of "truth," which the Pope promotes in the encyclical's title. But the Pope makes truth stand for Christ and in Christ's place himself, so for him truth represents the concrete values of fidelity and loyalty.[8]

To a great extent, the disagreements which occasioned the writing of the encyclical were over values, both abstract and particular, their hierarchies, and the ways in which they are used. Abstract values inspire change, so dissidents use the abstract value of truth to spell out inconsistencies in traditional moral teachings. Concrete values are resistant to change, so the Pope discusses truth understood as assent to what he teaches in response to those who challenge traditional teachings. At issue is whether change is appropriate.

Other important agreements used in the encyclical are *loci* of quality. *Loci* are "headings under which arguments can be classified" or "storehouses for arguments"; *loci communes* (commonplaces) are headings general enough to be used in any study or argument. For purposes of this study, *loci* "form the most general premises, actually often merely implied, that play a part in the justification of most of the choices we make."[9]

The presumption behind *loci* of quality is that 1) what something is has greater value than the numbers involved in its makeup or support, and 2) what is difficult has more value that what is easy. The pervasiveness of these emphases is evident in the encyclical's title, *The Splendor of Truth*, which lays claim to something more important than counting supporters and more magnificent than answering opponents. Its teaching on intrinsic evil— "man . . . can never be hindered from not performing certain actions, especially if he is prepared to die rather than to do evil"[10]—takes the principle to an ultimate conclusion: martyrdom for the sake of truth.[11]

Other elements for the argument of the encyclical are its selection and interpretation of data. One aspect of this process is the use of notions, qualifications and classifications which are applied to the topic. Notions do not have fixed meaning when used in argumentation. As designations of universal values, "instruments of persuasion *par excellence*,"[12] they are the most difficult to define in ways acceptable to all. Insofar as they are instruments of persuasion, their use is controversial.

The Pope gives certain meanings to notions like "teleologism," "consequentialism," and "proportionalism" in order to reject them; and he interprets the notion of "intrinsic evil" in such a way as to promote it. The formal audience of bishops would have no problem with this procedure. Others, however, might object that he makes opposing arguments into caricatures whose conclusions are ludicrous. The ways in which the Pope defines these controversial notions shows that he does not intend to discuss contentious moral issues in a strictly scientific way. Instead he uses extreme descriptions of dissent as a rhetorical tool in order to make his own teaching appear moderate and worthy of support.

3.
Structure

Veritatis Splendor is organized according to the classic structure for legal speeches in antiquity: exordium, narration, proof, refutation, conclusion, and epilogue.[13] The encyclical's introduction contains both the exordium and the narration, in which the Pope presents the topic (truth in moral matters), explains why it is important for consideration, and shows why he is the best person to discuss it. The proof is an extended reflection on the gospel story of the rich young man, and the refutation involves a complicated discussion of modern moral theories. The conclusion is a long exhortation on the Christian call to heroic obedience in living a moral life. The epilogue is a brief appeal to Mary, Mother of Mercy.

4.
Exordium and Narration

The encyclical begins by emphasizing truth and the importance of obedience to truth. Humans search for absolute truth, which is Jesus Christ, and the church interprets the "signs of the times" in each age to explain this truth. But some contemporary signs point to deviant moral teachings which threaten the church:

> spread of numerous doubts and objections . . . overall and systematic
> calling into question of traditional moral doctrine . . . currents of
> thought which end by detaching human freedom from its essential and
> constitutive relationship to truth . . . certain of the church's moral
> teachings are found simply unacceptable; and the magisterium itself is
> considered capable of intervening in matters of morality only in order
> to "exhort consciences" and to "propose values," in the light of which
> each individual will independently make his or her decisions and life
> choices.[14]

The encyclical proposes "to set forth . . . the principles of a moral teaching
based upon Sacred Scripture and the living apostolic tradition, and . . . to
shed light on the presuppositions and consequences of the dissent which that
teaching has met."[15]

The encyclical's specific audience (the bishops, whose teaching
authority is at stake) and express purpose (to reaffirm Catholic moral teaching threatened by dissent) account for its defensive tone. It is an internal
strategic document written by the commander-in-chief for his generals in
order to put down mutiny in the ranks and reassure those who are scandalized and confused. Because of this preoccupation with dissent, the letter's
positive aspects, such as "exhorting consciences" and "proposing values,"
attract less attention.

5.
The Triptych Core of the Encyclical

The central part of *Veritatis Splendor* begins with a moral exhortation
based on the gospels, a call to follow Jesus as the rich young man was
invited to do (Matthew 19:16-30). It ends with a challenge to heroic sacrifice, following the example of Christ. In the middle lies a discourse on the
fundamentals of moral doctrine.

From a rhetorical standpoint, this order of material is compelling. The
scriptural invitation, representing common ground accepted by all believers,
is made to include official teaching on moral doctrine, which some believers
might not accept completely. The invitation for all to accept the doctrine is
made equivalent to the call for Christians to imitate the sacrifice of Christ.
Living out the faith becomes a matter of living out the Pope's explanation of
moral doctrine.

The Pope's extended reflection on the call to evangelical perfection
and martyrdom is unusual for official Catholic moral instructions. Papal
documents typically use scriptural passages as "proof-texts," references
made in passing to quotations isolated from their contexts in order to reinforce ideas arrived at from other sources, especially natural law. In this
encyclical, however, the scriptural and theological bases at the beginning
and end of the triptych core demonstrate the encyclical's primary focus on

believers and its Christological context. Here moral doctrine appeals to reason, but reason enveloped by faith.

6.
Proof: A Parable Which Establishes Authority

The first chapter of the encyclical is an example of epidictic discourse, a style of presentation which reinforces basic ideas and values commonly accepted by the audience. The vehicle for this exposition is the gospel account in which Jesus stresses the importance of keeping the commandments and calls the rich young man to be his disciple, themes familiar to believers and reasonable even to those who might not live according to them. At first glance, then, the purpose of the story would appear to be exhortatory: people are invited to follow Jesus' teaching and consider his call.

The real function of the chapter is argumentative: like the "proof" in legal argument, it establishes the "case" in favor of the Pope and his message. What originally was a scriptural story designed to point out the problems of material wealth becomes a papal "parable" on the personal authority of church leaders. (Parable here refers to a developed comparison between two things in story form; in rhetoric, it is an extended analogy which grounds an argument about reality.) Jesus, the young man, and the bond between them form one term of the comparison, while the Pope, all people, and their relationship with each other form the other.

The characteristics of gospel parables are instructive for understanding the use of the rich young man story in the encyclical. Parables at first seem to be irrelevant: what does the story have to do with moral truth? They irritate: why is the Pope wasting time on this apparently noncontroversial part of the gospels? Parables make the audience seek and discover the meaning for themselves and, in the process, change their audience.[16] The papal parable based on the story of the rich young man leads to the conclusion that the Pope speaks in the place of Jesus, that people should listen to him as they would to Jesus, and that they should do what he says.[17]

The implicit comparison between Jesus in the gospel story and the Pope in the encyclical has the effect of embellishing the Pope's character and establishing his authority to speak definitively on moral matters. The comparison between the man and all people has the effect of showing that people need the Pope's help to know what is right and respond fully to the call. Thus "the magisterium . . . senses more urgently the duty to offer its own discernment and teaching in order to help man in his journey toward truth and freedom."[18]

The story establishes a feeling of presence because it treats the same subject which the encyclical addresses—morality. Bringing Jesus into the modern moral conversation helps anchor the discussion in the core of Christian experience and the reality of everyday life. The encyclical's various audiences are supposed to identify with the young man and learn from what Jesus, in the person of the Pope, has to say. Thus Jesus and the Pope represent concrete values, demanding fidelity and loyalty.

The first part of the story discusses the commandments, which are incarnations of universal value, principles which everyone accepts. The Pope interprets them in a maximalist way: "Jesus shows that the commandments must not be understood as a minimum limit not to be gone beyond, but rather as a path involving a moral and spiritual journey toward perfection, at the heart of which is love. . . ."[19]

The beginning of the journey, keeping the commandments, leads to the call to perfection, giving up worldly things and following Jesus. Discipleship is not a universal value but rather a particular one which is freely chosen by some as an outgrowth of keeping the commandments. The invitation to evangelical poverty brings out the full meaning of "love your neighbor," just as the call to discipleship is the fulfillment of "love your God."

The young man does not respond to the particular value proposed in Jesus' invitation. The hard teaching which discourages him and makes the disciples anxious highlights the distinction between two moral spheres— between responding to universal values and particular values, between obeying the commandments and answering the call. It also shows that the moral life goes beyond precepts and resides in values accessible only through God's help, thus demanding an openness to what is new and challenging. This distinction and this demand will form the basis for dividing the rest of the encyclical into Chapter 2 (dealing with moral precepts) and Chapter 3 (dealing with the call to follow Christ, even to the cross).

By retelling the story of the rich young man, the Pope lays claim to Jesus' role as the authentic interpreter of the commandments. The man represents everyone, but especially those who dissent from church teaching: "And ever since apostolic times the church's pastors have unambiguously condemned the behavior of those who fostered division by their teaching or by their actions."[20] They are not bad people (they may keep the commandments), but they fail to respond fully to the Pope's invitation to assent. This papal parable is an initial attempt at persuading them to change their ways.

7.
Chapter Two: The Moral Polemic

The triptych's central panel, which deals with moral doctrine, is made up of an introduction and four sections. The general structure is the same for most of these parts: 1) acknowledgement of theologians whose contributions have improved the expression of church teaching for different cultures in various historical periods; 2) mention of moral approaches which are extreme or unacceptable; and 3) delineation of the proper framework for subsequent discussion. The rhetorical procedures and techniques used are: 1) definition of agreements by association, 2) definition of disagreements by disassociation, and 3) clarification of theological qualifications or notions.

The Pope's argumentation throughout the section on morality is pragmatic: it evaluates dissenting moral theories in terms of their favorable or unfavorable consequences.[21] He counters them by laying out the direction of their thinking and emphasizing conclusions which are at odds with church teaching. There is a certain irony in this method of dealing with dissent because the Pope uses arguments from consequences to counter unnamed advocates of moral theories which he will say take consequences too much into account.

The Pope carefully crafts his arguments to condemn only extreme statements attributed to no one in particular. This practice makes future discussions possible because his extreme descriptions of dissenting positions let dissidents claim that his censure applies to others. Only approaches which exclude important considerations are unacceptable, while those which include all relevant factors may be acceptable. This procedure suggests a framework for future development.

1. Freedom and Law

The Pope says that the modern preoccupation with autonomy has led "Catholic moral theology . . . to undertake a profound rethinking about the role of reason and of faith in identifying moral norms with reference to specific 'inner-worldly' kinds of behavior involving oneself, others and the material world." He associates himself with these endeavors, but he rejects explanations of human freedom which are exaggerated:

> a *complete* sovereignty of reason in the domain of moral norms . . . the boundaries for a *merely* "human" morality . . . the expression of a law which man in an autonomous manner lays down for himself and which has its source *exclusively* in human reason.[22]

Such extreme claims to autonomy exclude God from the norms of morality reached by reason and reduce the word of God to exhortation, "a generic paraenesis," which reason would have to specify in concrete situations. The conclusion: "No one can fail to see that such an interpretation of the autonomy of human reason involves positions incompatible with Catholic teaching."[23]

The encyclical insists on the concordance between obligation and autonomy. "Human freedom and God's law meet and are called to intersect, in the sense of man's free obedience to God and of God's completely gratuitous benevolence toward man."[24] Human reason and will participate in God's wisdom and providence.

Other controversies surround human sexuality, where the function of the body in moral deliberations is at issue. One extreme, physicalism, makes moral laws out of biological laws and thus emphasizes the physical aspects of the natural more than the personal aspects of the human. The other extreme "ends up treating the human body as a raw datum devoid of any meaning and moral values until freedom has shaped it in accordance with its design."[25] This latter approach speaks of premoral goods which are extrinsic to persons, denies that these goods can determine the morality of actions, and thus emphasizes the role of the personal at the expense of the physical. The Pope rejects both extremes because the tension between freedom and nature in humans is reduced to an unacceptable division between the physical and the personal.

The Pope insists on the unity of rational soul and body, which "entails a particular spiritual and bodily structure . . . [and] implies respect for certain fundamental goods, without which one would fall into relativism and arbitrariness."[26] The natural law written in the hearts of humans and expressed in the commandments is universally valid in its negative precepts. Its norms remain unchanged, but their formulations adapt to different cultures and historical settings.

2. Conscience and Truth

According to the Pope, certain teachings on conscience share the same limitations as questionable teachings on freedom: a "concrete existential consideration . . . by taking account of circumstances and the situation, could legitimately be the basis of certain exceptions to the general rule and thus permit one to do in practice and in good conscience what is qualified as intrinsically evil by the moral law."[27] This unacceptable conclusion demonstrates the need to clarify the notion of conscience.

The Pope's explanation of conscience follows an arrangement of ideas which flows from St. Paul's reference to natural law in Romans 2:14-16. The order is noteworthy: conscience as the practical judgment of right and wrong; its imperative character; its recognition of the truth about moral good and evil; its possibility of being in error and thus not culpable; and its dignity. In this grouping, the Pope places the strongest arguments for his explanation of conscience at the beginning and end, with the weaker argument on error in the middle.

This development culminates in a discussion of the foundations of conscience: "knowledge of God's law in general is certainly necessary, but it is not sufficient: What is essential is a sort of 'connaturality' between man and the true good."[28] A virtuous life gives rise to the "moral sense" expressed by the word "connaturality," which helps overcome deficiencies in knowledge of God's law. Church teaching provides additional direction in the formation of conscience.

What root image underlies this explanation of conscience? The Pope mentions what Jesus said about the eye being the lamp of the body,[29] implying that conscience "sheds light" on truth, "gives witness" to it, and is the way in which humans "see" it. The image could also be magnetism, with truth being the magnet and conscience "connaturally" attracted to it. Although it is a modern concept, the image of radar bouncing waves off objects to detect what is what could also explain the way in which conscience "connaturally" perceives the true and the good.[30]

3. Fundamental Choice and Specific Kinds of Behavior

The Pope generally agrees with the concept of fundamental freedom but disagrees with specific explanations of it. He interprets unacceptable theories in ways which make his condemnation of them plausible. Thus he talks about "fundamental option" in this way: "Particular acts which *flow from* this option would constitute *only* partial and *never* definitive attempts to give it *expression*; they would *only* be its '*signs*' or *symptoms*."[31] He does not explain the role of particular acts, especially ongoing patterns of actions, in the *formation* of a fundamental option, and he reduces the rest of the description to extreme cases by using such words as "only" and "never."

This kind of description emphasizes the separation of "the transcendental dimension proper to the fundamental option" from "the choices of particular 'inner-worldly' kinds of behavior . . . "

> There thus appears to be established within human acting a clear disjunction between two levels of morality: On the one hand the order of good and evil, which is dependent on the will, and on the other hand specific kinds of behavior, which are judged to be morally right or wrong *only* on the basis of a technical calculation of the proportion between the "premoral" or "physical" goods and evils which actually result from the action.[32]

The conclusion of this way of thinking is that "the properly moral assessment of the person is reserved to his fundamental option, *prescinding in whole or in part* from his choice of particular actions, of concrete kinds of behavior."

Theories described in this way emphasize intention too much and do not pay enough attention to the content of the acts. These approaches lead to slavery because the moral agent gets used to doing objectively wrong acts by claiming good intention:[34]

> In point of fact, the morality of human acts is not deduced only from one's intention, orientation or fundamental option, understood as an intention devoid of a clearly determined binding content or as an intention with no corresponding positive effort to fulfill the different obligations of the moral life.[35]

Sin enslaves because it is denied; people don't even know that they are sinning seriously. As a result, they desensitize themselves to mortal sin: "The separation of fundamental option from deliberate choices of particular kinds of behavior disordered in themselves or in their circumstances, which would not engage that option, thus involves a denial of Catholic doctrine on mortal sin. . . ."[36] This extreme conclusion would seem to follow only from a complete and absolute disjunction of the fundamental option from all of the particular actions which constitute and express it.

4. The Moral Act

The Pope takes a firm teleological stand in his description of morality:

> The rational ordering of the human act to the good in its truth and the voluntary pursuit of that good, known by reason, constitute morality. . . . Activity is morally good when it attests to and expresses the voluntary ordering of the person to his ultimate end and the conformity of a concrete action with the human good as it is acknowledged in its truth by reason. If the object of the concrete action is not in harmony with the true good of the person, the choice of that action makes our will and ourselves morally evil. . . .[37]

Moreover, he explicitly acknowledges the importance of teleological studies and associates himself with them:

> This kind of investigation is legitimate and necessary, since the moral order, as established by the natural law, is in principle accessible to human reason. Furthermore, such investigation is well-suited to meeting the demands of dialogue and cooperation with non-Catholics and nonbelievers, especially in pluralistic societies.[38]

But he rejects teleological methods which reduce moral criteria to the wrong elements.

The crucial question is what constitutes the right ordering of human acts to God—circumstance, consequence, end, intention, proportion between good and evil effects, or the object of the act itself. The Pope's answer is the object of the act, "the proximate end of a deliberate decision which determines the act of willing on the part of the acting person."[39] An extreme teleological method—one which emphasizes elements other than the object of the act—becomes a teleologism, in which "free will would neither be morally subjected to specific obligations nor shaped by its choices, while nonetheless still remaining responsible for its own acts and for their consequences."

> This *teleologism*, as a method for discovering the moral norm, can thus be called . . . *consequentialism* or *proportionalism*. The former claims to draw the criteria of the rightness of a given way of acting solely from a calculation of foreseeable consequences deriving from a given choice. The latter, by weighing the various values and goods being sought, focuses rather on the proportion acknowledged between the good and bad effects of that choice, with a view to the "greater good" or "lesser evil" actually possible in a particular situation.[40]

The rhetorical devices employed here concern definition of the terms discussed, the agreements which can be presumed from special audiences, and disassociation from suspect approaches. The definition of consequen-

tialism with the exclusive and reductive word "solely" contrasts it with traditional teachings, which take into account intention, circumstances, and the
object of the act. These traditional teachings are agreements held by the
Pope, his formal audience of bishops, and all believers. The contrast between the definition and the agreements demonstrates why disassociation is
necessary.

The Pope wants above all to preserve the traditional teaching that certain actions are always and everywhere wrong. He says that analysis of
intention or circumstance cannot do this. Only attention to the species of
actions, the kinds of actions they are by reason of their object, can protect
the determination of intrinsic evil adequately.

> The teleological ethical theories . . . maintain that it is never possible to
> formulate an absolute prohibition of particular kinds of behavior which
> would be in conflict in every circumstance and in every culture with
> those values. . . .
>
> In this view, deliberate consent to certain kinds of behavior declared
> illicit by traditional moral theology would not imply an objective moral
> evil.[41]

The Pope lists the following acts as examples of intrinsic evil, known to be
such by consideration of their object:

> any kind of homicide, genocide, abortion, euthanasia and voluntary sui-
> cide; . . . mutilation, physical and mental torture and attempts to coerce
> the spirit; . . . subhuman living conditions, arbitrary imprisonment, de-
> portation, slavery, prostitution and trafficking in women and children;
> degrading conditions of work which treat laborers as mere instruments
> of profit, and not as free responsible persons. . . .[42]

The rhetorical approach used to promote consideration of the object as
decisive in moral analysis is the *locus* of essence, which refers to "the fact
of according a higher value to individuals to the extent that they embody
this essence."[43] The encyclical says that it is of the essence of moral systems to provide clear indication of intrinsically evil acts and adequate explanation why the acts are intrinsically evil. Only reference to the objects of
acts can entirely account for intrinsically evil acts.

What is involved in the Pope's emphatic teaching on intrinsic evil? At
issue is the way in which material events are looked at and talked about.[44]
An example from Thomas Aquinas quoted in the encyclical can illustrate the
point. "Let us say that someone robs in order to feed the poor: In this case,
even though the intention is good, the uprightness of the will is lacking.
Consequently, no evil done with a good intention can be excused."[45]

The most simple description of the material event in Aquinas' example
is that "others were deprived of their property." By using the word "robs,"
he adds elements which make the deed morally wrong ("by unlawful force
or threat of violence," where "unlawful" means "against the owners' reasonable will"). If he had used a word different from "robs," he would have

given a different description and reached a different evaluation of the conduct. For example, if in time of extreme emergency people forced open a food warehouse to feed the starving, their actions might be justifiable and they themselves even worthy of praise.

The way in which an action is described defines it in relation to a class of actions which has already received a moral determination, in this case intrinsic evil. How does the class of actions receive its moral determination? It is a generalization of concrete examples of actions similar enough to be grouped together and significant enough to be recognized as having a definitive moral character. "Robbery" covers all acts which involve taking what belongs to another by use of unjustifiable force. It is universally considered wrong because it is unreasonable: its toleration would make human life together in society impossible.

Once in place, the generalized class of actions becomes a paradigm which enjoys a certain self-evident status and imputes self-evident value to concrete acts which are like it. Contrary interpretations could not make sense. The strength of these self-evident qualities depends greatly on the generality of the paradigm, however. Once application is made to specific situations, self-evidence of moral quality depends on the possibility of establishing the almost identical similarity between a particular action and the paradigmatic class of actions.[46]

The Pope identifies "intrinsically evil acts" as the negative paradigm of morality and equates them with "self-evidently evil acts." These classes of actions are obviously "against human nature" (irrational) or "against nature common to humans and animals" (unnatural). Because these designations are self-evident insofar as they apply to the classes of actions, they are not open to deliberation but need only be applied to practical situations.

The application of the evaluations of moral paradigms to concrete acts is more complicated. These acts take on the character of being intrinsically and self-evidently evil only when they are described in ways which define them as being identical with the paradigmatic class of actions. The description of concrete acts thus becomes the key for determining whether or not they are intrinsically, that is self-evidently, evil.

If the designation of concrete acts as intrinsically evil is dependent on the description of the acts and their objects, "intrinsic evil" stands for the judgment that certain actions have been described in ways which make them "obviously wrong." The descriptions of particular actions, the judgment that these descriptions constitute objective wrong, and thus the designation of "intrinsic evil" itself would have to be open to deliberation. Otherwise empirical evidence would be imposed, not reported; moral quality would be prescribed, not evaluated; and self-evidence would be arbitrarily claimed, not persuasively argued.

The different audiences addressed in the encyclical will respond to these considerations in diverse ways. The elite audience of bishops accepts the prior agreements which are necessary for the Pope to speak of the intrinsic evil of concrete actions as self-evident moral truth. The audience of believers will agree with the use of "intrinsic evil" to designate certain paradigms of wrongful actions, but some will question applications of the paradigm to describe particular acts. The universal audience of all humans may or may not accept the Pope's explanation of the "intrinsic evil" paradigm and subsequent applications of it in particular contexts. It is only by arguing the case for the designation "intrinsic evil" and its application to specific acts that this can be done persuasively.

Instead of developing fully the notion of intrinsically evil acts, the moral core of the encyclical concludes by demonstrating how the *locus* of quality is used by the Pope throughout his teaching. Dissenting theologians may be numerous, and their numbers may constitute a basis for what casuists refer to as probable opinions—morally acceptable ways of proceeding in cases of doubt.[47] But these numbers (a *locus* of quantity) are not as fundamental as "that truth which is Jesus Christ himself"[48] (a *locus* of quality and a concrete value). Use of this *locus* also involves reference to the *locus* of person, to the effort which the person extends to achieve the quality, and to the difficulty involved in doing so. This theme forms the basis for the third part of the encyclical.

8.
Chapter Three: The Cross of Christ

The special Christian calling to uphold morality has a certain uniqueness which gives it great value. Difficulties incurred by Christians who try to follow Christ endow their activities with great value because value is connected with what is rare as an object and demanding of the agent. The problem is reconciling moral norms with the freedom of individuals. The solution is imitating Christ, even to death on the cross. The difficulty lies in applying the solution to the problem.

Christ crucified is the example which establishes the connection between observance of moral norms and ultimate self-sacrifice, and is normative for understanding how Christians should deal with moral rules. The Pope says that truth pitted against freedom and morality separated from faith are unfortunate dichotomies. The way to integrate freedom and morality into the challenge of truth and faith is to accept the call to follow Christ crucified, even to the point of martyrdom.

The difficulty with the example of Christ crucified to connect faith and morality is that Jesus did not die because of a moral stand, unless the Pope follows those who would interpret his death to be the result of organizing or revolutionary activities. Some potential and real martyrs to morality mentioned in the encyclical are relevant, for instance Susanna and John the Baptist. Less persuasive are other examples which the Pope gives—the deacon

Stephen, the apostle James, and early Christian martyrs, who all seem to be more martyrs of faith. The Pope's point in any case is clear:

> The unacceptability of "teleological," "consequentialist" and "proportionalist" ethical theories, which deny the existence of negative moral norms regarding specific kinds of behavior, norms which are valid without exception, is confirmed in a particularly eloquent way by Christian martyrdom. . . .[49]

Few are called to the extreme witness of martyrdom, but all are called to "a consistent witness . . . , even at the cost of suffering and grave sacrifice . . . [and] to a sometimes heroic commitment."[50]

The Pope identifies martyrdom, "accepted as an affirmation of the inviolability of the moral order,"[51] as the paradigmatic instance of moral self-sacrifice. He exhorts his audiences to acknowledge and respect that norm which is morality. Human weakness calls out for God's mercy, but it cannot become "the criterion of the truth about the good. . . ."[52]

The prototype for the sinner seeking mercy is not the Pharisee, who is self-satisfied and represents those today who "attempt to adapt the moral norm to one's own capacities and personal interests. . . ."[53] Rather the model is the tax collector of the gospel (cf. Luke 18:9-14), who is repentant for what he has done wrong. Having started out being identified with the rich young man who turned down Jesus' call, dissidents end up being compared to the unrepentant Pharisees who reject Jesus' teaching for selfish reasons.

Conclusion

> This is the first time, in fact, that the magisterium of the church has set forth in detail the fundamental elements of this teaching and presented the principles for the pastoral discernment necessary in practical and cultural situations which are complex and even crucial.[54]

As a first-time endeavor, how well does the encyclical succeed? From a rhetorical point of view, *Veritatis Splendor* is probably successful in convincing the bishops because their allegiance to the Pope can be presumed. This concrete value of loyalty is the rhetorical basis for his claim to truth. By explaining moral teachings in a traditional manner and avoiding difficulties in the applications of them, the encyclical reaffirms what the hierarchy is familiar with and ends up being an in-church document.

The broader value of the encyclical for Catholics and theologians lies in its persuasive scriptural and Christological focus. The document will have a general theological effect on the community of believers through the preaching and teachings of the hierarchy and the clergy, but the intricacies of the moral discussion will probably have little consequence in their moral life. The invitation to follow Jesus in the person of the Pope is the essential issue which believers will have to address.

Theologians will respond typically according to their positions on the questions dealt with in the encyclical. Their future moral discussions will benefit from the Pope's reflections on the gospel and the role of Christ in the moral life. They should have little trouble avoiding the traps of the "intrinsically unacceptable" positions which he condemns.

What is missing, however, is a way to move the discussion forward, a synthesis which goes beyond mere repetition of traditional teaching and out-right rejection of questionable theories. The Pope will not persuade dissent-ing theologians because he offers no new perspectives to address the gnaw-ing questions which gave rise to dissent in the first place. Believers will support the Pope in general but look to more practical considerations when engaging in moral discernment. The universal audience of all humans will respond to some of the values proposed insofar as they are understood ab-stractly, but not necessarily to the concrete values of fidelity and loyalty which are at the encyclical's heart. In this sense, the document fails even its primary audience, the hierarchy, because bishops will not find new ways to persuade those who don't share their perspective.

This deficiency means failure to convince the particular audiences which are the objects of the church's evangelization. Here theologians have an important rhetorical role:

> While recognizing the possible limitations of the human arguments em-ployed by the magisterium, moral theologians are called to develop a deeper understanding of the reasons underlying it teachings and to ex-pound the validity and obligatory nature of the precepts it proposes, demonstrating their connection with one another and their relation with man's ultimate end.[55]

Pope John Paul II evidently recognizes this need because he quotes the bish-ops of the Second Vatican Council, who encouraged theologians "to look for a more appropriate way of communicating doctrine to the people of their time. . . ."[56] In this sense, *Veritatis Splendor* is a dramatic plea for help.

Endnotes

1. Cf. John Paul II, "Veritatis Splendor," *Origins* 23 (14 October 1993): 297. The paragraph numbers of the original text will be used in all references except, as is the case here in the salutation, where there is none.

2. Ibid., n. 3.

3. Ibid., n. 1. Emphasis added.

4. Ibid., n. 93. Emphasis added. Are women excluded from the encyclical's teach-ing on morality but included in its teaching on martyrdom because they dissent less and put up with more than men? Should translations exclude audiences which origi-

nal texts don't? Whatever the answer, such choices in language are difficult to reconcile with the long practice in official Catholic documents of seeking common ground and union in the name of evangelization instead of promoting division and polarization.

5. This image is the one used by Pope Paul VI in his encyclical *Ecclesiam Suam* (n. 96), where he spoke of the concentric circles of humanity, worshippers of the one God, Christians and Catholics as various audiences for dialogue. See *The Pope Speaks*, vol. 10, no. 3 (Spring 1965) pp. 284-91.

6. Chaim Perelman and L. Olbrechts-Tyteca, *The New Rhetoric: A Treatise on Argumentation,* trans. John Wilkinson and Purcell Weaver (Notre Dame: University of Notre Dame Press, 1969), p. 75.

7. John Paul II, *Veritatis Splendor,* n. 41.

8. Cf. Perelman and Olbrechts-Tyteca, *The New Rhetoric,* p. 77, where concrete values are said to attach "to a living being, a specific group, or a particular object, considered as a unique entity . . . Such notions as obligation, fidelity, loyalty, solidarity, and discipline are of this kind."

9. Ibid., pp. 83 and 84.

10. John Paul II, *Veritatis Splendor,* n. 52.

11. Even though loci of quality predominate in this papal document, they are not always useful in other contexts. When arguing against induced abortion, artificial contraception, and fears of overpopulation, the hierarchy typically avoids references to "quality of life" because they have become identified with advocacy of reproductive choice, birth control, and population control. In those settings, church leaders often use *loci* of quantity to counter opposing claims.

The U.S. bishops' discussion before voting on the final draft of their pastoral letter on the U.S. economy illustrated this fact. Portland's Archbishop Levada, presenting various amendments from the floor on behalf of pro-life groups, argued against the following sentence from the third draft: "Our concern, however, must be as much for the quality of human life as for the number of human lives" because reference to "quality of life" had been used against pro-life groups in abortion discussions. The sentence was dropped from the final edition. (See videotape "Annual NCCB/USCC Meeting, Washington DC" [13 November 1986], tape #1, for the discussion of the amendment, and National Conference of Catholic Bishops, *Economic Justice for All: Catholic Social Teaching and the U.S. Economy,* [Washington DC: United States Catholic Conference, June 1986], n. 272, p. 77 for the quote from the third draft.)

12. Perelman and Olbrechts-Tyteca, *The New Rhetoric,* p. 140.

13. Cf. Ibid., p. 495.

14. John Paul II, *Veritatis Splendor,* n. 4.

15. Ibid., n. 5.

16. Cf. Jan Lambrecht, *Out of the Treasure: The Parables in the Gospel of Matthew* (Louvain: Peeters Press, 1992), p. 23.

17. Left out of the comparison in the encyclical is the point of the original gospel story, the hard saying about riches: "Truly I tell you, it will be hard for a rich

person to enter the kingdom of heaven. Again I tell you, it is easier for a camel to go through the eye of a needle than for someone who is rich to enter the kingdom of God." (Mt. 19:23-24; New Revised Standard Version.)

It is interesting to speculate about what results a fully-drawn comparison might have produced. The young man, as a Jew, could "have" eternal life by keeping the commandments (Mt. 19:16- 17). Does that mean that all people can "have" eternal life by keeping the commandments now? Does the call to follow Jesus in the gospel story correspond to a call to a Christian life in the encyclical? In the setting of the encyclical, what corresponds to the "riches" of the gospel story—deviant moral teaching? What would an application of this passage from the viewpoint of liberation theology look like, and how would it change the points the Pope is making?

18. Ibid., n. 27.

19. John Paul II, *Veritatis Splendor*, n. 15.

20. Ibid., n. 26.

21. Cf. Perelman and Olbrechts-Tyteca, *The New Rhetoric,* p. 266.

22. Ibid., n. 36. Emphasis added.

23. Ibid., n. 37.

24. Ibid., n. 41.

25. Ibid., n. 48.

26. Ibid.

27. John Paul II, *Veritatis Splendor*, n. 56.

28. Ibid., n. 64.

29. Ibid., n. 63. Cf. Mt. 6:22-23.

30. The encyclical cites Thomas Aquinas on connaturality. The phenomenon of magnetism, which he would have known, fits the teleology of his thought. But the phenomenon of radar, though unknown to Aquinas, helps interpret other aspects of his teaching, such as this statement from the *Summa Theologica,* I-II, q. 18, a. 2, ad 3: "Moreover, although the goodness of an action is not caused by the goodness of its effect, yet an action is said to be good from the fact that it can produce a good effect. Consequently, the very proportion of an action to its effect is the measure of its goodness."

31. John Paul II, *Veritatis Splendor,* n. 65. Emphasis added.

32. Ibid. Emphasis added.

33. Ibid. Emphasis added.

34. Cf. Ibid., n. 66. The identification of certain theories of the fundamental option with slavery seems to mean that people can easily deceive themselves into thinking that wrongful actions are right and thus become entrapped in harmful ways of living. This would happen if there were too much emphasis on subjective elements like intention (the will) and too little regard for objective elements, like the importance of particular actions and their intrinsic evil. Habituation to wrongful activity, rationalized as being acceptable because it is done in good faith, is moral self-enslavement. By using the metaphor of slavery as he does here, the Pope implies that

misguided intention explains the phenomenon of slavery. If this is so, why did the church take so long to change its moral assessment of the institution of slavery? Church teaching approved slavery for many centuries, especially during the massive abuses of the colonial period, on the grounds that slaveowners had justifiable property rights over their slaves. Slavery was finally condemned in the Second Vatican Council (cf. *Gaudium et Spes, #27*) as a crime against one's neighbor and against Christ, and in this encyclical the Pope refers to it as an example of intrinsic evil (see n. 80).

From the viewpoint of the history of church teaching on the subject, slavery would be more relevant in a discussion about misunderstanding the natural law than as an example of the effects of moralities based solely on intention. Unless the Pope wants to imply that church teaching was a deluded though well-intentioned "slave" to slavery for 350 years, his use of it would seem to point to conclusions different from the ones which he intends. Cf. John Francis Maxwell, *Slavery and the Catholic Church: The History of Catholic Teaching Concerning the Moral Legitimacy of the Institution of Slavery* (London: Barry Rose Publishers, 1975).

35. Ibid., n. 67.

36. Ibid., n. 70.

37. Ibid., n. 72.

38. Ibid., n. 74.

39. Ibid., n. 78.

40. Ibid., n. 75. Emphasis in original.

41. Ibid.

42. Ibid., n. 80. The passage quoted is from the Second Vatican Council document *Gaudium et Spes*, n. 27.

43. Perelman and Olbrechts-Tyteca, *The New Rhetoric*, p. 94.

44. Richard McCormick claims that this teaching is based on too limited a description of certain acts: "an action cannot be qualified morally simply by looking at the material happening, or at its object in a very narrow and restricted sense." Richard A. McCormick, "Document begs many legitimate moral questions," *National Catholic Reporter*, 15 October 1993, p. 17. McCormick makes the same point in "*Veritatis Splendor* and Moral Theology," *America*, 30 October 1993, p. 10.

45. Thomas Aquinas, *In Duo Praecepta Caritatis et in Decem Legis Praecepta. De Dilectione Dei: Opuscula Theologica*, II, No. 1168 (Ed. Taurinen, 1954), p. 250. Quoted in John Paul II, *Veritatis Splendor*, n. 78.

46. Cf. Thomas Aquinas, *Summa Theologica*, I-II, q. 94, a. 2 and a. 4 for a discussion of self-evident moral principles.

47. The encyclical acknowledges casuistry as part of the Catholic moral tradition but accepts its application only where the law is uncertain and the absolute validity of negative moral precepts is not questioned. See John Paul II, *Veritatis Splendor*, #76, p. 320.

48. Ibid., n. 83.

49. Ibid., n. 90.

50. Ibid., n. 93.

51. Ibid., n. 92.

52. Ibid., n. 104.

53. Ibid., n. 105.

54. Ibid., n. 115.

55. Ibid., n. 110.

56. Ibid., n. 29, quoting the Second Vatican Council document *Gaudium et Spes*, n. 62.

12

Judaism and Catholic Morality: The View of the Encyclical

John T. Pawlikowski

1.
The Revolution in Christian-Jewish Understanding

Jesus of Nazareth lived and died as a believing Jew. Moreover, as the church historian Franklin Littell has compellingly reminded us, if Jesus had been alive during the time when the Nazis were exterminating Jews in Europe, he would have gone to the crematoria with his people. Yet many Christians (and Jews as well) have been conditioned to regard Jesus as essentially anti-Jewish in the fundamentals of his teaching and preaching. As the 1985 Vatican *Notes* on the proper way to present Jews and Judaism in preaching and catechesis tells us, "Jesus was and always remained a Jew . . . Jesus is fully a man of his time, and his environment—the Jewish Palestinian one of the first century, the anxieties and hope of which he shared."[1] Cardinal Carlo Martini of Milan, formerly rector of the Biblicum in Rome, makes much the same point: "In its origins Christianity is deeply rooted in Judaism. Without a sincere feeling for the Jewish world, therefore, and a direct experience of it, one cannot understand Christianity. Jesus is fully Jewish, the apostles are Jewish, and one cannot doubt their attachment to the traditions of their forefathers."[2]

This new attitude towards Judaism and the Jewish people within Catholicism has its roots in Vatican II's Declaration on Non-Christian Religions (*Nostra Aetate*), whose fourth chapter set the Jewish-Christian theological relationship on a fundamentally new course. It also has resulted from significant new scholarship on the Hebrew Scriptures and the New Testament, as well as the reflections of individual Christian scholars such as Karl Barth and Johannes Metz who, in the light of the Holocaust, have recognized not only the need for a totally new approach to the Church's theology of Judaism but have understood that such a change will impact all theological statement within Christianity, not merely the Church's theology of Judaism and the Jewish people. Also contributing to this fundamental rethinking of Catholic thinking about Jews and Judaism have been many ecclesial documents, including official Vatican declarations in 1974 and 1985, as well as a series of important statements by Pope John Paul II, who has strongly emphasized the deep, continuing bonding between Jews and Christians at the very basic level of their identity.[3]

With regard to the Hebrew Scriptures, ample evidence exists that a major shift of emphasis is under way. More and more scholars are recognizing the value of studying these texts in their own right and not merely as a backdrop for the New Testament. The view, prevalent in most Christian churches for centuries, that the "Old Testament" materials have been retained merely as "foil" or "prelude" for the inherently superior wisdom found in the gospels and epistles is gradually receding. Surely the Hebrew Scriptures remain important for an adequate understanding of the New Testament. While Christian and Jewish scholars such as Lawrence Boadt, Eugene Fisher, John Collins, John Levenson and Roger Brooks[4] continue to debate whether we should stay with "Old Testament" as Christians (with a substantially revised meaning for the term) or whether we should turn to "Hebrew Scriptures," "First Testament," "Tanach," or some other term, it is nonetheless becoming apparent to a growing body of Christian biblical scholars that the Hebrew Scriptures contain revelatory insights which Jesus may have shared but which never became an explicit part of his public ministry. Few may be prepared at this point to go as far as a James Sanders who has said that "Without Torah the Christian gospel is hollow, gutless, and nothing but a form of hellenistic Palestinian cynicism,"[5] or an Andre LaCocque who considers the New Testament merely one among several possible commentaries on the Hebrew Scriptures which remain the central core of faith for the Christian.[6] But many are prepared minimally to embrace the words of Fr. Raymond Brown who has written: "Too often for Christians the proclamation of the word means the proclamation of the Jesus story. Yet that story can be easily misconstrued and distorted if one does not recite the story of Israel."[7]

Clearly, the new message is starting to penetrate the formidable barriers of Christian tradition. The recognition is growing that the New Testament's perspective remains incomplete in some important areas such as human responsibility for creation when it is not taken in tandem with the Hebrew Scriptures, and thus is not fully adequate by itself as a basis of Christian faith. Such a recognition quite obviously also carries profound implications for the basic approach to Christian morality which for centuries has been predicated in significant measure on the assumption of the superiority of the New Testament ethical perspectives rooted in the interiorization of a supposedly new "law of love."

Research growing out of the contemporary Christian-Jewish encounter has begun to impact even more profoundly on New Testament interpretation. It is no exaggeration to say that, however quietly, a genuine revolution is well under way in New Testament scholarship. Stimulating this revolution is an enhanced understanding of Hebrew and Aramaic in Christian circles and a greater exposure to materials from Judaism's Second Temple period, what Christians frequently term the "intertestamental period." We are currently experiencing the rapid dissolution of the dominance over New Testament interpretation held by Rudolf Bultmann and his disciples who highlighted the Hellenistic setting of Pauline Christianity. This exegetical approach to the New Testament resulted in a distancing of Jesus from his actual ties to biblical and Second Temple Judaism. Scholars working within the Bultmannian framework tended overwhelmingly to depict Jesus in heavily "universalist" tones. Intended or not, such portrayals opened the door for the development of theological anti-Judaism, which exercised considerable influence over the centuries in shaping Christian moral thinking.

The last decade or so has witnessed a profound shift of gravity in New Testament exegesis. Leading the directional shift have been scholars such as W.D. Davies, E.P. Sanders, Clemens Thoma, Anthony J. Saldarini, Cardinal Carlo Martini of Milan, James Charlesworth, Daniel Harrington, Robin Scroggs, James D.G. Dunn and others. The list continues to grow. Although their views do not coalesce at every turn, these exegetes nonetheless share the conviction that Jesus must be restored to his fundamentally Jewish milieu if the Church is to interpret his message properly. The title of one James Charlesworth's books captures well the central thrust of this new movement, *Jesus Within Judaism*.[8] Arthur J. Droge, in a review of E.P. Sanders' volume *Jesus and Judaism,* speaks of the impact of this movement in rather blunt terms: "Like Professor Sanders, I take this to be a positive development—a sign that New Testament studies is finally emerging from its 'Bultmannian captivity.'"[9]

Significant refinements in the positions of these scholars undoubtedly will emerge as time goes on, particularly regarding specific points such as Jesus' relationship to Pharisaic Judaism and the meaning of his parables. But there is little doubt that the increasing consensus among New Testament exegetes about Jesus' basic Jewish roots is rapidly transforming the Church's overall perspective on his ministry and person.

Considerable new thinking has begun to emerge within Pauline studies as well. An increasing number of scholars are now more willing to entertain the idea that Paul never intended to separate his newly formed Christian communities from the Jewish people. He may even have been far more positive towards the continued practice of Torah among Christians than Christians have traditionally been led to believe. Surely the sharp contrasts between grace and law, between law and Christian love, are increasingly coming into question in the light of new research. Pioneering scholars in this field, such as Bishop Krister Stendahl, have now been joined by the likes of E.P. Sanders, James D.G. Dunn, Peter Tomson, Daniel Harrington, Jewish scholar Alan Segal, John White and the scholars associated with the "Paul and Jewish Response Literature" project, coordinated by Hayim G. Perelmuter and Wilhelm Wuellner. While this reevaluation of Paul is not as far along as that of Jesus' basic relationship to Judaism, it is becoming clear that any systematic or moral perspectives within Christianity rooted in the classical contrasts between "law and love" or "law and grace" supposedly based on Pauline teaching stand on a crumbling foundation.

Several years ago Robin Scroggs attempted to summarize the major themes in this "re-Judaization" of Christian biblical scholarship. While this outline would not characterize all scholars associated with the movement and some might quarrel with one or more of the particular points, it is a useful summary of the general conclusions being reached.

Scroggs says that more and more scholars identified with this new perspective are depicting the movement launched by Jesus and continued after his death as fundamentally a reform effort within Judaism, with little or no consciousness of any basic rupture with its Jewish matrix. Paul's efforts in this line of thought are regarded as primarily a Jewish mission to the Gentiles, to include them in the ongoing covenant. It was not until sometime after the Jewish war with Rome that Christians began to develop a distinctive self-identity. But even then, as the later writings of the New Testament show us, there remained some sense of a continued link to the Jewish people[10] and, as Anthony Saldarini has shown, this situation continued for quite some time in many parts of the church, but especially in the East. For Saldarini the early Jesus movement and rabbinic Judaism started as two efforts to reform existing Judaism. The rabbis succeeded eventually in transforming Jewish life and practice in Mesopotamia and the Roman Empire. The movement based on Jesus' teachings impacted primarily the Gentile world and eventually became an independent, but closely related religion. "Yet," says Saldarini, "in the east, many believers-in-Jesus retained a close association with Jewish communities and shared with them many cultural characteristics . . . Despite Christian antisemitism, positive relationships continued between Jews and Christians." For Saldarini, then, this new scholarship regarding the first two centuries of the common era demonstrates the invalidity of any paradigm of two orthodox traditions dominating two independent religions from the second century onwards. The relationship between Jews and Christians in many parts of the world continued to remain fluid and complex in many regions for several more centuries.[11]

The developments in the area of scripture studies have begun to make some impact on the various theological disciplines. But their influence has been limited at best and confined to a select group of church leaders and scholars. Vatican II made new thinking on the theology of the Christian-Jewish relationship possible when, in its document on non-Christian religions *Nostra Aetate* (chapter four), it undercut the basis for the classical Christian theology of covenantal displacement by arguing that Jews could not be blamed collectively for murdering Jesus and insisting that, however one interprets the new revelation in Christ, it must include the notion that the original covenant with the Jewish people remains intact.

Pope John Paul II has led the way of proposing a reconstituted theology of the church's relationship with the Jewish people in light of *Nostra Aetate*. In numerous addresses he has stressed the inherent bonding that remains between Christians and Jews who are linked at the most basic level of their self-identity.[12]

As for individual theologians, we see several trends emerging. One prominent direction is the strong emphasis on a single covenant in which both Jews and Christians share. Paul van Buren, Bernard Dupuy, and Marcel Dubois have tended to emphasize this approach. It has also been the prevailing perspective in the writings of John Paul II. Cardinal Carlo Martini has spoken in a somewhat similar vein, though he has chosen to return to the "schism" model first proposed in 1948 by the Belgian Benedictine Dom Oehmen and recently endorsed by James D.G. Dunn, as well, in his *The Partings of the Ways*.[13] In reinterpreting this model, Martini underscores the fact that, theologically speaking, Christians need to recognize that they are not merely in a relationship of dialogue with Jews, but one of inherent bonding which carries implications for every aspect of Christian faith-expression.[14] Martini thus joins a growing list of Christian thinkers who are insisting that the theological restatement of the Christian-Jewish relationship launched by *Nostra Aetate* and similar Protestant documents[15] has profound significance for all of Christian theology (including ethical thought), not merely for Jewish-Christian relations. It touches upon basic ecclesial identity.

A second group of contemporary Christian thinkers involved in the dialogue with Jews continues to speak of two distinctive covenantal traditions in terms of Judaism and Christianity, even though most would stress strong, ongoing ties between them as well. Franz Mussner seems to move in this direction, and it is my basic framework as well. For both Mussner and myself, Christology as developed in the latter strata of New Testament materials, especially in Pauline literature and in the gospel of John, constitutes in the end the fundamental uniqueness of the revelation through Jesus. This revelation does not invalidate the earlier revelation given to the People Israel at Sinai; nor does it in any way signify a displacement of Jews by Christians in the covenantal relationship. Rather, it involves the creation of a second, parallel covenant which retains deep roots in the past. So most theologians leaning in the direction of a double covenant model do not necessarily reject all aspects of the single covenantal approach. On the contrary, they would join the single covenant proponents in stressing a high degree of continued bonding. But they feel that Christian theological particularity, especially as it emerges from Incarnational Christology, as well as Jewish distinctiveness resulting from 2,000 years of separate existence, are better safeguarded in the double covenantal model.

A handful of contemporary Christian theologians, most prominently Rosemary Ruether and Paul Knitter,[16] tend toward what might be termed a multi-covenantal orientation. Ruether is definitely more emphatic than Knitter on this point, viewing the Christ Event as one of many possible messianic experiences. Both agree, however, that Christians and Jews need to go beyond the parameters of their special bonding in exploring covenantal relationships with other faith traditions.

The process of rethinking theologically the Christian-Jewish relationship cannot be pursued successfully in isolation from parallel developments among Jewish and Christian scholars who are reexamining traditional assumptions about the growth and reconfiguration of Judaism in the period of Jesus' ministry and the emergence of the Christian churches. The works of Jacob Neusner, Efraim Shmueli, Gabriele Boccaccini and Hayim Perelmuter, to name only four, make it increasingly difficult to posit any simplistic vertical development from Judaism to Christianity.[17] Yet so much of Christian theological argumentation (including that found in *Veritatis Splendor*) assumes such a vertical development. When Jacob Neusner, for example, posits the existence of a multiplicity of Judaisms throughout history, including during the first century of the common era, Christian scholars will have to take notice. For if Neusner is correct, it will prove much more difficult to speak about the theology of the Jewish-Christian relationship in a way that presumes a certain basic homogeneity in Judaism at the time. If this basic homogeneity is in fact missing, then we may be compelled to accept an understanding of the relationship far more modest and nuanced in its claims. And when Irving Greenberg describes rabbinic Judaism as a more advanced stage of religious consciousness than Christianity (which remains tied far more to biblical forms of Judaism)[18] or when Hayim Perelmuter speaks of Jews and Christians as two new, distinctive "sibling" groups, both parented by biblical Judaism, the nature of the conversation about Jewish-Christian bondedness is significantly affected. Their conclusions also seriously challenge traditional models of Christianity's fulfillment of Judaism.

2.
The Encyclical and Judaism: Positive Aspects

There are a number of statements within *Veritatis Splendor* that show some influence, albeit indirect, of the fundamental rethinking of the theology of the Christian-Jewish relationship that has been underway for some four decades. When one compares this document to certain classical, or even 20th-century, treatises on Catholic morality, the positive advancement becomes striking, especially on the question of the continuing validity of the Jewish covenant.

The overall tone of the encyclical towards the Jewish tradition is quite positive, with occasional efforts made to counteract previously misleading Christian claims which distorted Judaism. In paragraph n. 14, for example, the Pope stresses that love of neighbor is an equally central value (as an indispensable component of authentic love of God) for both testaments, not merely something unique to the moral teachings of Jesus. This same point is also found in paragraph (n. 10) where the teaching of Deuteronomy is underlined. In paragraph (n. 15) we find the encyclical highlighting Mt 5:17, where Matthew has Jesus insisting that he has not come to abolish the law and the prophets. John Paul terms this passage the "Magna Carta" of Gospel morality, paraphrasing St. Augustine. And emphasis is given in paragraph (n. 16) to the profound connection between the original ten commandments found in the first testament and the gospel beatitudes. The latter are not to be viewed as an inherently superior form of morality. An especially strong affirmation of the continuing centrality of the original commandments for contemporary Catholic morality appears in paragraph (n. 97). Here the stress is on individual human dignity, with John Paul offering the following reflection:

> By protecting the inviolable personal dignity of every human being they (i.e., the commandments) help to preserve the human social fabric and its proper and fruitful development. The commands of the second table of the decalogue in particular—those which Jesus quoted to the young man of the Gospel (cf. Mt. 19:19)—constitute the indispensable rules of all social life.

Finally, in paragraph (n. 91) followers of the original law of God who suffered martyrdom (e.g., Susanna and John the Baptist) are singled out as authentic martyrs for the faith.

From the above examples it is obvious John Paul, while never making direct reference to any of his statements on Jews and Judaism, nor *Nostra Aetate* or its subsequent documents of implementation, is conscious of the need to incorporate the revised understanding of the Church's continuing linkage to the Jewish people into the core of Catholic morality. But the questions remain: Has the effort been successful, and does it leave Jewish covenantal tradition with a real, continuing purpose that has significance apart from the Christ Event? On this issue the overall assessment of the encyclical cannot be entirely positive. In many cases the document seems ambiguous, if not contradictory. It is to this dimension of *Veritatis Splendor* that we now turn.

3.
The Encyclical and Judaism: Negative Features

There are several paragraphs in which the encyclical regrettably does fall back into classical stereotypes of the Jewish tradition in contradiction to explicit recommendations in previous Vatican documents. The most glaring example of this are two references to the Pharisees (n. 77, 104), where this Jewish group is portrayed in the wholly prejudicial manner that has been commonplace in Christian preaching and teaching for centuries. And this occurs despite the explicit warning in the 1985 Vatican *Notes* that such mis-representations of Pharisaism should be studiously avoided. In fact, the 1985 document speaks of Jesus as standing closer to Pharisaism in his approach to basic religious values and practice than to any other Jewish group of the time.[19] Yet in the encyclical Jesus is described as being in "clear disagreement with the scribes and Pharisees, who prescribed in great detail certain outward practices without paying attention to the heart" (n. 77). And in paragraph #104 "the Pharisee" spoken of in Lk 18: 9-14 (parable of the Pharisee and the tax collector) is said to represent "a 'self-satisfied' conscience, under the illusion that it is able to observe the law without the help of grace and convinced that it does not need mercy."

This distorted picture of Pharisaism in *Veritatis Splendor* bears an impact on its presentation of Christian morality that may not be obvious at first glance. For the continuation of the classic stereotyping of Pharisaism inhibits Christians from exploring the profound constructive changes that this reform, perhaps even revolutionary (Ellis Rivkin's term), movement introduced into Jewish religious consciousness at the time of Jesus. Many of these changes directly affected the shape of Jewish ethics at the time, including the willingness to reinterpret the written Torah tradition, to increase focus on individual human dignity and equality and a growing desire to "internalize" the practice and appropriation of Torah.[20] Understanding these developments in Pharisaic Judaism are critical for grasping the fundamental inadequacy of the classical Christian paradigm which has Jesus preaching all these values as a supposedly new and unique moral teaching, a paradigm which unregrettably dominates a great part of this encyclical's basic outlook. More and more, scholarship is showing us that both Jesus' moral vision, as well as his direct ethical activity (e.g., invasion of the Temple precincts), were profoundly influenced by Pharisaism. He was a "son" of the movement, whatever disagreements he had with particular Pharisaic groups or individuals.

The failure to appreciate genuine, profound development in the moral perspective of Judaism during the Second Temple period, largely the result of Pharisaic creativity in interpreting the classical Torah tradition, results in repeated contrasts in the encyclical between the teachings of Jesus and Paul and those of their Jewish contemporaries. In the end the contrasts combine to produce a pervasive theme—through Jesus the law of God has been internalized far more than was ever possible within the Jewish perspective. This overarching theme does bring into question the ultimate significance of the occasional affirmations of the centrality of love in both testaments and the continuity of the Jewish covenant referred to above. That is why terms such as "ambiguous" and even "contradictory" come to mind when one reads this encyclical within the context of the new scholarship on Judaism at the time of Jesus and the emergence of the Christian movement. An overall assessment of *Veritatis Splendor* regrettably leads to the conclusion that at best the Jewish moral tradition served as an important seedbed for the development of a fully honed moral vision revealed by Jesus. Once Jesus has come, there is a real question as to the role remaining for Jewish ethics. The implication one receives is that it is definitely secondary, and inferior, by itself when compared to the Christian vision.

Any number of specific passages make the above point abundantly clear. Paragraph (n. 12) calls the Decalogue "a promise and a sign of the new covenant, in which the law would be written in a new and definitive way upon the human heart (cf. Jer. 31: 31-34), replacing the law of sin which had disfigured that heart (cf. Jer. 17: 1). . . ." Pope John Paul then goes on in the same paragraph to argue that the commandments only promised land here on earth, while in Christ's vision their observance was presented as leading to the Kingdom of heaven. He quotes St. Ambrose, who called the Mosaic law merely an "image of the truth" (n. 15). He also turns to St. John Chrysostom, who wrote that the new law given to the apostles at Pentecost was not engraved merely on tablets of stone, but given them in their very hearts through the Holy Spirit (n. 24). And in what is perhaps the boldest statement in this regard, the encyclical asserts that "Jesus brings God's commandments to fulfillment, particularly the commandment of love of neighbor, by interiorizing their demands and by bringing out their fullest meaning" (n. 15). Finally, in treating the writings of St. Paul on the law, the encyclical picks up the classical theme of contrasting the old law as a pedagogic devise which unmasks human sinfulness and powerlessness and grace with "the new law," which provides life in the Spirit. The text then continues that "Only in this new life is it possible to carry out God's commandments" (n. 23). Is this statement meant to imply that Jews, who seemingly lack this new life, cannot carry out the commandments today? If so, how does this relate to Catholicism's Vatican II-era assertions that the Jewish covenant remains in place (and presumably salvific) after the Christ Event? This is but another example of the ambiguity of this document.

It is not possible in this brief essay to present an indepth account of the varied ways in which recent scholarship has recast the fundamental Jewish-Christian relational paradigm, nor the shades of current opinion on Paul and the law. A brief overview was provided at the outset. Suffice it to say here that the encyclical will be found wanting in both areas. Its failure to take into account this scholarship, both Jewish and Christian, and to rely instead on patristic and classical interpretations of the relationship severely cripples its basic value, not merely in terms of the continuing conversation between Catholics and Jews but even more so in terms of forging an authentic Catholic moral self-identity for our time.

In approaching this question, Catholicism will need to begin by taking very seriously a cardinal statement of the 1974 Vatican Guidelines on Catholic-Jewish Relations—namely, that we in the church must come to un-

derstand Jews as they truly present themselves.[21] The overwhelming majority of Jewish scholars would not see in the encyclical's presentation of the
first testament an authentic interpretation of what that testament has meant
for them. The law of God was never predicated merely on external observance (as the encyclical itself occasionally acknowledges in its better moments), but on God's initial love for the covenanted people. Internalization
of Torah was held out as an ideal, even if not always faithfully observed.
And such internalization was especially stressed by Pharisaic Judaism. Torah observance was never viewed as an end in itself. Rather it was seen as
an integral part of preserving the basic covenantal relationship between God
and the Jewish people, a relationship that would one day culminate in the
promised land. What Jesus was teaching, what became evident through his
person, what Paul eventually preached in Jesus' name was that it was now
possible to participate in the covenant apart from Torah observance. This is
not to say that works were unimportant for Paul, only that the specific practices prescribed by Jewish law were no longer mandatory, even though they
may well remain redemptive for Jews. E.P. Sanders puts it well when he
says that:

> . . . it is easy enough to read Paul's *christological objections* to Judaism
> as if they were directed against Jewish *self-righteousness*. Thus the
> correct exegetical perception that Paul *opposed Judaism* and that he *ar-
> gued christologically* becomes—without argument or exegetical demon-
> stration, but on the ground of basic theological assumptions—an asser-
> tion that he opposed *the self-righteousness which is typical of Judaism.*

This step has doubtless been facilitated by more than a century of
reading Jewish literature as evidencing self-righteousness. But the supposed
objection to Jewish self-righteousness is as absent from Paul's letter as self-
righteousness itself is from Jewish literature.[22]

Gabriele Boccaccini's writings reveal yet another basic weakness in
the fundamental paradigm regarding Christ and the law adopted in the encyclical. He insists that separating early Christianity from other Jewish
groups of the time is far more the result of "confessional bias" than sound
scholarship. "The internal dialectic of the Judaism of that age," he says,

> . . . will continue to be deprived of an important element until we rec-
> ognize that historically Christianity is only one of the many Judaisms
> then active—nothing more and nothing else—and is as unique as each
> of its contemporary fellows.[23]

Another limiting aspect of *Veritatis Splendor*'s operative paradigm is
the impression it conveys that all significant aspects of moral understanding
have been deepened and enhanced through Christ. In fact this is not the
case, and even official Catholic documents have indirectly acknowledged
this by turning to the Hebrew Scriptures for their principal biblical texts on
some ethical questions. The clearest contemporary example of this is eco-
ethics, where the Catholic position on preserving creation and assuming the

appropriate human responsibility for sustaining life at every level has been argued morally by drawing heavily upon central texts from Genesis, not merely as prelude to a New Testament perspective, but in fact in lieu of a specifically stated New Testament position. One finds such argumentation, for example, in both John Paul II's *Laborem Exercens* as well as in the opening section of the U.S. Bishops' *Pastoral Letter on Economic Justice.* Yet the encyclical never makes mention of such a central use of the first testament.

Certainly we are far from a consensus regarding a replacement paradigm for the one that dominates this encyclical. If there is consensus in the midst of continuing scholarly ambiguity, it is about the basic inadequacy of this classical "fulfillment" model. Some scholars, in fact, see little unique moral teaching in the preaching of Jesus and Paul. Most do, however, see some fundamental differences, and I include myself among them. It is impossible here to lay out the details of the contrasts I would posit. I have presented that in other writings.[24] For me, the key to understanding the differences is to be found in the notion of the Incarnation.

4.
The Encyclical and Judaism: What's Not Said

In this concluding part of my analysis I would like to highlight briefly some aspects of the Church's dialogue with Judaism and the Jewish people affecting moral vision that are ignored in the encyclical. A number of these flow from reflection on the Holocaust, which has become a central theological question for many Jews and for some Christians.

David Tracy has raised two issues in light of the Holocaust which bear directly on the foundations of moral theology. The first is his emphasis that the Holocaust has brought us back to the recognition that the ultimate theological issue is the understanding of God, rather than Christology. Yet the current encyclical fails to address this most basic of questions in any meaningful fashion.[25] And next to the God problem, the most decisive challenge presented by the Holocaust, according to Tracy, comes in the area of theological methodology. After the Holocaust, says Tracy, neither a purely metaphysical approach to theology nor a mere emphasis on historical consciousness as abstract concept will suffice. Concrete historical events must now assume central significance for the whole of theology (including, by implication, the realm of moral theology).[26] Such an awareness is almost totally foreign to the current encyclical, which relies fundamentally on abstract philosophical methodology.

Elisabeth Schüssler-Fiorenza also takes the "return to history" theme as a central implication of the Holocaust for subsequent theology. We cannot speak of the suffering of the victims of the Holocaust as a "theological metaphor" for all human suffering. Instead, that suffering "must be named in its political particularity. The ideological heart of Nazi-fascism was racism, its ideological catchword was *Untermensch*, the-less-than-human, the subhuman being."[27] Nazism for her represents an extreme example of the Western capitalistic form of patriarchy, with origins in Aristotelian philosophy and subsequent mediation through Christian theology. The same ancient philosophical system, imported into Christian theology by Thomas Aquinas and others, that first subjugated women as people with "subhuman" nature, combined with religiously rooted bigotry and a new bio-theology to produce the Nazi cataclysm in Europe.

Schüssler-Fiorenza insists that overcoming biblical and theological anti-Judaism constitutes the first step in the complicated, rather wrenching process of cleansing Western society of its patriarchal basis. In an essay co-authored with David Tracy, she writes:

> Christian biblical theology must recognize that its articulation of anti-Judaism in the New Testament goes hand in hand with its gradual adaptation to Greco-Roman patriarchal society. Christian as well as Jewish theology must cease to proclaim a God made in the image and likeness of Man. It can do so only when it mourns the "loss" of women's contributions in the past and present and rejects our theological "dehumanization." Moreover, white Christian and Jewish theology must promote the full humanity of all non-Western peoples and, at the same time, struggle against racism wherever it is at work. In short the memory of the Holocaust must "interrupt" all forms of Western patriarchal theology if the legacies of the dead are not to be in vain.[28]

The continuing theological anti-Judaism which remains a regrettable feature of *Veritatis Splendor*, viewed through the lens of Schüssler-Fiorenza's analysis, takes on an additional disturbing dimension. For, if she is even partially correct, such theology continues to undergird a social framework that is inherently unjust and whose impact extends far beyond that of the Jewish community. Even if one does not fully agree with Schüssler-Fiorenza's analysis, the basic questions she raises deserve discussion, not silence. For they are profoundly related to the basic methodological change in all of theology, including ethics, for which David Tracy and others (including Johannes Metz) have called.

Yet another theologian who sees in the Holocaust a summons for Christian theology generally to return to the concrete historical matrix of its original Jewish roots is Rebecca Chopp. In her perspective the human person in history—especially the victimized and suffering human person—becomes the focal point for theological discourse. She points in particular to a profound connection she detects between Holocaust literature and liberation theology. This relationship she sees as unique among Western religious writings. Both Holocaust literature and liberation theology, as she interprets them, both agree on one foundational assumption:

> . . . the challenge to contemporary thought and action is the challenge
> of massive suffering. Christianity and Christian theology can no longer
> be content with addressing suffering on an individual level from Chris-
> tian texts, symbols, and traditions but must criticize, interrupt and trans-
> form both action and reflection in light of past, prevailing and potential
> events of massive suffering. Liberation theology and Holocaust litera-
> ture interrupt and disrupt Christianity and Christian theology with the
> question and the quest, "Who is the human subject that suffers his-
> tory?"[29]

Chopp goes on to add that both liberation theology and Holocaust literature force us to understand history not merely in terms of abstract notion
of evolution or process, but primarily in terms of the suffering realities of
that history caused by various forms of human exploitation. The history
that now must serve as the basis of theological reflection is not abstract
history, but the history of human victims. The voices and the memory of
the tortured, the forgotten, and the dead must become primary resources for
Christian anthropology. Obviously such an "anthropological reorientation"
will have significant implications for the shape of Christian morality.

Veritatis Splendor has some vague sense of this anthropological turn.
Following in the tradition of John Paul II's documents and speeches, considerable emphasis is placed on the importance of basic human dignity and
human rights. But the discussion becomes so abstract that the power of the
message tends to get lost. But on this point at least there seems to be some
basis for a productive interchange between the perspective of the encyclical
and that of Chopp and other liberation theologians.

But there is another aspect to Chopp's analysis, at least an implied
one, that does not lend itself to such a co-relation. Quite to the contrary in
fact. While Chopp does not herself develop this position, one could seemingly take her viewpoint in the same direction as Schüssler-Fiorenza and
Tracy take the feminist argument—that biblical anti-Judaism, with its inevitable dehumanization of concrete Jewish persons, paved the way for Western
colonialism to which liberation theology has been a prophetic response.
Seen in this light, *Veritatis Splendor* is what church historian Jaroslav Pelikan termed, in a May 1986 address to the 9th National Workshop on Christian-Jewish Relations in Baltimore, the Church's traditional "longing to be
saved from history." Expressing this same idea several years earlier, the
Austrian Catholic philosopher Friedrich Heer insisted that the Church's failure to challenge the Nazis in any effective way was symptomatic of how the
Church had dealt with other manifestations of evil, in particular war and the
possibility of a nuclear holocaust. For him, the main problem sprang from
the Church's withdrawal from history:

> The withdrawal of the church from history has created that specifically
> Christian and ecclesiastical irresponsibility towards the world, the Jew,
> the other person, even the Christian himself, considered as a human

being—which was the ultimate cause of past catastrophes and may be the cause of a final catastrophe in the future.[30]

As Heer sees it, antisemitism is the product of a persistent and deep-seated cancer within Christianity that began to grow in its classical period. The disregard on the part of Christians for the well-being of the Jewish people through history, especially between 1918 and 1945, can only be understood as part of a general disregard for humanity and the world. He attributes this attitude to the dominance in Christian theological thinking of what he calls the "Augustinian principle." This attitude views the world under the aspect of sin, and ultimately leads to a sense of fatalism and despair about the world. Heer is convinced that this fatalistic tendency constitutes as much a danger today as it did during the incubation of Nazism. The only cure for this centuries-long pattern in Christianity, according to Heer, is to relinquish the "Augustinian principle" and replace it with a return to Christ's own piety rooted in the Hebrew Bible, and to even older roots— namely, the original faith of Israel in which people felt themselves to be both God's creatures and responsible partners in the development of the earth. If Heer's analysis is correct, the encyclical's inadequate understanding of the Jewish Torah tradition deprives Christianity of a vital source for contemporary Catholic ethics.

Finally, in terms of the implications of a study of the Holocaust for contemporary Catholic morality, I would simply mention three issues which I have discussed far more thoroughly in other writings. The first is the importance of what Reinhold Niebuhr called the vitalistic side of the human being. For too long a time moral approaches have been strongly rationalistic in their fundamental orientation. *Veritatis Splendor* certainly fits that mold. But Niebuhr reminded us that both basic faculties of humankind—the rational and the vitalistic—were crucial for an effective ethic. Both were capable of inducing sinfulness as well as great virtue. The failure of many during the Nazi era lay in their inability to recognize the power of the vitalistic which the Nazis mastered through their public, liturgical-like rallies.

Recovery of Christianity's Jewish roots becomes important here, for in Judaism ethics was never isolated from other facets of Jewish life, especially worship. The central organizing reality was the covenant, not Torah by itself. Torah aimed to preserve the covenantal bonds which would be jeopardized if creational bonds were severed through sinfulness.[31] The encyclical's approach to Torah separated from the covenant in the end distorts its overall significance.

Secondly, there is the question of ecclesiology. When we examine the response of the Church during the Holocaust, we see that a prevailing "diplomatic model" severely impeded a strong moral stance on many occasions. Today, Christian scholars on the Holocaust, such as Johannes Metz and James Moore, argue that a "witness" ethic is required from the Church in the face of continued examples of mass human brutality that sometimes verge on the genocidal. Yet the encyclical gives scant attention to such a central issue for any authentic Catholic moral paradigm.

Lastly, several scholars have introduced the connection between the Holocaust and Hiroshima. Darrell Fasching and Robert Jay Lifton[32] are two prominent names in this regard. Their contributions serve as strong reminders that we live in a new era in which human power is now capable of unprecedented destruction to the whole of creation. All ethics must take this reality as a basic part of its starting point. *Veritatis Splendor* does not.

Overall, we can say that *Veritatis Splendor* surely is to be commended for challenging us on some fundamental perspectives. Without doubt many Christians and Jews would concur with its basic contentions that there is an urgent need to strengthen ethical foundations, especially in terms of public morality, and that freedom cannot be interpreted merely as "freedom from." Likewise substantial agreement would exist that the ten commandments provide a sound framework in this regard. Contemporary ethicists such as Arthur J. Dyck[33] have begun to reemphasize the centrality of duty, not merely rights, in ethics, and the importance of recognizing each person's moral obligations to community. The Torah tradition, I might add, has always been centered within a community framework rooted in the covenant, something this encyclical fails to notice. While some Jewish writers on ethics, such as David Novak, might have greater sympathy than most for the basic argumentation of the encyclical, even Jews sympathetic to the basic ethical values of *Veritatis Splendor* would find it too detached from the actual context of the world and the realities facing the contemporary faith community. And in continuing to present an inadequate, at times even distorted, image of Jewish morality it deprives Catholic ethics today of a valuable resource as this essay has tried to show.

In one sense this encyclical is not that much different from most Catholic documents and writings of individual theologians. The perspectives of the Jewish-Christian dialogue, emerging especially from Scriptural studies, have still not exercised a broad impact. But it is unfortunate that John Paul II, who otherwise has shown exceptional leadership on the Jewish question in word[34] and in action (e.g., historic visit to Rome synagogue, settlement of Auschwitz Convent controversy, recognition of the State of Israel), has not found it possible to extend this leadership to the question of Judaism's influence on Catholic morality. Hopefully those who advise him on ethical issues will soon take seriously his groundbreaking contributions to the dialogue itself.

Notes

1. Cf. Helga Croner, (ed.), *More Stepping Stones to Jewish-Christian Relations: An Unabridged Collection of Christian Documents*, 1975-1983 (Mahwah, NJ: Paulist Press, 1985), p. 226.

2. Cardinal Carlo Maria Martini, "Christianity and Judaism—A Historical and Theological Overview," in James H. Charlesworth (ed.), *Jews and Christians: Exploring the Past, Present, and Future* (New York: Crossroad, 1990), p. 19.

3. Helga Croner (ed.), *Stepping Stones to Further Jewish-Christian Relations: An Unabridged Collection of Christian Documents* (London/New York: Stimulus Books, 1977; Helga Croner (ed.), *More Stepping Stones*; Eugene J. Fisher and Leon Klenicki (eds.), *John Paul II On Jews and Judaism, 1979-1986*. Washington, DC: NCCB Committee for Ecumenical and Interreligious Affairs and Anti-Defamation League (USCC Publications), 1987. For a Collection of World Council of Churches' and Protestant regional and denominational documents, cf. Allan Brockway, Paul van Buren, Rolf Rendtorff, and Simon Schoon (eds.), *The Theology of the Churches and the Jewish People: Statements by the World Council and its Member Churches* (Geneva: WCC Publications), 1988.

4. Cf. Roger Brooks and John J. Collins, (eds.), *Hebrew Bible or Old Testament? Studying the Bible in Judaism and Christianity* (Notre Dame: University of Notre Dame Press, 1990); Jon D. Levenson, "Why Jews are Not Interested in Biblical Theology," in Jacob Neusner, Baruch A. Levine, and Ernest S. Frerichs (eds.), *Judaic Perspectives on Ancient Israel* (Philadelphia: Fortress Press, 1987), pp. 281-307; and the exchange between Eugene J. Fisher and Lawrence Boadt in *New Theology Review*, 4:4 (Nov. 1991), pp. 92-96 and 5:3 (August 1992) pp. 104-106.

5. James A. Sanders, "Rejoicing in the Gifts, " *Explorations* 3:1 (1986), p. 4.

6. Andre LaCocque. *But As For Me: The Question of Election in the Life of God's People Today* (Atlanta: John Knox, 1979).

7. Raymond Brown, S.S. *Biblical Exegesis and Church Doctrine* (New York: Paulist, 1985), p. 138.

8. James Charlesworth, *Jesus Within Judaism* (New York: Doubleday, 1988).

9. Arthur J. Droge, "The Facts About Jesus: Some Thoughts on E.P. Sanders' *Jesus and Judaism*," *Criterion* 26:1 (1987), p. 15.

10. Robin Scroggs, "The Judaizing of the New Testament," *Chicago Theological Seminary Register*, 76:1 (1986), pp. 42-43.

11. Anthony J. Saldarini, "Jews and Christians in the First Two Centuries: The Changing Paradigm," *Shofar*, 10:2 (Winter 1992), p. 34.

12. Cf. Eugene J. Fisher and Leon Klenicki (eds.), *John Paul II on Jews and Judaism*.

13. James D.G. Dunn, *The Partings of the Ways: Between Christianity and Judaism and Their Significance for the Character of Christianity* (London and Philadelphia: SMM Press and Trinity Press International, 1991), p. 269.

14. Cf. Cardinal Carlo Maria Martini, "The Relation of the Church to the Jewish People," *From the Martin Buber House*, 6 (1984), p. 9.

15. Cf. note n. 3.

16. Cf. Rosemary Ruether, *Faith and Fratricide: The Theological Roots of Anti-Semitism* (New York: Seabury, 1974) and Paul Knitter, *No Other Name?* (Maryknoll, NY: Orbis, 1985).

17. Cf. Jacob Neusner, *Death and Birth of Judaism: The Impact of Christianity, Secularism, and the Holocaust on Jewish Faith* (New York: Basic Books, 1987); Efraim Shmueli, *Seven Jewish Cultures: A Reinterpretation of Jewish History and Thought* (Cambridge: Cambridge University Press, 1990); Gabriele Boccaccini, *Middle Judaism: Jewish Thought 300 B.C.E. to 200 C.E.* (Minneapolis: Fortress, 1991); and Hayim G. Perelmuter.

18. Cf. Irving Greenberg, "The Third Great Cycle of Jewish History," in *Perspectives*, New York: CLAL (The National Jewish Center for Learning and Leadership), 1-7. *Siblings: Rabbinic Judaism and Early Christianity At Their Beginnings* (New York/Ramsey: Paulist Press, 1989).

19. Cf. Helga Croner (ed.), *More Stepping Stones*, pp. 227-228.

20. Cf. Ellis Rivkin, *A Hidden Revolution: The Pharisees' Search for the Kingdom Within* (Nashville: Abingdon, 1978).

21. Cf. Helga Croner (ed.), *Stepping Stones*, p. 11.

22. E.P. Sanders, *Paul, The Law, And The Jewish People* (Philadelphia: Fortress, 1983), p. 156.

23. Gabriele Boccaccini, *Middle Judaism*, p. 24.

24. Cf. my volume *Christ in the Light of the Christian-Jewish Dialogue* (New York/Ramsey: Paulist Press, 1982), pp. 108-147.

25. David Tracy, "Religious Values after the Holocaust: A Catholic View," in Abraham J. Peck (ed.), *Jews and Christians after the Holocaust* (Philadelphia: Fortress Press, 1982), p. 101.

26. David Tracy, "The Interpretation of Theological Texts after the Holocaust," unpublished lecture, International Conference on the Holocaust, Indiana University, Bloomington, Indiana, Fall 1982.

27. Elisabeth Schüssler-Fiorenza and David Tracy, "The Holocaust as Interruption and the Christian Return into History," in Elisabeth Schüssler-Fiorenza and David Tracy (eds.), *The Holocaust As Interruption*, Concilium 175 Edinburgh: T. & T. Clark, 1984, p. 36.

28. Schüssler-Fiorenza, "The Holocaust as Interruption," p. 36.

29. Rebecca Chopp, "The Interruption of the Forgotten," in Schüssler-Fiorenza And Tracy (eds.), *The Holocaust As Interruption*, p. 20.

30. Friedrich Heer, *God's First Love* (New York: Weybright & Talley), p. 406.

31. Cf. my essay "Christian Ethics and the Holocaust: A Dialogue with Post-Auschwitz Judaism," *Theological Studies*, 49: 4 (December 1988), pp. 649-669.

32. Cf. Darrell J. Fasching, *The Ethical Challenge of Auschwitz and Hiroshima: Apocalypse or Utopia?* (Albany, NY: State University of New York Press, 1993); and Robert J. Lifton and Eric Markusen, *The Genocidal Mentality: Nazi Holocaust and Nuclear Threat* (New York: Basic Books).

33. Arthur J. Dyck, *Rethinking Rights and Responsibilities: The Moral Bonds of Community* (Long Island City NY: Pilgrim Press, 1994).

34. Cf. Fisher and Klenicki (eds.), *John Paul II On Jews and Judaism*.

13

Natural Law and Personalism in *Veritatis Splendor*

Janet E. Smith

For centuries natural law was the backbone of the Church's teaching on moral issues, but in the mid-part of this century it began to be mixed with natural rights language. Then with the pontificate of Pope John Paul II, a new language, the language of personalism, already in evidence in the documents of Vatican II, particularly *Gaudium et Spes*, dominated magisterial documents, to the point where natural law language nearly disappeared. Now, in the *Universal Catechism* and in *Veritatis Splendor* we encounter a knitting together of the language and concepts of personalism, natural law and natural rights.

Those trained in natural law and in Thomism (and others!) have been a bit befuddled by "personalism" and "phenomenology," not knowing exactly what they mean and what their principles are. This essay will attempt to offer a brief explanation of personalism while contrasting it with natural law. It will also attempt to show how personalism and natural law are compatible and skillfully integrated into *Veritatis Splendor* (a consideration of the place of natural rights language is beyond the scope of this essay).

Although for most of the English-speaking world, *Veritatis Splendor* was available prior to the *Universal Catechism*, the issuance of *Veritatis Splendor* was delayed so that it would follow and be seen as building upon the Catechism. Thus, it seems appropriate to consult the Catechism to contextualize some of the elements of *Veritatis Splendor*. The first part of this essay will highlight the personalistic approach of the moral section of the *Universal Catechism* by comparing it with the *Roman Catechism* of the 16th century, a catechism entirely steeped in the natural law tradition. The second part of this essay will draw upon John Paul II's own explanations of how his phenomenological personalism draws upon but supplements the Thomistic metaphysical understanding of the person. He makes it clear that his anthropology and ethics are in no way incompatible with Thomism and indeed depend upon Thomistic metaphysics. The third and final portion of the essay will draw together the thematic concepts that distinguish a natural law approach to ethics and a personalist approach to ethics and show how they are integrated into *Veritatis Splendor*.

1.
A Comparison of the *Roman Catechism* with the *Universal Catechism*

A useful way to illustrate the difference between a natural law approach to ethics and a personalist approach to ethics is to compare the treatment of morality in the *Universal Catechism* with its treatment in the *Roman Catechism*. Such a comparison illuminates certain shifts of emphasis that the Church has made over the centuries, especially as a result of the second Vatican Council.

Cosmology vs. Christology

The new catechism expresses the Christological and personalistic emphasis of the Council, rather than the cosmological and natural law emphasis of the past. To oversimplify matters, one could say that the Church has shifted from an emphasis on God the father as Lawgiver who has written his will into the laws of nature to an emphasis on Christ as our model of perfection and human dignity as the grounding of morality. The new catechism does not reject or abandon a view of the cosmos as ordered by God or of natural law as a guide to morality but it incorporates them in a secondary way in its presentation of morality. Furthermore, the dignity of the human person is seen as rooted not so much in his status as a rational creature whose mind is able to grasp reality but in his status as a free and self-determining creature who must shape himself in accord with the truth. (I shall develop these observations below.)

Ten Commandments vs. Dignity of the Human Person

The shift in emphasis from natural law to a Christological and personalist emphasis is immediately apparent upon comparing the old and new catechisms. For instance, whereas the *Roman Catechism* began its moral section with the ten commandments, the *Universal Catechism* calls upon the Christian to "recognize your dignity" (1691) and calls him to a life in Christ. Whereas the *Roman Catechism* focused almost exclusively on the commandments and the law, the *Universal Catechism* sketches a Christian anthropology, begins with the beatitudes, and touches upon such topics as freedom and the conscience, and includes a long section on man as a member of a community. Again, these new emphases and starting points are not to be taken as a rejection of the old. The natural law themes of the moral act, virtue, sin and grace and, of course, the natural law itself are also covered in the new catechism but they are imbued with a personalist cast—that is, with a focus on man's dignity as manifested in his power to determine himself freely in accord with the truth. Whereas the *Roman Catechism* stressed God as the author of nature and the author of all moral laws, the *Universal Catechism* stresses that all moral law is in accord with the dignity of the human person. These are emphases that began to emerge in the documents of Vatican II and come to a fuller flower in the *Universal Catechism*.

The moral section of the *Universal Catechism* begins with this passage:

> The dignity of the human person is rooted in his creation in the image and likeness of God (*article 1*); it is fulfilled in his vocation to divine beatitude (*article 2*). It is essential to a human being freely to direct himself to this fulfillment (*article 3*). By his deliberate actions (*article 4*), the human person does, or does not, conform to the good promised by God and attested by moral conscience (*article 5*). Human beings make their own contribution to their interior growth; they make their whole sentient and spiritual lives into means of this growth (*article 6*). With the help of grace they grow in virtue (*article 7*), avoid sin, and if they sin they entrust themselves as did the prodigal son to the mercy of our Father in heaven (*article 8*). In this way they attain to the perfection of charity (1700).

In this passage we can see several of the main concepts that inform a personalist approach to ethics: man as made in the image and likeness of God, man as determining himself by his deliberate and free actions, a concern with the interior life, the need of conforming our actions to the good that is made known to us by our conscience, and the goal being attainment of perfect charity. These themes play a major role in both the *Universal Catechism* and in *Veritatis Splendor*. These concepts, of course, are also central to natural law ethics, but it is often the emphasis that is placed upon identical themes that distinguish the two approaches.

2.
John Paul II's Explanation of His Own Views

John Paul II, when he was the philosopher Karol Wojtyla, wrote several essays explaining the compatibility between personalism and natural law and the differences between them. In one essay "The Human Person and Natural Law," he asserts that any incompatibility between them is illusory and that any notion that they are incompatible stems from a faulty view either of what nature is or of what the person is.

Nature as Mechanistic vs. Nature as Rationality

The erroneous view of nature that Wojtyla combats is that held by phenomenalists and phenomenologists (and, may I add, of many nonphenomenological critics of natural law), that nature has nothing to do with rationality and freedom; that it simply refers to the rather mechanistic laws of nature, that is, to the natural impulses and responses of man's somatic and psychic nature; to what "happens in or to man" rather than what he himself does. Whereas nature seems deterministic or mechanistic to some extent, the person is free and thus it would seem that the person should be above nature and perhaps even in conflict with nature. (This is similar to the charge of biologism that is addressed in *Veritatis Splendor*). Wojtyla notes that this view of nature is not that held by Aquinas. Rather he states that Thomistic philosophy speaks of "nature" in the metaphysical sense: "which is more or less equivalent to the essence of a thing taken as the basis of all the actualization of the thing." Wojtyla notes that the phrase "all the actualization of the thing" is important, for he ever has his focus on man's self-actualization by his free and deliberate choices. Wojtyla does grant that on the somatic and psychic level, man is dominated by nature as something "happening" to him and exercises little creative control over these happenings. But he also draws upon the Thomistic distinction of the *actus humanus* (human action) and the *actus hominis* (act of a man): the former being acts that engage the rational and free powers of the human person; the latter being such acts as breathing. Natural law pertains not to acts of man but to human action.

Wojtyla insists that Aquinas' view of natural law rests upon his understanding of the person as "an individual substance of a rational nature." He notes that Aquinas defines law as "an ordinance of reason for the common good, promulgated by one who has care of the community" and that Aquinas defines natural law as "the participation of the eternal law in a rational creature." From this he extrapolates that man's rational nature, which defines his personhood, intimately links man with the "ordinance of reason" that defines natural law. He contrasts Aquinas' view of reason with that of Kant, who would have subjective reason "impose its own categories on reality." (Wojtyla's interest in subjectivity is not the same as Kant's subjectivism). Aquinas' reason has a "completely different orientation and attitude: that attitude of reason discerning, grasping, defining, and affirming, in relation to an order that is objective and prior to human reason itself." This objective order, this ordinance of reason, is no other than the eternal law; thus man through natural law, through his rational nature, participates in God's reason. With a proper understanding of nature, there should be no conflict between natural law and personalism. The person is not confined by natural law but indeed freely participates in God's governance; whatever subordination there is is to God. It is man's nature to be free and in that sense to transcend "nature"; he is not determined by any "natural law" to do the good; he may freely choose to do the good or not to do it.

The Person as Consciousness vs. the Person as Rational and Free

The definition of person that conflicts with natural law is the definition that elevates man's freedom unduly; it sees man as "some sort of pure consciousness" that makes the human being "a kind of absolute affirmed on the intellectual plane," subordinate to nothing. This definition of the person leads to the erroneous view of freedom that is rejected in *Veritatis Splendor*; this person is not subject to the "ordinances of reason" that point the way to objective, universal truths, but is free to form his own reality.

From this essay, we can discern what Wojtyla's understanding of the natural law is: it is the understanding that man's reason enables him to discover the "ordinances of reason" that govern the universe and is able to live in accord with it. Nature here does not have the mechanistic, determinative sense given to it by some modern philosophers. He also makes clear that his notion of person as a rational, self-determining creature does not entail that man's consciousness, and the subjective state is superior to objective truth; this notion is elaborated upon in other essays.

In the essay, "Thomistic Personalism," Wojtyla situates his own understanding of person *vis-à-vis* Aquinas and *vis-à-vis* the understanding of personalism devised by moderns such as Descartes and Kant. He accepts Aquinas' definition of the person, but integrates this definition into his ethics in a way significantly different from Aquinas. He notes that Aquinas develops his notion of the person largely in the theological context of an analysis of the Trinity and the Incarnation; as he notes, Aquinas' use of the term "person" is "all but absent from his treatise on the human being." In a theological context, the person is spoken of as being *perfectissimum ens*, the most perfect being, because it is a rational and free being. Despite its theological context, the definition of person used by Aquinas, taken from Boethius, is a philosophical one; it is that stated above, the person is an individual substance of a rational nature. Wojtyla restates the definition: "The person . . . is always a rational and free concrete being, capable of all those activities that reason and freedom alone make possible." Wojtyla notes that whereas Aquinas makes much use of the term "person" in his theological treatises, in his treatise on the human being, he adopts a hylomorphic view that sees man as a composite of form and matter. This definition does not, of course, conflict with the definition of man as a person, for man's form is a spiritual soul which is characterized by its rationality and freedom.

Wojtyla compares Aquinas' definition with that of Descartes, a definition which, like that of Kant mentioned above, tends to identify the person with consciousness and sees the body as a kind of mechanistic adjunct to the person. This view elevates freedom to a level of almost total independence. He observes that subjectivism is the most characteristic feature of such philosophy: "The person is not a substance, an objective being with its own proper subsistence—subsistence in a rational nature. The person is merely a certain property of lived experiences and can be distinguished by means of those experiences, for they are conscious and self-conscious experiences; hence, consciousness and self-consciousness constitute the essence of the person." Wojtyla notes that this is not the view of Aquinas, that he sees consciousness as something derivative of rationality.

Aquinas' Objectivity and Wojtyla's Subjectivity

While Wojtyla accepts Aquinas' view of the person, he supplements it. He summarizes Aquinas's view in this way:

> We can see here how very objectivistic St. Thomas' view of the person is. It almost seems as though there is no place in it for an analysis of consciousness and self-consciousness as a totally unique manifestation of the person as a subject. For St. Thomas, the person is, of course, a subject—a very distinctive subject of existence and activity—because the person has subsistence in a rational nature, and this is what makes the person capable of consciousness and self-consciousness. St. Thomas, however, mainly presents this disposition of the human person to consciousness and self-consciousness. On the other hand, when it comes to analyzing consciousness and self-consciousness—which is what chiefly interested modern philosophy and psychology—there seems to be no place for it in St. Thomas' objectivistic view of reality. In any case, that in which the person's subjectivity is most apparent is presented by St. Thomas in an exclusively—or almost exclusively—objective way. He shows us the particular faculties, both spiritual and sensory, thanks to which the whole of human consciousness and self-consciousness—the human personality in the psychological and moral sense—takes shape, but that is also where he stops. Thus St. Thomas gives us an excellent view of the objective existence and activity of the person, but it would be difficult to speak in his view of the lived experiences of the person.

Here is where Wojtyla moves beyond Aquinas. He shares the modern interest in consciousness and self-consciousness, though he does not share the modern view that the person *is* consciousness. Rather, in the *Acting Person* he uses an analysis of consciousness to unfold his notion of man as being free and self-determining. For it is his consciousness of himself as one who is an efficient cause of his own action and of his self-actualization that allows the human being to have a sense of responsibility for his actions and his character. In the *Acting Person*, particularly in chapters 3 and 4, Wojtyla maintains that to actualize himself properly the human person must have an authentic grasp of values or goods and must work to determine himself in accord with objective goods; only thus is his freedom truly exercised. (This, of course, is a major theme of *Veritatis Splendor*.) The dignity of the human person, for Wojtyla, lies in this determination of the self through the free choice of what is good.

Indeed, one of the chief differences between Wojtyla's interest in the human person and Aquinas is that Wojtyla begins with and returns to subjectivity and Aquinas focuses largely on objective truths. One might say that Aquinas' chief interest is in determining what acts are good and evil;

for Wojtyla, the chief interest is in showing that man's very subjectivity and
freedom requires that he be concerned with the truth. For instance, in the
Acting Person he states:

> For human freedom is not accomplished nor exercised in bypassing
> truth but, on the contrary, by the person's realization and surrender to
> truth. The dependence upon truth marks out the borderlines of the
> autonomy appropriate to the human person.

Aquinas' Metaphysical Interests and Wojtyla's Phenomenological Interests

Another difference between Aquinas and Wojtyla emerges from the
above comparison. Whereas Aquinas is interested in developing a metaphysical description of man, a description in terms of form and matter, and
rationality and animality, Wojtyla is interested in using man's experience of
himself, of his self-determining powers, to lead him to an awareness of his
dignity. Ultimately Wojtyla draws upon a Thomistic metaphysics, for Wojtyla finds Aquinas' appropriation of the Aristotelian concepts "potentiality"
and "actuality" (metaphysical terms) to be essential to a proper description
of man's power to determine himself; man's life is a process of bringing
into actualization various potencies that he has. But the fact remains that
Aquinas aims at a metaphysical description (one ultimately rooted in experience, but one which seeks to arrive at ultimate principles, described in terms
of universal categories), whereas Wojtyla aims at a phenomenological one,
one that remains as closely linked as possible to the lived experience of the
concrete human being of his own consciousness of himself as a self-determining person. A metaphysical analysis would lead one to see that man is
capable of being self-determining because he is a person, that is because he
is rational and free, but for Wojtyla this metaphysical analysis is of secondary interest.

Man as a Social Animal vs. Man as Self-Giver

Wojtyla also emphasizes another feature of the human person that
links his view more closely with the documents of Vatican II than with that
of Aquinas, and this is the portrait of man as a "self-giver". Wojtyla cites
the lines of Vatican II that express concepts and use terms that were characteristic of Wojtyla's thought before the council and that have played a major
role in his work after the council. He notes how these lines are in accord
with the tradition and with Thomism, but in a way moves beyond them
both:

> In Vatican II's Pastoral Constitution *Gaudium et Spes*, we read that "the
> human being, who is the only creature on earth that God willed for
> itself, cannot fully find himself or herself except through a disinterested
> gift of himself or herself" (24). The document of the last Council
> seems in these words to sum up the age-old traditions and inquiries of
> Christian anthropology, for which divine revelation became a liberating

light. The anthropology of St. Thomas Aquinas is deeply rooted in
these traditions, while also being open to all the achievements of human
thought that in various ways supplement the Thomistic view of the person and confirm its realistic character. The words of Vatican II cited
above seem chiefly to accentuate the axiological aspect, speaking of the
person as a being of special intrinsic worth who is, therefore, specially
qualified to make a gift of self.

In the tradition man was defined as a social animal; much was made of his
need to write human laws in accord with natural law to achieve harmony in
the state. The Wojtylan view of man as one who must give of himself to
perfect himself gives a much profounder cast to the traditional notion and
approaches a more theological understanding of the person who can only
perfect himself by imitating the total self-giving of Christ.

3.
Natural Law and Personalism in *Veritatis Splendor*

Now from the above analysis, let us draw together a list of the differences between natural law and personalism and see how the themes distinctive of each are integrated in *Veritatis Splendor*.

The Universal vs. the Concrete; the Objective vs. the Subjective

Natural law is interested in the abstract universal norm, whereas *Veritatis Splendor* is interested in the choices of the concrete individual. Natural
law is interested in the objectivity of moral norms; personalism is interested
in the subjectivity of the concrete individual, a subjectivity characteristic of
all human beings.

The presentation of *Veritatis Splendor* begins with what might be characterized as a dramatization of a personalist moment; it is the encounter of
one concrete individual, of one young man, with Christ, a young man who,
conscious of his own faithfulness to the commandments, further seeks the
truth about human action. *Veritatis Splendor* observes:

> For the young man, the *question* is not so much about rules to be fol-
> lowed, but *about the full meaning of life*. This is in fact the aspiration
> at the heart of every human decision and action, the quiet searching and
> interior prompting which sets freedom in motion. This question is ulti-
> mately an appeal to the absolute Good which attracts us and beckons
> us; it is the echo of a call from God who is the origin and goal of man's
> life (n. 7).[18]

The emphasis here on the human heart and human interiority and its need
for absolute truth for freedom are true to the emphases of personalism. In
(n. 8), *Veritatis Splendor* invites us to enter into the question asked by the
young man "allowing ourselves to be guided by [Jesus]." Here, in a sense,

we are invited as concrete individuals to have our own personalistic moment.

Natural law is not left far behind. Christ is first interested in the young man's allegiance to the commandments, to the Law, which laws are considered to be the precepts of the natural law (n. 12). The person must not be guided by his own subjectivistic understandings of what is good and evil, but must submit to the objective truth. Throughout *Veritatis Splendor* the universality of natural law is stressed, while care is taken to acknowledge the dignity of the individual. A passage from (n. 51) speaks especially to this point:

> . . . *the natural law involves universality.* Inasmuch as it is inscribed in the rational nature of the person, it makes itself felt to all beings endowed with reason and living in history . . . inasmuch as the natural law expresses the dignity of the human person and lays the foundation for his fundamental rights and duties, it is universal in its precepts and its authority extends to all mankind. *This universality does not ignore the individuality of human beings*, nor is it opposed to the absolute uniqueness of each person. On the contrary, it embraces at its root each person's free acts, which are meant to bear witness to the universality of the true good.

In this passage we see the parallel consideration of universality of natural law with the dignity of the human person and his individuality and uniqueness.

Refutation of Modern Interpretation of Natural law as Biologistic

The rejection of natural law ethics because it is "biologistic" is handled in a distinctively personalistic way in *Veritatis Splendor*.

As we saw, Wojtyla was concerned to refute interpretations of natural law that portrayed man as slavishly subject to the mechanistic laws of nature. This view of natural law is addressed in (n. 47) of *Veritatis Splendor*. *Veritatis Splendor* mentions that modern theologians tend to reject many of the Church's teachings on sexual issues as based on a "naturalistic" understanding of natural law. They hold that man should be free to determine the meaning of his behavior and not be constrained by "natural inclinations." In (n. 48), *Veritatis Splendor* argues that such an objection to natural law fails to correspond to the Church's teaching of the human being as unity of body and soul. Indeed, *Veritatis Splendor* holds the view that man's very subjectivity is dependent upon his bodily state:

> . . . reason and free will are linked with all the bodily and sense faculties. *The person, including the body, is completely entrusted to himself, and it is in the unity of the body and soul that the person is the subject of his own moral acts.* The person, by the light of reason and the support of virtue, discovers in the body the anticipatory signs, the expression and the promise of the gift of self, in conformity with the wise

plan of the Creator. It is in the light of the dignity of the human person—a dignity which must be affirmed for its own sake—that reason
grasps the specific moral value of certain goods towards which the person is naturally inclined. And since the human person cannot be reduced to a freedom which is self-designing, but entails a particular
spiritual and bodily structure, the primordial moral requirement of loving and respecting the person as an end and never as a means also
implies, by its very nature, respect for certain fundamental goods, without which one would fall into relativism and arbitrariness (n. 48).

In other writings, most notably in *Love and Responsibility*, *Familiaris
Consortio* and his series of teachings on the theology of the body, John Paul
II has laid out the connection between the dignity of the human person, the
self-as-gift and the need to respect the life-giving power of the sexual act.
In those writings, he holds that to reject the life-giving power of the sexual
act is to reject a fundamental part of human dignity and to treat one's beloved as an object or a means rather than as an end. Here, he simply states
in general terms his observation that natural law is not tied so much to the
mechanistic laws of nature as it is to certain fundamental human goods that
are embedded in certain natural inclinations.

God as Lawgiver vs. the Good as Perfective of Human Dignity

Natural law stresses that God is the source of what is good and that we
ought to seek the good and obey the law because of God's authority. Sections 10 and 11 of *Veritatis Splendor* speak of the decalogue as having been
delivered by God who declares, "I am the Lord your God," and *Veritatis
Splendor* asserts that "*Acknowledging the Lord as God is the very core, the
heart of the Law*, from which the particular precepts flow and towards
which they are ordered" (sec. 11). The personalistic emphasis on morality
as perfective of the dignity of the human person is seen in the comment on
the commandment: "You shall love your neighbor as yourself" (Mt 19:19;
cf. Mk 12:31). *Veritatis Splendor* states:

> In this command we find a precise expression of *the singular dignity of
> the human person*, 'the only creature that God has wanted for its own
> sake.' The different commandments of the Decalogue are really only
> so many reflections of the one commandment about the good of the
> person, at the level of the man, different goods which characterize his
> identity as a spiritual and bodily being in relationship with God, with
> his neighbor and with the material world." (n. 13)

Throughout the document, it is stated that acts ordained to God are
also acts that bring about the perfection of the person. For instance, in (n.
78) we read:

> The reason why a good intention is not itself sufficient, but a correct
> choice of actions is also needed, is that the human act depends on its
> object, whether that object is *capable or not of being ordered* to God,

to the One who "alone is good", and thus brings about the perfection of the person. An act is therefore good if its object is in conformity with the good of the person with respect for the goods morally relevant for him. Christian ethics, which pays particular attention to the moral object, does not refuse to consider the inner "teleology" of acting, inasmuch as it is directed to promoting the true good of the person, but it recognizes that it is really pursued only when the essential elements of human nature are respected.

Man as Rational Creature vs. Man as Self-Determined

It could be said that whereas natural law ethics emphasizes the objective goodness or evil of exterior acts and man's ability as rational creature to discern that objective goodness, personalism is concerned with subjectivity and the effect that one's choices have on the self that one is forming with one's choices. This statement of the difference between the two approaches to ethics is certainly fair to neither one, for natural law ethics has as its proximate end the formation of man in virtue so that he can achieve his ultimate end of salvation. And personalist ethics certainly does not downplay the necessity for man to act in accord with objective truths. Nonetheless, with natural law's emphasis on the rationality of man's personhood and its rootedness in the "ordinances of reason" that govern the world, and with personalism's emphasis on man's responsibility for his free determination, such a contrast can be pushed to some extent. A passage very true to a natural law emphasis is the following:

> The rational ordering of the human act to the good in its truth and the voluntary pursuit of that good, known by reason, constitute morality. Hence human activity cannot be judged as morally good merely because it is a means for attaining one or another of its goals, or simply because the subject's intention is good. Activity is morally good when it attests to and expresses the voluntary ordering of the person to his ultimate end and the conformity of a concrete action with the human good as it is acknowledged in its truth by reason (n. 72).

A passage from (n. 71) reflecting the personalist emphasis is the following:

> Human acts are moral acts because they express and determine the goodness or evil of the individual who performs them. They do not produce a change merely in the state of affairs outside of man, but to the extent that they are deliberate choices, they give moral definition to the very person who performs them, determining his profound spiritual traits.

Man as Social Animal vs. Man as Self-Giver

The Aristotelian definition of man adopted by Aquinas defined man not only as a rational animal, but also as a social animal. His individual good was dependent upon the common good. Thus, in keeping with this view of man, *Veritatis Splendor* states: "The commandments of the second table of the Decalogue in particular—those which Jesus quoted to the young man of the Gospel (cf. Mt 19:19)—constitute the indispensable rules of all social life" (n. 97). The portion of *Veritatis Splendor* in which this statement appears speaks much of the state and civil authorities. *Veritatis Splendor* makes it clear that the good of society requires the recognition of absolute moral norms. The personalistic emphasis of *Veritatis Splendor* goes beyond this notion of obedience to the law being necessary for "social life"; it portrays man in his deepest ontological core as being one who should make a "gift of himself." Talk of "gift of self" is nearly always linked to the imitation of Christ: "*Jesus asks us to follow him and to imitate him along the path of love, a love which gives itself completely to the brethren out of love for God. . . .*" (n. 19, cf. 85, 87, 89). Indeed, Christ himself is the ultimate integration of the law and the gift of self: as *Veritatis Splendor* states:

> *Jesus himself is the living "fulfillment" of the Law* inasmuch as he fulfills its authentic meaning by the total gift of himself: *he himself becomes a living and personal Law,* who invites people to follow him; through the Spirit, he gives the grace to share his own life and love and provides the strength to bear witness to that love in personal choices and actions (cf. Jn 13:34-35)" (n. 15).

4.
The Centrality of Conscience
to both Natural Law and Personalism

Again, it would be a distortion to say that natural law is concerned with rationality and truth whereas personalism is concerned with freedom, but such an assertion allows us to discern certain distinctive concerns and emphases of these two approaches to ethics. The point at which these two approaches most manifestly overlap is in their understanding of the centrality of conscience to the moral life. Both natural law and personalism find truth and freedom meeting in the human conscience. Conscience and its relation to truth and freedom is a major theme both in the writings of Pope John Paul II and in *Veritatis Splendor*. Because the natural law is perfective of the human person, and because it is through his free choices that man perfects himself, conscience is central to the moral life. In "obeying" his conscience (a rightly formed conscience), which is, indeed, his inner self, man is simultaneously living in accord with the truth and freely determining himself. Paragraph 52 of *Veritatis Splendor* states: ". . . universal and permanent laws correspond to things known by the practical reason and are applied to particular acts through the judgment of conscience. The acting subject personally assimilates the truth contained in the law. He appropriates this truth of his being and makes it his own by his acts and the corresponding virtues." Paragraph 54 states: "The relationship between man's freedom and God's law is most deeply lived out in the 'heart' of the person, in his moral conscience." Paragraphs 57 and 58 make powerful statements of the subjectivity of the conscience combined with its link with God himself:

> According to Saint Paul, conscience in a certain sense confronts man with the law, and thus becomes a *"witness" for man*: a witness of his own faithfulness or unfaithfulness with regard to the law, of his essential moral rectitude or iniquity. Conscience is the *only* witness, since what takes place in the heart of the person is hidden from the eyes of everyone outside. Conscience makes its witness known only to the person himself. And, in turn, only the person knows that his own response is to the voice of conscience (n. 57).
>
> The importance of this interior *dialogue of man with himself* can never be adequately appreciated. But it is also a *dialogue of man with God*, the author of the law, the primordial image and final end of man. Thus it can be said that conscience bears witness to man's own rectitude or iniquity to man himself but, together with this and indeed even beforehand, conscience is *the witness of God himself*, whose voice and judgment penetrate the depths of man's soul, calling him *fortiter et suaviter* to obedience.
>
> Moral conscience does not close man within an insurmountable and impenetrable solitude, but opens him to the call, to the voice of God. In this, and not in anything else, lies the entire mystery and the dignity of the moral conscience: in being the place, the sacred place where God speaks to man.

The creativity of man, the freedom of man, is expressed not in inventing law, but in living out the law "written on his heart," conscious that in doing so he is either living in accord with his dignity or not, he is either forming himself in accord with his innate dignity or not.

Conclusion

Perhaps the passage of *Veritatis Splendor* that best brings together the themes of the encyclical while showing the overlap of natural law and personalism is the first paragraph of n. 90:

> The relationship between faith and morality shines forth with all its brilliance in the *unconditional respect due to the insistent demands of the personal dignity of every man*, demands protected by those moral norms which prohibit without exception actions which are intrinsically evil. The universality and the immutability of the moral norm make manifest and at the same time serve to protect the personal dignity and inviolability of man, on whose face is reflected the splendor of God (cf. Gen. 9:5-6).

In all written by Pope John Paul II, the theme of the dignity of the human person, freedom, subjectivity, and self-determination are prominent.

The above analysis has attempted to show that in the most recent publications of the magisterium, particularly in the *Universal Catechism* and in *Veritatis Splendor*, we begin to see a blending of natural law themes with those of personalism. One can only think the Church is so much the richer for both approaches to ethics, approaches that are ultimately thoroughly compatible.

Notes

1. That part of the purpose of *Veritatis Splendor* was to reassert the centrality of natural law to Catholic moral teaching is clear from the introduction, n. 4.

2. *Catechism of the Catholic Church* (San Francisco: Ignatius Press, 1994).

3. In Karol Wojtyla, *Person and Community: Selected Essays,* trans. by Theresa Sandok, OSM (New York: Peter Lang, 1993); hereafter *PC*.

4. Wojtyla refers to followers of Kant as "phenomenalists" and to those who use the philosophic method of phenomenology as "phenomenologists." See *PC*, p. 32-33.

5. *PC*, p. 182.

6. *PC*, p. 182.

7. *PC*, p. 183.

8. *PC*, p. 184.

9. *PC*, p. 184.

10. *PC*, p. 185.

11. *PC*, p. 166.

12. *PC*, p. 167.

13. *PC*, p. 168.

14. *PC*, p. 169.

15. *PC*, pp. 170-171.

16. *PC*, p. 189.

17. Karol Wojtyla, *The Acting Person* (Boston: D. Reidel Publishing Co., 1979), p. 154.

18. Passages from *Veritatis Splendor* are taken from the edition published by Libreria Editrice Vaticana. All italicization in this passage and other is not mine, but is found in the original text.

14

Veritatis Splendor and Sexual Ethics

James P. Hanigan

In the first encyclical letter of his pontificate, *Redemptor hominis*, Pope John Paul II laid down what he would later describe as the charter or program for his papacy.[1] In clear, somewhat novel and quite forceful language, the pontiff offered to the Church his version of Christian humanism.[2]

> Man in the full truth of his existence, of his personal being and also of his community and social being. . .this man is the primary route the Church must travel in fulfilling her mission: *he is the primary and fundamental way for the Church*, the way traced out by Christ himself, the way that leads invariably through the mystery of the Incarnation and redemption.[3]

With the publication of *Redemptor hominis*, the Church, in the person of its official leader, again went on public record as acknowledging and embracing a fundamental moral responsibility to champion the dignity of the human person and to explore the ethical and practical import of the doctrinal truths proclaimed by the Church for the promotion of this cause. Indeed, John Paul II affirmed that "the human person's dignity itself becomes part of the content of that proclamation" with the consequence that "the Church, because of her divine mission, becomes all the more the guardian of [human] freedom, which is the condition and basis for the human person's true dignity."[4]

In subsequent encyclicals the Pope has explored and developed this basic program in a variety of ways.[5] In *Laborem exercens*, for example, he reflected at length on the importance of work as an essential need and expression of human dignity.[6] In *Dives in misericordia* he explored the relationship between the divine mercy and human dignity, going so far as to say that the "relationship of mercy is based on the common experience of that good which is man, on the common experience of the dignity that is proper to him."[7] *Veritatis splendor*, the tenth encyclical authored by John Paul II, takes up the same theme in terms of how fundamental moral theology bears on the dignity of the human person, once again exploring, in another area of human experience, the relationship between the truth of the human person and the uses of human freedom. In this way the Pope has continued to make theological anthropology and ethics central themes of his papal teaching.

The central importance of theological anthropology and ethics in the contemporary world is not a new emphasis for Pope John Paul II. As early as 1954, when Karol Wojtyla joined the philosophy faculty at the Catholic University of Lublin, it was the conviction of that newly reconstituted faculty, a conviction shared by its new ethics professor, that the tragic abuses of human dignity and the complete obliteration of human rights, which Poland had experienced under Nazism during the war and was continuing to experience under communist rule, were rooted in a false view of the human person. What had to be salvaged and reconstituted, as the philosophy faculty saw things, was the full truth about the human person.[8]

The truth that is splendid, for Karol Wojtyla then and for Pope John Paul II now, is the truth about the human person. This is a truth revealed by God in Christ who not only reveals to us the mystery of the mind and heart of God, but also, and at the same time reveals to us the truth about ourselves. It is precisely this truth, that each human being in his or her own unique unrepeatability is made for God in the image of God and, though fallen and sinful, has been redeemed and joined to Christ, and so has the capacity as a free, rational, acting subject to respond in knowing love to the Divine invitation, that John Paul II sees to be imperiled by a wide variety of philosophies and theologies in the modern world. *Veritatis splendor*, then, whatever its intrinsic merits, is the papal effort to renew in all our societies the age-old wisdom that we can know the truth and it is the truth that shall make us free.

The above background, it seems to me, is the essential context for reading and interpreting *Veritatis splendor*. While the more immediate occasion for the document may well be the continuing vocal disagreement among Catholics throughout the world over substantive moral questions like contraception and over the methods appropriate to Catholic moral theology, I suggest that there is a larger cultural and pastoral context to the letter which must be attended to if we are to give it a fair reading. Contrary to the interpretations of some commentators on the letter who read it, for good or ill, as a vigorous and uncompromising exercise of Vatican authority designed to stifle all dissenting voices and so bring Catholic theologians under the control of the Roman magisterium,[9] contrary to those who see in the encyclical an attempt to reestablish official control over the sexual views and behaviors of the Catholic faithful,[10] I do not think the letter is properly read from such a narrow perspective. In any case, it is not the way in which it is being read here.

I do not think, therefore, that *Veritatis splendor* is about sexual morality as such, nor do I think that an obsessive concern with sexual morality is a hidden subtext or agenda in the letter. Indeed, there are only five passing references to sexual behaviors in the entire letter.[11] Nonetheless, the letter is not without great significance for moral theology in the area of human sexuality. I find that significance to lie, mainly but not exclusively, in at least four areas which I intend to develop briefly in this essay.[12]

The four areas I intend to discuss are the following: first, the letter proposes an ideal of moral perfection as normative for the Christian life; second, it considers Catholic morality to be a revealed morality in which reason plays an important but decidedly secondary role; third, it challenges Catholic moralists of the so-called "revisionist" stripe to articulate more clearly both their understanding of intrinsically evil acts as well as the alternative methodological proposals they have been advancing, concerns which are treated in the encyclical under the headings of fundamental option and proportionalism; fourth, the encyclical invites all moral theologians to greater clarity about the cultural situation out of which their concerns arise and to which they choose to speak.

1.
The Ideal of Moral Perfection

The papal meditation on the story of the rich young man which opens the encyclical, and which John Paul II has used in a similar fashion on previous occasions,[13] makes it clear that the rich young man stands for every follower of Jesus, indeed for every human person. The initial question of the young man, "Teacher, what good must I do to have eternal life?," is, says the Pope, a question every human person must ask in view of both the human condition and the human situation. The conclusion of the story, Jesus' final words, "If you wish to be perfect, go, sell your possessions and give the money to the poor, and you will have treasure in heaven; then come follow me," represent for the Pope a normative truth of every human life. These words are a call to moral perfection, to an unconditional love of God and neighbor, to a whole-hearted following of Christ, to a complete self-giving in love by the moral agent to the person of Jesus after the example of Jesus' own self-giving to the Will of his Father.

This ideal of moral perfection as the normative standard for faithful Christian living and behavior is stated explicitly in any number of places in the encyclical.[14] It is also reflected throughout the entire document, but nowhere more clearly than in the concluding papal meditation on the significance of martyrdom in the Christian life. This reflection on martyrdom in the context of the entire letter enables us to bring at least three points to clear expression.

The ideal of moral perfection is of supreme worth, of vital importance to salvation. It is not an optional ideal, but a basic requirement of Christian discipleship, not limited to an elite few but mandatory for all the faithful. This ideal of moral perfection which is the truth of human existence is certainly worth dying for, worth forsaking all other human goods and values for its sake. And to choose not to do so, when placed by circumstances in a position where such an either/or choice must be made, is to miss the mark, it is to sin.[16] For the Church to proclaim anything less than the ideal of moral perfection as the normative truth of human existence for all followers of Christ, indeed for all human persons, would be to betray her evangelical mission.

Second, the ideal of moral perfection, while having its concrete, temporal embodiments in the lives of particular persons in history, looks to an eschatological fulfillment of human life. Such a fulfillment means that human persons may well have to forego various and otherwise quite legitimate forms of present temporal human happiness or human fulfillment as they search for and strive to grow in moral perfection. The ideal of moral perfection never admits of temporal completion, and overrides morally all human claims of rights to temporal goods.[17] Hence, morally speaking, human rights are always inseparable from human obligations, and from the perspective of the acting subject, one's own moral obligations have a moral primacy.

Third, the pursuit of and adherence to the ideal of moral perfection takes place in a world of sin and evil, in a world that makes the pursuit difficult and the adherence often dangerous. Consequently, the life of the disciple of Jesus will be one of struggle and conflict.[18] This dangerous, conflict-laden situation highlights the urgency and the normativity of the ideal. It also highlights the most fundamental of Christian truths, that both the call to perfection and the ability to respond to the call are gifts of grace.[19]

What does this ideal of moral perfection have to do with sexual ethics? Clearly, for Pope John Paul II, it adds a depth of seriousness and absoluteness, an almost harsh and categorical quality to our most basic moral obligations that removes them from the calculus of temporal consequences. For one example, the marriage bond demands absolute fidelity from those who pursue moral perfection in that way of life. He says so explicitly.[20] Divorce and remarriage in the interests of the temporal happiness or sexual fulfillment of the partners is ruled out as a moral consideration. For a second example, arguments in favor of contraceptive intercourse based on the difficulty of practicing natural family planning carry little moral weight for him. Or again, theories of a morality of compromise with the moral ideal appropriate to human sexuality that have been used by some[21] to justify homosexual relationships and behaviors lose their force in the face of the rigor of the normative ideal. In general, experiential objections to the Church's teaching on a variety of sexual practices which appeal to the practical difficulties or unrealistic nature of such teaching in the conditions of modern life, or which invoke pastoral compassion against Church teaching, are dismissed as excuses. After all, even the rich young man went away sad.[22]

The birth control issue might serve here as a most useful illustration of the point being made. Among the arguments offered against the teaching of *Humanae vitae* on the immorality of all contraceptive practices in marriage, two seem central in the context of contemporary Roman Catholic moral theology. One argument, more theoretical in nature, accepts the claim that human sexual activity has an essential procreative dimension or meaning. It therefore acknowledges that there is, indeed, some ontic evil present in all nonprocreative sex acts, including contraceptive marital intercourse.[23] But it fails to find persuasive or well-grounded the insistence that every act of sexual intercourse in marriage must be open to the possibility of new life, for it fails to see how one can rule out absolutely and antecedently in every possible situation the existence of a proportionate reason for allowing the ontic evil. That insistence has been described by Richard McCormick as "a prohibition in search of an argument."[24]

The second argument against the teaching of *Humanae vitae* is more practical in nature. It claims that once the idea of responsible parenthood, i.e., the control of births, is accepted as a serious moral obligation, as it was in Pope Paul VI's encyclical,[25] then the effectiveness of the means to exercising the obligation becomes a major moral consideration.[26] The practice of natural family planning (NFP), while it may work well for some couples, can hardly be normative for all for a host of circumstantial reasons. To be effective, NFP requires knowledge about the female reproductive system and access to the use of technological devices to acquire that knowledge in particular cases that is not available to many people. It also requires a high degree of motivation and mutuality on the part of the couple which cannot be readily presumed, training in the practice of the method and a good deal of self-knowledge and self-discipline on the part of the couple.

Ironically, if one considers the virtues and relational dynamics needed to practice NFP effectively, one discovers many of the values and virtues advocated for marital relationships by revisionist and feminist theologians who emphasize "quality of relationship" norms to evaluate the morality of human sexual behaviors.[27] NFP, more than any other means of birth control, calls for honest communication, for mutuality and equality, and for shared responsibility and joint decision-making between the sexual partners. The burden of responsible parenthood through the techniques of NFP, while still heavier on the woman than on the man,[28] is not placed exclusively on the woman. Sexual intercourse, whether in fertile or nonfertile periods, is and must be a mutually agreed upon and self-conscious choice that acknowledges and respects the procreative potential of human sexuality. It cannot be a one-sided insistence on "conjugal rights" or a concession to satisfy a "need," or a spontaneous but unreflective act that ignores or wishes not to be troubled by the procreative meaning of the act.[29] Neither does NFP ask one of the partners to undergo health risks as a result of interfering with the natural processes of the female body or to suffer a surgical mutilation of the body.

In short, NFP embodies very high moral ideals about the marital relationship, requires the practice of sometimes difficult moral virtues, and sees something other than genital sexual fulfillment as the goal of marriage or as the exclusive way to realize the unitive good of sexuality. For the present pontiff, this lofty—some would say impractical and unrealistic, others would say bloodless and inhuman—moral idealism about marriage is precisely what married couples, men as well as women, are called to live in their following of Christ. While he acknowledges, at least abstractly, the practical difficulties of living out the ideal,[30] they hold no weight for him as objective moral reasons justifying something less than the ideal. He is not prepared to excuse anyone from objective moral failure because the ideal has been found to be too difficult, due either to character weakness or circumstantial difficulties. He is, of course, more than willing to recognize that such actual or virtual impediments[31] may mitigate or even abolish subjective moral responsibility. That something appears to be too hard, too difficult in the face of the demands of modern life, however, is no reason for accepting the objective moral rightness of actions that contravene the normative ideal of moral perfection.

What I think this example illustrates is that John Paul II uses an appeal to the essential cross-bearing aspect of Christian discipleship for more than motivational purposes. All moral theologians recognize the legitimate paranetic character of appeals to the cross in the moral life of the Christian. Certainly the writings of the Pope have this strong paranetic flavor. But in addition to calling upon the cross for homiletic or motivational purposes, it seems to me that the Pope John Paul II also seeks to derive substantive moral content from his understanding of the cross. He does so at least to the extent that he uses such appeals to rule out or deny the weight of certain kinds of experiential appeals as providing objective, justifying reasons for certain kinds of human action. He also uses the cross to advocate and to sustain the normativity of the development of certain virtues and the normativity of certain practices.

To be as clear as possible, I am not suggesting that the pope engages in a form of argument that defends a course of action as right because it is hard or even heroic. I am suggesting that *Veritatis splendor*, in continuity with the earlier encyclicals of John Paul II, finds the full truth about the moral capabilities and moral fulfillment of the human person to be most fully manifested in the cross of Christ and so to be normative for the moral life. This truth is for him a matter of revealed faith far more than a conviction derived from human experience, though it is a truth that has a kind of experiential confirmation in the lives of the saints. This truth about the moral capacity of the human person, in which human dignity is rooted and through which it is most clearly expressed and respected, is also the normative moral message the Church is required to proclaim in its proclamation of the good news of Jesus. It is good news owed to human beings if the Church is, indeed, to be the champion of human dignity.

2.
Revelation and Reason

The previous discussion of the relevance of the ideal of moral perfection to sexual ethics leads readily into a second point of fundamental importance. *Veritatis splendor* clearly understands Christian morality to be a revealed morality and says so explicitly.[32] Reason has an essential role to play in the human effort to understand the full range of the moral demands of the Christian life, but reason operates in the light of revelation and in the service of faith, not as an independent and primarily critical agent.[33] While the truths of revelation pertinent to morality are summed up by the Pontiff in a rather general fashion,[34] it is clear that his understanding of what is revealed about our moral conduct is not limited to these general affirmations. Furthermore, the content of revelation pertinent to the moral life is neither exhausted nor fully understood merely by specific references to biblical texts. It finds its fullness only by attending to the ongoing tradition of the Church as that has unfolded and been handed down under the guidance of the magisterium.

The Pope has stated clearly in the encyclical that the Church does not and cannot bind the faithful to any one theological or philosophical system.[35] For those systems are the work of human reason. Yet the Church can and must bind the faithful in conscience to the truths of revelation. These truths of revelation pertain not only to matters of doctrine but also to morality. It is not surprising, therefore, that more than one commentator on *Veritatis splendor* sees the issue raised by the encyclical as one of revelation versus dissent,[36] or that a good deal of the theological ink spilled over the past 25 years on disputed sexual issues has been mainly concerned with the questions of the competence and scope of ecclesial authority to teach about matters of mortality.

Again, an example here will be helpful. The issue of the moral permissibility of same-sex genital acts has been a matter of considerable theological and cultural debate in the last 25 years. Fundamentalist Christians are confident that homosexual acts are clearly condemned in Scripture. The moral wrongness of such acts is, for them, a simple matter of divine revelation. The Catholic natural law tradition, which affirmed procreation as the primary goal and good of human sexual behavior, argued the moral wrongness of such acts on the grounds of their unnaturalness as perceived by reason. But this tradition also found this conclusion to be confirmed by both the teaching of Scripture and the tradition of the Church, and it was surely deeply influenced in its "reasoning" by the scriptural and ecclesial tradition which was the cultural context in which it worked.

It should not be necessary here to rehearse the ways in which the historical-critical method of biblical interpretation and a more personalist and historically sensitive understanding of natural law, as well as a more scientific understanding of homosexuality, all of which are the work of human reason, called this simple certainty about God's Will into question. But the Catholic understanding of revelation and its relationship to reason, at least as laid out in *Veritatis splendor*, is too complex to allow theologians to simply dismiss the traditional teaching as wrong on the basis of the findings of critical reason alone. Theological reason in the person of moral theologians may very well and rightly point out that the arguments advanced in defense of such teaching are inadequately or even falsely grounded.[37] But such critical observations are not the end of the matter.

Those Catholic moralists who would argue for the moral rightness of homogenital acts and relationships, however conditioned and limited their rightness might be, will have to do so on more specifically theological grounds. They will have to appeal not only to critical reason's inability to ground their moral wrongness, but also to revelation's positive affirmation of their moral rightness. That is to say, they will have to reconstruct a 2,000-year theological tradition of thought about the meaning of human sexuality in human life to show that the procreative dimension of sexuality is only accidentally or gratuitously related to the unitive dimension. At least they will have to do so if they wish to meet the challenge laid down by *Veritatis splendor*.

3.
Intrinsically Evil Acts

Toward the conclusion of *Veritatis splendor,* John Paul II summarized for his fellow bishops what he had done in the encyclical and stressed its importance:

> Each of us knows how important is the teaching which represents the central theme of this encyclical and which is today being restated with the authority of the successor of Peter. Each of us can see the seriousness of what is involved, not only for individuals but also for the whole of society, with the reaffirmation of the universality and immutability of the moral commandments, particularly those which prohibit always and without exception intrinsically evil acts.[38]

Undoubtedly the Pope sees the contemporary cultural and intellectual challenge to the universality and immutability of the moral commandments to be a major danger facing the Church and society at large. He is zealous to reestablish the idea in both Church and society that there are some kinds of actions that ought never, under any circumstances, to be done. It is also clear that he—or his advisors—have read fundamental option theory, proportionalist method, and some unnamed theories of conscience to be among the challenges to the universality and immutability of the commandments.

These challenges are of particular concern for they have arisen from within the Church community itself.

Like other commentators on the encyclical,[39] I, too, am at a loss to recognize, in the writings of any specific Catholic authors with whom I am familiar, the description given in the encyclical of the theories the Pope finds so troublesome and wrong-headed. I must also admit that I find it difficult to understand, from the account in the encyclical, precisely what constitutes a particular action as intrinsically evil.[40] The list of such actions presented in the encyclical and drawn from Vatican II are specific enough,[41] but they are not without their own ambiguity. Only two of the practices listed pertain at all to the area of sexual ethics—prostitution and trafficking in women and children—and I know of no Catholic moral theologians writing today who are interested in defending even a limited objective moral rightness for such practices. In addition, there is a reference to *Humanae vitae* that obliquely associates contraceptive practices and intrinsically evil acts.[42]

A number of writers have commented upon the inadequacy of the encyclical's understanding of proportionalism and fundamental option, and have insisted that the real issue is not whether there are intrinsically evil acts. The real question is what must be taken into account in order to provide an adequate description of the object of an act before it can properly be labeled intrinsically evil.[43] It is not to the point here to rehearse that discussion, though it surely is of great consequence for sexual ethics. The point I wish to raise has to do with the perceived inability of proportionalism and fundamental option theory to affirm that some moral prohibitions bind absolutely. Why is it, I ask, that so many critics of proportionalism especially, including the Pope and his advisors, read proportionalism as if it were a crude form of situation ethics in the mode of Joseph Fletcher or a crass utilitarianism that had not progressed beyond Jeremy Bentham?

The reason seems to lie somewhere in the conviction that all these methods and theories deny the possibility of absolute negative prohibitions, even if they might allow for the possibility of virtually exceptionless rules.[44] The scriptures and the long tradition of theological thought in the Church surely affirm that there are some kinds of behaviors that are simply not compatible with the gospel, some human activities that inevitably degrade those who do or approve of them, that must be judged unworthy of the human person no matter what good intentions may inspire them or what good consequences they aim at or effect.

While I do not think very many Catholic moralists would dispute that claim in principle, it seems to me that it is now the burden of those who use fundamental option theory or proportionalist method to illuminate the moral status of human choices and actions to show how their theories and methods are concretely and specifically able to affirm the claim in fact. Once again an example may be helpful.

Among the clearest absolute negative prohibitions to be found in scripture, tradition, and the magisterial teaching is the prohibition against adultery. One of Joseph Fletcher's more famous and dramatic examples in his book, *Situation Ethics*, had to do with a Mrs. Bergmeier and an adulterous act which Fletcher called sacrificial adultery.[45] The example was clearly intended to provide an objective justification for a particular act of adultery in terms of intention, situation and consequence. Using traditional moral categories, Catholic moral theologians could readily find in Fletcher's example a number of factors which would mitigate or even abolish the subjective guilt of the moral agents involved in the act. But their judgment would remain that the act was objectively morally wrong, for it was an act of adultery by any traditional definition.

The questions I raise here are whether and how proportionalists would or could establish adultery in a case such as Fletcher's as an action that ought never to be done. Or if they could not or would not wish to defend such a judgment, how would they argue that, despite traditional definitions and understandings of the sixth commandment, this action is not to be described morally as adultery? Or is the Pope correct in reading proportionalists to say that the Church has been and is wrong to teach that there are some actions "which per se and in themselves, independently of circumstances, are always seriously wrong by reason of their object?"[46]

For some reason any number of people are reading proportionalists to agree with authors like Joseph Fletcher. While I am convinced that such a reading is incorrect, and while I acknowledge that serious efforts have been made to clarify the method of proportionalism,[47] I suggest that *Veritatis splendor* challenges proportionalists to a clearer and more specific account of their method and conclusions. For if adultery, as commonly and traditionally defined, is not always an objective moral wrong, if it is not one of those kinds of actions that is beyond the pale for those asking Jesus what they must do to be saved and who wish to start on the path to perfection, then what is the Church to do with the sixth commandment and with Jesus' initial response to the rich young man?

4.
Theology and Culture

From my limited reading of both the present encyclical and other prepapal and papal writings of John Paul II, as well as of the history of John Paul II and several commentaries on *Veritatis splendor*, the biggest point at issue, to my mind at least, is the cultural, pastoral context out of which moral theology arises and to which it addresses itself. Several readers of the encyclical who are not professional moral theologians have greeted the letter appreciatively and with an enthusiasm not matched by many moral theologians. One such commentator even suggested that moral theologians might be the worst audience for the letter. Given their professional and technical concerns, theologians were likely to miss the forest for the trees. Their own particular interests and professional training would blind them to other and more significant features of the letter. This possibility seems to have touched both so-called "liberal" and "conservative" moral theologians.

Bernhard Häring, for one example, has good reason for seeing in the encyclical one more instance of Vatican mistrust of bishops, priests and theologians. He reads the letter almost exclusively as one more attempt on the part of Rome to limit dialogue and to control any dissenting voices, especially among bishops, pastors and theologians.[49] John Finnis, on the other hand, finds good reason to rejoice that the encyclical is finally cracking down on dissenting moral theologians within the Church who distort the tradition, confuse the faithful and so promote moral skepticism and an unwarranted moral pluralism in the Church.[50]

But each of these thinkers brings a very different cultural context and set of pastoral concerns to their reading of the encyclical. For Häring, there is presently far too much mistrust in the official Church, far too much centralization of authority, far too many restrictions on the people who preach and teach the Gospel and carry out the ministry on a daily basis among and in cooperation with the faithful. For Finnis, there is too much moral confusion among the people of God, too little respect for authority, too much arbitrary moral sentiment passing itself off as conscience, too much pastoral sentimentality ignoring the truth the Church proclaims in the name of compassion. And it is quite possible that both men are correct.

American Catholics quite naturally tend to read the letter as if it were addressed to the American Catholic Church and more specifically, perhaps, as if it were directed against some of the better known moral theologians in the United States, despite the encyclical's silence in that regard. Many American Catholics, deeply concerned for the faith and the future of their Church, but not involved in either ecclesiastical life or the intricacies of the discipline of moral theology, read the document as a badly needed correction of the worst features of American culture—its individualism, its crude obsession in the public media with sex, wealth and violence, its moral and philosophical relativism, its tendency to define all values, especially moral and religious values, in exclusively pragmatic terms. Such readers are attending to the obvious moral shortcomings in American society—the breakdown of family life, the shockingly high number of abortions, the sexual promiscuity so common among teenagers and young adults, the outrageous number of instances of rape, spousal and child abuse, the growing number of single parent families, and the list could go on. Many, though certainly not all, of these ills are related to human sexuality.

In short, peoples' concern about Christian faith and life always has a particular understanding of the cultural context and a particular set of pastoral needs in which the concern operates and to which they think Church teaching is or ought to be addressed. It is against this cultural context that the teaching is received and interpreted. As a teacher of college undergraduates for almost a quarter of a century, for example, I have long been puzzled by the seeming reluctance of so many pastors and theologians to speak to college students about their sexual practices and drinking habits in blunt and absolute terms. The students I have taught did not need to be persuaded that premarital sex might be an acceptable moral choice under certain circumstances, or that their weekend drinking practices could be situationally or consequentially justified. What they needed to learn, and I am deeply afraid they did not, was that their sexual and drinking practices were morally wrong, humanly degrading to themselves and their partners, serious obstacles to their growing in love of God and neighbor, and that there are solid, objective grounds in both faith and reason for that judgment. If there are, in fact, exceptions to the Church's teaching on the objective immorality of premarital sexual intercourse, I have yet to come across any case of an exception among the undergraduates I have taught. In that cultural context and with that set of pastoral concerns, *Veritatis splendor* is both well-named and vitally needed.

On the other hand, academic and pastoral concerns have also led me into attending to the difficulties experienced by homosexual persons who are deeply committed to the faith and who struggle to understand the meaning of their sexuality. In that particular and somewhat narrow cultural context, a simple insistence on absolute negative moral prohibitions is less than fully helpful. It is not that such insistence is wrong; it is, however, very often pastorally insensitive and intellectually tyrannical. Given that set of pastoral concerns, *Veritatis splendor* seems less well-named, and certainly requires more extensive mining to bring forth the splendid truth it proclaims.

My own reading of the encyclical has tried to place it in the context of a larger papal program for the Church, a program that emerges from a background of fierce struggle against Nazism, Communism, and western materialism and individualism, a struggle that continues today, despite the apparent defeat of Hitler and the collapse of the Soviet Union. My reading suggests that the world, and inevitably the Church which lives in the world, daily experiences an incredible number of human actions that betray human dignity, violate human rights, and deny, fundamentally and of their very nature, the truth of the human person as proclaimed in the Gospel. Such actions, and the philosophies which justify and give rise to those actions, cannot, must not, ought not to receive specious justifications or be allowed to pass unchallenged, whether those justifications appeal to political expediency, economic necessity, cultural differentiation or historically conscious methodologies.

In the American context and with specific regard to sexual ethics, both within and without the Church, it seems highly implausible that the most pressing need is for moral justifications of greater sexual license, of more divorce and remarriage, or of single-parent families. It seems most unlikely that teenagers will be helped to grow in moral perfection by being told that masturbation is fine because everyone does it or that the avoidance of sexually transmitted diseases is the sole or even primary moral concern they should have about their sexual behaviors. There is little reason to think that married couples will find greater marital stability, unity and joy or the wisdom to be better parents by learning moral justifications for easier technological ways to avoid conception. The meaning of human sexuality as it is portrayed in the mass media, on television shows, in the movies and the best sellers, must be challenged as a lie. Sex is not a biological need like hunger and thirst, it is not a game or a recreation in which one scores at the expense of the other, nor is it a purely private matter of no social consequence or concern. If the moral truth about human sexuality is not spoken clearly and without compromise, then the virtues that must be cultivated and the social institutions that must be developed to live and sustain the truth cannot be supported. Certainly there are obvious trends in American culture that point to the urgency and necessity of speaking the moral truth about human sexuality. The necessity and urgency of that truth is a major way in which *Veritatis splendor* is relevant to sexual ethics.

Notes

1. John Paul II, *Redemptoris missio* 4; cited from *Origins* 20, 34 (January 31, 1991), p. 453.

2. Avery Dulles, S.J., "The Prophetic Humanism of John Paul II," *America* 169, 12 (October 23, 1993), pp. 6-11.

3. Pope John Paul II, *The Redeemer of Man* 14, (Washington, DC: United States Catholic Conference, 1979), p. 43.

4. Ibid., 12, p. 36.

5. In each of the 10 encyclicals of his pontificate to date, John Paul II has explored the theme of human dignity in one way or another, has emphasized the foundations of that dignity in human freedom, and insisted that respect for the truth of the human person is a necessary condition for the flourishing of human dignity. The text of the present essay restricts itself to two examples in the interest of space, but the papal interest in human freedom and its relationship to truth is no novelty in the writings of John Paul II, any more than it is in the pre-papal writings of Karol Wojtyla.

6. Pope John Paul II, *The Priority of Labor* 4, ed. Gregory Baum (New York/Ramsey: Paulist Press, 1982), pp. 100-102.

7. John Paul II, *Dives in misericordia* 6; cited from *Origins* 10, 26 (December 11, 1980), p. 407.

8. Stefan Swiezawski, "Introduction: Karol Wojtyla at the Catholic University of Lublin," in Karol Wojtyla, *Person and Community: Selected Essays,* trans. Theresa Sardok, OSM (New York: Peter Lang, 1993), pp. ix-xvi. See also George Huntston Williams, *The Mind of John Paul II: Origins of His Thought and Action* (New York: The Seabury Press, 1981), p. 150.

9. This reading of the letter is shared by both traditional and revisionist moral theologians, by so-called "conservative" and "liberal" writers. Herbert McCabe, *"Veritatis Splendor* in focus: 10: Manuals and rule books," *The Tablet* (December 18, 1993). "Now it seems to me that the encyclical . . . is, in great part, an attack on those who want to read the rule book as though it were a training manual by those who want to read the manual as though it were a rule book." Or Germain Grisez, *"Veritatis Splendor* in focus: 1: Revelation versus dissent," *The Tablet* (October 16, 1993). "In claiming that the received teaching concerning intrinsically evil acts is a revealed truth, the Pope also implicitly asserts that it is definable. That implicit assertion will be denied by those rejecting the teaching. This argument is undeniably over essentials, and cannot long go unresolved. It cannot be settled by theologians. Only the magisterium's definitive judgment will settle it."

10. Nicholas Lash, *"Veritatis Splendor* in focus: 5: Teaching in crisis," *The Tablet* (November 13, 1993). "And it is not war or poverty, atheism or the dead hand of the 'commodity form' which most preoccupies the Pope, but sex."

11. John Paul II, *Veritatis splendor* 15, 22, 47, 49, 80; cited from *Origins* 23, 18 (October 14, 1993), pp. 303, 305, 312, 313, 321.

12. There is a fifth area of importance in a negative sense: the letter continues a pattern in the papacy of John Paul II of side-stepping some of the critical questions and challenges raised by the contemporary movement of women toward full social and personal equality. Lisa Sowle Cahill, *"Veritatis Splendor* in focus: 9: Accent on the masculine," *The Tablet* (December 11, 1993), has commented on this dimension of the letter admirably.

13. See the Apostolic Letter of Pope John Paul II, "To the Youth of the World," *Origins* 14, 43 (April 11, 1985), pp. 701-713.

14. *Veritatis splendor* n. 17-18.

15. Ibid., n. 90-94.

16. Ibid., n. 90, offers examples from both the Old and the New Testament.

17. Ibid., n. 92.

18. Ibid., n. 93, "Although martyrdom represents the high point of the witness to moral truth, and one to which relatively few people are called, there is nonetheless a consistent witness which all Christians must daily be ready to make, even at the cost of suffering and grave sacrifice."

19. Ibid., n. 93, "Love and life according to the Gospel cannot be thought of first and foremost as a kind of precept, because what they demand is beyond man's abilities. They are possible only as a gift of God . . ."

20. Ibid., n. 22.

21. Charles E. Curran, "Dialogue with the Homophile Movement: The Morality of Homosexuality," *Catholic Moral Theology in Dialogue* (Notre Dame: Fides Publishers, 1972), pp. 184-219, and "Moral Theology, Psychiatry and Homosexuality," *Transition and Tradition in Moral Theology* (Notre Dame: University of Notre Dame Press, 1979), pp. 59-80, was a leading exponent of this view, one which I believe he no longer holds.

22. *Veritatis splendor,* n. 95.

23. Philip S. Keane, S.S., *Sexual Morality: A Catholic Perspective* (New York/Ramsey: Paulist Press, 1977), pp. 121-134, reflects this approach to the question.

24. Richard A. McCormick, S.J., "A Response," *America,* 169, 8 (September 25, 1993), p. 14.

25. *Humanae vitae,* 10.

26. Effectiveness was a fundamental aspect of the argument advanced in the majority report of the pontifical birth control commission, though hardly something that would stand by itself. See Robert Blair Kaiser, *The Politics of Sex and Religion* (Kansas City: Leaven Press, 1985), p. 158.

27. Quality of relationship norms were first made popular in Catholic theology by the study authored by Anthony Kosnik, et. al., *Human Sexuality: New Directions in American Catholic Thought* (New York/Paramus: Paulist Press, 1977), pp. 83-88. An excellent summary of feminist proposals in this regard is Sandra Friedman and Alec Irwin, "Christian Feminism, Eros and Power in Right Relation," *Cross Currents* 40, 3 (Fall 1990), pp. 387-405.

28. The nature of the male and female reproductive systems makes this inevitably the case. Attention to aspects of human sexuality such as this is part of what the Pope means when he speaks about the truth of the body. See *Veritatis splendor* 48, p. 312, where the Pope defends the magisterium against charges of biologism and physicalism, and rightly so, I think, at least as far as the writings of John Paul II go.

29. To make the case for the intrinsic evil of all contraceptive practice, one must identify an objective defect of the will inevitably present in the practice. NFP manages to avoid many of the more likely and obvious defects, which is the point of the paragraph in the text. That is no minor matter. However, the paragraph is not, and is not intended to be, a conclusive argument for the teaching of *Humanae vitae,* though some advocates of NFP seem to think it is. See the article by McCormick cited in note 24 and the article to which he is responding: Kevin Flannery, S.J. and Joseph Koterski, S.J., "Paul VI Was Right," *America* 169, 8 (September 25, 1993), pp. 7-11.

30. *Veritatis splendor* n. 104.

31. James P. Hanigan, *As I Have Loved You* (New York/Mahwah: Paulist Press, 1986), pp. 54-57, develops how virtual impediments relate to character and actual impediments to situation.

32. *Veritatis splendor* n. 4, "the intrinsic and unshakeable bond between faith and morality . . . "; n. 8, "It is [Christ] who opens up to the faithful the book of the Scriptures and, by fully revealing the Father's will, teaches the truth about moral action."

33. This is not to deny the critical function of reason; it is to suggest that there is more to the work of reason than a hermeneutic of suspicion, and that something more is the discovery of the truth of being, a far more fundamental task. Nor is the legitimate autonomy of reason called into question so long as reason acknowledges its own orientation to the truth, a truth reason itself does not create. *Veritatis splendor* n. 31-32.

34. *Ibid.* n. 28, "Our meditation on the dialogue between Jesus and the rich young man has enabled us to bring together the essential elements of revelation in the Old and New Testament with regard to moral action. These are: the subordination of

man and his activity to God, the one who 'alone is good'; the relationship between the moral good of human acts and eternal life; Christian discipleship, which opens up before man the perspective of perfect love; and finally the gift of the Holy Spirit, source and means of the moral life . . ."

35. Ibid., n. 29.

36. Grisez, *The Tablet*; see note 9; Robert P. George, Hadley Arkes, both writing separately in "The Splendor of Truth: A Symposium," *First Things* 39 (January 1994), pp. 24-29.

37. Both Paul VI and John Paul II have recognized that the arguments advanced by the magisterium are not always as solid as one might wish. *Veritatis splendor* n. 110, very gently acknowledges this possibility.

38. Ibid., n. 115.

39. Richard McCormick, "*Veritatis Splendor* in focus: 3: Killing the patient," *The Tablet* (October 30, 1993); Joseph Fuchs, "*Veritatis Splendor* in focus: 4: Good acts and good persons," *The Tablet* (November 6, 1993).

40. I also find the account of intrinsically evil acts in John Finnis, *Moral Absolutes: Tradition, Revision and Truth* (Washington, DC: Catholic University of America Press, 1991), especially pp. 31- 57, to be no more clarifying. The difficulty in comprehension may, of course, be mine, not the author's.

41. *Veritatis splendor* n. 80, the list is cited from *Gaudium et spes* 27.

42. Ibid.; the obliqueness of the reference is noted by Mary Tuck, "*Veritatis Splendor* in focus: 8: A message in season," *The Tablet* (December 4, 1993). Ms. Tuck describes herself as "an ordinary lay Catholic," not a moral theologian, and is strongly positive about the virtues of the encyclical.

43. See McCormick, as cited above in *The Tablet*.

44. See Donald Evans, "Paul Ramsey on Exceptionless Moral Rules," in *Love and Society: Essays in the Ethics of Paul Ramsey,* eds. James T. Johnson and David H. Smith (Missoula, Montana: Scholars' Press, 1974), pp. 19-46.

45. Joseph Fletcher, *Situation Ethics* (Philadelphia: The Westminster Press, 1966), pp. 165-165.

46. *Veritatis splendor* n. 79. The Pope is quoting himself here from his Apostolic Exhortation *Reconciliatio et poenitentia* 17, in *Origins* 14, 27 (December 20, 1984), p. 442.

47. None have done more in this regard than Richard McCormick in his work in "Moral Notes" in *Theological Studies*. See also the useful work by Bernard Hoose, *Proportionalism: The American Debate and Its European Roots* (Washington, DC: Georgetown University Press, 1987).

48. See Tuck, cited above in note 42 from *The Tablet*.

49. Bernhard Häring, "*Veritatis splendor* in focus: 2: A distrust that wounds," *The Tablet* (October 23, 1993).

50. John Finnis, "*Veritatis Splendor* in focus: 10: Beyond the encyclical," *The Tablet* (January 8, 1994).

15

Veritatis Splendor:
A Revisionist Perspective

Charles E. Curran

Pope John Paul II's encyclical, *Veritatis Splendor*, officially signed on August 6, 1993, has the "central theme" of the "reaffirmation of the universality and immutability of the moral commandments, particularly those which prohibit always and without exception intrinsically evil acts" (n. 115).[1]

The pope directs his remarks primarily to the state of Catholic moral theology today, but since the Catholic approach always saw its moral teaching affecting society as a whole the encyclical makes important remarks about life in the world today. The pope had publicly mentioned his intention of writing such an encyclical on August 1, 1987, the second centenary of the death of Alphonsus Liguori, the patron saint of moral theologians and confessors (n. 5). Rumors about the preparation, the primary authors, the central themes, and even the possible scrapping of the whole idea surfaced in the intervening years. The pope himself refers to the encyclical as "long awaited" and proposes as one reason for the delay that the *Catechism of the Catholic Church* should be published first (n. 5).

1.
Overview of the Encyclical

The encyclical is addressed to "the venerable brothers in the episcopate who share with me the responsibility of safeguarding 'sound teaching' " (n. 5).

The occasion for the new encyclical is the "new situation" within the Catholic Church itself. "It is no longer a matter of limited and occasional dissent, but of an overall and systematic calling into question of traditional moral doctrines on the basis of certain anthropological and ethical presuppositions" (n. 4). These dissenting positions are heard even in seminaries and theological faculties with regard to questions of the greatest importance for

---

Note: This article first appeared in David P. Efroymson and John C. Raines, eds., *The Open Church: A Festschrift for Gerard S. Sloyan* (Collegeville, MN: Liturgical Press, 1995).

the life of the church and souls (n. 4). This reality constitutes "a genuine crisis" for the church (n. 5).

At the root of these unacceptable presuppositions causing the present crisis are currents of thought which end by detaching human freedom from its essential and constitutive relationship to truth (n. 4). This explains the whole thrust of the encyclical, with its title of the "Splendor of Truth" and with the very first paragraph of the introduction citing 1 Pt 1:22 about the need for "obedience to the truth." The whole structure of the document with its three chapters follows logically and coherently from the understanding of the occasion for it and the root causes of the problem.

The first chapter involves an extended reflection on the story in Mt 19:16ff. of the rich young man who came to Jesus with the question, "What good must I do to have eternal life?" Jesus' response is to obey the commandments and to give up all his possessions and come follow Jesus. This comparatively long biblical reflection involves a somewhat new approach in papal teachings on moral matters. Catholic moral theology is traditionally based on human reason and natural law. However, similar but shorter reflections on biblical passages can be found in other encyclicals of the pope.[2] The pope uses this scriptural passage to point out that God's revelation includes moral commandments and the moral life is intimately connected with faith. However, in no way does the pope abandon the Catholic emphasis on natural law, as the second chapter makes abundantly clear.

The real import of the first chapter comes from its relationship to the purpose of the entire document. "Jesus' conversation with the rich young man continues in a sense in every period of history including our own" (n. 25). The church ('the pillar and bulwark of the truth'—2 Tm 3:15) continues the teaching role of Jesus with the "task of authentically interpreting the word of God . . . entrusted only (sic) to those charged with the church's living magisterium, whose authority is exercised in the name of Jesus Christ" (n. 27).[3] These quotations come from the end of the first chapter and make the point that the pope today continues the work of Jesus in teaching the commandments to guide the moral life of all the followers of Jesus.

The way in which scripture is used depends on the purpose of the one using it. Here the pope's purpose has shaped and limited the use of the scripture. The moral life is understood primarily in terms of commandments (to the exclusion and underplaying of other elements, such as the change of heart, virtues, vision, attitudes, moral imagination, goals, etc.), and the role of Jesus and consequently of the church is reduced to teaching commandments. Jesus as exemplar or paradigm is left out. The risen Jesus through the Spirit as the enabler and empowerer of the Christian life is not mentioned. The moral life itself is understood in light of a legal model, with the pope following the role of Jesus proposing the commandments "with the reaffirmation of the universality and immutability of the moral commandments, particularly those prohibiting always and without exception intrinsically evil acts" (n. 115).

The second chapter has an entirely different feel and approach. The pope, carrying on the moral teaching function of Jesus, points out and condemns certain interpretations of Christian morality which are not consistent with sound teaching. The pope explicitly denies any intention "to impose upon the faithful any particular theological system, still less a philosophical one" (n. 29). However, in reality John Paul II strongly reasserts the nineteenth and twentieth century Neo-Scholasticism of the manuals of moral theology within his more personalistic framework.

The general error pointed out in this section is a failure to recognize the importance of truth in moral theology and absolutizes freedom or conscience, cutting off their basic relationship to truth. The pope specifically mentions and condemns the most important aspects of the so-called revisionist school of Catholic moral theology (he does not use that term) that has been evolving since the Second Vatican Council—an autonomous ethic, the charge of physicalism made against the accepted Catholic teaching in sexual and medical ethics, the theory of fundamental option, and the ethical theory of proportionalism. All these in their own way have called into question the existence of some intrinsically evil acts. *Veritatis Splendor* in this chapter also strongly criticizes in the broader context the absolutization of freedom, false autonomy, subjectivism, individualism, and relativism.

Chapter three develops a number of related points. The first stresses the bond between freedom and truth. Commitment to the truth above all shows forth in the willingness of people to give their lives for the truth of the gospel of Jesus. Although martyrdom represents the high point of witness to moral truth, and one to which few people are called, all Christians must daily be ready to make a consistent witness at the cost of suffering and sacrifice (n. 93). Second, universal and unchangeable norms are at the service of persons and of the society, thus showing the necessary connection between freedom and truth. Only a morality which acknowledges certain norms and rights as valid always, everywhere, and without exception can guarantee an ethical foundation of social coexistence on both the national and international levels (n. 95-101). Third, the chapter recalls that God's grace transforms and strengthens weak and sinful human beings to be able to obey God's law (n. 102-105). A final section on morality and evangelization contains an important section dealing with the roles of the magisterium and of moral theologians who are called to be an example of loyal assent, both internal and external, to the magisterium's teaching (n. 106-117).

Reaction to the encyclical has followed a somewhat predictable course.[4] Proponents of what has been called revisionism in Catholic moral theology have tended to be quite negative,[5] whereas more conservative moral theologians have been quite positive, although some want the pope to go even further to a definitive and infallible magisterial judgment on the received teaching on intrinsically evil acts, and to the same kind of judgment on certain under-standings of faith and revelation which are even more fundamental.[6] Some more evangelically rooted scholars have lauded the pope's great emphasis on scripture and the gospel, but perhaps they do not give enough importance to how strongly the second chapter of the documents holds on to Neo-Scholastic philosophy.[7] Feminists readily find fault with the methodology involved.[8] A good number have been appreciative of the pope's dealing with the broader societal issues.[9] All of us interpret and react to the document in the light of our own understandings and interests, but we all must be careful to try to understand precisely what the pope is saying before entering into dialogue with him. In this spirit I recognize that I am coming from a revisionist posi-tion and have disagreed over the years with the papal teaching on intrinsi-cally evil acts and dissent in the church. One commentator has pointed out that the encyclical is directed at my work.[10] However, I also find myself in agreement with many points made in the encyclical.

2.
Positive Evaluation

I find myself in agreement with many of the pope's problems with some contemporary ethical thinking, with the positive points he makes against them, and with the applications especially in the area of social eth-ics. Moral truth is most important. Freedom and conscience can never be absolutized. There are many things one should not do (nn. 35-53). The Catholic tradition in the past often failed to give enough importance to free-dom, as exemplified in its long-standing opposition to religious freedom and the continuing problems with academic freedom. However, as the twentieth century developed, the Catholic Church in reaction to the danger of totali-tarianism began to give a greater role to human freedom. A very significant development occurred in Pope John XXIII's writings within two years. In *Mater et Magistra* in 1961 he claimed that the ideal social order was founded on the values of truth, justice, and love.[11] In *Pacem in Terris* in 1963 he added freedom to this triad.[12] Freedom is very significant, but it must be seen in its relationship to other values. The pope in *Veritatis Splen-dor* is concentrating on freedom's relationship to truth, but it is fair to say he is not denying the other important relationships of freedom with justice and charity. One is not free to deny fundamental human rights.

Just as freedom cannot be absolutized, so too conscience cannot be absolutized. Conscience cannot make something right or wrong (n. 54-64). Adolph Eichmann claimed that he only followed his conscience, but he was rightly convicted of crimes against humanity. Conscience is called to recog-nize and respond to moral truth.

Intimately connected with the absolutization of freedom or conscience is the false autonomy of the individual. The individual is not autonomous in the sense that the individual makes something right or wrong on her own. Here too, however, the Catholic tradition has not given enough importance to the role of creativity and the initiative of the individual. But one cannot go to the other extreme and proclaim the absolute autonomy of the individual. Any theistic morality sees the individual in relationship to and dependent on God.

The challenge is to avoid both a one-sided autonomy or a one-sided heteronomy. *Veritatis Splendor* deals well with this aspect of autonomy in the first part of the second chapter (n. 38-42). To its credit the Catholic tradition, with its emphasis on participation, has been able to provide a very satisfactory approach to this question. Too often the issue is proposed in terms of a competition between the divine and the human. If you have 100 points to assign to both, then you might assign eighty to God and twenty to the human. But maybe human beings should have more and God less. The traditional Catholic emphasis on participation and mediation as mentioned in the encyclical avoids such an either-or approach. The glory of God is the human person come alive. God wants us to attain our happiness and our perfection. The basic insight of Thomas Aquinas well illustrates this approach. In the Second Part of the Summa, Aquinas treats of the human being. The human being is an image of God because, like God, she is endowed with intellect, free will, and the power of self-determination.[13] The human person imitates God by using her intellect, free will, and the power of self-determination. Traditional Catholic moral theology, following the teaching of Thomas Aquinas, sees the natural law as the participation of the eternal law in the rational creature. Human reason reflecting on God's created human nature can arrive at the plan of God for us which involves our own fulfillment.[14] All theists and even some nontheists would join the Catholic tradition in denying the absolute autonomy of the human being. But the Catholic tradition does not want to embrace a heteronomy which downplays the place of self-direction and human fulfillment.

Likewise, the pope properly points out the related danger of individualism in our society (n. 33). The absolutization of freedom, conscience, and autonomy logically lead to individualism. The individual becomes the center of all reality, and not enough importance is given to the community in general, the various communities to which we all belong, and the relationships that tie us to other human beings. In the past, again, the Catholic tradition has not given enough importance to the individual, and sometimes in the name of community restricted the role and rights of the individual. Think of the acceptance of torture in some cases and the failure to recognize the right of the defendant not to incriminate oneself. Until this century it was universally held that the state could and should use capital punishment to protect itself, but now many Catholics, recognizing more the dignity of the person, strongly oppose capital punishment. A greater emphasis is being given to the rights of the individual vis-à-vis the state, but contemporary

Catholic thought, in keeping with the best of its own tradition, rightly rejects individualism. In the United States society today, many are criticizing American individualism in the name of a more communitarian understanding of human anthropology.[15] The Catholic tradition strongly supports such a communitarian critique of individualism.

Subjectivism logically follows from all the above-mentioned approaches. The pope correctly condemns the subjectivism that makes the subject the center of right and wrong and does not give enough significance to objective reality (n. 32). Here again the Catholic tradition in the past has not given enough importance to the subject, and many recent developments in Catholic theology and philosophy have embraced the turn to the subject, but this does not entail a radical moral subjectivism.

This radical subjectivism often appears in our society, but without much philosophical grounding. The morality accepted by many people today proclaims that you do your thing and I'll do my thing. Just don't interfere with each other. Such subjective individualism destroys any possibility of a community of shared truths and values. To have a community, one needs such shared moral values. The pope rightly points out there are rights that are always and everywhere to be acknowledged and protected. There are actions such as torture, arbitrary imprisonment, and treating workers as mere instruments of profit that should never be done (n. 95-97). The dangers of individualism and subjectivism are present in our contemporary American society.

Finally, John Paul II points out the danger of relativism for human social living (n. 96-101). The Catholic tradition by definition stands opposed to relativism. Catholic means "universal," and the pope insists on the existence of universal principles and norms. The danger in the Catholic tradition has been not to give enough importance to diversity in all its different forms. Think, for example, of the insistence on the universal language for liturgical prayer before Vatican II, so that almost no Catholic understood the language of the Eucharist. The Catholic emphasis on universality too easily claimed universality for what was a historically or culturally conditioned reality. Feminism reminds us how easy it was for those in power to impose patriarchy in the name of universality.

One of the most significant debates in contemporary ethics focuses on the possibility of universality in ethics, with many either theoretically or practically denying the possibility of such universality.[16] However, the Catholic tradition, with its emphasis on the one God who is Creator, Redeemer, and Sanctifier of all, can never accept a relativism. We are brothers and sisters of all other human beings and called to live together with them in peace and harmony. In the midst of the pluralism and diversity of our world, universalism is more chastened than in the past and more difficult to ground and explain. I think that the pope tends to gloss over too easily some of the objections to universalism, too readily grounds it in Thomistic natural law, and at times claims too much for it. However, the Catholic tradition has correctly insisted on universality.

The signs of the times also demand some universality. We experience the lack of unity in many countries in the world, including our own. Religious, ethnic, and tribal differences are the cause of war and disintegration in many nations. In our own United States' society, the divisions based on color and economic class are evident in every one of our cities. In our world with its growing interrelatedness, we badly need to be able to communicate with one another despite, religious, linguistic, ethnic, and cultural differences. In many ways the challenge to our society today is how to achieve unity in the midst of the great diversity that exists on all levels.

3.
Negative Evaluation

My strong disagreements with the papal letter center on his understanding of and approach to contemporary Catholic moral theology, and what might be described as the churchly aspect of moral theology as distinguished from Catholic social ethics. Having already identified myself as a revisionist Catholic moral theologian, one would expect such differences to be there. Naturally, I disagree with the position that condemns the revisionist developments in moral theology, but I am even more disturbed by other aspects of the papal document.

1. The Role and Understanding of Law. The first objection comes from the moral model which the pope proposes in *Veritatis Splendor.* Here John Paul II understands morality primarily on the basis of a legal model. Such an approach, which characterized the manuals of moral theology in vogue until very recent times, sees morality primarily in terms of obedience to the law or the commandments of God. No one can doubt that *Veritatis Splendor* employs such a model. The very first paragraph emphasizes the need for obedience to the truth, but recognizes that such obedience is not always easy. The pericope of the rich young man stresses Jesus as the teacher proposing the commandments that are to be obeyed. The first and longest of the four parts of chapter two deals with freedom and the law (n. 35-53). Chapter two especially emphasizes the role of the natural law. Positive precepts of the natural law are "universally binding" and "unchanging." The negative precepts of the natural law oblige always and in every circumstance—*semper et pro semper* (n. 52). The third chapter continues this approach with its emphasis on laws and commands and the church's firmness in defending the universal and unchanging moral norms (n. 96).

In the judgment of many, the legal model is not the best and most adequate model for moral theology or any ethics. At the very minimum the legal model cannot adequately cover all the moral decisions that a person makes. In fact, the vast majority of moral decisions are not made on the basis of existing laws. Law directly enters into comparatively few of the moral decisions by which we live our lives. In addition, the legal model tends to restrict moral considerations only to acts and forgets about the more important realities of change of heart, vision, attitudes, dispositions, etc. Thomas Aquinas did not follow a legal model, but rather a teleological model, based on what is the ultimate end of human beings. For Aquinas, the ultimate end of human beings is happiness, and actions are good if they bring one to that end and evil if they prevent one's arriving at that end. Reality, of course, is quite complex so there exists not only the ultimate end but also other ends which are not ultimate and interrelated with one another. In addition, Thomas Aquinas developed the moral life primarily in terms of human powers and habits and only brings in law at the end of his discussion of what we call fundamental moral theology.[17] The manuals of moral theology, the textbooks in the field before Vatican II, did adopt a legal model. Much has been said about the legal model, but for our present purposes it suffices to point out the inadequacy of the model and the fact that Thomas Aquinas himself adopted a different approach.

One might defend the legal model in *Veritatis Splendor* precisely because the pope is dealing primarily with the existence of universal and immutable moral commandments, especially those which prohibit always and without exception intrinsically evil acts. However, at the very minimum the encyclical should have pointed out that the legal model is not the most adequate model for moral theology, and this document is dealing only with one aspect of moral theology. Neither explicitly nor implicitly does the pope make such an admission. *Veritatis Splendor* thus gives the impression that it is describing the model for moral theology in general.

Ironically, someone in the Catholic tradition using the legal model tends to weaken the basic assertion of the entire encyclical that there is no opposition between freedom and law. Historically, the manuals of moral theology, with their legal model ever since the seventeenth century and later debates over probabilism, tended to posit an opposition between law and freedom. This assertion needs further explanation.

The Catholic tradition as illustrated in Thomas Aquinas has always insisted on an intrinsic morality. Something is commanded because it is good. For Aquinas the ultimate end of human beings is happiness. Morality involves what is good for me as a person and ultimately makes me flourish. There is no opposition between freedom and moral obligation, because the moral obligation is based on what is good for the individual. This is the central point to which the pope so frequently returns in his document. However, in the manuals of moral theology ever since the probabilism controversy, a greater opposition rather than harmonious agreement exists between freedom and law. Probabilism maintains that one may follow a truly probable opinion going against the existence of a law, even if the opinion favoring the existence of the law is more probable. The so-called reflex principle used to defend this position holds that a doubtful law does not oblige—an adage more attuned to human law than anything else. The individual starts out with freedom and this freedom can only be taken away by a certain law.[18] Ironically, the law model, as it was employed in the manuals of Catholic moral theology in the light of the probabilism controversy, emphasized the tension and apparent opposition between freedom and law, rather than the harmony which the pope wants to emphasize.

2. Laws which Always and Everywhere Oblige. The major thrust of the encyclical insists on universal, immutable moral commandments which prohibit always and without exception intrinsically evil acts. In this context note that the pope never cites the fifth commandment, "Thou shalt not kill." Everyone recognizes that killing is not always and everywhere wrong. We have justified killing in cases of self-defense and war. In fact, after much discussion and nuancing the manuals of moral theology came to the conclusion that the intrinsically evil act which is always forbidden is the following: direct killing of the innocent on one's own authority. Thus we allowed indirect killing, killing in self-defense or in war, and capital punishment.[19]

Notice the difference between the two. Killing is a physical act which in some circumstances can be permitted. The second rule tries to account for all the possible justifying circumstances and thus states the norm that admits of no exceptions. But one has to circumscribe quite severely the generic "no killing." The pope himself in this document does not cite this very specific absolute norm that was developed in Catholic moral theology.

What then is the papal example of the universal, immutable condemnation of an act that is always and everywhere wrong? The answer: murder. Thus in the passage about the rich young man in Matthew, Jesus begins the commandments with, "You shall not murder" (n. 13). All would agree that murder is always wrong because by definition murder is unjustified killing. Thus we have here three different types of norms dealing with killing. The pope cites only the very formal norm of no murder.

But there is a problem in *Veritatis Splendor* from the pope's own perspective because of a fourth formulation that is proposed. The pope wants to illustrate the point that there are intrinsically evil acts which are always and *per se* such on account of their very object and quite apart from the intention of the agent and circumstances. He quotes the *Pastoral Constitution on the Church in the Modern World,* paragraph 27, to illustrate this thesis (n. 80). The quote begins: "Whatever is hostile to life itself such as any kind of homicide. . . ." However, homicide is not an intrinsically evil act. Homicide is the physical act of killing a human being. Our language recognizes that homicide can be justifiable in certain circumstances.

But the problem might not come primarily from the pope. The official Latin version of the encyclical, in its citation from the *Pastoral Constitution on the Church in the Modern World,* uses the word *homicidium.*[20] Homicid-

ium in the Latin can refer either to murder or to homicide. As mentioned above, in this case the pope is citing a text from the *Pastoral Constitution on the Church in the Modern World* of the Second Vatican Council. Two unofficial English translations of the Vatican II documents translate *homicidium* as "murder."[21] However, the official translation of the papal encyclical that came from the Vatican uses the word "homicide." The error might rest with the translator and the approval of that translation by the Vatican. However, at the very minimum this goes to show how intricate and difficult it is to speak about norms that are always and everywhere obliging without any exception.

In fact, the list of actions found originally in the *Pastoral Constitution on the Church in the Modern World* and quoted in *Veritatis Splendor* contains some actions which are not always and everywhere wrong. Both documents include abortion under the category of "what is hostile to life itself." However, the Catholic tradition has always recognized the existence of some conflict situations and concluded that direct abortion is always wrong. Indirect abortion can be justified for a proportionate, reason so that abortion is not always and everywhere wrong. One would have to be stretching the point beyond belief to claim that the original clause of "whatever is hostile to life itself" means that homicide is murder and abortion is direct murder. The reality is that any homicide or abortion is hostile to life itself, but in some circumstances might be justified.

The second category of those actions in both documents which are now claimed by the pope to be always and everywhere wrong concerns "whatever violates the integrity of the human person such as mutilation. . . ." However, Catholic moral theology has consistently recognized justified mutilation. In fact, the primary precept in medical ethics justifies a mutilation of a part of the body for the sake of the whole.[22] Here again, one cannot appeal to the opening clause "whatever violates the integrity of the human person" to show that the mutilation in such a context excluded medical mutilation for the good of the whole person. If the heading were the dignity or total good of the human person then one could make such a claim. By definition all mutilation goes against the integrity of the person, but the Catholic tradition does not say that all mutilation is wrong. The pope's efforts to uphold laws that are intrinsically or always and without exception wrong by reason of the object is fraught with difficulties. There are such actions when the act is described in merely formal terms, such as murder. One could also make the case that there are such acts when the significant circumstances are included. In reality, *Veritatis Splendor* itself does not succeed in making a consistent case to prove its own position about acts that are always and intrinsically evil by reason of the object alone.

3. Evaluation of Contemporary Moral Theology. Veritatis Splendor strongly disagrees with and condemns many of the developments in Catholic moral theology since Vatican II and stands opposed to the revisionist moral theology in general.

However, *Veritatis Splendor* distorts and does not accurately describe the various positions attributed to so-called revisionist moral theologians. The first part of the second chapter disagrees with a school of autonomous ethics which first arose in Germany (n. 36, 37). I have disagreed with the name autonomous but accept the reality proposed in the sense that the moral content for life in this world is the same for Christians as for non-Christians. In my judgment, this position is in keeping with the traditional assertion that the Christian life brings the human to its perfection and fulfillment. Like *Veritatis Splendor* I have also disagreed with the contention that the scripture provides only *parenisis*, or exhortation, as some hold.[23] However, the supporters of autonomous ethics in the Catholic tradition would strongly disagree with the following description of their position. "Such norms . . . would be the expression of a law which man (sic) in an autonomous manner lays down for himself and which has its source exclusively in human reason. In no way could God be considered the author of this law except in the sense that human reason exercises its autonomy in setting down laws by virtue of a primordial and total mandate given to man by God" (n. 36).

Veritatis Splendor, in the same first part of chapter two, points out that some Catholic moral theologians have disagreed with the teachings of the hierarchical magisterium in the area of sexual morality because of their "physicalism" and "naturalistic" argumentation (n. 47). Such a statement is correct. In my opinion physicalism is the *a priori* identification of the human or the moral aspect with the physical, natural, or biological process. So far, so good. But the pope goes on to explain this theory in this way. "A freedom which claims to be absolute ends up treating the human body as a raw datum devoid of any meaning and moral values until freedom has shaped it in accordance with its design. Consequently, human nature and the body appear as presuppositions or preambles, materially necessary for freedom to make its choice, yet extrinsic to the person, the subject, and the human act. . . . The finalities of these inclinations would be merely 'physical' goods, called by some *premoral*. To refer to them, in order to find in them rational indications with regard to the order of morality, would be to expose oneself to the accusation of physicalism or biologism. In this way of thinking, the tension between freedom and a nature conceived of in a reductive way is resolved by a division within man (sic) himself" (n. 48).

Those who charge the hierarchical magisterium's teaching on sexuality with physicalism do not "treat the human body as a raw datum devoid of any meaning." The physical is one aspect of the moral or the fully human. The moral or the fully human must embrace all the aspects of the human— the physical and the spiritual, the sociological and the psychological, the eugenic and the hygienic, etc. In keeping with the Catholic tradition, one should never be guilty of a reductionism that reduces the fully human to just one aspect of the human, no matter what that aspect is. Yes, there are times when the physical is the same as the moral and the truly human, but this needs further justification to make the point.[24] In this very citation the pope contradicts his own assertion. *Veritatis Splendor* refers to this physical aspect as physical or premoral goods. Note the word "goods." They are not just "raw datum" or "extrinsic to the person." Those making the charge of physicalism take seriously the position of Pius XII that the physical and the bodily exist to serve the higher spiritual good of the person.[25] That one in theory can interfere with the physical or biological process because of the good of the total person as a whole seems to be very much in accord with any kind of personalism. But at the very least *Veritatis Splendor* distorts the position of those who characterize hierarchical Catholic sexual teaching as guilty of physicalism. We do not absolutize freedom and we do not deny any value or meaning to the physical. In our judgment, the hierarchical magisterium in this matter has absolutized the physical and the biological at the expense of the truly and the fully human.

The second part of chapter two deals with the relationship between conscience and truth. However, John Paul II also dealt with that question earlier in the encyclical. The pope claims that those who invoke the criterion of conscience as "being at peace with oneself" (he puts the words in quotation marks) are guilty of absolutizing freedom, forgetting the claim of truth, and subjectivism (n. 32).

I have proposed a theory of conscience which "attempts to explain in a more systematic and reflective way the traditionally accepted notion that joy and peace mark the good conscience which is the adequate criterion of good moral judgment and decision."[26] I explicitly point out that my approach disagrees with the position of the manuals that the judgment of conscience is based on conformity with the truth "out there." I developed this theory in dialogue with the transcendental approaches of Karl Rahner and Bernard Lonergan. However, I insist that one's judgment has to attain the true and the real value. I do put great emphasis on the subject but insist that "thus we have established the radical identity between genuine objectivity and authentic subjectivity."[27] Such an approach is proposed as a theory, and others might readily disagree with it, but it does not "exalt freedom to such an extent that it becomes an absolute" nor "adopt a radically subjectivistic conception of moral judgment" (n. 32).

In the second part of chapter two on conscience, it seems that the pope's insistence on the relationship between conscience and truth has influenced him to take a position which at the very least is in opposition to the generally accepted position in Catholic moral theology. *Veritatis Splendor* states: "It is possible that the evil done as the result of invincible ignorance or a nonculpable error of judgment may not be imputable to the agent; but even in this case it does not cease to be an evil" (n. 63). Thomas Aquinas maintained that invincible ignorance renders the act involuntary and excuses from sin. In other words, the evil act done in invincible ignorance is never imputable to the agent. The encyclical does not go as far as Aquinas and simply says that it "may not be imputable to the agent." However, St. Alphonsus Ligouri, the patron saint of moral theologians and confessors, goes even further than Aquinas. Alphonsus maintains that an act done out of invincible ignorance is not only not imputable but it is actually meritorious. This opinion of Alphonsus became the more common position among Catholic theologians.[28] Louis Vereecke, now an emeritus professor of the history of moral theology at the Academia Alfonsiana in Rome and a consultor to the Holy Office, concludes his article on conscience in Alphonsus Liguori by claiming that Alphonsus' moral doctrine on conscience embraces three values—the importance of truth, the importance of reason and conscience, and the importance of freedom.[29] By so emphasizing and perhaps even absolutizing the relationship of conscience to truth, *Veritatis Splendor* not only does not accept the position of Alphonsus, but does not even accept the position of Thomas Aquinas that does not go as far as Alphonsus.

The third part of chapter three addresses the theory of the fundamental option. Here also the theory is distorted. For example, the encyclical speaks of the theory as separating "the fundamental option from concrete kinds of behavior" (n. 67, see also n. 70). The theory of fundamental option distinguishes the different levels of human freedom and of transcendental and categorical acts, but it does not separate them. As Joseph Fuchs, who has written much on the fundamental option, points out, the encyclical distorts the meaning of the theory by failing to recognize that the fundamental option and categorical acts happen on different levels, and thus the fundamental option does not occur in the area of reflex consciousness.[30]

The fourth part of chapter three deals with the moral act, insists on acts that are intrinsically evil by reason of their object, and condemns teleological and proportionalist theories which hold "that it is impossible to qualify as morally evil according to its species—its 'object'—the deliberate choice of certain kinds of behavior or specific acts apart from a consideration of the intention for which the choice is made or the totality of the foreseeable consequences of that act for all persons concerned" (n. 79). On a number of occasions the pope points out that a good intention is not sufficient to determine the morality of an act (n. 67, 78). But no Catholic moral theologian I know has ever claimed that the intention alone suffices to determine the morality of an act.[31] Above, I pointed out that as a revisionist I accept some acts as always and everywhere wrong if the significant circumstances (not the totality of the foreseeable consequences) are included.

I have no doubt that the pope disagrees with all these recently developed theories in Catholic moral theology, but the encyclical tends to distort them and thus does not reflect their true meaning. In a certain sense, they are made into straw people which then are much easier to reject. However, this is not the worst distortion in the encyclical about the present state of Catholic moral theology.

The pope claims that the "root of these presuppositions [of the dissenting Catholic moral theologians] is the more or less obvious influence of currents of thought which end by detaching human freedom from its essential and constitutive relationship to truth" (n. 4). This sentence is found in the opening introduction to the entire document. The introduction to chapter two points out "these tendencies are at one in lessening or even denying the dependence of freedom on truth" (n. 34). Note some qualification in these statements, but the fundamental problem the pope has with revisionist Catholic moral theologians is their tendency to detach or lessen human freedom's relationship to truth. Such an assertion itself is not accurate. I know no Catholic moral theologian who absolutizes freedom or detaches conscience from truth. The real question remains the proverbial one: What is truth?

As a result of this misreading of the present state of Catholic moral theology, the pope apparently sees no difference between Catholic revisionist moral theologians and the proponents of absolute freedom, conscience separated from truth, individualism, subjectivism, and relativism. Non-Catholic colleagues or any fair-minded interpreter of the present state of Catholic moral theology would readily recognize that revisionist Catholic moral theologians are not absolutizing freedom or conscience and are not supporting individualism, subjectivism, and relativism. Catholic revisionist moral theologians strongly agree with the pope in opposing these positions. That is why I made it a point earlier in this essay to stress my strong agreement with the pope on these points.

All recognize that the pope strongly disagrees with and condemns revisionist Catholic moral positions, but the problem here is the understanding of revisionist moral theologians. Their theories are caricatured, but even worse, the pope falsely accuses them of absolutizing freedom and separating it from truth and wrongly identifies them with subjectivists, individualists, and relativists.

What is going on here? I do not know. Some have blamed the pope's advisors.[32] Such an approach is a familiar Catholic tactic. When Catholics disagree with the pope it is always easier to blame it on the advisors than on the pope. On the other hand, I have never heard anyone who agreed with a papal statement say that they agreed with the pope's advisors! Popes obviously have advisors but the final document is the pope's and not the advisors. More worrisome is the fact that the pope's area of expertise is ethics. Does he really think that Catholic moral theologians who dissent on some church teachings (especially in the area of sexuality) are subjectivists, individualists, and relativists?

A realistic assessment of the contemporary state of Catholic moral theology differs considerably from the picture painted in *Veritatis Splendor*. The differences between the pope and revisionist moral theologians are by no means as great as *Veritatis Splendor* states. Yes, different methodologies are often at work, but revisionist moral theologians have generally agreed with the papal teaching in the area of social ethics. Likewise, revisionist moral theologians are willing to accept some intrinsically evil acts when the object of the act is described in formal terms (murder is always wrong, stealing is always wrong) or when the act is described in terms of its significant circumstances (not telling the truth when the neighbor has no right to the truth).

The primary area of disagreement concerns the understanding of the moral object. The encyclical claims that morality is determined by the three sources of morality—the object, the end, and the circumstances—and that some actions are intrinsically evil by reason of their object (n. 71-83). The question is, how does one describe the object? As mentioned above, revisionist theologians would be willing to admit intrinsically evil acts by reason of the object if the object were described in a broad or formal way or with some significant circumstances. The earlier discussion about always obliging laws pointed out a very significant problem in the encyclical itself in describing the moral object.

Revisionists in general object to those cases in which the moral act is assumed to be identical with the physical structure of the act. These areas occur especially in the area of sexuality. As pointed out, not every killing, mutilation, taking something that belongs to another, and false speech are always wrong. Contraception, however, describes a physical act. The physical act described as depositing male semen in the vagina of the female can never be interfered with. Some people have mistakenly thought that the hierarchical teaching against contraception was based on a pronatalist position. Such is not the case. The hierarchical teaching also condemns artificial insemination with the husband's seed (AIH) even for the good end of having a child. The reason why both contraception and AIH are wrong is because the physical act must always be there and one can never interfere with it, no matter what the purpose.[33]

The charge of physicalism is intimately connected with the theory of proportionalism. Rather than describe the physical act or object as morally wrong, this theory speaks of premoral, ontic, or physical evil that can be justified for a proportionate reason. This challenges the hierarchical teaching on contraception, but also explains the existing hierarchical teaching on killing, mutilation, taking property, etc. There is no doubt that Catholic moral theologians are calling for a change in hierarchical teaching, especially in the area of sexuality, but they are precisely challenging these areas in which the moral aspect has been *a priori* identified with the physical aspect of the act. Thus the differences between these revisionist moral theologians and the pope are much less than the encyclical recognizes. The problem is not that dissenting moral theologians absolutize freedom and/or conscience or separate them from truth. The question remains: What is moral truth?

4. Hierarchical Magisterium and Theologians. The confrontation and differences within Catholic moral theology in the last few decades have centered not only on the moral issues themselves but on the ecclesiological questions of the role and functioning both of the hierarchical magisterium and of theologians. *Veritatis Splendor* explicitly addresses these issues in the third chapter (n. 106-117), although the role of the hierarchical magisterium is mentioned throughout the document.

The encyclical itself deals primarily with moral truth. The ultimate questions for both the hierarchical magisterium and for moral theology are "What is moral truth?" and "How do we arrive at moral truth?" *Veritatis Splendor* condemns many approaches in moral theology and in the broader ethical world, but it never really explicitly addresses the question about how the hierarchical magisterium itself arrives at moral truth. In fact, the encyclical gives the impression that the hierarchical magisterium just has the truth. However, the hierarchical magisterium like everyone else has to learn the moral truth. How is this done? The most frequently used phrase in this regard in the encyclical is the "assistance of the Holy Spirit." Mention is also made of the revelational aspect of morality and the hierarchical magisterium's role as the protector, guarantor, and interpreter of revelation.

The entire second chapter, with its discussion of very complex theories and positions, shows that the hierarchical magisterium also uses human reason in its attempt to know and explain moral truth. The Catholic insistence on mediation means that God works in and through the human and does not provide short circuits around the human. The assistance of the Holy Spirit does not exempt the hierarchical magisterium from using all the human reason necessary to arrive at moral truth. The tradition of Catholic natural law, once again affirmed and developed in this encyclical, maintains that its moral theology is based on human reason and is accessible to all human beings. Yes, the encyclical reminds us (correctly) that human sin affects all our reasoning processes, but sin does not take away human reason's ability to arrive at moral truth (n. 86-87). In learning moral truth, the hierarchical magisterium must use human reason like everyone else.

In the last few decades, many theologians have also pointed out the experience of Christian people as a source of moral knowledge. Once again, sin affects human experience and a proper discernment is required. One cannot just work on the basis of a majority vote. However, the hierarchical magisterium itself, in its *Declaration on Religious Freedom of the Second Vatican Council*, recognized the experience of Christian people as a source of moral wisdom by saying that the fathers of the council take careful note of these desires for religious freedom in the minds of human beings and proposes to declare them to be greatly in accord with truth and justice.[34] However, *Veritatis Splendor* never mentions even implicitly that the hierarchical magisterium can and should learn from the experience of Christian people. The pope explicitly says the fact that some believers do not follow the hiercharchical magisterium or consider as morally correct behavior that their pastors have condemned cannot be a valid argument for rejecting the moral norms taught by the hierarchical magisterium (n. 112).

The Thomistic moral tradition which the hierarchical magisterium claims to follow has insisted on an intrinsic morality: something is commanded because it is good, and not the other way around. The hierarchical magisterium does not make something right or wrong, but the hierarchical magisterium must conform itself to the moral truth. Thus the hierarchical magisterium must use all the means available to arrive at that truth.

In addition, the Thomistic tradition recognizes that one cannot have the same degree of certitude about practical truths as about speculative truths.[35] The hierarchical magisterium has a role in guaranteeing and protecting revelation under the inspiration of the Holy Spirit, but must also use all the human means available to arrive at moral truth and live with the reality that practical truths do not have the same degree of certitude as speculative truths. One cannot expect an encyclical to say everything on the subject, but a document dealing with the splendor of truth might have been expected to say something about the nature of moral truth, and how the hierarchical magisterium itself learns and knows this moral truth.

History points out that the teaching of the hierarchical magisterium in moral matters has been wrong in the past and has developed or changed. John Noonan has recently documented this change in the areas of usury, marriage, slavery, and religious freedom.[36] The fact that past teachings of the hierarchical magisterium in morality have been wrong must have some influence on how one understands the pronouncements of the hierarchical magisterium today.

The Catholic tradition itself has rightly recognized a hierarchy of truths,[37] and even the pre-Vatican II theology developed a system of theological notes to determine how core and central teachings are in Catholic faith.[38] All interpreters would admit that most of the papal teaching (I would say all, as would many others) on specific moral issues involves the noninfallible teaching office of the pope. The fact that something is noninfallible does not mean that it is necessarily wrong or that Catholics can disagree with it, but by definition it means that it is fallible. Catholic moral theologians, as well as the hierarchical magisterium, today must do more work to develop and talk about these different categories in the light of the general insistence on the hierarchy of truths and the older theological notes. At the very minimum, the hierarchical magisterium itself must also be willing to recognize the more tentative and peripheral nature of some of its pronouncements. In addition, the hierarchical magisterium has never come to grips with the fact that some of its teachings in the past have been wrong and subsequently changed.

Veritatis Splendor understands the role of the moral theologian in the light of its understanding of the hierarchical magisterium. The assumption is that the hierarchical magisterium, with the assistance of the Holy Spirit, has the moral truth and proclaims it. Therefore moral theologians are to give an example of loyal assent, both internal and external, to the hierarchical magisterium's teaching (n. 110).

Veritatis Splendor in an adversative clause acknowledges "the possible limitations of the human arguments employed by the magisterium," but calls moral theologians to develop a deeper understanding of the reasons underlying the hierarchical magisterium's teaching and to expound the validity and obligatory nature of the precepts it proposes (n. 110). Thus there might be limitations in the arguments proposed by the hierarchical magisterium, but these in no way affect the validity of the precepts it proposes.

In condemning dissent, the present document follows the approach of *Donum Veritatis,* the 1990 document of the Congregation for the Doctrine of the Faith on the role of theologians.[39] Dissent, in the form of carefully orchestrated protests and polemics carried on in the media, is opposed to ecclesial communion and to a proper understanding of the hierarchical constitution of the people of God. Opposition to the teaching of the church's pastors cannot be seen as a legitimate expression either of Christian freedom or of the diversity of the Spirit's gifts (n. 113). I know no Catholic moral theologian who dissents from church teaching who would propose what she or he has done in those terms. One might argue that such a definition of dissent leaves the door open for a different type of dissent. However, the encyclical itself calls for moral theologians to give an example of loyal assent, both internal and external, to the magisterium's teaching (n. 110).

The consideration here of the hierarchical magisterium does not intend to be a thorough discussion of the role of the hierarchical magisterium or of the moral theologian. This discussion is sufficient to point out the differences that exist. Revisionist Catholic moral theologians recognize the role of the hierarchical magisterium, but insist that its teachings cannot claim an absolute certitude on specific moral issues, have been wrong in the past, and might in some circumstances be wrong today. In this light dissent is at times a legitimate and loyal function of the Catholic moral theologian. However, *Veritatis Splendor* at the very minimum does not admit any kind of tentativeness or lack of absolute certitude about the teachings of the hierarchical magisterium, and in no way explicitly recognizes a positive role for dissent.

Ever since the pope announced his intention in August 1987 of writing an encyclical dealing more fully with the issues regarding the foundations of moral theology in the light of certain present-day tendencies, any student of moral theology had a pretty good idea of what the encyclical would do. The pope was certainly not going to change any of the teachings that have recently been reinforced, nor was he going to abandon the reasoning process behind those teachings. As a result, then, no one should be surprised by those aspects found in *Veritatis Splendor.*

What is surprising is the fact that the pope caricatures the positions of Catholic revisionist moral theologians and refuses to recognize the great areas of agreement between them and himself. One can only wonder why

Veritatis Splendor proposes such an either-or or all-or-nothing under-standing of the positions taken by Catholic revisionist moral theologians. The fundamental question remains:　what is moral truth?

Notes

1. Pope John Paul II, *Veritatis Splendor, Origins* 23 (1993), pp. 297-334.　References will be given in the text to the paragraph numbers in the encyclical.

2. E.g., the parable of the prodigal son in *Dives in misericordia,* nn. 6-7.　See Pope John Paul II, *"Dives in misericordia,"* in Michael Walsh and Brian Davies, eds., *Proclaiming Justice and Peace:　Papal Documents from Rerum novarum through Centesimus annus* (Mystic, CT: Twenty-Third Publications, 1991), pp. 344-47.

3. This passage is a citation from *Dei Verbum,* the *Constitution on Divine Revelation* of the Second Vatican Council, n. 10.

4. Symposia on *Veritatis Splendor* have appeared in *Commonweal* 120 (October 22, 1993), pp. 11-18; *First Things,* 39 (January 1944): 14-29.　*The Tablet* (London) devoted a series of eleven articles to the encyclical beginning with the October 16, 1993 issue, pp. 1329ff.

5. E.g., Bernhard Häring, "A Distress that Wounds," *The Tablet* 247 (October 23, 1993), pp. 1378-79; Richard A. McCormick, "Killing A Patient," *The Tablet* 247 (October 30, 1993), pp. 1410-11; Daniel C. Maguire, "The Splendor of Control," *Conscience* 14: 4 (Winter 1993/1994), pp. 26-29.

6. John Finnis, "Beyond the Encyclical," *The Tablet* 248 (January 8, 1994), pp. 9-10; Robert P. George, "The Splendor of Truth: A Symposium," *First Things,* 39 (January 1994), pp. 24-25; Germain Grisez, "Revelation vs. Dissent," *The Tablet* 247 (October 16, 1993), pp. 1329-31.

7. Stanley Hauerwas, *"Veritatis Splendor,"* *Commonweal* 120 (October 22, 1993), pp. 16-17; L. Gregory Jones, "The Splendor of Truth: A Symposium," *First Things,* 39 (January 1994), pp. 19-20; Oliver O'Donovan, "A Summons to Reality," *The Tablet* 247 (November 27, 1993), pp. 1550-52.

8. Lisa Sowle Cahill, "Accent on the Masculine," *The Tablet* 247 (December 11, 1993), pp. 1618-19.

9. E.g., Mary Tuck, "A Message in Season," *The Tablet* 247 (December 4, 1993), pp. 1583-85.

10. Maguire, p. 28.

11. Pope John XXIII, *Mater et Magistra,* n. 212, in David J. O'Brien and Thomas A. Shannon, eds., *Catholic Social Thought:　The Documentary Heritage* (Maryknoll, NY: Orbis Books, 1992), p. 118.

12. Pope John XXIII, *Pacem in Terris,* n. 35, in O'Brien-Shannon, *Catholic Social Thought,* p. 136.

13. Thomas Aquinas, *Summa Theologiae* (Rome: Marietti, 1952), $I^a II^{ae}$, Prologue.

14. Ibid., q. 91, a. 2.　John Paul II cites this passage in *Veritatis splendor,* n. 43.

15. E.g., Robert Bellah et al., *The Good Society* (New York: Alfred A. Knopf, 1991); Amitai Etzioni, *The Spirit of Community* (New York: Crown Publishers, 1993).

16. For my response to this debate, see *The Church and Morality: An Ecumenical and Catholic Approach* (Minneapolis, MN: Fortress Press, 1993), pp. 96-109.

17. Thomas Aquinas, *Prima Secunda* I^a II^{ae}.

18. See, for example, John Mahoney, *The Making of Moral Theology* (Oxford: Clarendon Press, 1987), pp. 224-45.

19. P. Marcellinus Zalba, *Theologiae Moralis Summa II: Tractatus de Mandatis Dei et Ecclesiae* (Madrid: Biblioteca de Autores Cristianos, 1953), nn. 243-66, pp. 255-86.

20. *Acta Apostolicae Sedis* 85, n. 12 (December 9, 1993), p. 1197.

21. Walter M. Abbott, ed., *The Documents of Vatican II* (New York: Guild Press, 1966), p. 226; Austin Flannery, ed., *Vatican Council II: The Conciliar and Post-Conciliar Documents* (Northport, NY: Costello Publishing, 1975), p. 928.

22. Zalba, n. 251-52; pp. 263-68.

23. Charles E. Curran, *Toward an American Catholic Moral Theology* (Notre Dame, IN: University of Notre Dame Press, 1987), pp. 57-59.

24. Charles E. Curran, *Directions in Fundamental Moral Theology* (Notre Dame, IN: University of Notre Dame Press, 1985), pp. 127-37; 156-61.

25. Pope Pius XII, "The Prolongation of Life," (November 24, 1957), in Kevin D. O'Rourke and Philip Boyle, eds., *Medical Ethics: Sources of Catholic Teachings* (St. Louis, MO: Catholic Health Association, 1989), p. 207.

26. Curran, *Directions in Fundamental Moral Theology,* p. 244.

27. Ibid., p. 242.

28. Louis Vereecke, *De Guillaume d'Ockham à Saint Alphonse de Liguori* (Rome: Collegium S. Alfonsi de Urbe, 1986), pp. 555-60; James Keenan, "Can a Wrong Action Be Good? The Development of Theological Opinion on Erroneous Conscience," *Église et Théologie* 24 (1993), pp. 205-19. However, Aquinas, Alphonsus, and Pope John Paul II all recognize that the external act remains an objective disorder and is wrong.

29. Vereecke, *De Guillaume d'Ockham*, p. 566.

30. Joseph Fuchs, "Good Acts and Good Persons," *The Tablet* 247 (November 6, 1993), p. 1445.

31. McCormick, "Killing a Patient," pp. 1410-11.

32. Fuchs, p. 1445; McCormick, p. 1411.

33. See "Artificial Insemination" and "Contraception," in O'Rourke and Boyle, eds. *Medical Ethics,* pp. 62, 92-95.

34. *Declaration on Religious Freedom*, n. 1, in Abbott, *Documents of Vatican II*, p. 676.

35. Thomas Aquinas, I^a II^{ae}, q. 94, a. 4.

36. John T. Noonan, "Development in Moral Doctrine," *Theological Studies* 54 (1993), pp. 662-77.

37. *Decree on Ecumenism*, n. 11, in Abbott, *Documents of Vatican II,* p. 354.

38. Sixtus Cartechini, *De Valore notarum theologicarum* (Rome: Gregorian University Press, 1951).

39. Vatican Congregation for the Doctrine of the Faith, "Instruction on the Ecclesial Vocation of the Theologian," *Origins* 20 (1990), pp. 117-26.

16

The Nature of Christian Love

John Giles Milhaven

The encyclical *Veritatis Splendor* generates its presentation of Christian morality and spirituality out of its description of Christian love. What does it understand Christian love to be?

Love, says the encyclical, is not only the calling of the Christian. It is his life. He has no other true life. In this life everything is love or flows from love or supports love. The life of the Christian is presently a life of faith and hope as well as love, but faith and hope feed the love only so long as this is necessary (n. 15). Then, as Paul says, faith and hope pass away; only love remains. This love that makes up the substance of Christian life is nothing but a share, however imperfect, of God's love. God gives men a share in his love; it is communicated and revealed in Jesus (n. 11). In presenting the encyclical's theology and spirituality, I maintain respectfully the English translator's use of "man," "men," and masculine pronouns to designate persons of both genders. In speaking for myself I will do otherwise.

The word "love" has many meanings. Humanly speaking, there are many kinds of "loves," many ways of "loving." What is Christian love? Inasmuch as the Christian loves, he becomes like God, who is Love (n. 24, 10). The love with which the Christian loves must then be somewhat like God's love. What then is the nature of Christian love? As does the encyclical, so I focus this question mainly on love for other men. How does the Christian love other men? The Christian loves them as God loves them and him (n. 24). Correspondingly, the Christian loves them as Jesus Christ loved and loves him and them (n. 20, 22, 24). What then is the nature of Christian love for other men? As the encyclical stresses, Christian love for other men is a giving because God's love for men is a giving. Since he gives them a share in this love, he gives them a giving. He empowers and energizes them to give. He enables them to give to other men in some small degree as he does. This love communicated in Jesus and shared thereby with men is above all a giving of self. God in creating or redeeming gives himself. In this earthly life, the ideal human love lived by Jesus is a giving of self epitomized in beneficent sacrifice. Christ imitates the Father's love by giving himself, i.e., his life, for men. If the Christian loves as fully as a man can, he will, like Christ, give his whole life for others, by continual sacrifice and even martyrdom if need be (n. 120; also n. 15, 17, 20, 22, 85, 87, 89, etc.).

That true love of another person, whether the lover be divine or human, is a giving which undergirds the whole message of the encyclical on love. Since the encyclical says little else of the nature of this love, that love is a giving could convey that the one who loves is, at least in any given act of love, superior to the one loved in that the *whole* loving is the lover giving and the loved one able to receive. For the same reason the lover would be in loving relatively independent while the loved one depends on him.

This superiority and independence of the lover vis-à-vis the beloved is obviously intended by the encyclical to be true of God vis-à-vis men. The lack of any other indication for the case of men loving men would seem to imply that it is true here, too. I will shortly argue that these two possible implications for men loving men need to be eliminated. Here the picture of good human love drawn by the encyclical must be completed. But note first that this love extolled by the encyclical is not selfless. The encyclical makes this clear and it is, of course, traditional in Catholic Christianity. For one thing, the Christian, in loving his fellow men, is motivated principally by his desire to be with God for all eternity, for loving his neighbor is essential to his getting there. In the total reality of their act, Jesus on Calvary and Christian martyrs do not "give themselves" or "give their life." Their faith is difficult and admirable, and by it they know that they are only superficially, most briefly giving self or life, while at the same moment *gaining* self and life eternally in blissful security with God.

The Christian is motivated here also by a second, good kind of self-love. The Christian, in striving to love others as God does, strives consciously to be like God who loves men for their own sakes (n. 13). If he gives lovingly, he thereby, however minimally, becomes like God and this is pure gain for him. He knows it and wants it very much. As the encyclical asserts repeatedly, the Christian by loving strives knowingly, appropriately, and successfully to attain perfection (e.g., n. 17, 18, 20, 34, 38, 39, 51, 71, 78, 79).

Both these motives are completely satisfied whether or not the loved one actually receives, i.e., takes what the lover gives. I agree with this traditional understanding of good human love so far as it goes. Good love for another person is never selfless but is always self-loving, too. In loving you well, I always love me, too. At very least, in willing you some good for your sake, I cannot help willing and annealing my so willing. I love you for your sake, but also for my own sake, for loving is a good thing, and I want and am glad to be doing it. Moreover, I gain peace and satisfaction at your getting the good I want you to get. Modern Christian exalting and urging of "selfless" love leave me bewildered. But good human loving is more than self-loving. It is other-loving, too. Curiously, though the encyclical affirms this repeatedly, it explicates it hardly at all.

What is good human love of the other for his or her sake? What is the conscious reality of good, genuine love of another person? Whenever we give, of course, we intend the other to receive what we give. But the other's receiving may not be a real motive of ours in this giving. We may not really care. For example, the two self-loving motives which I sketched above are perfectly good in themselves and may be our only motive. We know by theory and experience that this can happen. When it does, then "giving myself" to others, helping them perhaps at my cost and pain, is narcissistic. It is only self-loving. I give to others only because I will it as a good thing for me to do so. I take satisfaction only in my deliberately willing and acting this way. I may thus admire myself self-giving, and trust that others, too, admire me for this. That the object of my love actually receives my gift is also my intent, but only superficially so. I am not deeply disappointed nor frustrated if he or she does not. I have achieved my sole real goal, satisfied my operative motive: I have been a loving person with this person. That he did not take what I gave disappoints me a bit, but I serenely plan to be giving again to him or to someone else. I will continue to be a loving person and that alone is important!

The encyclical does not endorse any such narcissistic view of Christian giving love. But neither does it bring out traits of good human love that exclude such narcissism. In good human giving love one not only wants to be a loving, giving person but one wants very much that the other take the gift. The father saw his returning prodigal son while he was yet at a distance (Lk 15:20ff). Did he perhaps often look up the road for him? In any case, the father was moved in his inner organs (*esplagxnisthe*), ran to his son, fell upon his neck and embraced him. The son blurted out his guilt and unworthiness, but the father said only,

> Bring quickly the best robe and put it on him! Put a ring on his hand
> and shoes on his feet. And bring the fatted calf and kill it and let us eat
> and make merry. For this my son was dead and is alive again, was lost
> and is found.

And they began to make merry.

When the elder son protests afterwards that no such celebration was ever given him who stayed at home and served the father faithfully, the father replies,

> Son, you are always with me and all that is mine is yours. It was fitting
> to make merry and be glad, for this your brother was dead and is alive;
> he was lost and is found!

In telling of the love of the father for the prodigal son, Jesus shows dimensions of good love that the encyclical does not exclude but fails to present. For one thing, in loving, the father wants not so much himself loving as—much more!—his son's return. His love is satisfied little by itself, i.e., by his steadfast loving, but mainly by his son's return. The father's new, happy feelings and actions arise from his son, once dead and lost, being now alive and found. The father exults, not in his own love, but in his son's return.

Welcoming his son extravagantly, he invites all the others to join him in making merry and being glad of what his son has done. The father's love, though centered on his returned son, is not selfless: the father makes himself, too, merry and he is glad. He is merry, yes, principally, because his son is alive once more. But he is merry also because he has found his son. They are now together again. Satisfied is now his aching longing for him over the years, the longing with which, I assume, he kept looking up the road. I imagine, too, that he has in all the merrymaking a dim, underlying satisfaction that he is being a good, loving father.

The story of the prodigal son makes clear another dimension of good human love, again a dimension passed over by the encyclical. The other-centered nature of the father's love makes him dependent on his returning son. By returning, the son gives a great gift, himself, to the father. Because of his love, the father happily receives from the son. Yet the son did not return out of a love to give himself to the father. His giving himself to his father was not his motive or purpose, but a means to a self-centered end. "How many of my father's hired servants have bread enough and to spare, and I perish here with hunger?" (v. 17). He returned so he could, as hired hand, have enough to eat. But because the father loved the son truly for his own sake, his return, whatever his motivation, was for the father a precious gift from the son to the father. Jesus stresses how glad the father was and that this merry gladness comes mainly because the son in fact returned and now profits from the father's bounty.

The father's love for his son made him deeply dependent on his son. This receiving dependency essential to loving another truly for her or his own sake emerges as well when someone loves another for his own sake and the other does not take the offered gift. Jesus weeps over Jerusalem for what will befall it and its inhabitants because they did not recognize his visiting them (Lk 19:41). He compares himself to a mothering hen, "How often would I have gathered your children together as a hen gathers her brood under her wings, and you would not!" (Mt 23:37). Jesus feels the pain that a giving love that is not narcissistic feels. It is not enough that one loves and gives. One wants absolutely, primarily, that the other receive! It is painful, at times agonizing, devastating, if the other does not. In the Middle Ages there arose through Western Europe countless images of the *pietà* drenched in pain, holding her lifeless son. In her love she wants him to be there alive, but he is not. She wants him to feel her embrace, but he cannot. In the *pietàs* of northern Europe there is little peace or hope in the sculpted lines of Mary. Only sinking grief. His assurances of his rising again are not in her mind. How many women identified in prayer with this love of Mary?

I have perhaps blurred two kinds or phases or dimensions of good love of the other for her or his own sake. Permit me to repeat and better distinguish. My goal is much less a more precise, coherent conceptualizing than a more revelatory pointing to differing contours of two important, precious experiences. First, there is in love a ground that precedes its being a giving. This ground within all good love is that I will the loved one, simply for his or her own sake, to be well in some concrete way. Mary most basically wanted just that her son thrive, that he do well what he do and that he be satisfied therein. I picture her at times listening to him from the edge of the crowd and rejoicing at his powerful, exciting words. Most basically, the father wanted the son to prosper truly and be happy, whether he return to the father or not.

What this ground-love adds importantly to the picture drawn by the encyclical is that by this ground of other-love I depend on my loved one. I seek to receive from her or him. What I depend for and want to receive is that they are well. Inasmuch as my primary willing and wanting is of this, I take on a profound dependency and radical receiving. We recognize this in the movement of the "innards" of the father of the prodigal son, in Jesus weeping over Jerusalem and in the grief-stunned *pietà*. It will not be an important dependency or receiving if my main will is not for the loved one's happiness but for myself to so will and thus be admirably loving.

I am trying to identify a common, banal fact of experience. My daughter and her family have moved off to Las Vegas. They seem to me, after difficulties and setbacks, to be moving now towards new happiness and strength and familial unity. I think often of them there and want wholeheartedly their prosperity, growth, and happiness. When I do, I miss them keenly but I feel warm satisfaction since I believe that such is their life now beginning to be. Quite apart from anything else, herein I receive from them the satisfaction that I feel when I think of them. It is of course a bit frightening. Things could turn bad. I fear this bad turn mainly for their sake, but I am aware that it would also upset me terribly. My happiness depends in good part on their happiness.

But there is a second ground in all good love of the other for himself or herself. The encyclical mentions several times that good love desires "communion" of persons, but it does not develop in what the "communion" consists (n. 51, 52, 72, 86, 88, 118). We want not only that the loved one prosper and be happy. We want to be with her. The father wished not only that his prodigal son prosper but that he come home. The grieving mother not only wanted her Son to be alive; she wanted to be there with him. Jesus not only wanted the people of Jerusalem to turn to God. He wanted to gather them to himself as a hen her chicks.

I phone my daughter every night. When we so want to be with the loved one and want it for its own sake and strongly, then we depend in this way, too, on the loved one. We depend on the loved one's response to us. We depend thus much more on him and her than if we were just willing their good. We want to receive the other's presence simply for itself. In thus simply wanting the two of us to be together, we obviously are willing something for ourselves as well as for the other. The father wills the return of the prodigal son and their new life, both for his son and for himself. Neither aspect is subordinated to the other. He wants both for their own sake. So, too, Jesus, Mary and myself in the examples above! Selflove and other-love are intertwined in a beautiful, though painful, loving. There is here a certain mutuality even though only one is loving.

It is, however, a very limited mutuality. My examples, so far as I have described them above, are of one-sided love. The parable says nothing of what goes on in the prodigal son at his loving reception by his father. The people of Jerusalem are still ignoring Jesus. The pieces of sculpture make dramatically evident that Mary holds in her lap a dead body. I have said nothing of my daughter's feelings or actions in my regard. But the best human love is two-sided, reciprocal.

One of the most valuable contributions of contemporary women writers to Christian morality and spirituality is to bring out the full *mutuality* of the best human love. In other words, the best human love is when two or more persons *love each other* with the other-loving, self-loving, giving, receiving, dependent love that I have tried above to identify. This mutuality of full human love is as undeveloped by the encyclical as are the two aspects of one-sided love I sketched earlier. The picture drawn by the encyclical of good human love fits rather the ideal of Greek and Hellenistic philosophers. The wise person is self-sufficient and gives of his abundance serenely. He gains nothing from his wisdom being received. His giving is a simple over-flow. Though it is one of his intents, he in no way needs or wants urgently that these individuals receive his giving love. Recall Socrates, at the anger of his enemies and the grief of his friends, drinking the hemlock insouciantly. So, too, the Stoic facing serenely the death imposed on him because he persisted in speaking the truth to others. These heroes feel little pain at those who did not heed them. Little pain for those who have heeded, now love them and grieve at losing them by their death. And little pain at losing these friends.

From the third century through the middle ages of western Christianity, the *Song of Songs* grew in being esteemed for its metaphors of true love. No book of the Bible received more commentaries from the medieval cloister. The two lovers of the *Song of Songs* were seen as God or Christ and the Church or the individual Christian. In their burning desire to be with each other and their pleasure when they succeed, the lovers abundantly give to and receive from each other. For their happy being together they manifestly depend on each other, though I doubt that any commentary dares affirm explicitly that God depends on those he loves and seeks and enjoys. Systematic theologians throughout the course of Christianity wrestle with how God can love humanity for its own sake and yet still be totally independent. Hardly any theologians take the route of Hadewijch of the 13th century or Carter Heyward of the 20th and depict God loving human individuals in mutual interdependence. But Christians through the Song of Songs or countless other imaginations—in devotion to the Sacred Heart, for instance—have experienced their personal love for God and God's personal love for them as mutually giving, receiving, dependent. Whether lettered or unlettered, they knew this was the best kind of love and trusted that God had somehow taken them up into this mutual, interdependent love with Himself. It is sad, misleading, that the encyclical proposes so incomplete a picture of this traditional, fundamental, lived Christian love. The encyclical simply omits the mutuality, complete or partial, that I have sketched. This impoverishment carries over into the encyclical's exposition of Christian social morality. Social union, harmony, cohesion, etc., are grounded correctly by the encyclical in rights, duties, personal dignity and other properties of the individual. But the encyclical stops there (n. 96-101). The peculiar value and intrinsic demands of interpersonal mutuality are not discussed. Yet, for example, it is crucial for good family life that its members work not only to observe duties and rights and each other's personal dignity but also to grow among themselves a strong, live, giving-receiving, interdependent love as I have outlined above. A father might with all good will and intellectual honesty strive to observe all rights and dignity of family members and to "give" lovingly, even to "give himself" to them in loving devotion. But he is a sorely lacking father if in the daily flow of family life he does not also receive from the others and depend substantially on them. Similarly a teacher or social worker or church authority or leader and those to whom they give. One who envisages his responsibilities as regularly and profoundly involving both his giving and his receiving will understand those responsibilities differently from one who does not. This is obvious, of course. Why does the encyclical omit it?

The encyclical affirms the sexual and its value principally as simply an instance of the bodily and its value. The value of the body is discussed principally in term of current false interpretations of it. Only briefly does it identify positively what is the value of the bodily. Reason and free will, it notes repeatedly, are linked with all the bodily and sense facilities. In the unity of body and soul the person is the subject of his own moral acts. If he loves morally, he respects certain fundamental spiritual and bodily goods. He respects purposes, rights and duties based upon the bodily and spiritual nature of the human person (n. 48, 50). In this context the encyclical does not answer any question on the nature of the love at work here. An exception: As subject of his own moral acts, the person, by the light of reason and the support of virtue, discovers in the body "the anticipatory signs, the expression and promise of the gift of self, in conformity with the wise plan of the Creator" (n. 48). But if the best love is not merely to give but to give in receiving and receive in giving, in mutuality and interdependence, then certain bodily goods of nature can lie in being simply that. They are not "expression" and "promise" but the reality of intrinsically good and worthwhile embodied, mutual loving. They can be a meal shared or a playing together or a walking together or a working together or a making love together. No further goal is needed to constitute this supreme good. Going to sleep with my wife or talking with my friend, Dick, or teasing and being teased by my granddaughter, Stephanie, are great in themselves. They need no further justification. One place where this understanding of the best love would challenge sweeping prohibitions by traditional Christian morality is obviously contraceptive sex or sex between two lovers of the same gender. What if the two are in their lovemaking thoroughly loving, mutually giving and receiving? This sexual activity is then in itself good and fine. But the positive implications of this understanding of the supreme good of loving, embodied mutuality are a million times broader than the sexual. As I said above, Christian women thinkers, particularly over the last 30 years or so, have kept pushing back the frontier in this direction. But all of us who study Christian morality and spirituality—and that includes all Christians—can go further in uncovering in experience and spelling out these implications.

Note

See Hadewijch, *The Complete Works*. tr. Mother Columba Hart, O.S.B (New York: Paulist Press, 1980), and Carter Heyward, *Touching Our Strength: The Erotic as Power and the Love of God* (San Francisco: Harper & Row, 1989). Cf. my *Hadewijch and Her Sisters: Other Ways of Loving and Knowing* (Albany, NY: State University of New York Press, 1993).

17

Veritatis Splendor:
Some Implications for Bioethics

B. Andrew Lustig

Although *Veritatis Splendor* was issued only in October 1993, it has already provoked significant reaction, as exemplified by the present collection. In this essay, I will focus on the ways that the encyclical's discussion of fundamental themes and general questions of methodology sheds light (or casts shadow) on issues in bioethics. The essay falls naturally into four parts. In Part 1, I review six basic themes the encyclical develops and briefly consider their implications for matters of method in moral theology and for particular issues in bioethics and sexual ethics. In Part 2, I review the encyclical's analysis of certain methods it characterizes as "teleology, proportionalism, and consequentialism" in recent Catholic moral theology. In this section, I assess the fairness of the encyclical's criticisms in light of the work of Richard McCormick and conclude that *Veritatis Splendor* fails to depict accurately either the general spirit or the subtle particulars of the tendencies it criticizes, at least as reflected in his writings. (The fairness of the encyclical's depiction of those methods as practiced in secular ethics I set aside as a separate issue, though one that would be useful to consider on its own merits). Nonetheless, in concluding Part 2, I argue that proportionalism has not fully answered the criticisms that can legitimately be raised against it, although these more nuanced criticisms do not appear in the encyclical's discussion. In Part 3, I consider two concrete issues—artificial contraception and artificial insemination by husband—in light of the discussion in *Veritatis Splendor*. I suggest that specific differences between the encyclical's approach and proportionalist alternatives raise further questions about the appropriate sources of authority for moral theology and about the criteria at work in the different conclusions reached on the issues I consider. Finally, in Part 4, I identify several controverted questions about the sources and bindingness of the Church's teaching authority.

Veritatis Splendor is relatively modest in its discussion of concrete moral issues. Indeed, specific conclusions require its readers to do significant further work in applying its fundamental theological and methodological themes to concrete matters. This is especially so in considering the implications of *Veritatis Splendor* for issues in bioethics. However, if one situates the encyclical within the ongoing discussion of the past 25 years, from the issuance of *Humanae Vitae*[1] through the 1987 instruction *Donum Vitae*[2] by the Congregation for the Doctrine of the Faith, a number of issues— those involving the legitimate ends of and constraints on sexuality in mar- riage, the nature of parenting, and the assessment of new reproductive tech- niques—can be assessed, through the lens of *Veritatis Splendor*, by extend- ing the focus of inquiry back to earlier documents and positions. In this way, the broader emphases of the encyclical on general matters of method in moral theology can be applied to particular questions about which it may have little expressly to say.

1.

In this section, I set forth six fundamental themes developed in *Verita- tis Splendor*. To varying degrees, each theme has implications for matters of general ethical method and for specific issues in bioethics. This strategy will enable me, in Part 3, to rehearse those implications for specific issues in bioethics. Despite my desire to be brief, I will discuss the fourth theme in more extended critical fashion, because it bears directly on the issues I dis- cuss in Part 3.

First, the encyclical reaffirms a theme long fundamental to John Paul II's writings. Freedom is not an absolute value to be celebrated in the way so often developed in secular literature and philosophy. Rather, freedom in the Christian sense can only be seen in the light of truth, a truth developed in *Veritatis Splendor* as the truth of Christ, indeed, the truth that is Christ. This freedom is an embodied freedom. The facts of embodiment relate cen- trally to general natural law claims about the purposes of rightly ordered human choices and actions, and about the licitness of particular bodily ac- tions as expressive, or distortive, of a unitary perspective.

Second, the encyclical emphasizes the necessary connection between faith and morality. Faith cannot be separated from morality, nor, given the role of the Church in speaking as moral teacher to both the people of God and the world at large, can a properly interpreted morality be separated from faith. This theme raises unsettling questions about how best to understand the Church's teaching authority, especially about how revelation and reason are seen to interact as sources of moral authority and about how these sources are to be interpreted in drawing moral conclusions about specific actions.

Third, the encyclical underscores that Church teachings on moral is- sues are grounded in a commitment to objective, universal truth, most fully manifested in the person of Jesus Christ. This same alliance—between genu- ine moral freedom and the reality of objective moral truth—also underlies the natural law tradition in a more "minimal" sense than its full expression in Christ. Faith based on revelation and a "natural" human morality based on right reason (i.e., practical reason teleologically directed toward proper human ends) are not compartmentalized in the Catholic tradition, either in social teaching since the time of Leo XIII or in issues of sexual ethics or bioethics. Hence, in n. 52,[3] John Paul sets forth the links in the tradition between natural law as a source of moral insight and the goods that human beings share in common:

> Precisely because of this truth, the natural law involves universality. Inasmuch as it is inscribed in the rational nature of the person, it makes itself felt to all beings endowed with reason and living in history. In order to perfect himself in his specific order, the person must do good and avoid evil, be concerned for the transmission and preservation of life, refine and develop the riches of the material world, cultivate social life, seek truth, practice good, and contemplate beauty. . . . Inasmuch as the natural law expresses the dignity of the human person and lays the foundation for his fundamental rights and duties, it is universal in its precepts and its authority extends to all mankind.

This third motif, of course, draws again upon the first theme, here through a discussion of natural law. *Veritatis Splendor* affirms that freedom cannot be an end in itself, unfettered to rightly ordered choice, because as Christians we acknowledge that we participate in a teleologically shaped created order. We have ends that we can know and goods against which we should never directly choose. This teleological orientation, as a general tendency, may be obvious enough; however, as I will indicate in Part III, its moral implications for particular issues are not.

Fourth, the encyclical stresses that morality must be understood according to revelation and reason, and in light of the Church's magisterial authority as teacher. In this context, the encyclical draws specific conclusions about the nature of certain acts that the Church deems intrinsically evil, i.e., acts that allow for no justified exceptions. Positive precepts (for example, to worship God, to honor one's parents) "which order us to perform certain actions and cultivate certain dispositions, are universally binding; they are unchanging" (n. 52). So, too, the negative precepts of the natural law are ". . . universally valid. They oblige each and every individual, always and in every circumstance." As examples of the latter, the encyclical observes: "The Church has always taught that one may never choose kinds of behavior prohibited by the moral commandments expressed in negative form in the Old and New Testaments" (n. 52).

Such assurances regarding the unchanging and universally binding nature of the negative precepts of the natural law leave a great deal unaddressed, especially when one considers implications for particular issues in sexual ethics and bioethics. To speak of the moral law as "in principle" accessible to human reason is, on Roman Catholic terms, unobjectionable. But how that moral law will be accessible to all persons everywhere at all times, independent of a revelation-informed faith and independent of the Church's teaching authority, remains unclear. Here the issue goes to the heart of ecclesiological understanding and the way that respective sources of moral authority are employed to draw moral conclusions, even about putatively shared natural law precepts. Especially problematic is the encyclical's linkage of quite general natural law directives to particular judgments about concrete acts, especially in reproductive ethics. For example, most secularists of good will, indeed, most other Christians, do not view artificial contraception or artificial insemination by husband as essentially disordered. The bridgework between the basic moral prohibitions that John Paul, like John Calvin, finds in the second table of the Decalogue and specific judgments about particular acts is not provided, but assumed. Granted, the encyclical's lack of detailed argument presumes upon the history of 25 years of discussion since *Humanae Vitae*. But even focused discussion, as in *Donum Vitae*, has failed to address systematically how general teleological appeals to natural law should be understood in their specific applications.

In *Donum Vitae*, the unclarity was compounded. That document invoked the "obviousness" of natural law, clarified by the Church's interpretation of revelation, both for Catholics and, in its final section, for society at large in its specific recommendations for legislation.[4] By contrast, *Veritatis Splendor*, unlike encyclicals addressed to all persons of good will, is specifically written to the bishops as teachers of the Church. The encyclical thereby avoids the confusion that plagued *Donum Vitae* in its use of revelation and reason as sources of authority for its prescriptions to the larger culture. Nonetheless, *Veritatis Splendor* faces difficulties of its own. The document remains unclear about which sources of moral interpretation are to be seen as normative for specific judgments. Here the question is not the bindingess of faith premises for a secular culture: revelation clarifies natural law, to be sure, but only for those who acknowledge the premises of revelation as relevant to secular recommendations. Rather, the questions raised by *Veritatis Splendor* implicate a fundamental issue of ecclesiology—how to understand the relationship between magisterial teaching and the *sensus fidelium*.[5]

As a fifth foundational theme, *Veritatis Splendor* emphasizes a personalism that keeps intact the link between one's basic orientation, one's "fundamental option," and the way this option is related to particular moral decisions. As an extension of the principle of "embodiedness" and a specific remonstrance against a "dualism" that would separate one's fundamental convictions from the way those convictions are expressed, the encyclical, in Number 67, underscores the need to view morality from a unitary perspective:

> To separate the fundamental option from concrete kinds of behavior means to contradict the substantial integrity or personal unity of the moral agent in his body and in his soul. . . . Judgments about morality cannot be made without taking into consideration whether or not the deliberate choice of a specific kind of behavior is in conformity with the dignity and integral vocation of the human person.

As a sixth theme, the encyclical elaborates a sophisticated understanding of the way that claims of conscience function in the moral life. In
keeping with the first theme—that responsible freedom must be yoked to
truth—the encyclical emphasizes that conscience, freely exercised, is not
self-validating; freedom of conscience must be understood in light of the
"object" of one's choice. Number 78 of *Veritatis Splendor* speaks directly to
this point:

> The reason why a good intention is not itself sufficient, but a correct
> choice of actions is also needed, is that the human act depends on its
> object, whether the object is capable or not of being ordered by God, to
> the "One who alone is good," and thus brings about the perfection of
> the person. . . . Christian ethics, which pays particular attention to the
> moral object, does not refuse to consider the inner "teleology" of act-
> ing, inasmuch as it is directed to promoting the true good of the person;
> but it recognizes that it is really pursued only when the essential ele-
> ments of human nature are respected.

This final theme conveys profound truths: that the moral licitness of
acts is not determined by intentions alone; that morality requires an intentionality in keeping with the "object" of choice; and that the "true good" of the
person requires a respect for the "essential elements" of human nature. But
again, problems of specification emerge: namely, what are the factors relevant to describing accurately the "object" of moral choice? A statement unexceptionable as a general claim about conscience becomes controversial when
applied to particular issues, depending on how legitimate "objects" of choice
and "essential elements" of human nature are described in each instance.

2.

Because the encyclical seeks to develop the notion that certain actions
are *mala in se*, i.e., intrinsically evil because intrinsically disordered in the
light of right reason, it turns its attention to a trend in recent moral theology
it identifies as "proportionalism." In Number 75, the encyclical characterizes
proportionalism (and other teleological ethical theories) in this way:

> The teleological ethical theories (proportionalism, consequentialism),
> while acknowledging that moral values are indicated by reason and by
> revelation, maintain that it is never possible to formulate an absolute
> prohibition of particular kinds of behavior which would be in conflict,
> in every circumstance and in every culture, with those values.

And again, in n. 79, the encyclical asserts the following:

> One must therefore reject the thesis, characteristic of teleological and
> proportionalist theories, which holds that it is impossible to qualify as
> morally evil according to its species—its object—the deliberate choice
> of certain kinds of behavior or specific acts, apart from a consideration

of the intention for which the choice is made or the totality of the foreseeable consequences of that act for all persons concerned.

Proportionalism as a method has involved a rather complex, at times
even arcane, discussion.[6] Nonetheless, the force of the encyclical's criticism
depends crucially on the adequacy of its depiction of proportionalism as a
method, i.e., is it a fair and nuanced assessment or a caricature? Most proportionalists, after all, are not arguing that the end always justifies the
means; rather, they are suggesting, as one of them puts it, "that an action
cannot be judged morally wrong simply by looking at the material happening, or at its object, in a very narrow and restricted sense."[7]

Why this point is important for issues in sexual ethics and bioethics
becomes clear when one appreciates that the Roman Catholic tradition has
assessed sexual matters in remarkably narrower fashion than issues in other
areas. For example, as McCormick develops the point, in the tradition, a
"theft" cannot be equated simply with "taking another's property," but only
with taking that property "against the reasonable will of the owner."[8] The
latter addition widens the moral compass; it suggests that exceptional circumstances—severe deprivation or hunger—legitimate the "taking" of another's property, since that action comports with what a "reasonably willed"
owner should conclude on the basis of the natural-law directives at work.
Here the additional phrase qualifies the moral judgment of what constitutes
theft; more than a narrow definition of "taking" another's property is required before we judge a given act to be morally culpable. By contrast, in
sexual matters, the tradition has generally seen no need to add any qualification: the "matter" of the act is described as a given, independent of further
reflection about what "reasonableness" might require in light of the good
being served. As McCormick comments,

> When the tradition deals with masturbation or sterilization, for example,
> it adds little or nothing to the material happening and regards such a
> materially described act alone as constituting the object. If [the tradi-
> tion] were consistent, it would describe such an object as "sterilization
> against the good of marriage." This all could accept.[9]

At the core of the debate, then, is an argument about how one interprets, in specific instances, the proper "object" of an action in its strict
Scholastic sense. What McCormick and other proportionalists rightly note is
the quite different range of factors deemed relevant to the moral assessment
of various types of acts. As a further example, the object of moral choice is
invoked quite differently in considering the morality of homicide (which
requires intentions and circumstances to be specified before a moral assessment can be made) as compared with the morality of sterilization, artificial
contraception, or artificial insemination (where the tradition has not included
intentions and circumstances as relevant to describing the object of the act).
In the latter cases, a narrow description, independent of intentions and circumstances, has led to moral disapproval of such acts as essentially disor-

dered. McCormick is correct in his observation: the Church serves to narrow the focus of what materially constitutes the "object" of choice and action only for certain issues of sexual ethics. As Section III will suggest, that narrowed focus requires justification, which *Veritatis Splendor* fails to offer.

1. McCormick as a Concrete Example: A Nuanced Proportionalist

To best appreciate proportionalism as developed by McCormick, one must return to his chapters in a 1978 volume he co-edited with Paul Ramsey, *Doing Evil to Achieve Good*.[10] McCormick makes a number of claims there, but two are especially important for assessing the fairness of the criticism of proportionalism in *Veritatis Splendor*. First, in "reinterpreting" the principle of double effect, McCormick argues that the traditional doctrine has never been as nonconsequentialist as it may have appeared, because it has employed the notion of "proportionate reason" to assess when an action may be performed despite foreseen but unintended side effects. McCormick criticizes the traditional understanding of double effect for "overemphasiz[ing] the importance of the physical effect in judging the moral value of . . . human action."[11] Second, McCormick stresses the central role of proportionate reason in determining the *moral* good in all cases where *nonmoral* evils can be foreseen. This last emphasis has two important implications. First, it raises questions about the relevance of the tractional vocabulary of "direct" and "indirect" intentionality. Second, it maintains the appropriateness of the traditional distinction between moral and nonmoral evils.

It is clear, in upholding the distinction between moral and nonmoral evils, that McCormick is not a "consequentialist" in the ordinary sense. Although he stresses proportionate reason as decisive, it plays that pivotal role only in cases where one weighs consequences that are deemed, in the first instance, as nonmoral. One finds in McCormick a careful attention to a distinction that the tradition has long considered important—the difference between moral and premoral evils—even as he questions the way that the tradition has chosen to define the members of each class and the initial description of the goods at stake when invoking proportionate reason in harder cases. Thus the characterization of proportionalism in *Veritatis Splendor* does not fairly reflect the nuances of McCormick's discussion. Moreover, the central questions that McCormick raises remain important for particular issues in bioethics, as I will suggest in Part 3.

Still, while *Veritatis Splendor* fails to do justice to the subtlety of McCormick's discussion, I would be remiss here in letting my criticism of the encyclical's discussion be interpreted as unqualified support of proportionalism. There are two areas where further clarification from proportionalists would be helpful.

First, although McCormick is right to stress the importance of proportionate reason for judging nonmoral evils, the tendency to describe values initially as premoral or ontic may fail to capture an important element of traditional moral evaluations. For example, Albert R. Di Ianni emphasizes the traditional distinction between a nonmoral evil (e.g., death) and the causation of that evil (e.g., homicide). Of homicide, Di Ianni argues that "the concept of the free causation of death has at least minimal moral meaning in itself prior to consideration of intention and circumstances."[12] And this already moral meaning (though a minimal one) makes the act "intrinsically evil though in a weaker sense than that of the tradition." For Di Ianni,

> To treat [homicide] as a mere nonmoral evil leans too far in the direction of act-utilitarianism or situationism which demands the voiding of the intrinsic moral meaning of all action concepts.[13]

Di Ianni is correct to ascribe at least minimal moral meaning to acts such as homicide, prior to considerations of intentions and circumstances. Thus the "decisive" role of proportionate reason McCormick develops must account for resultant moral duties and obligations in a manner at once subtler and more respectful of that *moral* meaning than the recourse to intentions and consequences may suggest.

Second, while McCormick acknowledges that proportionalism is limited to a consideration of nonmoral values and that the moral disvalue of sin does not provide an occasion for proportionate reason to function, the nagging question remains: how and when do nonmoral or premoral disvalues become moral evils? Granted, McCormick argues that an adequate answer must be couched in terms of proportionate reason. But his depiction of the way that proportionate reason works remains murky. As I have said, McCormick is not, as his critics charge, a consequentialist in the strict sense, since proportionate reason functions only in choices to be made concerning nonmoral evils. Where absolute disvalue is involved, proportionate reason is not free to operate. However, the way that McCormick understands the relationship between legitimate moral choice and relative disvalues distinguishes his approach. The case of an abortion to save a mother's life (rather than letting both mother and fetus die) is instructive of the difference in his method. Thus he says:

> An act is wrong because its very description, when carefully made (and not without some intuitive elements) entails an attack on the value it seeks to serve. The acceptance of such an act as right will, of course, have deleterious consequences. But these do not constitute its wrongfulness. Bad consequences occur because the act was in itself disproportionate in some way. I trace this disproportion, this "attack on the value it seeks to serve," to the fact that the harm done in realizing the good is unnecessary. . . . Harm done stands in a necessary relationship to evil to be avoided or good achieved when it is the only way possible, essentially and deterministically, for the evil to be avoided or the good achieved—as in the case of saving the mother versus allowing both mother and child to die when these are my only alternatives.[14]

It is clear that proportionate reason has a decisive function for McCormick in cases involving relative, rather than absolute, disvalue. It remains less clear, however, how elements other than consequences actually function in his judgments of actions involving relative disvalues. For example, the minimal moral meaning that Di Ianni ascribes to homicide, independent of other considerations, is not echoed in McCormick's account. A more careful attention by both proponents and critics of proportionalism to the way that practical reason acts to "balance" the consequentialist and nonconsequentialist features of choice and action would help to clarify the reasons for their different conclusions in particular cases.

3.

What one does not discover in *Veritatis Splendor*, except briefly in passing, is any focused discussion of the "hot topics" that so often make the headlines in reporting on Catholic developments. To be sure, the encyclical refers to abortion, artificial contraception, homosexual acts, euthanasia, genocide, the abuse of workers, and a number of other explicit prohibitions which exemplify negative precepts that are putatively never to be violated. (See James Gaffney's essay for trenchant criticism of this discussion). However, as I have said, the tenor of the encyclical discussion is at a level of generality that, while it has implications for each of these issues, leaves much underdeveloped. Especially lacking is a sense of precisely how such actions as those listed above are to be understood as *intrinsically* disordered (i.e., as immoral independent of intentions and consequences) and thus always and everywhere prohibited.

Nonetheless, when *Veritatis Splendor* is read in light of earlier documents, there are obvious judgments that follow for particular issues in bioethics. I will focus here on certain implications for artificial contraception and new reproductive technologies.

The passages most relevant to bioethics are found in Numbers 47-50 of the encyclical. Numbers 47 and 48 respond to the charge, raised by a number of critics of *Humanae Vitae* and *Donum Vitae*, that the natural law tradition commits the fallacy of "physicalism," i.e., that merely biological laws are presented as moral laws, especially in the realm of sexual ethics. In Number 47, the encyclical characterizes the arguments of its critics in this fashion:

> According to certain theologians . . . [i]t was . . . on the basis of a naturalistic understanding of the sexual act that contraception, direct sterilization, autoeroticism, pre-marital sexual relations, and artificial insemination were condemned as morally unacceptable. . . . The workings of typically human behavior, as well as the so-called "natural inclinations," would establish at the most—so they say—a general orientation towards correct behavior, but they cannot determine the moral assessment of individual human acts, so complex from the viewpoint of situations.

In Number 48, the encyclical offers a number of rebuttals. First,

> This moral theory does not correspond to the truth about man and his freedom. It contradicts the Church's teachings on the unity of the human person, whose rational soul is *per se et essentialiter* the form of his body.

Second,

> . . . since the human person cannot be reduced to a freedom which is self-designing, but entails a particular spiritual and bodily structure, the primordial moral requirement of loving and respecting the person as an end and never as a mere means also implies, by its very nature, respect for certain fundamental goods, without which one would fall into relativism and arbitrariness.

Finally, quoting *Donum Vitae*, the encyclical in Number 50 asserts that,

> The natural moral law expresses and lays down the purposes, rights, and duties which are based upon the bodily and spiritual nature of the person. Therefore, this law cannot be thought of as simply a set of norms on the biological level; rather it must be defined as the rational order whereby man is called by the Creator to direct and regulate his life and actions and in particular to make use of his own body.

Taken together, these responses to critics are quite useful, and at times quite eloquent, in identifying certain tendencies in bioethics that would surely be unacceptable. To reduce the body to merely manipulable nature, to treat the person who is embodied, or the biological substratum of personhood, as "mere" matter, would be a denial of an incarnational ethic. We do have dominion over ourselves, but it remains a rational dominion, one that requires careful reflection upon the facts of our embodiedness, our purposes as embodied beings.

At the same time, it is difficult to recognize any moral theologian within the Church who would deny such obvious general truths about Catholic understandings. Does any Catholic moral theologian embrace the tendencies that John Paul paints in broad strokes? Does any Catholic moral theologian in fact exemplify the problem John Paul identifies as human freedom unfettered from its essential relationship to truth? Does any recognizable individual advocate that freedom should be absolutized as an end in itself, independent of the facts of our embodiedness?

The differences between John Paul and the unnamed critics he caricatures are not, then, at the level of generalizations about embodiedness, but at the level of particular judgments about licit actions involving the body. And it is not a matter of all-or-nothing choices, but of what moral responsibility entails in particular contexts of decision-making. It is one thing to say that Christ reflects the truth, that Christ is the truth, as John Paul does in the encyclical's first chapter. It is quite another to move from that, with all the requisite theological and moral bridgework, to offer formulations of putatively clear, unambiguous, immutable, exceptionless, and universally binding moral truths.

It is, therefore, difficult to know what specific implications are meant to follow from the quite general theological truths developed in Numbers 48-50. To be sure, the subtext to the encyclical is that certain sexual acts—artificial contraception, sterilization, artificial insemination, even by husband—are always wrong, always essentially disordered as a rupturing of the conjugal and procreative aspects of marital love. This understanding was clearly reflected in the connection between procreation and the conjugal act set forth in *Donum Vitae*:

> The Church's teaching on marriage and human procreation affirms the "inseparable" connection, willed by God and unable to be broken by man on his own initiative, between the two meanings of the conjugal act: the unitive meaning and the procreative meaning.

As the earlier *Humanae Vitae* asserted the inseparability of the unitive and procreative goods of marriage, applying that principle to proscribe artificial contraception, so *Donum Vitae* asserted the inseparability principle to argue against artificial fertilization, even by husband:

> Contraception deliberately deprives the conjugal act of its openness to procreation and in this way brings about a voluntary dissociation of the ends of marriage. Homologous artificial fertilization, in seeking a procreation which is not the fruit of a specific act of conjugal union, objectively effects an analogous separation between the goods and meanings of marriage.[16]

It is fair to characterize the debate about artificial contraception and new reproductive practices, both inside and outside the Church, as one that involves different interpretations of what has been called the "inseparability principle." Most (though not all) Christian denominations affirm the inseparability of the conjugal and procreative aspects of marriage. The Roman Catholic magisterium alone interprets this general relational principle as applying to each and every act of marital intercourse. What is also at stake, at the methodological level, is whether the "object" of an act can be defined differently according to circumstances and intentions in *sexual* ethics as it is in other areas of Catholic moral theology. For example, is in-vitro fertilization an "illicit" separation of the goods of marriage, or an affirmation of those goods for couples otherwise infertile? Is masturbation by a husband to obtain sperm for artificial insemination "essentially disordered" in the same sense as masturbation for merely hedonistic motives? To critics, an act-centered analysis that reduces moral judgments to biological ones, seemingly without remainder, appears paradoxically depersonalized, despite its insistence on a "holistic" view of ourselves as embodied persons.

In their book-length analysis of *Donum Vitae*, Thomas Shannon and Lisa Cahill develop several points of critical leverage; two are especially germane to an assessment of magisterial teaching on sexual ethics. First, Shannon and Cahill identify the "intricacy of the method of Catholic moral theology, especially if understood as a 'natural-law' method"; and second, "the difficulty or at least complexity of moving from general principles to persuasively presented specific conclusions in the area of sexuality and parenthood."[17]

The central problematic for recent magisterial discussion concerns the sources of legitimate authority, as understood in the context of natural law appeals. Shannon and Cahill ask:

> What defines an authoritative "natural-law" teaching, if not self-evidently reasonable argumentation about the relatively clear application of shared values? For whom is an argument persuasive if it is proposed by an ecclesiastical or religious body, and premised on that body's authority, but not so clearly on values and specific applications acknowledged as legitimate beyond the religious community?[18]

The affirmation by the magisterium that the procreative and conjugal aspects of marital love must be present in each and every act of intercourse is central to the traditional arguments reaffirmed in *Donum Vitae* and *Veritatis Splendor*. Clearly, "responsible parenthood" is a central theme in recent magisterial discussion. However, as Shannon and Cahill suggest, the "question not completely answered is where and why the line should be drawn in distinguishing morally acceptable means of seeking a child from those which are morally objectionable."[19]

In their analysis of the inseparability principle, Shannon and Cahill pose two questions: (1) "How are arguments about what 'nature' requires to be validated, and how does concrete human experience fit into the process?" and (2) "What is the moral status of actions that fall short of the ideal, that do not fulfill essential human values to the highest degree?"[20]

In answering these questions, Shannon and Cahill argue that decisions about reproduction should be contextualized within the overall relationship of a loving marriage. Their method affirms the centrality of the experience of married couples for interpreting of natural law directives. In turn, the fundamental values of conjugal intimacy and procreative potential, always central to magisterial teaching on sexual issues, are best understood in relational, rather than act-centered terms. Shannon and Cahill therefore conclude:

> It is dubious . . . that the experience of married persons, parents or not, clearly warrants the assertion that the love which their sexual relationship expresses must be incompatible both with occasional artificial avoidance of conception and with the use of artificial means to bring about conception without a sexual act. It is the committed love relationship of the couple in its totality that gives the moral texture both to their sexuality and to their subsequent roles as parents. It is from the wholeness of the relationship that their specific acts of sex and conception take their moral purpose.[21]

Although Shannon's and Cahill's more holistic approach is a welcome and needed response to magisterial teaching, it fails to address adequately a key aspect of the inseparability debate. As Joseph Boyle perceptively observes, the central issue posed by the inseparability principle is whether "anything about the dissociation of reproduction from a given act of marital intercourse . . . morally flaws any act of reproduction which involves that dissociation."[22] Thus, Shannon's and Cahill's argument, "which denies that such a flaw should be morally decisive, does not help us to see whether or not such a flaw is present."[23]

Richard McCormick's response to *Donum Vitae*, which Boyle also cites, directly confronts the central issue, i.e., whether or not the separation of reproduction and marital intercourse constitutes a moral flaw. Although McCormick acknowledges the force of the inseparability principle as "arguably a legitimate aesthetic or ecological (bodily integrity) concern," he challenges the *moral* relevance of that aesthetic feature:

> All artificial interventions, whether to promote or to prevent conception, are a kind of "second best." They involve certain disvalues that, absent sterility or fertility, respectively, we would not entertain. In this sense we can agree with the Congregation that conception achieved through in vitro fertilization is "deprived of its proper perfection." Much the same can be said of contraception. However, a procedure "deprived of its proper perfection" is not absolutely wrong in all cases—unless we elevate an aesthetic-ecological concern into an absolute moral imperative.[24]

In overview, Shannon and Cahill insist upon the relevance of the lived experience of married couples to the formulation of natural-law appeals. McCormick, in turn, emphasizes that proportionate reason should be central to moral judgments in sexual ethics as elsewhere. None of these critics find the magisterial interpretation of the inseparability principle to be compelling. All three would be likely to pose the same questions to *Veritatis Splendor* as they did earlier to *Donum Vitae*. Why should an arguably aesthetic concern be elevated to an intrinsically moral one? And even if granted moral force, why should the inseparability principle be seen as decisive without careful attention to the context, say, of an infertile couple's desire to achieve procreation as a good of marriage in the only way that their less-than-ideal circumstances allow? Should we view their choice to avail themselves of technically assisted reproduction as a frustration of the goods of marriage or as an affirmation of marital goods under exceptional circumstances?

At present, the force of this internal critique remains unclear. Neither the Vatican nor its critics have offered fully developed positions. *Donum Vitae* and *Veritatis Splendor* can rightly be accused of betraying a physicalist bias in their reading of natural law on sexual and bioethical issues. But critics of the documents have failed to offer systematically constructive positions of their own. As Boyle aptly concludes,

The discussion during the past few years concerning the dignity of procreation is not complete. But it has led to a more precise formulation of the issues in controversy, sufficient to allow a more focused, and perhaps, definitive discussion to begin.[25]

4.

With the foregoing said about matters of sexual ethics and bioethics, the heart of the encyclical remains foundational moral theology. John Paul is concerned by a crisis he perceives, both within the Church and in secular culture, one brought about by what he sees as a widespread lack of responsible freedom, a freedom celebrated for its own sake rather than as a capacity to be exercised within the acknowledged context of God's purposes for humanity.

Nonetheless, there remain persistent unclarities in the encyclical, and more broadly within the tradition, about the appropriate hierarchy of truths under discussion. Because the vocabulary of natural law remains central to the encyclical, *Veritatis Splendor* is deficient in failing to discuss the degrees of certainty associated with various types of natural law directives. After all, very little about the natural law is unambiguously obvious beyond the general injunction to do good and avoid evil. The so-called secondary prescriptions of the natural law, as specifications of that fundamental injunction, may well involve judgments of prudence and habits of virtue fostered by the Church as a resurrection community. Once one moves from the most general normative claims, the relations between natural law as the basis of moral authority and the practice of moral discernment become much more complex and, I would suggest, much less certain than the discussion in *Veritatis Splendor* implies.

In this light, a second unclarity persists throughout the document. The relations between revelation and reason are not sufficiently integrated to provide clear guidance on specific matters. For example, the Catholic manualist tradition tended to view natural law as a source of moral authority readily available to all.[26] There are tendencies within the tradition to make sweeping claims for the moral force of natural reason available to believers and unbelievers alike. It is as if revelation, invoked by John Paul in Chapter One's discussion of Christ and the rich young man, were simply a "motivational" addition to a set of obvious truths known to all on independent grounds. Although John Paul attempts to provide nuance to his discussion of the relations between divine and natural law, still greater nuance is required. Precisely how are we to understand the claims of natural law independent of revelation, i.e., what bindingness do such claims have for those who do not see in Christ the perfect expression of the demands of morality? Here, of course, the answer to that question depends crucially upon one's evalu-

ation of the effects of sin upon the function of natural reason unaided by
revelation.

As a third and final point, a word is in order about John Paul's discussion of conscience. Clearly, John Paul concludes that individual conscience
should *not* function for Catholics in determining which moral principles are
inviolable. Rather, such principles are to be determined by the Church's
teaching authority on natural law matters in the light of revelation. Conscience, he argues, should play a role only in applying such principles to
concrete circumstances.

Here, then, we are back to basic matters of ecclesiology and theology
regarding the nature and sources of moral authority in the Church. How are
we to understand the experience and reflection of the faithful, the *sensus
fidelium*, in relation to the Church's moral teaching? Richard McCormick
describes two very different approaches to that question:

> The first approach asserts that the experience and reflection of the faith-
> ful (and I include in that term all of us—lay people, theologians,
> priests, and even bishops, for bishops must be numbered among the
> *fideles*) ought to be listened to, but it is ultimately the responsibility of
> authoritative teachers to determine the truth. For example, if huge seg-
> ments of the Church believe that the ordination of women is compatible
> with the gospel and doctrinal development, yet the Congregation for the
> Doctrine of Faith determines otherwise, then the Congregation . . . is
> right because authoritative.
>
> The second view is that the *sensus fidelium* is absolutely essential to
> a certain and binding proclamation of the truth. Concretely, if large seg-
> ments of the community do not see the analyses and conclusions of an
> authoritative teacher, it is a sign (a) either that the matter is not suffi-
> ciently clear, sufficiently mature for closure, or (b) that it is badly for-
> mulated, or (c) that it is wrong.[27]

The Roman Catholic Church has long held, in creative tension, a dual
allegiance to the claims of revelation and the conclusions of right reason. In
principle, of course, the natural law is seen by Thomas as reflecting the
divine law. In practice, however, the application of general first principles
has always required a careful attention to circumstances, a certain tentativeness, a recognition that few truths, beyond first principles, are of the lapi-
dary sort. Judgments of prudence require, of right-minded persons, reflection
upon the way that the good is to be realized and how the commandments are
to be followed in particular circumstances. Yet what remains contested, despite the assertions of *Veritatis Splendor*, is the way that reasonable reflection on experience, brought to bear upon new circumstances, is to be fully
respected as a source of authority within the Church.[28] Which model, of the
two just cited, better avails itself of the insights of all faithful persons
within the Church? Which approach better appreciates that the demands of
faith must ever be specified anew for the moral life? Which perspective
better acknowledges that moral theology, especially within a tradition so

respectful of reason, should be reasonably modest in its sense of absolute certainty about deeply conflicted matters? I leave these questions with my readers as I close, although I assume that they will have a strong sense of how I would answer each of them.

Notes

1. Pope Paul VI, *Humanae Vitae* (Washington, D.C.: United States Catholic Conference, 1967).

2. The Congregation for the Doctrine of the Faith, "Instruction in Respect for Human Life in Its Origin and on the Dignity of Procreation," in Thomas A. Shannon and Lisa Sowle Cahill, *Religion and Artificial Reproduction: An Inquiry into the Vatican Instruction on Respect for Human Life* (New York: Crossroad, 1988). pp. 140-47.

3. John Paul II, *Veritatis Splendor* (Washington, D.C.: United States Catholic Conference, 1993). All numbers quoted in this essay are from the U.S.C.C. edition.

4. Vatican Congregation for the Doctrine of the Faith, "Moral and Civil Law," Section III, in Shannon and Cahill, pp. 169-72.

5. For a useful discussion of the *sensus fidelium* and its role in legitimate dissent in the Church, see Richard A. McCormick, *The Critical Calling* (Washington, D.C.: Georgetown University Press, 1989), Chapter 2.

6. Bernard Hoose, *Proportionalism: The American Debate and its European Roots* (Washington, D.C.: Georgetown University Press, 1987).

7. Richard McCormick, "*Veritatis Splendor* and Moral Theology," *America* (October 30, 1993), p. 10.

8. Ibid.

9. Ibid.

10. Richard McCormick and Paul Ramsey, eds., *Doing Evil to Achieve Good* (Chicago: Loyola University Press, 1978).

11. Ibid., p. 17.

12. Albert R. Di Ianni, "The Direct/Indirect Distinction in Morals," *Thomist* 41 (1977), p. 362.

13. Ibid.

14. McCormick and Ramsey, p. 261.

15. Shannon and Cahill, p. 161.

16. Ibid.

17. Ibid., p. 103.

18. Ibid., pp. 106-7.

19. Ibid., p. 113.

20. Ibid., p. 120.

21. Ibid., p. 138.

22. Joseph Boyle, "The Roman Catholic Tradition and Bioethics," in B. Andrew Lustig, ed., *Bioethics Yearbook. Volume 1. Theological Developments in Bioethics: 1988-1990* (Dordrecht: Kluwer, 1991), p. 9.

23. Boyle, p. 9.

24. McCormick, *Critical Calling,* p. 348.

25. Boyle, p. 11.

26. Edwin Healy, *Medical Ethics* (Chicago: Loyola, 1956).

27. McCormick, *Critical Calling,* p. 37.

28. Shannon and Cahill, p. 115, on *Donum Vitae:* "The authors of the instruction may be inadequately attuned to the fact that their *statements* about what marriage and parenthood require do not constitute *arguments,* especially for those who do not share their basic frame of reference. This includes many Catholics who may look to the Church for guidance, but are also committed enough both to the Western norm of individual intelligence and responsibility and to the Catholic commitment to an objective and reasonable moral order, to reject magisterial conclusions devoid of arguments whose reasoning they can follow."

18

Veritatis Splendor
and Our Cover Stories

John C. Haughey

Our pope is getting poor grades for his recent encyclical on moral theology from many moral theology professors. Some are flunking him, others are barely passing him. I was prepared to join this chorus of umbrage takers but, in the reading of it, I concluded that a different standard needs to be applied to judging it than that being used by the moral theology academy. The standard I will use to evaluate *Veritatis Splendor* is that of a work of pastoral discernment.

The reason for not grading him as a moral theologian (even though he might be considered as the *primus inter pares* of that group) is because of what he says he is doing again and again in this document, namely discerning. "The magisterium . . . senses more urgently the duty to offer its own disernment" about the "new tendencies and theories" presently affecting the Church (n. 27). Since he doesn't define what he means by it, I assume his is a common understanding of discernment, namely, that it is an act of perception involving more than thinking or judgment, though it includes these. It is thinking done open to and imploring the active assistance of the Holy Spirit. As the pope indicates in the letter, that means thinking with one's affections affected by (or open to being affected by) that same indwelling presence (n. 28). Discernment is a form of supernatural prudence. If discernment is done well, one's perceptions and judgments are being assisted by the Holy Spirit. If poorly, the best that can be said about the effort is that it is done by a would-be discerner.

Since claims to be discerning and to do discernment are made more frequently than the results warrant, what proof is there that this document goes beyond the claim and is in fact a product of discernment? Would that this question was as easy to answer as it is to ask! The main reason why the answer is difficult is because evidence of discernment must come from the same source as the gift itself. There will be a consonance between the heart and mind of the reader and the text itself if both are moved by the same Spirit.

One way to get at an answer is to ask what the encyclical is trying to discern. In general "the encyclical will limit itself to dealing with certain fundamental questions regarding the church's moral teaching, taking the form of a necessary discernment about issues being debated by ethicists and

269

moral theologians" (n. 5). More specifically, it is the character of the rationality that has been used by many moral theologians and faithful to argue for particular positions that the encyclical is calling into question because it is seen as being at odds with "Sacred Scripture and the living apostolic tradition" (n. 5). This encyclical does not argue at any great length for the positions it takes nor does it argue against the positions it rejects. Its preferred mode of discourse is to assert and claim for its assertions that they are more faithful to the Roman Catholic tradition than the opposite position. In this first ever papal spelling out of a fundamental moral theology the elaboration does not proceed from a position of rationality but from a position that sees "a genuine crisis" because of the growing gap between the way Christian morality is being construed and practiced by many in the Church and the living tradition as the pope understands it. "It is no longer a matter of limited and occasional dissent, but of an overall and systematic calling into question of traditional moral doctrine. . . " (n. 4). Some would refer to this as restorationist thinking. I believe remnant thinking is closer to the mark because he is consciously excluding the majority's form of moral rationality.

It is significant and somewhat surprising that *Veritatis Splendor* is not addressed to those it was expected to address: people of good will or the Church at large or moral theologians. Rather it is addressed to bishops the world over, i.e., to those who have positions of pastoral responsibility to teach and guard "the living apostolic tradition." "The task of interpreting (the moral catechesis) was entrusted by Jesus to the apostles and to their successors, with the special assistance of the Spirit of truth" (n. 25). There is an ecclesiology undergirding this document. He sees himself and his brother bishops as in a line stretching all the way back to the apostles "who were vigilant over the right conduct of Christians, just as they were vigilant for the purity of the faith and the handing down of the divine gifts in the sacraments" (n. 26)

In brief, there are two things that seem to be the keys to understanding what the pope sees himself doing in this document, namely, discerning and addressing his discernment to the episcopacy first and foremost. Hence, the reader would be well advised to let this document speak for itself, bearing in mind what it says it is doing, not what one presumes it would or should do.

If I have interpreted the mind of the author correctly, the pope is not first and foremost addressing moral theologians, nor is he positioning himself as an intellectual critiquing other intellectuals. Rather, he is a pastor whose primary concern is with the moral praxis of the Church's membership. Their spiritual and moral condition is also what he sees himself and the rest of the episcopacy primarily responsible for. He sees them together as responsible for the strengthening of the bonds of those entrusted to their care with God. If this is so, then the document can be read not as seeking to address, correct, or win the approval of the guild of moral theologians, but as trying to help pastors to pastor their flocks in obedience to the Good Shepherd. Insofar as their pastoring responsibility extends to what the People of God think is the morality called for in following the Good Shepherd, only to that extent are extant moral theories addressed and evaluated.

If all of this is so, then the immediate question arises: Is he competent to judge this aspect of the Church? Specifically, does he have some special *munus* by reason of his office that enables him to take on the questions he is asking about the moral life of those who follow Christ? Rather than answer this question doctrinally, *sine additone*, I would prefer to answer it more empirically. It would seem he is more competent to know the moral condition of the People of God than any of the rest of us since his daily, *ad limina* visits from his brother bishops give him an unparalleled, on-the-ground, near universal font of information. So, even if one doesn't want to address the question of the authority of his office, just the simple fact of his regular briefings would make him more informed, I would think, about the subject he's addressing than the information of the rest of us, possibly even those whose special competence is moral theology. The best informed person may not be the most discerning, but the less informed person is at a disadvantage with respect to the skill.

What is it he sees when he looks into the spiritual and moral condition of the People of God? A very mixed scene, surely. Heroic virtue, but not in such strong supply that moral laxity and dereliction of duty is not also an alarming part of the evidence. But this is as it has always been, I presume. His sense is that there is something more radically wrong that cannot be explained simply by people becoming more sinful. He locates the problem, therefore, in what I would call self-deception. This is my term, but I believe it fairly sums up what he is saying. He even implies that those who should be unearthing it, namely those who traditionally teach the morality expected of followers of Christ, are either not knowledgeable about what this following entails or are part of the problem of self deception and purveyors of it.

One of the uniquenesses and strengths of this text becomes evident early (n. 6). It takes for granted that a marriage that many have seen as strained or inoperative is still a marriage, namely, the marriage between spirituality and moral theology. This remark requires a brief excursus. Somewhere in our deep, dark past, these two aspects of Christian life that once were and should have always stayed together came apart. Moral theology eventually became a specialization that produced a whole new network of relationships with other traditions of moral reasoning. Spirituality, on the other hand, has developed its own kind of independence and fecundity, producing many different families of spirituality in the church. Although the separation between moral theology and spirituality has not been altogether infelicitous, it has produced some bad fruit. John Paul is still acting like there should never have been a separation or a divorce. Or, better, he doesn't seem to recognize its validity, since he folds the two back into the one living tradition with each of a piece with the other.

He effects this reconciliation, not in the abstract, but by introducing the distinctiveness of the moral life of Christians with the story of the young man who sought out Jesus to know "what good must I do to have eternal life?" (Mt 19:16), Jesus' answer was to keep the commandments. These commandments and this foundation haven't changed their stripe in all the centuries since their articulation, according to *Veritatis Splendor*. The young man claimed to "have kept all these; what do I still lack?" Jesus' answer was that dispossessing himself of all else he was to follow him. Christ was to become his wealth, as it were. The would be follower of Christ was to "appropriate and assimilate the whole of the incarnation and redemption" in order to find oneself (n. 8). Or, more starkly, the moral life of the Christian "involves holding fast to Jesus, partaking of his life and his destiny, sharing in his free and loving obedience to the will of the Father" (n. 19).

It is through his Christology that he rejoins morality and spirituality. "Jesus brings the question about morally good action back to its religious foundations" (n. 9). "Come, follow me is the new specific form of the commandment of love of God" (n. 18). "The moral life presents itself as the response due to the many gratuitous initiatives taken by God out of love for man (sic). . . . Thus, the moral life caught up in the gratuitousness of God's love, is called to reflect his glory. . . ." (n. 10)

Not that one has to be a Christian to be moral. The Pope would give an affirmative answer to his question: "Do the commandments of God which are written on the human heart . . . have the capacity to clarify the daily decisions of individuals and entire societies?" "Is it possible to obey God and thus love God and neighbor without respecting these commandments in all circumstances?" (n. 4). To this question the pope would answer in the negative.

In the second chapter the pope makes a move that is the source of irritation to many in the community of moral theologians. He doesn't take them seriously, at least seriously enough to be thorough with what they have written. Rather, he takes the general direction of some of their positions and unearths the self-deception their work can be used for. The encyclical is at pains to reveal what it takes to be the rationalizations and self-justifying ways of being inured against the fully heard moral call of the Gospel. It skewers not what the best moral theologians have written but unnuanced reductions of these teachings that are being used to compromise the following of Christ, as the pope understands this walk. The way "moral" is conceived is one thing; the way it is received and acted upon is something else. Wrongheaded conceptions as well as self-interested receptions of good conceptions both lead to bad morals.

For example, the version of the fundamental option described in *Veritatis Splendor* so disjoins "the transcendental dimension proper to the fundamental option" from "choices of particular inner worldly behavior" that it can only condemn it (n. 65). The transcendental dimension which claims to be *ad Deum* is used to justify immanent disorders. The problem, therefore, is not with the well-honed understanding of "fundamental option" of a Rahner, for example, but with its received understanding (n. 65-67). If what the Pope says about the fundamental option is the way it is being taught or used, he should have a problem with it.

A good question to ask would be whether the caricature of the fundamental option that the encyclical contains is fair to the moral theologians who have done a more careful version of it. It wouldn't be fair if the document were addressing moral theologians and their efforts. It would be fair and is fair if the document is discerning the ways in which the fundamental option has been twisted into being a cover story for the moral agent to use while acting in ways clearly proscribed by the moral tradition. In general, some of the encyclical's characterizations of positions taken by moral theologians are more like caricatures than actual accounts of what careful moral theologians have actually written. The only way one can understand this is to believe that the pope is more interested in how their writings are being used than in the writings as such or with the specialized dialogue that takes place within the moral theology guild. What could be read as a disdain for the guild is more understandable if one recalls the ecclesiological presuppositions mentioned earlier.

If my reading of this document has been accurate so far, I would take a further step in interpreting it, though without the comfort of its actual language. I see the pope uncovering cover stories. Cover stories spread like a contagion without their real character being detected. Cover stories can be used to cover our actual moral condition in our communications with others. But they frequently go beyond that to conceal our real condition even from ourselves. With this double cover the truth is twice concealed, first from the truth we allow others to know about us, then from the truth we need to admit to about ourselves. This condition I have referred to above as self-deception. I believe it is this condition that *Veritatis Splendor* is trying to discern and uncover.

But this is also, in part, what moral theologians are supposedly doing. There is a difference, however, in the responsibilities, the one being pastoral, the other academic. The first is concerned first and foremost with people's religious condition, the second with the world of ideas, cultures, methodologies, theories, contemporary disciplines. These are not airtight. The moral theology guild's purview is wider, taking in contemporary cultures, ideas, questions with varying degrees of competence in the behavioral sciences. Sometimes their reflections are not successful. Pastoring can be inept or successful; doing moral theology can also be one or the other. At issue for both pastor and moralist is whether their culture so biases them that, though their work is always being done within a culture, to do what they must each do, they must also transcend it. Presumably both these professionals will be aware of the dangers of acculturation while the non-professional will be less aware of the possibility of accommodating the Gospel to the culture. But either can create a package of moral reasoning which legitimates a version of morality that enables one to live according to an accommodated Christian morality.

How to do right reasoning with a right heart and avoid self-deception whether as a pastor, a moral theologian, or an ordinary follower of Christ is, *inter alia*, a matter of developing the gift of discernment. Interestingly, *Veritatis Splendor* states that "moral theologians . . . have a *grave duty* to train the faithful to make this moral discernment (of the church's moral doctrine), to be committed to the true good and to have confident recourse to God's grace" (n. 113). Training the faithful in discernment is not a duty moral theologians have ordinarily seen themselves as having.

I have not seen anyone comment on the significance of this grave duty being laid on moral theologians for interpreting this document. Why would this be a grave duty if one reads the document as calling only for obedience? Why would people need to be trained in discernment if it has already been done for them here? If all we need to know about our moral lives is to find the authorities who will tell us what we ought to do and what not to do, discernment could hardly be a grave duty; indeed, it would be a waste of both party's time.

Ignatius of Loyola's rules for discernment would be useful to recall, not only because of this duty moral theologians are being told they have, but also because skill in discernment is helpful in interpreting this encyclical. Ignatius instructs those guiding people through the Spiritual Exercises to notice that there are two very different ways "the enemy of their soul" works. It works relative to their spiritual condition. When they are going from serious sin to serious sin this enemy functions as a false consoler, lulling them by every possible means to stay the course in which they are mired. It seeks to keep them in a denial mode of morality.

But when they are in a spiritual condition of striving to go from good to better in their union with God, this enemy of their soul works differently, namely by whispering "good" advice into their ears. When this advice can be traced to a source inimical to God, it is easier to detect its character than when its genesis is from those who are in positions of leadership, theological or pastoral, in the Church. Then it had better be good advice, i.e., of a piece with or in continuity with the moral tradition of the Church. It is this "good" advice that the pope is at pains to discern. When he sees that its fruit is undesirable, he is in a position to say it is bad advice and that it has its genesis in some darker place than the moral tradition rightly understood.

More specifically, the rules for discernment, for those who are sincerely following the Lord, caution that "the enemy of our soul" fights our state of joy in the Lord by "using specious reasonings, subtleties and persistent deceits" to bear on the personal issues we are trying to sort out (Rules for Discernment: Second Week; 1st rule). These "specious reasonings, etc." can be intellectually appealing and pose as light while very subtly drawing us away from following the light and toward following our own constructs of light into a course of action that posits us in a darkness, removed from the truth. If *Veritatis Splendor* is seen as pointing out some of the deluded uses to which moral theology has been put, it will be read very differently than if it is seen as prescinding from use and as an exercise in chastising moral theologians by constructing "straw men" to strike down.

Although he was not a consequentialist, Ignatius suggests that one of the ways of discerning is to check out the consequences of following what at first appears to be good advice (Rules for Discernment: Second Week; 6th rule). Not without reason the pope concludes that there is something radically wrong with some of the ways the faithful go about making moral choices. He traces this to bad advice, specifically to some of the methods and moral theories the faithful are either being taught or deriving from wherever.

One of the ironies of moral theology is that moral formulae can be used by the unrepentant heart to keep it unrepentant but self-righteous. The problem then would be with the heart, not with the moral formula. Its misuse can keep one from dealing with the core of the problem. For example, the just war formula can be used with thoroughness to decide the rightness or wrongness of using force while leaving untouched the complicity in fomenting violence of the party attempting to employ the formula, howsoever sincerely. One of the bad fruits of the estrangement of moral theology from spirituality is that people can be supplied with moral formulae and think that their accurate use makes their choices good.

Proportionalism and consequentialism are two moral theories the encyclical judges negatively. Its negative judgment is guided by means of discernment—but not solely by means of discernment. There is also the issue of competing moral theories about what constitutes a moral or immoral act, more specifically, its object. *Veritatis Splendor* invests the contents of the moral object with a different content than the proportionalists and consequentialists do. For *Veritatis Splendor* the object "is the proximate end of a deliberate decision which determines the act of willing on the part of the acting person" (n. 78). For the teleologists, by contrast, the object alone and "materially" cannot be considered moral or immoral until the intentions and the circumstances have been taken into account. *Veritatis Splendor* accords these latter two a subsidiary importance and claims that for teleologists "the moral goodness (of an act) would be judged on the basis of the subject's intention in reference to moral goods, and its rightness on the basis of a consideration of its foreseeable effects or consequences and their proportion" (n. 75).

As *Veritatis Splendor* sees it, the choices made under these teleological moral systems are more like "a process or an event of the merely physical order, to be assessed on the basis of its ability to bring about a given state of affairs in the outside world" (n. 75). The encyclical's discernment about this way of choosing is that both of these "teleological" moral theories are too much the product of an autonomous or rational morality (n. 75). "They believe they can justify as morally good deliberate choices of kinds of behavior contrary to the commandments of the divine and natural law" (n. 75).

Both the encyclical's treatment of these two theories and my treatment of the text's assessment of it are perhaps overly simple but rather than deepening the issues separating the pope and these teleologists, I will make only one further comment. Proportionalism and consequentialism had developed as moral theories that focused on infrequent quandaries where there was considerable conflict about the goods, values, and unavoidable evils. But when used for day-to-day moral issues which involve character and virtues they can be misused. They mislead if one overlooks one's conscience and instead follows the good advice produced by "specious reasonings, subtleties and persistent deceits." The misuse of these theories shapes people into being moral calculators rather than moral agents.

One of the strengths of *Veritatis Splendor* is its casting of moral issues on a wider and deeper horizon than morality alone. By making spirituality a constitutive part of moral theology it advocates that moral choices be made in the light of a "participated theonomy." From this perspective moral agents would not act in terms of norm centeredness or moral theories or as autonomous weighers of moral goods. Rather, seeing themselves as followers of Christ they would seek to discern what love calls for and they would make their choices in a way that was more explicitly accompanied rather than solitary or rational. For personal, simpler issues, this optic can go a long way in assisting the would-be discerner. But complexity is never far from the human condition. In real quandaries where the issue to be discerned is not whether one has the character to do the right thing but what the right thing to do is, teleological ethics can be helpful.

Although *Veritatis Splendor* addresses the bishops, it can also address any reader who wishes to subject his or her own moral and spiritual condition to its scrutiny. *Veritatis Splendor* will speak to readers in their personal moral history not to a *tabula rasa* or mind empty of some at least implicit moral theory. A fair reading will force the reader to meet the Pope's discernment with a review of and discernment of the spirits moving in oneself. Those whose professional work is in moral theology or ethics may find it harder to accept that one's personal condition of spirit is in play in reading such a document, since their social location has them try to read with a critical objectivity whatever is written in their field, without it seeming to pass through the matrix of their own moral condition—which it does.

If one of the strengths of the document is its ability to pull off cover story after cover story by exposing some of the more frequent ways of rationalizing done by the church's members, it also has several weaknesses. It is too pat about morality. While it is true that we are not free to create our own moral truths and that by obeying your informed conscience, (its) "truth will make you free" (Jn 8:32), it is also true that "where the Spirit of the Lord is, there is freedom" (2 Cor 3:16). Once spirituality and morality are linked as they are here, one must expect followers' responses to Christ to be more differentiated, not less, if for no other reason than the fact that each has been personally called to follow him from their own history, affectivity, culture, generation, with their particular gifts. Once spirituality and morality are linked, it becomes more obvious that there is more going on between the self and the Spirit than obedience. If we know anything about the saints, it is that they were neither conformists nor predictable. The Spirit invariably produces a different kind of pluralism than dissent does. It produces more nonconformity than this document appears to expect. Any effort to morally homogenize the following of Christ must remember St. Thomas' distinction between universal principles (formal norms) which are absolute, and secondary or concrete precepts (material norms) which *"valent ut in pluribus,"* i.e. not always (ST I-II q.94,a.4).

A clearer weakness of the document is the quality of severity which develops toward the end. It begins to lose its pastoral discernment focus as it takes on the managerial roles of controlling dissent, threatening the removal of legitimations and inviting incursions into academic freedom. But more troubling: when one thinks of Jesus as a teacher of morals and recalls the way the sinners flocked to him, one realizes how far the quality of mercy of the Good Shepherd is from at least this last part of *Veritatis Splendor*. Attracting sinners to accept God's mercy while exercising responsible clarification of the morality entailed in following him might be too much to ask for in one document.

One last point. While discernment is key to reading the document, it is also affirmed that discernment is not a *munus* that is peculiar to the author(s) of the document. In n. 109 we are told that "the whole church" has been made "a sharer in the munus propheticum of the Lord Jesus through the gift of his Spirit." Further, the pope adds that "the universal body of the faithful who have received the anointing of the holy one cannot be mistaken in belief." Finally, he asserts that the whole church "displays this particular quality (of not being mistaken) . . . when from the bishops to the last of the lay faithful it expresses the consensus of all in matters of faith *and morals*."

My interpretation of the fact that there is a discernment basis for the moral teaching herein contained is that, though authoritative, it is not the last word on the subject. Its teaching must be completed by being received. It is received when it is confirmed by the same gift of discernment from which it purports to have arisen, but this time in the faithful. In n. 53 the document acknowledges that "the truth of the moral law—like that of the deposit of faith—unfolds" and that the magisterium's understanding of this moral law "is preceded and accompanied by the work of interpretation and formulation characteristic of the reason of individual believers and of theological reflection." Until we hear an "amen!" from the pews, at least from those in the pews who are well disposed and have been attentive to this extremely important discernment, the process of discernment will not have been completed.

19

The Moral Act in *Veritatis Splendor* and in Aquinas's *Summa Theologiae:* A Comparative Analysis

Jean Porter

Are there some kinds of actions which are never morally justifiable, whatever the circumstances or the foreseen consequences of acting otherwise? Traditionally, Catholic moral theologians have held that there are: for example, murder, theft, or adultery. Actions of these kinds are said to be intrinsically evil by virtue of the nature of the object of the act, and they can therefore never licitly be done, for any reason whatever. Over the past 30 years, however, this view has increasingly been questioned by moral theologians, variously described as proportionalists or revisionists, who argue, in the words of Richard McCormick, that "we must look at all dimensions (morally relevant circumstances) before we know what the action is and whether it should be said to be [morally wrong]."[1] These theologians, in turn, have been sharply criticized by Germain Grisez, John Finnis, and their followers, collectively known as deontologists or traditionalists, who insist that it is always morally wrong to act against certain basic goods such as life, knowledge, and the like.[2]

The encyclical *Veritatis Splendor* represents the long-anticipated official intervention in this debate. While the Pope is careful not to condemn or to endorse the views of any particular theologian, and while he foreswears any attempt to "impose on the faithful any particular theological system, still less a philosophical one" (n. 29), nonetheless, his own position in the debate between revisionists and traditionalists is clear enough:

> One must therefore reject the thesis . . . which holds that it is impossible to qualify as morally evil according to its species—its "object"—the deliberate choice of certain kinds of behavior or specific acts apart from a consideration of the intention for which the choice is made or the totality of the foreseeable consequences of that act for all persons concerned (n. 79).

In the process of elaborating and defending this conclusion, the pope offers an encyclical that only a moral theologian could love. One commentator remarks that the second chapter of the encyclical "is very tough going, even for theologians, unless they specialize in moral thought or ethics,"[3] and another remarks on "their [i.e., moral theologians'] delight at its ponderously convoluted and technical second chapter, which will provide ample opportunity for scrutiny, exegesis, distinctions, comments and modifications of the papal animadversions. . . ."[4] These commentators are quite right; the arguments of the encyclical *are* hard going. To some extent, the difficulties that the reader encounters are generated by its distinctive ecclesial style, but it is also the case that this encyclical is hard going because the issues that it addresses are difficult and complex.

Veritatis Splendor takes up other issues besides the question of intrinsically evil kinds of actions, including the grounding of moral norms (n. 42-53 and n. 71-75), the role of conscience in moral judgment (n. 54-64) and the religious significance of persons' actions (n. 65-70). Of course, all these issues are interconnected, but it is also the case that a short discussion must be focused, if it is to be of any use. Accordingly, in this essay I will limit myself to the task of identifying and clarifying the issues which underlie the discussion of intrinsically evil actions, beginning at number 79. I do not intend to offer a detailed commentary on the encyclical itself, or much less on the extensive and complicated debate between proportionalists and deontologists which forms its context. Rather, I hope to offer a brief guide to some of the relevant concepts and questions, which will enable the reader to make her own way through both the encyclical and the relevant theological literature more easily.

In what follows, I have structured my discussion around Thomas Aquinas's account of the moral act in the *Summa Theologiae*. In doing so, I do not mean to suggest that Aquinas's thought should be normative for the encyclical or for Catholic moral theology, nor do I hold that his account of morality is without limitations or errors. Nonetheless, Aquinas offers one of the most insightful accounts of moral judgment that is available to us, and his account, moreover, has set the framework for all subsequent moral theology. Both the current debate among moral theologians and the encyclical itself are cast in terms which Aquinas set. Thus, a review of Aquinas's exposition will provide a framework within which to sort out and to reflect upon the issues at hand, in terms of an idiom which is distinctively Catholic.

1.
The Moral Act: A Preliminary Consideration

In his discussion of the moral act in the *Summa Theologiae*, Aquinas identifies three criteria in terms of which human acts are to be evaluated. That is, an act must be evaluated in terms of its object (I-II 18.2), the circumstances in which the act is done (I-II 18.3), and the agent's aim in acting (I-II 18.4).[5] In order for an act to be morally justifiable, it must be good in every respect; that is, good or at least neutral in its object, with due consideration of circumstances, and directed towards a good, or at least an innocent aim (I-II 18.4 *ad* 3). Thus, an action which is bad with respect to its object cannot be redeemed by a good aim, and yet an act which is generically good will be corrupted by a bad aim, or by the agent's failure to do what she should in the circumstances in which she acts.

The object of an act, as Aquinas understands it, is expressed in terms of that description which indicates its species, or as we would say, indicates the kind of act that it is, considered from a moral point of view (I-II 18.2); that is, it is an act of murder or theft or adultery, or alternatively, an act of capital punishment, or making use of what is one's own, or marital intercourse. Neither the agent's end in acting nor the circumstances of the act can be collapsed into the object for Aquinas. Thus, to take his own example, someone who steals in order to commit adultery is guilty of a twofold transgression in one act; that is, the object of his act of theft cannot be elided into his aim in that act, namely, to have the means to commit adultery (I-II 18.7). Similarly, the circumstances in which the agent acts do not change its object, unless they have some intrinsic relation to it. Thus, an act of theft is an act of theft, whether one steals from the rich or the poor, whether one walks off with a television set or appropriates funds by electronic transfer, whether one steals a valuable work of art or a painting on black velvet. These circumstances may well mitigate or exacerbate the wrongness of a given act of theft, but they do not alter its essential character or its wrongness (I-II 18.10, 11).

It might seem that on Aquinas's own terms, the aim for which an agent acts would always be a positive factor in the evaluation of the act since, as he frequently reminds us, every agent necessarily acts in pursuit of something that is perceived to be good (for example, at I 5.4,5; 6.1; 60.3,4; I-II 1.2). However, it is also the case, according to Aquinas, that the aim of the agent is determined by what the agent knowingly does, and if what she does is wrong in itself, her aim is *ipso facto* bad (I-II 19.1, especially *ad* 1). Thus, for example, someone who aims to sleep with a woman whom he knows to be someone else's wife has the intention of committing adultery, even though what he wants is not the act of adultery *per se*, but the pleasure which he anticipates from the act. Thus, a morally bad intention cannot be redeemed simply by the fact that the agent acts with a view to securing some good.

So far, the terms of moral analysis which Aquinas sets forth would seem to correspond, more or less, to the teaching of *Veritatis Splendor*. According to the latter, "The primary and decisive object for moral judgment is the object of the human act, which establishes whether it is capable of being ordered to the good and to the ultimate end, which is God" (n. 79). For Aquinas, too, the object of an action provides a criterion for moral judgment that cannot be elided into a consideration of circumstances or the agent's aim. Moreover, if the object of the action is bad, the action cannot be redeemed morally by any other sort of consideration, although the evil of an action which is wrong by virtue of its object can be mitigated by the presence of a good aim or difficult circumstances. Thus, Aquinas would appear to agree with the encyclical that

> the opinion must be rejected as erroneous which maintains that it is impossible to qualify as morally evil according to its species the deliberate choice of certain kinds of behavior or specific acts, without taking into account the intention for which the choice was made or the totality of the foreseeable consequences of that act for all persons concerned (n. 82).

Yet it would be misleading, at best, to say that Aquinas would agree without qualification with the encyclical at this point. The difficulty is this: *Veritatis Splendor* reflects a widely shared assumption that Aquinas's criteria for the evaluation of an action can be applied to specific acts prior to and independently of the process of determining the moral evaluation of a specific action. On this view, Aquinas's analysis of these criteria would provide us with a methodology for evaluating particular actions; we determine the object of the act, we take note of the agent's aim and the circumstances, and we then arrive at a moral evaluation, by means of an application of the formula, *quilibet singularis defectus causat malum, bonum autem causatur ex integra causa* (any single defect causes evil; good, however, is brought about through a complete and intact cause; I-II 18.4 *ad* 3).[6]

Yet matters are more complex than that. Aquinas does not in fact hold that the criteria for moral judgment set forth in I-II 18 jointly provide a methodology or a formula for the moral evaluation of specific actions. In order to draw out a methodology for moral decision-making from the criteria of object, circumstances, and aim, we would first need to be able to identify which component of a particular action is which, *prior to* forming a moral evaluation of the action. Yet as Aquinas recognizes, this is just what we cannot do. In order to determine the object of an action, distinguishing it in the process from circumstances and from the agent's aim in acting, it is *first* necessary to arrive at a correct description of the act from the moral point of view. That process, in turn, depends on prior evaluative judgments, in terms of which we determine what is morally relevant and what is not, and how the different components of the action should be interrelated to one another. Description is not prior to evaluation; to the contrary, to describe an action from the moral point of view *is* to form a moral evaluation of the action.

This point will be clearer once we have looked more closely at the relation between object and circumstances, on the one hand, and object and aim, on the other.

2.
Object and Circumstances

The language of "the object of the act" is so familiar, at least in Catholic circles, that it is easy to assume that this language is clear and straightforward, forgetting just how puzzling it can be. *Veritatis Splendor* appears to reflect this assumption, since it does not offer any extended discussion of just what the object of an act is. We are told that:

> By the object of a given moral act, then, one cannot mean a process or an event of the purely physical order, to be assessed on the basis of its ability to bring about a given state of affairs in the outside world. Rather, the object is the proximate end of a deliberate decision which determines the act of willing on the part of the acting person. Consequently, as the *Catechism of the Catholic Church* teaches, "There are certain specific kinds of behavior that are always wrong to choose, because choosing them involves a disorder of the will, that is, a moral evil" (n. 78).

But surely this gets matters backwards. If the object of the act qualifies the will, surely that is *due to* the moral significance of that object.

Further on, we are told:

> The primary and decisive element for moral judgement is the object of the human act, which establishes whether it is capable of being ordered to the good and to the ultimate end, which is God. . . . It is precisely these which are the contents of the natural law and hence that ordered complex of "personal goods" which serve the "good of the person": the good which is the person himself and his perfection. These are the goods safeguarded by the commandments, which, according to St. Thomas, contain the whole natural law.
>
> Reason attests that there are objects of the human act which are, by their nature, "incapable of being ordered" to God because they radically contradict the good of the person made in his image. These are the acts which, in the church's moral teaching, have been termed "intrinsically evil" (*intrinsece malum*): they are such always and per se, in other words, on account of their very object and quite apart from the ulterior intentions of the one acting and the circumstances (n. 79-80).

In other words, the objects of some actions, that is, those which are wrong by virtue of their object, are characterized by their intrinsic inconsistency with the good of the human person; moreover, such acts are contrary to the natural law.

This is more helpful. At least we now have some substantive criteria by which to determine which kinds of actions are intrinsically evil, and which are not. Yet questions remain. It is far from clear, for example, which specific kinds of actions are those which "radically contradict" the good of the human person, especially since the Catholic moral tradition has traditionally acknowledged that there are some kinds of actions which involve inflicting harm, and which are yet morally justified (for example, capital punishment). The difficulties involved in determining the content of the natural law are notorious and longstanding. Apart from these, however, there are additional problems associated with applying this language to the logic of the language. These problems are less frequently acknowledged, but they are, for that very reason, potentially more troublesome. These are the difficulties on which we will focus in this section and the next.

In the first place, it is not at all clear how we are to distinguish object from circumstances in the description of a particular action. Consider some examples: if one person kills another, it is surely circumstantial that the act takes place at dawn, or in the evening, in the city or in the countryside, quickly or slowly. The means that the killer uses are also circumstantial, as for example, whether the act is done with a knife or a gun or poison or a garrotte. But what about the personal characteristics of the killer and the victim? It is surely circumstantial that the killer is a woman and the victim is a man, that the killer is young and the victim is old, and so forth. But it is *not* a mere circumstance that the killer is an authorized executioner and the victim is a duly convicted criminal. Those details change the essential description of the act, from murder to legal execution; or to be more exact, they do, *if* we accept the traditional Catholic account of murder and justifiable homicide (cf. II-II 64.2).

Consider another example, this time from Aquinas himself:

> The process of reason is not determined to any one thing, but when anything is given, it can proceed further. And therefore, that which is considered in one act as a circumstance added onto the object, which determines the species of the act, can be considered a second time by ordaining reason as a principle condition of the object that determines the species of the act. And so, to take what is another's has its species from the formal notion of "another" [*ratione alieni*], and by this fact [the act] is constituted in the species of theft; and if the notion of place or time should be considered beyond this, [such a notion] would fall under the formal description of a circumstance. But since reason can ordain also with respect to place or time, and other things of this sort, it happens that the condition of place is considered with respect to the object, as contrary to the order of reason; as for example, that reason ordains that no damage should be done to a sacred place (I-II 18.10).

In other words, it is not generally relevant to a description of a particular act of taking what is another's that the object is taken from a museum, or a private house, or from the street; in all these instances, the act is still an act of theft, and qualifications of place are circumstantial to that act. But for Aquinas, at least, it is not just a circumstantial detail that something is stolen from a church; that fact qualifies our essential understanding of the act itself, in such a way as to change its moral description, in this case, from an act of simple theft to an act of sacrilege.

As these examples suggest, the object of an action is not simply given perspicuously in the description of an act. It certainly cannot be equated with "what is done," described in a simple, nonmoral way. For one thing, any action allows for indefinitely many possible true descriptions of "what is done."[7] More to the point, whatever precisely is meant by the object of the action, as understood by Aquinas or by traditional moral theology, this is surely a *moral* concept. Thus, the object of an act is the generic moral concept in terms of which the act is correctly described from the standpoint of moral evaluation (or in Aquinas's terms, it determines the species of the act; I-II 18.2). Once the object of an act has been correctly determined, *then* it is possible to identify other components of the act as mere circumstances, which can mitigate the badness of the action (if it is objectively bad) but cannot alter its fundamental moral character.

Correlatively, it is not the case that the object of an action can serve as an independently given datum for moral evaluation. The determination of the object of an act presupposes that we have described the act correctly, from a moral point of view, and that process requires normative judgments about the significance of different aspects of the action. In other words, the determination of the object of an act is the *outcome* of a process of moral evaluation, not its presupposition.

How, then, are we to determine the object of the act? Aquinas's response to this question, as given in the treatise on action in the *prima secundae*, is not immediately clear. We are told that the object is determined by reason, which determines whether what is done is appropriate (as, for example, to use what is one's own) or inappropriate (to take what is another's: I-II 18.5; cf. I-II 18.10). But what, specifically, does this mean?

In order to answer this question, it is necessary to turn from the programmatic analysis of I-II 18 to the *secunda secundae*, where we find Aquinas's discussion of the specific details of the moral life. It is here that he repeatedly raises and addresses questions of the form, "What kind of act is this?" or, in other words, what is the moral species of this or that kind of action? And since the species of the act determines its object (I-II 18.5), it follows that the generic descriptions which give the species of actions will also describe their objects.

When we turn to an examination of the relevant texts (especially, but not exclusively, found in the treatise on justice, II-II 57-122), it becomes apparent that the generic concepts in terms of which Aquinas identifies the objects of acts are taken from the same basic moral notions that serve as the starting points for moral reflection for nearly everyone else: for example, murder (II-II 64), injury (II-II 65), theft and robbery (II-II 66), fraud (II-II 77), usury (II-II 78), and lying (II-II 110). These basic concepts of kinds of actions are associated with widely accepted moral prohibitions (theft, murder, lying, adultery) or with stereotypical ideals of good behavior (almsgiving, restitution, prayer). Since the precepts of morality can all be traced to the natural law, which is contained (in diverse ways) in the precepts of the Decalogue (I-II 100.1,3), he would agree with the encyclical that the intrinsic wrongness of some kinds of actions is given by the natural law; moreover, he would agree that these acts are such because they involve some kind of harm to another (I-II 100.5, II-II 72.1).

Thus, Aquinas takes his examples of objects of actions from those generic moral concepts which are the common currency of moral reflection, and which, in the case of morally bad kinds of actions, can be correlated with basic moral prohibitions. Yet how does this help him, or us, to distinguish the object from the circumstances in the description of particular actions? In order to answer this question, we must turn to those articles in which Aquinas considers whether some more specific kind of action, suspicious on its face, should be subsumed under the wider category of a prohibited kind of action; for example, does capital punishment, or killing in self-defense, count as murder (II-II 64.2,7)? In these and similar cases, Aquinas clarifies and extends the meaning of the basic moral concepts, such as murder or theft, through an extended reflection on the point of the prohibitions or injunctions connected with them. Thus, he distinguishes murder from legitimate forms of killing through an extended reflection on the point of the prohibition against killing, and the ways in which different sorts of killing do or do not fit within the rationale for the complex concept of murder (see especially II-II 64.2,3,5-7). This reflection, in turn, allows him to determine, in some detail, which aspects of an act of killing would be relevant to determining the object of the act; those, namely, which are relevant to the point of the prohibition against murder. Thus, it is determinative of the object of an act of killing that the victim is a duly convicted criminal, or conversely, is innocent (II-II 64.2,6), and it is similarly so determinative that the killer is a duly authorized executioner or soldier, or conversely, is a private citizen (II-II 64.3). Other features of the act, on the other hand, are circumstantial, for example, the gender and age of killer and victim (cf. I-II 18.10, quoted above).

Of course, it follows that someone with a different understanding of the point of the prohibition against murder would draw the lines between murder and permissible forms of killing in a different way. For example, someone who does not accept the traditional arguments for capital punishment might well insist that an act of execution *is* a form of murder and, therefore, the officially sanctioned position of the executioner would be merely circumstantial in her view.

It is sometimes assumed that the object of an act can be equated with some form of behavior which can be described in terms that make no reference to cultural conventions or to particular institutional forms of life, and which is therefore natural in the sense of being comprehensible in nonconventional terms. This is the view of those moral theologians who defend a version of the traditional doctrine of intrinsically evil actions along the lines set out by Grisez and Finnis, and it appears to be the view of the encyclical as well (cf. n. 48). It is also Aquinas's view with respect to some kinds of actions, specifically lying and the so-called unnatural sexual sins (II-II 110.3; II-II 154.11). But Aquinas does not understand the object of every morally significant act in this way, as his discussions of murder, theft and robbery would suggest. To the contrary, in the majority of cases, he does *not* equate the object of an action with a form of behavior that is natural in the sense of being comprehensible in nonconventional terms (cf. I-II 1.3 *ad* 3, I-II 18.7 *ad* 1, I-II 20.6). Thus, every murder involves killing a human being, but not every act of killing is a murder. Every act of theft involves taking what is another's (which already builds in a reference to a convention), but not every form of taking what is another's counts as theft (to take a modern example, taxation does not). In most cases, the moral concept which gives the object of an action includes some essential reference to the institutional, or more broadly, the cultural context in which the act takes place, within which it takes on its distinctively rational and human meaning. Aquinas has specific arguments for not understanding lying and certain forms of sexual activity in this way, as an examination of the relevant questions makes clear. These arguments may or may not be convincing, but it would be a mistake to assume that all moral concepts must be analyzed in the same terms; Aquinas himself does not think so, and the view is in any case quite implausible.

There is one further point that must be made, before turning to an examination of the aim of an action and its relation to the object. We have already observed that the concepts of morally significant kinds of actions, in terms of which Aquinas identifies the objects of actions, are generic concepts. For that reason, they cannot be applied with absolute certainty in every case. While the correct description of an action in terms of its object will usually be straightforward, it will always be possible that we will find that we cannot arrive with certainty at the correct moral description of a particular act, even though we know all the morally relevant facts of the matter, and attempt in good faith to arrive at a correct evaluation of the act in question. This limitation to moral judgment is not a feature of positive injunctions only, as the encyclical suggests (see n. 67 in particular). Rather, it is a specific instance of the logical limitations inherent in any kind of knowledge of singulars; that is, we cannot apply generic concepts to concrete individuals with certainty in every instance. That is why Aquinas holds that there will always be some uncertainty with respect to the application of the precepts of the natural law:

> As was said above, those things pertain to the law of nature, to which the human person is naturally inclined; among which, it is proper to the human person that he is inclined to act according to reason. However, it pertains to reason to proceed from what is general to what is specific. . . . The speculative reason is constituted in one way with respect to this [procedure], however, and the practical reason, in another way. Since the speculative reason deals chiefly with necessary things, concerning which it is impossible that it should proceed otherwise [than it does], the truth is found without any defect in specific conclusions, as also [it is found] in general principles. But practical reason deals with contingent things, among which are human operations, and therefore, even though there is some necessity in [its] general principles, the more one descends to specif-

ics, the more defect is found. . . . With respect to things that are done, there is not the same truth or practical rectitude for all people with respect to specifics, but only with respect to general principles; and with respect to those things about which there is the same rectitude in specifics for all, it is not equally known to all (I-II 94.4).[8]

If Aquinas is right to insist on the indeterminacy of all moral concepts, as I believe him to be, then it follows that there are logical limits to the certainty and the degree of consensus that can be attained in moral judgment, even among those who share the same basic moral concepts and attempt to apply them in all good faith. The presence of moral uncertainty and disagreement in our society cannot be attributed without remainder to bad faith, or to moral pluralism, or to the effects of consequentialism (which in any case has not had all that much effect in the wider culture). There will always be some hard cases about which we, as individuals, just cannot judge, or about which we, collectively, cannot agree.[9]

3.
Object and Aim

The philosopher Alan Donagan has divided the norms of common morality into what he calls first and second order precepts, which have to do with the evaluation of moral actions and the attribution of moral responsibility, respectively.[10] Intention, purpose, voluntariness and other such notions generally pertain to our second order evaluations, and thus, they normally presuppose that we have already evaluated the act that is in question.

In order for a person to be responsible for an action, the act must be hers in some fundamental way; that is to say, it must be voluntary. Almost everyone who has reflected on the moral life, from Aristotle to the present time, would agree on this much; Aquinas joins the general consensus at I-II 6. Moreover, the voluntary status, or otherwise, of a particular item of behavior would seem to be easy to determine. There is a basic difference between killing someone deliberately, and killing her inadvertently, say, by falling on her from a great height. In the latter case, an individual may be the material means by which something occurs, which is nonetheless not her action in any sense.

Yet it is possible for an act to be voluntary in one respect, and yet to be involuntary in another sense. Medieval moral theologians were fond of the somewhat implausible example of someone who has sex with a woman whom he believes, wrongly, to be his wife; the act in question is not a *voluntary* act of adultery, and the man is not an adulterer, because in one respect, he does not know what he is doing (Aquinas uses this example at I-II 19.6; cf. I-II 6.8). Or consider the case of an actor who fires at her fellow performer in the course of the play. Unknown to her, a very nasty person has loaded the gun with live ammunition and so, to her horror, her fellow actor falls dead at her feet. Did she kill him? In one sense, she did, since he dies as the result of an action of hers. But in another sense, she did not, since she did not know that she was killing him, and did not intend to kill him. Her act is voluntary under some descriptions (in this case, acting a part, doing her job), but under the crucial description of killing a man, it is involuntary, that is, it is not *her* action.

On the other hand, there is a general presumption that a person *is* responsible for what she knowingly does. That is, if someone is aware that her act falls under a particular description, she is responsible for the action, so described, even if she does not particularly want to do *that*, but rather, chooses to do what she does under another description. We have already mentioned the example of the adulterer; what he wants is not to commit adultery, but to have a good time; yet his action is nonetheless adultery if he knows the relevant fact that his partner is someone else's wife. To turn to our second example, if the actor knew that her gun was loaded with live ammunition, her act would be an intentional act of murder, even if it were the case that she did not especially *want* to bring about the death of her unfortunate colleague. (She may just have said to herself, "Well, this is hard luck for Fred, but the show must go on.")

Aquinas's views on what we would describe as voluntariness, intention, and purpose, which he discusses in terms of voluntariness, the aim for which an act is done, and the object of the will, are quite complex. It would take us too far afield to attempt to sort them out in any detail; suffice it to say that for him, the goodness or evil of the will is determined by any morally relevant description of the act, which the agent herself knows, and which is therefore an appropriate description for her *voluntary* act (in general, see I-II 19.1,3 and I-II 20.1-3). Thus, if it is the case that an action falls under one of the generic concepts of morally wrong kinds of actions, and the agent knows that it does, that fact corrupts her will, even if her purpose in acting is praiseworthy (I-II 20.4).[11] On the other hand, a bad aim corrupts an action that is generically good if, for example, someone gives alms to the poor out of vainglory (I-II 20.1).

The examples that we have been considering would suggest that the object of the action, considered as an external action, can be determined independently and prior to any consideration of the agent's aim in acting. This is indeed generally the case, for Aquinas, but it is not always so. In some cases, the agent's aim forms an essential component which must be taken into account, in order to determine the object of the action. Ordinarily, any act of killing another, carried out by a private citizen (as opposed to a soldier or public executioner) counts as murder. But it is not murder to kill another in self-defense, because in such a case the agent's intention, to preserve her own life, determines the correct description of what is done (II-II 64.7). Similarly, it is ordinarily either theft or robbery to take what is another's (theft, if done secretly; robbery, if done by force). But if someone takes what is another's in order to sustain her own life, if this is indeed the only way in which she can do so, then the act in question does not count as either theft or robbery, because the point of the institution of property is to provide the necessities of life for all persons (II-II 66.7).[12] What is decisive in each case is the naturalness of the intention to preserve life, taken in conjunction with some consideration of what it is reasonable to expect someone to endure (II-II 64.7), or of what the point of a widespread human institution should be taken to be (II-II 66.7).

Thus, just as we cannot determine the object of an act, and distinguish it from its circumstances, prior to some normative evaluation of the different aspects of the action, so we cannot always determine the object of an act prior to some moral assessment of the agent's intention.

4.
Moral Judgment and Consequentialism

Two points emerge from our assessment of Aquinas's account of the moral act. First, if Aquinas is correct, then we cannot derive a judgment about the moral value of an action from a determination of the object of the act because we cannot determine what the object of the act *is* without some prior consideration of the action, taken as a whole. Secondly, for Aquinas, there can be no formula which enables us to arrive with certainty at the correct moral assessment of individual acts. The difficulty of moral knowledge, as Aquinas understands the matter, should not be exaggerated. In most cases that he foresees, the correct assessment of a particular action will be obvious, or will follow with only a little reflection (cf. I-II 100.3). Nonetheless, it is always possible, on his terms, that we might encounter a particular action that is so difficult or complex that we cannot say with certainty whether it is right or wrong.

This latter point is worth underscoring, because it is easy to assume that Aquinas's analysis of the different components of an action is meant to provide a formula by which to determine whether a particular action is morally licit or not. In Aquinas's view, there can be no such formula, and his account of the moral act at I-II 18 is not meant to provide one. What he offers here, rather, is an analytic account of the different components of moral judgment, which is meant to indicate the different factors that must be considered in any assessment of a particular action.

If Aquinas holds that an action cannot be evaluated prior to some consideration of all its different aspects, and if, furthermore, he acknowledges that we cannot always arrive with certainty at the correct moral assessment of a particular action, then does it follow that his account of morality is a version of consequentialism? In answering this question, the first thing that must be noted is that Aquinas himself does not either endorse or reject consequentialism in so many words. He does consider the moral significance of consequences at I-II 20.5, but in my view, his remarks in this article do not settle the question of whether he should be considered to be a consequentialist as we understand the term.

At this point, we come to another question that must be addressed before we proceed. That is, how *do* we understand the term "consequentialism"? It is difficult to answer this question, because almost no one has denied that consequences have *some* moral relevance. Yet it is perhaps not too important to arrive at a definition of "consequentialism" that would satisfy everyone; it is enough, for our purposes, to arrive at some sense of the point of those theories of morality which are generally brought together under the rubric of consequentialism. In this way, we will be able to see more clearly what it would mean to describe Aquinas as a consequentialist, and more importantly, we will see what is at stake in affirming or rejecting a consequentialist account of morality.

Although consequentialism is a wider category than utilitarianism, the latter is the best known, the most influential, and probably also the earliest version of consequentialism. Thus, in order to arrive at a better understanding of consequentialism, we would do well to consider the thought of another moralist, the so-called father of utilitarianism, Jeremy Bentham.

As the title of Bentham's great work, *The Principles of Morals and Legislation*, suggests, utilitarianism began as a response to growing pressures for social and legal reform during the late 18th and early 19th centuries.[13] Bentham himself was trained as a jurist, and in the *Principles*, he attempts to place the laws of England on a rational and scientific basis by subjecting actual and proposed norms to the test of the utility principle. Thus, this book is as much a treatise on jurisprudence as it is a work of moral philosophy.

The central idea of the utilitarian challenge to traditional mores, as Bentham developed it, is quite simple. The first task of the legislator, says Bentham, is to attempt to secure the well-being of every member of society; therefore, all norms should be evaluated by the test of what he calls the principle of utility, according to which an action is good if and only if it produces the greatest possible balance of happiness over unhappiness for all concerned.[14] But of course, so formulated, this criterion is *too* simple. It is one thing to assert in general terms that the first concern of the legislator should be the overall happiness of the community, but it is quite another thing to attempt to translate this ideal into a scientific method for evaluating moral and legal norms. Bentham attempts to do so by developing a formula for analysis whereby alternative courses of action in a given situation are to be assessed in terms of which one produces the greatest quantitative measure of pleasures over pains. As Henry Sidgwick would later make clear, this procedure implies that pleasures and pains are homogeneous, that is, that there are no qualitative differences among diverse pleasures or pains, and it furthermore implies that pleasures and pains can be quantified. And as Sidgwick also acknowledges, it is exceedingly difficult to carry out the latter task (although he himself attempted it), even if we grant this particular conception of mental states. Much of the subsequent debate over utilitarianism has focused on the cogency or the practicality of the "greatest happiness" principle.[15]

There is another aspect of the utilitarian account of morality that is more directly relevant to the subject of our inquiry. If particular actions are to be evaluated in terms of the overall balance of pleasures and pains that they produce, then clearly the basic moral concepts, which are correlated with generally accepted moral rules, cannot have *ultimate* validity for moral analysis. Some utilitarians have indeed attempted to argue that a utilitarian analysis can be applied to general rules, which, if so validated, should then be obeyed by individuals, but the cogency of this argument is questionable.[16] Others have admitted that there are advantages to sustaining an agreed-upon system of rules, and correspondingly, we are likely to bring about some pain through the infraction and weakening of a received norm, which should be factored into any utilitarian calculus. Nonetheless, as Sidgwick observes, this consideration does not, in itself, imply that the general norms of morality can never be broken, particularly by sophisticated and discreet persons who can appreciate the implications of what they are doing.[17] At any rate, whatever the details of particular versions of utilitarianism may be, it is clear that for the utilitarian, the norms of morality can never have ultimate and exceptionless validity.

This point is critical for understanding the significance of affirming or denying a consequentialist account of morality. We have already noted that almost no one denies that consequences have some moral significance. The critical difference between utilitarianism and other versions of consequentialism, on the one hand, and most other accounts of the moral life, on the other, lies in the kind of significance that is given to consequences. For the consequentialist, the moral evaluation of specific acts will always be determined by some assessment of consequences, as determined by one or more general criteria. The basic moral concepts, such as murder, theft, and the like, can never play anything other than a secondary and derivative role in such a system; at most, they might function as reminders of kinds of actions that generally turn out badly, on a consequentialist calculus.

For almost everyone else, on the other hand, there are at least some basic moral concepts (not necessarily the traditional ones) which are irreducibly significant for moral evaluation. Generic moral concepts of whatever kind stand in need of interpretation if they are to be applied to actual cases, and this process of interpretation and application will often include some assessment of consequences. But for most moralists, except for consequentialists, the considerations which govern the assessment of consequences, and which determine, more fundamentally, which consequences are morally relevant, will be derived from some reflection on the meaning and point of the basic moral concepts themselves. A Kantian will ask herself whether a particular dubious act does or does not involve some kind of failure to respect rational autonomy; a rights theorist will determine whether some action violates a right through a consideration of the forms of freedom that the right was meant to protect; and so on.[18]

It is at this point that we see the critical difference between Aquinas's account of morality and different versions of consequentialism. For Aquinas, like most other moralists, but unlike Bentham and his followers, the generally accepted concepts of morally significant kinds of actions (murder, theft, adultery and the like) are of basic and irreducible moral significance. Aquinas does not attempt to analyze these basic concepts in terms of more fundamental units of moral analysis, such as units of happiness, or values, or basic goods, in terms of which moral judgments can be given a more precise or certain formulation. Rather, for Aquinas, the basic moral concepts, which form the essential moral vocabulary for theologians and everyone else alike, are themselves basic units of moral analysis. Once it is determined that a particular action can be correctly described in terms of one of these generic concepts, then that fact alone may determine the moral value of the act (depending on which generic concept the act falls under).

Yet if it is the case that we cannot determine the object of the act prior to some consideration of the act as a whole, then perhaps there is no *practical* difference between Aquinas's view and some version of consequentialism. This would seem to be suggested by an interpretation of Aquinas's account of the object of the act offered by John Dedek in an influential essay published in 1979.[19] On Dedek's reading, the meaning of the basic moral concepts, as Aquinas understands them, is purely formal; so, for example, "murder" should be understood as "unjust or undue killing," "theft" as "unjust/undue taking," and so forth.

Dedek does not say that Aquinas is a consequentialist, and even if his interpretation were correct, it would not necessarily imply such a conclusion. Dedek's interpretation is based on Aquinas's discussion of the so-called sins of the patriarchs (for example, Abraham's intended killing of Isaac, discussed in the *Summa* at I-II 100.8 *ad* 3), and given this context, it would be more plausible, on Dedek's terms, to read Aquinas as an exponent of a radical version of a divine command theory of ethics.[20] Yet Dedek's interpretation would also be consistent with a reading of Aquinas as a consequentialist, on the further assumption that our human efforts to determine whether an act of killing (for example) is unjust could be made solely on the basis of an assessment of the overall balance of good and bad that would result from this particular killing. That is, on this reading, Aquinas would be a consequentialist, because the application of the basic moral notions to particular actions would be determined wholly on the grounds of considerations that could be formulated independently of any mention of those basic notions.

But in fact, this is not Aquinas's view. As we have already seen, the basic moral concepts do have a substantive meaning for him. He does not present these meanings in terms of formal definitions, but he does indicate his understanding of them by the terms in which he argues throughout the *secunda secundae*. That is, when Aquinas considers whether a specific kind of action should fall under the scope of a more general prohibition, he never argues in terms of the overall balance of good versus bad that is attained by the kind of act in question.[21] Rather, he couches his argument in terms of the *point* of the prohibition in question. Some kinds of acts, which look suspiciously like instances of (for example) murder or theft, are in fact justified, for reasons which are drawn from the point of the prohibitions in question themselves. Others, however, are not justified, because they *do* violate the point of the relevant prohibition. For example, Aquinas argues that it is not morally permissible to baptize the infant children of non-Christian parents against their (the parents') consent, because this would be a violation of natural justice, even though, on Aquinas's terms, the good that might thereby be secured, that is, the salvation of the children, would infinitely outweigh any misfortune whatever (II-II 10.12).

The point is this. Aquinas is not a consequentialist because he does not subject the basic moral concepts to any sort of reductive analysis, in terms of which moral judgments can be given a more precise meaning or a more certain foundation. This is significant for us, in turn, because it helps us to see what is at stake in either affirming or rejecting some version of consequentialism. It is not the case that Aquinas's analysis brings more certainty to individual moral judgments than does consequentialism; to the contrary, most consequentialists would assert what Aquinas more than once denies, namely, that we can arrive at a certain moral judgment about every specific moral act. Nor is it the case that Aquinas's account is more stringent than consequentialist alternatives. Again, it is at least arguable that the reverse is the case. Consequentialism is generally associated with perfectibilism, the moral doctrine that one is obliged to do the greatest and most perfect good that one can do. Aquinas not only does not claim this, he denies it (I-II 19.10).

The implication of affirming the independent significance of the object of an action, for Aquinas, is that moral judgment must be carried out in terms of the meanings of the basic moral concepts, such as murder and legitimate execution, for example, which form the framework for moral judgment and discourse for the whole society. Our understanding of these basic notions can be refined, and we can and do change our minds, individually and collectively, about the moral quality of some kinds of actions. Yet we cannot "get behind" the basic moral concepts to some simpler and more fundamental units of moral analysis. The wisdom and the commitments to the good that are embodied in these basic notions set the fundamental terms for moral judgment, whether that wisdom and those commitments are seen as coming from the human community and natural reason alone, or we trace them ultimately, as Aquinas himself would do, to the wisdom and love of God.

Notes

1. Richard A. McCormick, *"Veritatis Splendor* and Moral Theology," *America* 169:13 (Oct. 30, 1993), pp. 8-11, 10.

2. The literature generated by this debate is enormous. Bernard Hoose offers a helpful and sympathetic exposition of proportionalism in his *Proportionalism: The American Debate and Its European Roots* (Washington, D.C.: Georgetown University Press, 1987), and John Finnis discusses the same issues from the deontologists' perspective in *Moral Absolutes: Tradition, Revision and Truth* (Washington, D.C.: Catholic University of America Press, 1991). Germain Grisez has commented on the encyclical; see his "Revelation vs. Dissent," *The Tablet* 247 (Oct. 16, 1993), pp. 1329-31.

3. Richard P. McBrien, "Teaching the Truth," *Christian Century* (Oct. 20, 1993), pp. 1004-5.

4. Lawrence S. Cunningham, et al., *"Veritatis Splendor,"* *Commonweal* (Oct. 22, 1993), pp. 11-18.

5. These and all subsequent references to Aquinas's work are taken from the *Summa Theologiae*; all translations are my own.

6. Aquinas is here quoting, approvingly, pseudo-Dionysius's *The Divine Names.*

7. This point is frequently made by philosophers who deal with action or the philosophy of language; the most influential of such treatments would include G.E.M. Anscombe, *Intention,* 2nd ed., (Ithaca: Cornell University Press, 1963) and the essays of Donald Davidson on action theory, many of which are collected in Donald Davidson, *Essays on Actions and Events* (Oxford: Clarendon University Press, 1980/1982). Eric D'Arcy offers a very useful discussion of this point seen in the context of moral theology in his *Human Acts: An Essay in Their Moral Evaluation* (Oxford: Clarendon Press, 1963).

8. For a helpful discussion of Aquinas's views on the general logical problem of knowledge of particulars, see Anthony Kenny, *Aquinas on Mind* (London: Routledge, 1993), pp. 111-18.

9. This point has been made by more than one contemporary moral philosopher; see, for example, J. M. Brennan, *The Open-Texture of Moral Concepts* (New York: Barnes and Noble, 1977), and Julius Kovesi, *Moral Notions* (London: Routledge, 1967). I have also defended this account of moral judgment, in considerably more detail, in *Moral Action and Christian Ethics* (Cambridge: Cambridge University Press, forthcoming).

10. Alan Donagan, *The Theory of Morality* (Chicago: The University of Chicago Press, 1977), pp. 112-42. Donagan's treatment of the issues discussed in this section is extremely helpful, and I am indebted to it at a number of points.

11. There is an ambiguity that should be noted here. It is one thing to know, or to reasonably believe, that an action falls under the description of an intrinsically evil kind of action. In such a case, the agent knows the relevant features of the action which bring it under the category in question, and furthermore, she has no reason to believe that there is any other aspect of the act which would alter its description. It is something else to draw the further conclusion that the act is, in fact, morally wrong; the agent may not believe that an act of kind X is wrong, or she may believe, wrongly, that some feature of the act changes its moral description. Aquinas does not, in fact, believe that a mistaken judgment of the latter sort excuses; see I-II 19.5,6. However, it seems to me that he is too quick to draw this conclusion.

12. This passage is often taken as an early statement of the principle of double effect, but in my view, that would be a mistake. Aquinas does not say that the causal relationship between what the agent aims at, and what she does, is morally determinative; rather, it is the nature of her intention, seen within a context of what we can reasonably expect of ourselves and one another, that is decisive.

13. Jeremy Bentham, *The Principles of Morals and Legislation*, with an introduction by Laurence J. LaFleur (New York: Hafner Press, 1948/1989).

14. Ibid., pp. 1-7.

15. Henry Sidgwick, *The Methods of Ethics,* 7th ed. (New York: Hackett Press, 1981), pp. 123-98 and pp. 460-95.

16. This position has often been traced to John Stuart Mill, but this seems not to have been Mill's view; see the discussion in Donagan, pp. 193-94.

17. On both points, i.e., the utility of generally respecting moral rules, and the legitimacy of breaking them, secretly or not, see Sidgwick, pp. 475-95.

18. There is no one contrast position to consequentialism, but in addition to Aquinas's own account (as I argue below), Kantianism, classical human rights theories, and most forms of intuitionism would all fit the description that I have just offered. On the other hand, it is not so clear to me that the so-called deontological theories of Grisez and Finnis would answer to this description. For Grisez and Finnis and their followers, the fundamental units of moral analysis are basic goods, such as life and knowledge, which are self-evidently such to all mature persons. Generic moral concepts can be analyzed without remainder in terms of forms of behavior which either tend to, or absolutely do not respect these basic goods. Thus, the Grisez/Finnis theory of morality is closer to consequentialism than it is to Kant's classical deontological theory of morality; what saves it from being consequentialist without remainder is the stipulation that there are some kinds of consequences, namely, the destruction of basic goods, which are never morally permissible. In addition to Finnis's *Moral Absolutes,* cited above, see Germain Grisez, *The Way of the Lord Jesus,* Vol. 1, *Christian Moral Principles* (Chicago: Franciscan Herald Press, 1983); John Finnis, *Natural Law and Natural Rights* (Oxford: Clarendon Press, 1980), *Fundamentals of Ethics* (Washington D.C.: Georgetown University Press, 1983); and Germain Grisez, Joseph Boyle, and John Finnis, "Practical Principles, Moral Truth and Ultimate Ends," *American Journal of Jurisprudence* 32 (1987), pp. 99-151.

19. John Dedek, "Intrinsically Evil Acts: An Historical Study of the Mind of St. Thomas," *The Thomist* 43 (July, 1979), pp. 385-413.

20. This does, in fact, appear to be Dedek's view, although he does not say so explicitly; see Dedek, pp. 401-06.

21. As an examination of I-II 100.8 *ad* 3 indicates, Aquinas attempts to justify even the so-called sins of the patriarchs in this way; that is, he does not just appeal to the power of God, as Supreme Legislator, to dispense from the natural law, but he argues, as far as possible, in terms of the point of the relevant prohibitions. Thus it would not have been murder had Abraham killed Isaac at God's command, because God has supreme authority over life and death, just as the leaders of a human community have authority over the life of malefactors. Ultimately we all die at God's command, and yet we cannot say that God is the murderer of us all. Dedek does recognize that Aquinas argues in this way, but he does not seem to me to appreciate the full significance of this fact; see Dedek, p. 404.

20

The Splendor of Truth:
A Feminist Critique

Kathleen Talvacchia
Mary Elizabeth Walsh

As we approach the end of the second millennium, few fail to realize that these are exciting times for the Roman Catholic Church. We who live and work a mere 30 years in the wake of the Second Vatican Council know the challenges that present themselves to the People of God as we struggle together to better understand ourselves as "Church." In the midst of this sometimes daunting and often fractious realignment of our self-understanding lies tremendous possibility. Fed by a renewed awareness and attention to our biblical roots, Catholic Christians are inspired to take up Jesus' command to "Come, follow me," with a renewed evangelical authenticity. Catholic biblical and theological scholarship has blossomed while it has at the same time broken out of the insular Catholic academic world of much preconciliar discourse. As Catholic scholars, we now count Protestants, Jews, Buddhists, and Hindus among our conversation partners, enriching our understanding of faith while clarifying the distinctiveness of our Catholic identity. Moreover, Catholic scholarship has been enriched by the voices of those within the church who previously had little opportunity to contribute, by the peoples of Latin America, Africa and Asia (what we sometimes call the Third World), and by women across the globe. With an irony that perhaps only the Holy Spirit herself fully understands, the exclusion of women from the ordained ministry has led many committed Catholic women into theological scholarship. From the earliest days of feminist theological work in the United States to the present, Roman Catholic women have been centrally involved in defining the discourse.[1] It is within this flourishing of Catholic feminist scholarship that we take up the task of examining the most recent papal encyclical, *The Splendor of Truth*.

We are interested in *The Splendor of Truth* in part precisely because there are so few commentaries on the document from a feminist-liberationist perspective. While some explicitly feminist assessments of the document exist,[2] we suspect that many feminist and liberation theologians agree with Richard McCormick's commentary: "What will be the effect of this encyclical letter? On the public, zero."[3] We disagree.

We would offer three reasons feminist and other liberation theologians should examine seriously *The Splendor of Truth*. First, while the primary concern of this encyclical letter is to respond to certain contemporary issues in moral theology, one could read this letter and still have no idea that the vast body of literature on feminist and liberation theology had ever been penned. To judge from this document, two decades of critical and constructive theological work by liberation and feminist theologians that seriously challenges both traditional theological content and method has made little impact at the highest offices of the church. At the very least, this is discouraging to the many Catholics who have found a renewed and vibrant faith in the work of liberation and feminist theologians. It remains important for those of us committed to a liberationist perspective to examine *The Splendor of Truth* and ask what difference it makes that our voices and concerns have been omitted here.

Second, the third section of the encyclical makes clear its intent to make a difference in the day-to-day life of the church. From its circumscribed delineation of the role of the moral theologian to its admonition to bishops to exercise vigilance in defense of church teaching, this document is meant to affect the faithful. By contrast, liberationist and feminist theologies begin by looking at the actual experiences of people, at the lived reality of church, and especially at the sort of lived contradictions this experience often engenders. Insofar as this encyclical aims to influence the lived reality of church, it warrants close examination by feminists and other liberation theologians.

The Splendor of Truth requires our attention for a third and related reason. Liberation and feminist theologians begin their reflection with attention to the lives and experiences of the poor and of women; at the same time, the institutional church in its hierarchical organization has an undeniable impact on those lives and experiences. Papal teaching and statements affect the grassroots profoundly at the diocesan seminary and in the parish confessional. Genuine concern for the grassroots of the church, for the poor, and for women necessitates a careful reading of papal teachings with just these people in mind.

This essay then will approach *The Splendor of Truth* with two questions in mind. First, how would this encyclical be different had it taken seriously feminist and liberationist concerns? And second, how will this encyclical actually affect our lived experience of church?

1.
Feminist Liberationist Concerns

The first section of *The Splendor of Truth* is a meditation on the story of the rich young man (Mt 19:16-26). It appears here, the encyclical tells us, to "serve as a useful guide for listening once more in a lively and direct way to [Jesus's] moral teaching" (n. 6). The rich young man's question to Jesus, "What must I do to have eternal life?" reminds the reader precisely what is at stake in the discussion of moral theology that follows. Commentators on the encyclical agree that this opening meditation is fruitful, calling it "beautiful, Christ-centered,"[4] characterized by "rhetorical genius."[5] Our question is: How might this story be read differently in light of the insights liberation or feminist theologies offer?

A rich young man approaches Jesus and asks, "Teacher, what must I do to gain eternal life?" Jesus responds, "Why ask me what is good, there is only one who is good. If you wish to enter into life, keep his commandments." The rich young man asks Jesus which ones he means, and Jesus responds, "You shall not murder, you shall not steal, you shall not commit adultery, you shall not bear false witness, honor your father and mother, also you shall love your neighbor as yourself." The rich young man replies that he has already done all these; what more must he do? Jesus tells him, "If you want to be perfect, go sell your possessions and give the money to the poor, and you will have treasure in heaven; then come, follow me." And the rich young man goes away grieving since, as the writer of Matthew tells us, he had many possessions.

A feminist-liberation reading would highlight the commandment to love one's neighbor as one's self, as well as Jesus' final word to those seeking perfection. Someone committed to the liberation of the oppressed of the world would probably understand the admonition to sell one's possessions and give the money to the poor as the heart of the story. Using some of the gospel verses as headers on various parts of this first chapter, the encyclical emphasizes other aspects of the story. It highlights the following verses: "Teacher, what must I do to gain eternal salvation?"; "There is only one who is good"; "If you wish to enter into life, keep the commandments"; "If you wish to be perfect"; "Come, follow me"; and "With God all things are possible." Jesus' exhortation to sell what one has, give the money to the poor, and follow him is briefly noted in the text. The encyclical states that this advice "must be read and interpreted in the context of the whole moral message of the Gospel and in particular in the context of the Sermon on the Mount, the Beatitudes (Mt 5:3-12), the first of which is precisely the beatitude of the poor, the 'poor in spirit' as St. Matthew makes clear (Mt 5:3), the humble" (n. 16). The pope seems to suggest here that when Jesus said "the poor," he did not mean those actually struggling in poverty, but rather the poor in spirit, those who are humble. Yet, how much sense does it make for Jesus to tell the rich young man to sell all that he has and give the money to the humble and the poor in spirit? Not much.

It is worth noting that the pope urges us to read the story within its greater context and within the context of the whole of Matthew's gospel. Far too often in the past, official church documents have used scripture selectively, citing verses out of context and distorting the text. However, one is forced to ask why we need to return to the Sermon on the Mount to understand what Jesus meant by the poor in this verse, when the very next verse sheds some light on the subject.

After the rich young man goes away grieving (for he had many possessions), Jesus tells the disciples, "Truly I tell you, it will be hard for a rich person to enter the kingdom of heaven. Again I tell you, it is easier for a camel to go through the eye of a needle than for someone who is rich to enter the kingdom of God (v. 24)." The disciples, alarmed upon hearing this, ask "Then who can be saved?" and Jesus answers, "For mortals it is impossible, but for God all things are possible." (Mt 19:26) This additional mention of the rich in Mt 19:24, appears to clarify Jesus' intention (in v. 21) to invoke those who were economically poor. The encyclical resists this interpretation by not including verse 24; in fact, this is the only verse from Mt 19:16 to Mt 19:26 that is left out of the encyclical's reflections. Liberation theologians have long argued that it is a distortion of Jesus' message to view the poor and poverty only in spiritualized terms. And yet this document does just that.

It is also useful to step back from the biblical text and consider the question that frames the encyclical: What must I do to gain eternal life? The centrality of this concern points up one of the major themes of the document, namely the integral relationship between one's beliefs and one's actions: "No damage must be done to the harmony between faith and life: the unity of the church is damaged not only by Christians who reject or distort the truths of faith but also by those who disregard the moral obligations to which they are called by the gospel (cf. I Cor 5:9-13)" (n. 26). Liberation theology, which has long called for a transformation of orthodoxy into orthopraxis, would applaud such an insight. Both the pope and liberation theologians want to reject a comfortable faith that rests assured in its beliefs and pietistic practices. Both call for a living faith that infuses all of one's life and all of one's actions. Both agree that the meaning of being Christian is demonstrated in the actions of our lives and not simply in our faith statements.

And yet a tension remains between the focus of the encyclical and that of liberation. While the pope asks, "What must I do to gain eternal life?" the liberation theologian is more likely to ask, "What must we do to bring about the kingdom of God?" The encyclical, while insisting that faith and life be linked, nonetheless approaches the question in terms of the individual and answers it with a focus on the afterlife. Both in its individualism and in its otherworldliness, the encyclical fails to grasp the significance of communal life and suffering in the world. A liberationist vision is deeply concerned with people's lived experiences in the world and with alleviating the suffering that constitutes that lived experience for too many of the world's people. As Jon Sobrino reminds us, our "theological concern is not to explain as accurately as possible what the essence of sin is, or what meaning a sinful world has, or what meaning human existence has in such a world. The concern is to change the sinful situation."[6]

The Splendor of Truth fails to take seriously the ways that an authentic Christian faith will result in social action, and it perpetuates the separation of the church's moral and social teachings. This is ironic for a document that argues so forcefully for the overcoming of so many other polarities, among these faith and life, and freedom and truth. A liberationist perspective, while accepting the encyclical's insistence of overturning these dualities, would also press for a vision that does not separate the individual from society or this world from the next. Many feminists would agree. As Lisa Sowle Cahill recognizes,

> For Christian feminists, virtue consists not only in the integrity and rectitude of the rational self. It also requires a relational concern for building communities on which all can contribute to mutual fulfillment, communities secured on a base of justice and ascending toward the completion and transformation of love.[7]

The Splendor of Truth would have made a stronger argument for the ultimate significance of moral actions if it had made its case with respect to the social and communal life of human beings.

Liberationist and feminist theologians would also raise some questions about the use of the concept of natural law in the encyclical. *The Splendor of Truth* claims that the norms of natural law "in fact represent the unshakable foundation and solid guarantee of a just and peaceful human coexistence, and hence of genuine democracy, which can come into being and develop only on the basis of the equality of all its members, who possess common rights and duties" (n. 96). Certainly in many ways liberation and feminist theologians have much to gain from such claims. In many ways the most basic beliefs of liberation and feminist theology are undergirded implicitly by the view of the human person that is found in natural law.[8]

A question remains, however, of exactly how the natural law is made known. All may agree that the natural law is a universal, objective account of how we should be as human beings that may be ascertained through the proper use of reason. This is what we believe God wills for us. But has the natural law been fully revealed and clarified in the teachings of the church, or is there still more for us to come to know? Are our understandings, even of something objective and universal, subject to historical conditioning? To say that we understand the natural law in a way that is shaped by our historical and social limitations does not call into question the objective and universal character of natural law itself. Liberation theologians might say that a particular sort of reason developed through reflection on liberating praxis sheds new and important light on the body of natural law as we have come to understand it in the church. Feminists would also claim that we have learned certain universal and objective truths about God's will for us that have not been included in the historical descriptions of natural law precisely because women and women's experience have not been included. In two places *The Splendor of Truth*, citing Vatican II documents, does refer to humanity's gradual discovery of natural law (n. 38, 43). Yet, overall, the document evidences little awareness of the ongoing nature of humanity's struggle to comprehend more fully all that God wants for us on the basis of our being human. Too often natural law is spoken of as a fully revealed and received deposit of truth.

Had the encyclical taken account of more explicitly feminist theological concerns, it would look quite different than it does. The first difference would show up in the translation of the document. "Humanity" and "human beings" are almost always referred to as "mankind" and "man." It may be useful to recall why this usage is objectionable. Compare the following two sentences: *Man's true end is union with God. Man's vocation on earth may be lived out in the priesthood.* Both are grammatically correct. But the word "man" actually means something different in each sentence. In the first, it means human beings, people both male and female. In the second, it means only males, as women are excluded from the priesthood. Whenever a woman reads the word "man," she has to stop and think, *Am I included here?* This reminds her of the many times she has not been included, consulted, or considered in the history and life of the church. Even if one is unpersuaded by feminist concerns to be more linguistically inclusive, the case can also be made that simply for the sake of clarity one should use unambiguously inclusive nouns when one means to be inclusive. The English language is blessed with many felicitous words for "man" and "mankind," among them human being(s), humans, people, persons, humanity, humankind. Inclusive language is seldom awkward, and as it becomes more and more the norm in daily usage, one must ask what purpose it serves for official church documents to continue to use pseudo-generic male language? What goal is achieved by giving this sort of offense?

Along similar lines, feminist readers of *The Splendor of Truth* will note the few places where female images or people are actually referenced. To explain and defend the church's insistence on absolute moral norms, the pope contrasts the church's motherhood to the church's role as bride of Christ. While in the church's motherhood we find compassion and understanding, it is in the church's role as bride of Christ that the church acts as teacher. In fact, "in obedience to the truth which is Christ," the church must faithfully convey Christ's message, although "she in no way is the author or arbiter of this norm" (n. 95). The image of mother is set in contrast to the image of teacher, as though mothers were not teachers. Further, the image of the church as teacher rests on the identification of the church as the bride of Christ, suggesting that the role and function of a bride is that of faithful service to the husband. The use of this metaphor here is based on the assumption that the bride is an obedient conduit of the message of her husband. The images of marriage are clearly hierarchical. If the church wants to teach the mutual self-giving of the married couple as the basis of married life, then we will have to face the fact that the image of church as bride of Christ no longer works.

Feminist sensibilities also mandate attention to the last pages of *The Splendor of Truth*, which conclude with a brief meditation on "Mary, Mother of Mercy." At this time when our Protestant sisters are beginning to take seriously the religious significance of the mother of God, and Catholic women are working to better understand and reinterpret Mary's place in our theology and lives,[9] it is discouraging to have her here lauded for her "perfect docility to the Spirit" (n. 120). In fairness, the pope also praises Mary because "she sheltered in her womb the Son of God who became man; she raised him and enabled him to grow, and she accompanied him in that supreme act of freedom which is the complete sacrifice of his own life" (n. 120). It is encouraging to see Mary's "gift of herself" commended at the same time Jesus' gift of himself is recognized. And yet it is difficult not to see, too, the opportunities missed here. One searches in vain for interpretations of Mary as the original and most faithful disciple. Or for reflection on her strength and clarity of vision in living a life free from sin. Or for the ways in which she modeled a relationship to God which her son would learn from her. It is lamentable that the pope has passed up an opportunity to encourage the renewed and feminist attention to the Mother of God about which women now speak.

2.
Influence on Our Lived Experience of Church

Another important aspect of a feminist liberationist critique involves concern for the practical implications of this encyclical on the faithful's lived experience of church. This next section considers this key issue.

Practically speaking, this encyclical wants to face squarely the challenges to the faith brought by the currents of critical theory and ideological deconstruction present in contemporary thinking. These post-modernist movements, according to the encyclical, result in "relativism and skepticism" (n. 1), especially in regard to the universal nature of moral norms and the legitimacy of magisterial authority. They "exalt freedom to such an extent that it becomes an absolute," and conscience is seen to be "a supreme tribunal of moral judgment" (n. 32). Truth is relativized, and this in turn creates a "radically subjectivistic conception of moral judgment" (n. 32), and an individualistic ethic, in which individual conscience determines the criteria for good and evil according to the person's particularity of context or culture. These ideas are the origin of other currents which state that moral law and conscience, truth and freedom are radically opposed. "Despite their variety," the encyclical warns, "these tendencies are at one in lessening or even denying the dependence of freedom on truth" (n. 34). In fact, the document argues, freedom finds its authentic and complete fulfill-ment in the acceptance of truth, which is the Divine Law inscribed in our hearts and known to us through reason and the natural law.

The majority of believing Catholics would probably accept the encyc-lical's reassertion of the tradition that radically links human freedom with the law of God. However, a feminist critique must question the encyclical's patriarchal interpretation of law and freedom, an interpretation which is re-moved from the context of people's lives. Specifically, feminists should challenge the way in which the encyclical interprets moral principles with-out consideration of the contexts and circumstances of human experience.

In its concern to clarify doctrine, the document focuses on the role of church as magisterial teacher, rather than as pastor. In doing so, it fails dra-matically to consider in any depth or nuance the difficulty of contradictory or conflicting moral choices in real life. Lived experience sometimes con-fronts believers with choices that are not as neatly packaged as moral theory might indicate. The married woman with a chronic crippling disease who gets pregnant; the hospital executive who must decide on the proper alloca-tion of limited budgetary funds among equally necessary programs; and the parents who must decide how far to extend hydration to a comatose, termi-nally ill child are only some of the conflicting moral situations and norma-tive choices that people of faith contend with in their attempt to live moral lives. This encyclical, in failing to acknowledge the conflicting norms that often are part of moral judgment, sets up an often burdensome and unreach-able moral goal for many people. This burden is not the burden of living up to moral norms that seriously challenge persons. Moral norms should chal-lenge persons to live out of their best selves, no matter how difficult, so that they may be authentically free. Rather, this burden is the burden of trying to adhere to moral norms that are often unreasonable, and quite possibly rooted in an unjust social structure or oppressive ideology.

The lived experience of conflicting moral norms, and the sometimes contradictory choices they pose, require a pastoral sensitivity. In order to make wise moral judgments, one must have the ability to engage in nuanced moral reasoning, as well as the compassion to understand human limitation. Such pastoral concern is not especially evident in the document, nor is it intended as its primary concern:

> The church's teaching, and in particular her firmness in defending the universal and permanent validity of the precepts prohibiting intrinsi-cally evil acts, is not infrequently seen as the sign of an intolerable intransigence, particularly with regard to the enormously complex and conflict-filled situations present in the moral life of individuals and of society today. . . . The church, one hears, is lacking in understanding and compassion. . . . In fact, genuine understanding and compassion must mean love for the person, for his true good, for his authentic free-dom (n. 95).

The message comes from a stern "for your own good" perspective. A more pastoral message could hold people accountable to moral standards, while acknowledging that the "enormously complex and conflict-filled situations" one experiences require compassionate guidance.

In its attempt to clarify the doctrinal truths that underlie moral theology, the encyclical passes over the pastoral issues that are germane to moral discernment. As the editors of the *National Catholic Reporter* observe: "This encyclical sacrifices the church's pastoral tradition, which responds to the murky circumstances in which people live imperfect lives, for the sake of its doctrinal tradition, which proclaims truths and judges how and who lives by those truths."[10]

This encyclical implies that a pastoral approach to moral discernment—one that considers the conflicts of lived experience, and one in which moral norms are not the only consideration—will inevitably relativize the norms. The following passage, quoted at length, clearly illustrates the logic operating in the encyclical. In considering theological positions about the role of conscience, the encyclical states:

> In order to justify these positions, some authors have proposed a kind of double status of moral truth. Beyond the doctrinal and abstract level, one would have to acknowledge the priority of a certain more concrete existential consideration. The latter, by taking account of circumstances and the situation, could legitimately be the basis of certain exceptions to the general rule and thus permit one to do in practice and in good conscience what is qualified as intrinsically evil by the moral law. A separation, or even an opposition, is thus established in some cases between the teaching of the precept, which is valid in general, and the norm of the individual conscience, which would in fact make the final decision about what is good and what is evil. On this basis, an attempt is made to legitimize so-called "pastoral" solutions contrary to the teaching of the magisterium and to justify a "creative" hermeneutic according to which the moral conscience is in no way obliged, in every case, by a particular negative precept (n. 56).

The encyclical appears to denigrate the genuine struggles of people of faith (including moral theologians) to grapple with the sometimes very real contradictions of lived experience, and the conflicting understandings of what qualifies as intrinsic evil. It denigrates conscientious decisions which, although they outwardly appear to contradict the negative precept, in fact honor the intended purpose of the norm, and allow persons to live with integrity. For those who in genuine moral conscience cannot abide by a strict interpretation of some of the precepts of the moral law, an agonizing decision must be made: to live in the tradition, dissenting from the strict interpretation of its precept, or to follow the precept absolutely to the harm of one's personal integrity and dignity. For many persons, the choice is exile, that is, leaving the tradition altogether. This is the lived experience of many Catholic persons who, for example, are homosexual, divorced, or who experience inordinate guilt over the use of artificial birth control.

Through its articulation of a key question for the human community, "How can obedience to universal and unchanging moral norms respect the uniqueness and individuality of the person and not represent a threat to his freedom and dignity?" (n. 85), the encyclical shows an awareness of the reality that one's lived experience and the strict interpretation of God's law are sometimes in conflict. The encyclical proposes heroic suffering and martyrdom as answers to that lived contradiction:

> There is . . . a consistent witness which all Christians must daily be ready to make, even at the cost of suffering and grave sacrifice. Indeed, faced with the many difficulties which fidelity to the moral order can demand even in the most ordinary circumstances, the Christian is called, with the grace of God invoked in prayer, to a sometimes heroic commitment (n. 93).

The elevation of martyrdom and heroic sacrifice in this context is particularly problematic from a feminist-liberationist point of view. Liberationists would agree that often the cost of true discipleship is martyrdom. Yet in the context of this encyclical, which does not have a critical analysis of the presence of structural discrimination and oppressive ideologies, such an exhortation should be viewed with a "hermeneutic of suspicion." By linking heroic suffering and martyrdom with the maintenance of a patriarchal social order and ideology, the encyclical undermines the meanings of these witnesses. Rather than instruments for the transformation of injustice, they become instruments to maintain an unjust system which actively works against the full humanity of women. Heroic sacrifice and martyrdom are the proper responses to resist unjust social, economic, and political structures, and the individual actions of persons in maintaining them. They are not the proper response when such action would lead to a repressive status quo.

Liberation theologies take as their starting point the lived experiences of marginalized persons, challenging the ways in which the dominant culture imposes unjust suffering on disempowered persons. Feminists and womanist authors, specifically, have begun to challenge theologies which promote women's continued suffering, rather than resistance to their dehumanization and victimization.[11] In this regard, it is imperative to ask several questions of moral theology that promotes suffering as its only, or its chief, response: *Who benefits from this suffering? Whose needs are left out in this suffering? What end will the suffering serve?* Unfortunately, in a work in which the experiences of women are ignored, exhortations to heroic sacrifice and martyrdom cannot promote the transformation of injustice, but may promote a greater injustice. A fuller discussion of the complex issue of a feminist/womanist critique of Christian theologies about suffering is beyond the scope of this work.[12] What follows describes some basic themes these critiques raise.

Feminist and womanist theologians rightly reject theologies that view suffering as a value in itself. Such theologies present victimization as the normal experience of living; therefore, enduring the suffering of victimization becomes part of the expectation for living a normal life. Sometimes this oppressive understanding of normality is viewed as divinely ordained. Marie Fortune refers to this type of theological thinking, which teaches that it is God's will that we suffer and therefore we must endure it, as "doormat theology."[13] By contrast, a feminist/womanist perspective understands suffering as a reality that cannot be avoided in the work of justice. Suffering is not a value in itself, but is only a value in the work of solidarity.

Feminists and womanist theologians also reject suffering that is coerced onto a group or individual. Marie Fortune articulates the difference between voluntary and involuntary suffering. "Voluntary suffering," she writes, "is a painful experience which a person chooses in order to accomplish a greater goal."[14] It is optional and part of an ongoing strategy for personal or social change. Involuntary suffering, however, "is not chosen and never serves a greater good; it is inflicted by a person(s) upon another against their will and results only in pain and destruction."[15] A feminist/womanist viewpoint rejects involuntary suffering as coercive, exploitive, and oppressive.

Finally, feminist and womanist theologians insist that the suffering that one takes on leads to a greater good which involves the alleviation of the suffering. This is conditioned by the previous two statements: that solidarity is the goal, rather than suffering, and that the suffering is voluntary.

A feminist-liberationist method[16] begins with lived experience, and in the praxis of the struggle for liberation from oppressive structural realities, it evaluates traditional norms and understands them according to whether the norms promote the full humanity of women, or deny it.[17] Feminist and womanist perspectives hold that so-called universal norms have been articulated without taking into account the lived experience of these marginalized persons, who suffer inordinately under the authority of these norms. Those who uphold such norms spiritualize the suffering of these groups in order to ignore the reality of their suffering. As Frances E. Wood reminds us, "Elevating women's suffering to a form of martyrdom for the cause (of others) virtually guarantees that it will remain unexamined."[18]

Two recent beatifications by Pope John Paul II provide a particularly vivid example of this tendency to spiritualize the suffering that a patriarchal norm imposes on a disempowered group; they also provide an example of involuntary suffering toward an end which seemingly leads to no transformation:

> Pope John Paul II beatified two women, a Zairian and an Italian who, he said, were examples of fidelity and care for others. Dr. Gianna Beretta Molla of Zaire, a pediatrician, was pregnant when a uterine tumor was discovered. Instead of undergoing a lifesaving operation that would have led to the death of the fetus, Molla carried the baby to term.

She died at age 39 a week after the infant's birth in 1962. Elisabetta Canori Mora, born in Rome in 1774, was beatified as an example of a Christian mother who cared for her children and helped the poor despite the hardships she faced after her husband abandoned the family. A brief biography published by the Vatican praised her fidelity to her marriage vows despite the physical and psychological abuse to which her husband subjected her.[19]

This account shows quite clearly the patriarchal thinking that assigns undue suffering to women in the name of strict adherence to a moral precept—a precept which no woman had any voice in articulating. One wonders what these women who were beatified thought about their suffering, or what choices and options they or their families had. Their suffering is literally spiritualized through beatification and is held up as a model of Christian faithfulness. Such a questionable interpretation is, in part, the result of excluding lived experience in the discernment of moral norms and precepts.

Because *The Splendor of Truth* does not acknowledge contextual perspective and particular lived experiences as valid components of moral reasoning—perspectives common to liberationist thinking—the norms it articulates are viewed as objective and universal, without any awareness of the oppressive ideological overlay they carry. When one's experience challenges the norm, according to such a viewpoint, then one's experience necessarily must be wrong; the only moral choice one has is to obey the norm. This creates a situation in which, to be a moral Christian, one may have to embrace involuntary, coercive suffering toward an oppressive end. Since these norms are interpreted as the law of God, the coerced suffering is viewed as divinely ordained. This presents an internal conflict in the document itself, which presents God as the one who "brings the question about morally good action back to its religious foundations, to the acknowledgement of God, who alone is goodness, fullness of life, the final end of human activity and perfect happiness" (n. 9).

A major consequence of this encyclical for the faithful's lived experience of church (understood as the people of God) is the reassertion of a theology that is unconcerned with the complexities of human experience and the contradiction of moral norms that the faithful must face. The document prefers to deal with those complexities dogmatically, rather than pastorally— legalistically, rather than compassionately. According to this patriarchal logic, obedience to a norm must often equal unnecessary suffering toward no transformative end. In its articulation of universal norms, the encyclical is not self-critical about the limitations of its patriarchal interpretations, and how those interpretations have been used against women and other disempowered groups in the church's history. The encyclical depends upon the coercion of authority to make its point: "Only by obedience to universal moral norms does man find full confirmation of his personal uniqueness and the possibility of authentic moral growth" (n. 96).

A feminist analysis of this "power-over" model of relationship must conclude that the underlying agenda of this encyclical is a reassertion of a patriarchal structure of moral norms. In this paradigm women, as well as other marginalized groups, are disempowered through the promotion of heroic suffering and martyrdom which is removed from a transformative end. Such suffering is viewed as the only moral response to a disagreement in conscience with the strict interpretation of a moral precept. The intention of this reasoning, whether conscious or unconscious, is to maintain the unjust and unequal power relations that exist between the dominant and marginalized group.

This is especially evident in the previously noted exhortation of Mary as a model of "perfect docility to the Spirit." Mary is lauded as "the radiant sign and inviting model of the moral life," who "lived and exercised her freedom precisely by giving herself to God" (n. 120). This portrayal of Mary as submissive and docile exemplifies a theology that has been used in Christian history to oppress groups of persons according to race, gender, class and sexual orientation. Specifically referring to racial oppression, M. Shawn Copeland views such theology as "inculcating caricatures of the cardinal virtues of patience, long-suffering, forbearance, love, faith, and hope."[20] She warns that in order to avoid a Christian masochism, a theology of suffering from a womanist perspective must reevaluate those caricatured virtues in the light of black women's experience. Similarly one must critically analyze the caricature of Mary's virtue and the implication of this model on the lived experience of church.

In conclusion, the effect of this encyclical on the faithful's lived experience of church may be quite negative, for it dismisses the complex contradictions of lived moral discernment, crushing them within absolute, unchanging principles. Personal integrity could be sacrificed to those rules; pastoral support is owed only to those who accept any resulting "heroic suffering" (toward non-transformative ends). This sounds strangely like the extremes of Catholic theology that the Second Vatican Council sought to renew. Rather than a step forward, this document represents a backlash against the vicissitudes of postmodernism. Rather than helping us find our way through deconstruction's challenge to traditional norms—its very real confusion and shifting of perspectives about what is absolute and what is contextual— this encyclical begs the question by answering it with a reassertion of universal interpretations of truth and, therefore, blunts the effectiveness of its message.

Conclusion

The exclusion of the disempowered voices in the Catholic Church in this document, particularly of women, and its exclusion of lived experience challenge its credibility as moral teaching. We agree with Lisa Sowle Cahill that the encyclical's "defense of moral objectivity" is "fatally wounded by a too-visible male point of view, and by a tendency to resolve genuinely difficult questions by resort to authority."[21] The inclusion of the voices of women and other marginalized groups, and of the particularity of their lived experiences in the articulation of moral norms, would go a long way toward nurturing a genuine justice realized both in society and in the church.

Notes

1. Early examples include Mary Daly, *The Church and the Second Sex* (New York: Harper and Row, 1968), and essays by Daly, Rosemary Ruether and Elisabeth Schüssler-Fiorenza in *WomanSpirit Rising,* Carol Christ and Judith Plaskow, eds. (San Francisco: Harper and Row, 1979). A recent excellent collection of essays by Catholic feminists: Catherine Mowry LaCugna, ed., *Freeing Theology* (New York: HarperCollins, 1993).

2. Lisa Sowle Cahill, "Accent on the Masculine," *The Tablet* 11 (Dec. 1993), pp. 1618, 1619. Also Lisa Sowle Cahill, "Veritatis Splendor," *Commonweal* 120 (Oct. 22, 1993), and Anne E. Patrick, "Veritatis Splendor," *Commonweal* 120 (Oct. 22, 1993).

3. Richard A. McCormick, *"Veritatis Splendor* and Moral Theology," *America* 169 (Oct. 30, 1993), pp. 10-11.

4. Ibid., p. 9.

5. L. Gregory Jones, "The Splendor of Truth: A Symposium." *First Things* (Jan. 1994), p. 19.

6. Jon Sobrino, *The True Church and the Poor,* translated by Matthew J. O'Connell (Maryknoll, NY: Orbis Books, 1983), p. 16.

7. Lisa Sowle Cahill, "Feminism and Christian Ethics," in *Freeing Theology,* p. 216.

8. For many reasons Latin American liberation theologians may be less quick to agree with this assessment than most feminists. See Thomas L. Schubeck, "The Reconstruction of Natural Law Reasoning: Liberation Theology as a Case Study," *Journal of Religious Ethics* 20 (1992), pp. 149-78. Also useful is Schubeck's *Liberation Ethics* (Minneapolis: Fortress, 1993).

9. See Chung Hyun Kyung, *Struggle to be the Sun Again* (Maryknoll, NY: Orbis, 1990), esp. Chap. 5. Also Ivone Gebara and Maria Clara Bingamer, *Mary Mother of God, Mother of the Poor* (Maryknoll, NY: Orbis, 1988).

10. "John Paul II's Truths Sacrifice Tradition of Pastoral Concern," editorial, *National Catholic Reporter* (October 15, 1993), p. 28.

11. See, for example, Emilie M. Townes, ed., *A Troubling in My Soul: Womanist Perspectives on Evil and Suffering* (Maryknoll, NY: Orbis Press, 1993); Joanne Carlson Brown and Carole R. Bohn, eds., *Christianity, Patriarchy and Abuse: A Feminist Critique* (New York: The Pilgrim Press, 1989); Susan E. Davies, "Reflections on the Theological Roots of Abusive Behavior," in Susan E. Davies and Eleanor H. Haney, eds., *Redefining Sexual Ethics* (Cleveland: The Pilgrim Press, 1991).

12. For a more detailed discussion, see Kathleen T. Talvacchia, "Compassionate Solidarity: Toward a Feminist Pedagogy of Justice" Ed.D. diss., (Columbia University, Teachers College, 1992), pp. 49-59.

13. Marie Fortune, "The Transformation of Suffering: A Biblical and Theological Perspective," in *Christianity, Patriarchy and Abuse,* Brown and Bohn, eds., 144.

14. Ibid., p. 141.

15. Ibid., p. 142.

16. The interracial Mudflower Collective, in understanding the conditions necessary for an intellectually honest feminist theological praxis, cite the following factors: 1. accountability to certain particular people who are marginalized; 2. collaboration with others rather than lone researching; 3. beginning with lived experience in relation to others; 4. a diversity of cultures represented; 5. a shared commitment to the transformation of oppressive structures into just structures. The Mudflower Collective, *God's Fierce Whimsy: Christian Feminism and Theological Education* (New York: The Pilgrim Press, 1985), pp. 23-27.

17. Ruether articulates, "The critical principle of feminist theology is the promotion of the full humanity of women. Whatever denies, diminishes, or distorts the full humanity of women is, therefore, appraised as not redemptive. Theologically speaking, whatever diminishes or denies the full humanity of women must be presumed not to reflect the divine or an authentic relation to the divine, or to reflect the authentic nature of things, or to be the message or work of an authentic redeemer or a community of redemption." Rosemary Radford Ruether, *Sexism and God-Talk* (Boston: Beacon Press, 1983), pp. 18-19.

18. Frances E. Wood, " 'Take My Yoke Upon You': The Role of the Church in the Oppression of African-American Women," in Townes, ed., *A Troubling in My Soul,* p. 39.

19. *National Catholic Reporter* (May 6, 1994), p. 10.

20. M. Shawn Copeland, "'Wading Through Many Sorrows': Toward a Theology of Suffering in Womanist Perspective," in *A Troubling in My Soul,* p. 122.

21. Cahill, "Accent on the Masculine," p. 1618.

Name Index

Ambrose, St., 16, 123, 130, 185
Ambrosiaster, 109
Anthony of Egypt, St., 17, 31
Aquinas, Thomas, St., 62, 65, 67, 72, 76, 88, 93, 98, 112, 114, 140, 149-50, 168, 188, 194, 197-201, 228-29, 231, 235-36, 240, 266, 277; the moral act, 279-81; moral judgment and consequentialism, 289-93; object and aim of a moral act, 287-89; object and circumstances of a moral act, 281-87
Aristotle, 98, 150, 188, 200, 204
Athanasius, St., 76
Augustine, St., 16-17, 20-24, 26-28, 30-33, 88, 93, 139, 183, 190

Balthasar, Hans Urs, von, 85
Barth, Karl, 99, 177
Benedict, St., 109-10
Boadt, Lawrence, 178
Boccaccini, Gabriele, 182, 186
Boethius, 198
Bentham, Jeremy, 216, 290, 292
Bonhoeffer, Dietrich, 95
Boyle, Joseph, 264-65
Brooks, Roger, 178
Brown, Raymond, 178
Bultmann, Rudolf, 179
Buren, Paul, van, 181
Burke, Ronald R., 119-31

Cahill, Lisa S., 262-64, 300, 308
Caiger, B. J., 110
Calvin, John, 255
Campbell, Joseph, 145
Cassian, John, 108
Catherine of Siena, St., 108

Charlesworth, James, 179
Chopp, Rebecca, 188-89
Collins, John J., 178
Constantine, 18, 32
Copeland, M. Shawn, 308
Curran, Charles E., 224-42
Cyril of Alexandria, St., 16

Damasus, Pope, 109
Daniel, 56
Davies, W. D., 179
Decius, Emperor, 3
Dedek, John, 292
Descartes, René 198
Di Ianna, Albert R., 259-60
Dionysius, St., 149
Donagan, Alan, 287
Donatists, 24, 27, 30, 32
Droge, Arthur J., 179
Dubois, Marcel, 181
Dulles, Avery, 12
Dunn, James D.G., 179-81
Dupuy, Bernard, 181
Dyck, Arthur J., 191

Eusebius, St., 27-28

Fasching, Darrell J., 191
Finance, Joseph, de, 149
Finnis, John, 218, 278
Fisher, Eugene J., 178
Fletcher, Joseph, 216-17
Fortune, Marie, 306
Freud, Sigmund, 147
Fries, Heinrich, 12
Frohlich, Mary, 106-16
Fuchs, Josef, 84-85, 88, 236

Gaffney, James, 60-70, 260

311

Gerson, Jean, 110-11
Gilleman, Gerard, 84
Gnostics, 76
Greenberg, Irving, 182
Gregory of Nyssa, St., 16, 24-25, 52
Gregory Palomas, 76
Grisez, Germaine, 278, 285

Hadewijch, 249
Hanigan, James P., 208-20
Häring, Bernard, 84, 218
Harrington, Daniel, 179
Haughey, John C., 269-77
Heer, Friedrich, 189-90
Heidegger, Martin, 147
Heyward, Carter, 249
Hildebrand, von, 143
Hitler, Adolf, 219
Hopkins, Gerard Manley, 137

Ignatius of Loyola, St., 112-14, 150, 274-75

James, St., 171
Jerome, St., 24
Jesus Christ, 1-3, 5, 10, 12, 19, 23, 30, 48-51, 62, 77, 83, 85, 90, 92, 94, 96, 102, 124, 160-62, 177, 179-81, 195, 205, 208-10, 245, 249, 253, 261, 272, 298-99; his cross, 170-71, 213; and Pharisaism, 184
John the Baptist, St., 170, 183
John Chrysostom, St., 76, 185
John of the Cross, St., 55
John the Evangelist, St., 84, 90, 98
John XXIII, Pope, 76-77, 227
John Paul II, Pope, 1, 3, 5-6, 8-11, 16-26, 32-33, 39, 48, 50, 65-68, 72-73, 83, 86, 91, 106-7, 109, 111-13, 115-16, 119, 121-28, 130-31, 157-58, 162-68, 196-201, 214, 217, 226, 229-30, 235, 241, 253, 255, 261, 217, 226, 229-30, 235, 241, 253,255, 261, 265-66, 272,

276, 278, 306; and conscience, 205-6; images of perfection, 48-57; just war, 40-45; and moral perfection, 210-13
Jovinian, 30
Jung, Carl Gustav, 146

Kant, Immanuel, 85, 88, 142, 197-098, 291
Knitter, Paul, 181-82

La Cocque, Andre, 178
Lammers, Stephen E., 38-46
Las Casas, Bartolomé de, 75
Leo XIII, Pope, 254
Levenson, John, 178
Levinas, Emmanuel, 138-40, 142-48, 152
Lifton, Robert Jay, 191
Liguori, Alphonsus, St., 224, 236
Littel, Franklin, 177
Lonergan, Bernard J.F., 114, 139-42, 150, 235
Luke, St., 53, 87, 90-91, 95, 108
Lustig, B. Andrew, 252-67
Luther, Martin, 87-88

MacNamara, Vincent, 84
Maloney, John J., 116
Mark, St., 90-91
Markus, Robert, 26, 28, 30-31
Martini, Carlo, Cardinal, 177, 179, 181
Mary of Nazareth, 54-57, 160, 249, 302, 308
Matthew, St., 1-2, 17, 19-22, 31-32, 49, 53, 83, 85, 90, 95, 183, 225, 298
Maximus the Confessor, St., 76
McBrien, Richard P., 7
McCormick, Richard A., 6, 16, 22, 99, 212, 252, 257-58, 264, 266, 278, 296; a nuanced proportionalist, 258-60
Metz, Johannes, 177, 188, 190
Milhaven, John Giles, 244-51

Molla, Gianna Beretta, 306
Moore, James, 190
Mora, Elisabetta Canori, 307
Moses, 90, 95
Mussner, Franz, 181

Neusner, Jacob, 182
Newman, John Henry, 76, 80nn4,6, 139
Nicolas, Adolfo, 115
Niebuhr, H. Richard, 5
Niebuhr, Reinhold, 190
Noonan, John T., Jr., 89, 240
Novak, David, 191
Novation, 33-34

Oehman, Dom, 181
O'Keefe, John J., 16-34

Parmenides, 114
Paul, St., 21, 23, 26, 31, 65, 87, 93, 139, 154, 179-80, 185-86, 206
Paul VI, Pope, 50, 65, 124
Pawlikowski, John T., 177-91
Pelagius, 17, 20, 24, 30-31
Perelmuter, Hayim G., 179, 182
Peter Abelard, 61
Pius X, Pope, 129
Pius XII, Pope, 235
Platonists, 76, 145
Porter, Jean, 278-93

Rahner, Karl, 88, 114, 137-39, 148-51, 235
Ramsey, Paul, 258
Ratzinger, Josef, 85
Ricoeur, Paul, 144, 146-48
Rivkin, Ellis, 184
Ruether, Rosemary, 181-82
Ryan, Maura Anne, 1-13

Saldavini, Anthony J., 179-80
Sanders, E. P., 179, 186

Sanders, James, 178
Sartre, Jean-Paul, 147
Scheler, Max, 143
Schillebeeckx, Edward, 12
Schopenhauer, Arthur, 145
Schuller, Bruno, 85
Schüssler-Fiorenza, Elisabeth, 12, 187-89
Scraggs, Robin, 179-80
Segal, Alan, 179
Shannon, Thomas A., 262-64
Shmueli, Efraim, 182
Sidgwick, Henry, 290-91
Sirach, 52
Smith, Janet E., 194-207
Sobrino, Jon, 97
Socrates, 249
Spohn, William C., 83-102
Stendahl, Krister, Bishop, 179
Stephen, St., 171
Stevens, Clifford, 72-79
Stoics, 249
Sunshine, Edward R., 157-72
Susanna, 56-57, 92, 170, 183
Sylvester II, Pope, 76-77, 81n11

Tallon, Andrew, 137-52
Talvacchia, Kathleen T., 296-308
TePas, Katherine M., 48-57
Teresa of Avila, St. 111
Thoma, Clemens, 179
Tomson, Peter, 179
Tracy, David, 187-89

Vereecke, Louis, 236
Voegelin, Eric, 114-15

Walsh, Mary Elizabeth, 296-308
White, John, 179
Wojtyla, Karol. *See* Pope John Paul II
Wood, Frances E., 306, 310
Wueller, Wilhelm, 179